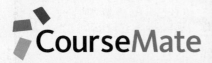

WADSWORTH
CENGAGE Learning·

TEACH 2
Janice Koch

Editor-in-Chief: Linda Ganster

Executive Editor: Mark Kerr

Developmental Editor: Caitlin Cox

Assistant Editor: Joshua Taylor

Editorial Assistant: Greta Lindquist

Media Editor: Elizabeth Momb

Executive Brand Manager: Melissa Larmon

Senior Market Development Manager:
   Kara Kindstrom

Content Project Manager: Samen Iqbal

Art Director: Jennifer Wahi

Manufacturing Planner: Doug Bertke

Rights Acquisitions Specialist: Don Schlotman

Production Service: Lindsey Anderson, Integra

Photo Researcher: XX

Text Researcher: XX

Copy Editor: XX

Cover Designer: Kate Scheible

Cover Image: Red Pencil/White notebook
   © iStockphoto 98054315, Yellow Legal Pad
   © iStockphoto 138091461

Compositor: Integra

For product information and technology assistance, contact us at
Cengage Learning Customer & Sales Support, 1-800-354-9706.

For permission to use material from this text or product,
submit all requests online at **www.cengage.com/permissions**.
Further permissions questions can be e-mailed to
permissionrequest@cengage.com.

Library of Congress Control Number: 2012938235

ISBN-13: 978-1-133-96339-4

ISBN-10: 1-133-96339-0

Wadsworth
20 Davis Drive
Belmont, CA 94002-3098
USA

Cengage Learning is a leading provider of customized learning solutions with office locations around the globe, including Singapore, the United Kingdom, Australia, Mexico, Brazil, and Japan. Locate your local office at **www.cengage.com/global.**

Cengage Learning products are represented in Canada by Nelson Education, Ltd.

To learn more about Wadsworth, visit **www.cengage.com/wadsworth**

Purchase any of our products at your local college store or at our preferred online store **www.CengageBrain.com.**

Printed in the United States of America
1 2 3 4 5 6 7 16 15 14 13 12

Brief Contents

GET ONLINE

HE DID

Access CourseMate for **TEACH** at **login.cengagebrain.com**.

You'll find everything you need to succeed in your class.

- Interactive Games
- Quizzes
- Flash Cards
- Videos
- Audio
- And more

www.cengagebrain.com

Contents

© Brian Powell/iStockphoto

© Claudia Dewald/iStockphoto

PART 2   THE EVOLUTION OF SCHOOLS AND TEACHING PRACTICES   42

CHAPTER 3   A HISTORY OF SCHOOLING IN AMERICA   44

PART 3   LOOKING AT TODAY'S SCHOOLS   86

© Ju-Lee/iStockphoto

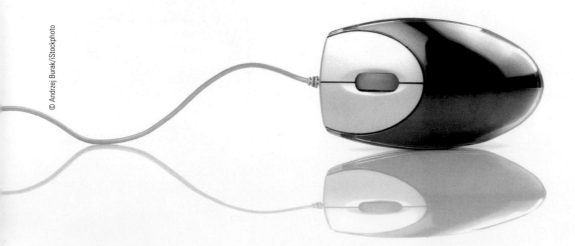

© Andrzej Burak/iStockphoto

© geopaul/iStockphoto

PART 4 CLASSROOMS, COMMUNITIES, AND YOU 162

© Rafa Irusta/iStockphoto

CHAPTER 10 MAKING THE DECISION TO BECOME A TEACHER 180

© Joey Boylan/iStockphoto

PART 1
THINKING ABOUT TEACHING: MAKING THE DECISION

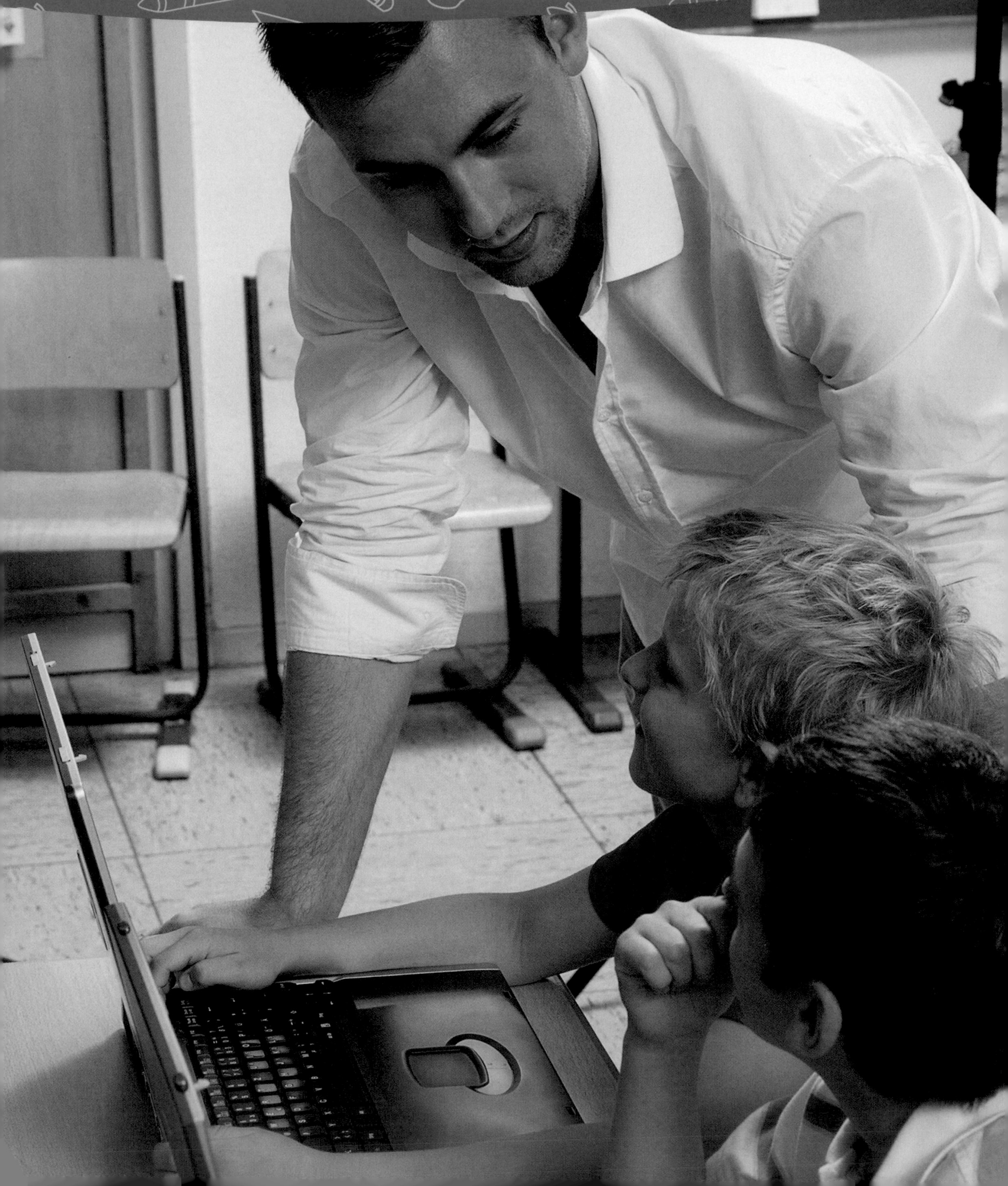

This book invites you on a personal journey of reflection about education—your own education, the education of people you know, and the education of children who will become the future of the United States. It is a journey of self-exploration, during which you will be asked to look inside your mind and heart and consider what it takes, emotionally and intellectually, to become a teacher who experiences joy and satisfaction through service to others.

Any plan to improve educational outcomes is dependent on the teachers who carry it out and on the abilities of those attracted to the field. In this book, you will have the opportunity to explore some of the attributes that will make you successful as a classroom teacher.

We will examine the specific challenges of becoming a teacher in today's social and political context, which raises issues such as testing, standards, and the effect of digital technology on the lives of young people and their teachers. Although much about teaching and learning remains the same year after year, technology has significantly changed the ways students communicate, learn, and spend their time outside of school. As we experience the second decade of the twenty-first century, compelling truths about our world *must* be considered.

- The world is rapidly changing and is a far different place than it was only ten years ago.
- The global economy and the technological innovations of the past decade demand a well-educated citizenry.
- The best teachers grow and change with rapidly shifting social and cultural conditions, thereby becoming lifelong learners.
- Online education is a significant presence in K–12 schools all over the country.
- Technology occupies a great deal of time for students of all ages.
- Every single student has the ability to learn, and becoming a teacher means accepting the daily responsibility to take all students, at whatever level and place in their lives they may be, and help them to learn.
- Education provides students with the opportunity to become productive and contributing members of society.
- Teachers make a difference. The quality of the teacher in the classroom is one of the most important influences on student achievement.
- Preparing to teach involves personal reflection and a commitment to understanding yourself and the world around you.

Part Outline

CHAPTER 1   Becoming a Teacher: Looking Forward and Backward at the Same Time

CHAPTER 2   Teaching Stories

CHAPTER 1

BECOMING A TEACHER:
LOOKING FORWARD AND BACKWARD AT THE SAME TIME

© LWA/Dann Tardif/Getty Images

> *Everyone who remembers his own education remembers teachers, not methods and techniques. The teacher is the heart of the educational system.*
> —Sidney Hook, American philosopher (student of John Dewey), 1902–1989

This book is designed to guide your thinking about entering the field of education. It is about schools and schooling, teachers and teaching, learners and the process of learning. It is also about you. What do you already know about classrooms, and how can you apply that knowledge to the complex experience of being a classroom teacher? Your answers to these questions will play a big role in deciding the kind of teacher you will become. Research has shown that out of all the factors that contribute to a student's school day, the single most important one in improving students' performance is the effectiveness of the teacher. Yes, the teacher makes all the difference.

You have within you everything you need to become the kind of teacher you want to be. You will be challenged to identify the attitudes, skills, and dispositions that teaching requires. You will need to make a commitment to becoming a lifelong learner— that is, expanding your ideas by what you learn from your students, your research, and your own personal growth. Donald Schön (1983), an educational researcher, used the term **reflective practitioner** to refer to a teacher who consistently and consciously modifies his or her own teaching practice based on the active consideration of events in his or her classroom. You are invited to conceptualize teaching as a personal activity requiring a large capacity for reflective thought and deliberate action and experimentation.

Teaching, which requires such a heightened sense of self and a commitment to the social good, demands nothing less of its professionals than an ongoing examination of their authentic motives for teaching. Hence, in addition to *knowledge* about schools, curriculum, and instruction, this text provides a *venue* through which you can actively consider your skills, attitudes, and dispositions as they relate to becoming a teacher.

We begin by examining your interest in education. This chapter will encourage you to reflect on your own educational background as you explore the possibility of forging a career as a teacher.

reflective practitioner A teacher who consistently reflects on classroom events (both successes and problems) and modifies teaching practices accordingly.

© Brian Powell/iStockphoto

LEARNING OUTCOMES

After reading this chapter, you should be thinking about the following ideas:

1-1 Reflect on your own educational history and its implications for your future as a teacher.

1-2 Examine the "goodness of fit" between your own personal qualities and the demands of teaching.

1-3 Explain the effect that a committed teacher has on the climate and culture within a school.

1-4 Examine the importance of being a reflective practitioner.

WRITING & REFLECTION

Draw Yourself as a Teacher

Draw a picture of yourself teaching a lesson. You do not have to be an artist; stick figures are fine (see Figure 1.1). Just imagine yourself in a classroom. Be sure to include the students! This is a way to explore your images of teaching. Close the book while you work. When you finish your drawing, return to this section.

As you analyze your drawing, you may want to reflect on the following questions:

- How is your classroom arranged?
- Are desks in rows? Or are tables grouped around the room?
- What are you doing? What are your students doing?
- Are you standing in front? In the middle? To the side?
- Are students raising their hands?
- Judging from your drawing, what mental models do you have of yourself as a teacher?

1-1 Looking Backward: Talking about Teaching

I recently asked a number of new teachers what made them decide to enter teaching; some of them remarked that they had always loved school. School was, for them, the happiest place to be. But several others shared not-so-glorious stories about their experiences. They decided to go into teaching to make a difference, to teach others in ways they wish they themselves had been taught. Still others had no specific personal calling to teach. They "fell into" teaching because they needed a job. And some are trying to figure out if teaching is for them. Whichever of these categories you feel you may fit, with this book you can discover if teaching is for you.

Laura and Sharyn pursued teaching careers because they loved school and loved learning. Laura explained that from her earliest years in school, she was excited when the school year began and sad when it ended.

School was her happiest place, so she decided to pursue a career that would keep her there. Sharyn described similar feelings:

She remembered how, as a child, she could not wait for summer camp to be over because she wanted to go back to school. In high school, she was part of a peer tutoring program and also privately tutored friends and classmates. When they did well, she was actually happier than when she did well because she knew she had helped her friends to succeed. Sharyn's love for school and learning, combined with the joy she felt when her friends (whom she tutored) succeeded, led her to teaching. Sharyn wanted to enable children to love learning as much as she did.

A third teacher, Derrick, told me that most of his teachers were female. Not until sixth grade did he experience his first male teacher—the music teacher. He gained an appreciation of music from this teacher and started to imagine that he might teach as well. He played school with his younger brother and began to consider a career in education. Later, a male history teacher encouraged him to study that subject, and he majored in history in college while also pursuing a professional program in elementary education. A kindergarten teacher today, Derrick is firmly convinced that men are needed in early-childhood education so children can see that men are able caretakers.

Are you like Laura, Sharyn, or Derrick in your conviction that teaching is a career you want to pursue? Or are you more ambivalent? The "Writing & Reflection" activity will help you think about ways in which your educational past, and your thoughts and feelings about it, may influence your future career.

1-1a Your Educational Autobiography

What was school like for you? What kind of a student were you? When you think of teaching, which teacher or teachers do you conjure up?

© Cengage Learning

FIGURE 1.1

Drawing a Teacher
These samples show how three teacher candidates responded to the challenge to draw a teacher. What ideas about teaching do the drawings suggest?

You may think questions like these are irrelevant at this stage of your life. But examining your early experiences as a student is an important task:

Who you are as a person, the kinds of experiences you had inside and outside of school, your values, beliefs and aspirations shape what you will be as a teacher and how you will teach and how you will respond to the changing contexts of teaching. (Bullough & Gitlin, 2001, p. 45)

Thinking about your own story and telling it is an important step in looking backward.

An **educational autobiography** is your story of your life as a student. It has no definite length but usually responds to the following questions:

- What do you think of when you think of school?
- Where did you attend school?
- When you walked in the building, did you have a sense of comfort? Fear? Anxiety?
- Close your eyes and imagine you are back in elementary, middle, or high school. What was school like for you? Do you remember what school *smells* like? *Sounds* like?
- Try to imagine specific teachers. What grades did they teach? Who were your friends in those grades?

My story begins with kindergarten:

I remember starting kindergarten at the age of four years and six months. Arbitrary calendar cutoff dates, typical of many public school districts, allowed me to enter school well before my fifth birthday. Neighbors would say, "She made the year." That referred to being allowed to commence kindergarten prior to turning five. Other children, born four weeks later, had "missed the year" and began kindergarten after their fifth birthday. They would be the oldest in the grade, whereas I was the youngest.

I remember being frightened and throwing up every day for the first two months of kindergarten. But I also recall my kindergarten teachers' accepting and welcoming me each day, regardless of my physiological reaction to my separation from home. I was a "young" four-and-a-half year old and would probably have been better served by missing the year. How patient and kind my two kindergarten teachers were! They saw me coming and intuitively knew that I was not ready for school. After

WRITING & REFLECTION

Teaching Is Like . . .

Think of one or more comparisons for teaching. If you need some leads, visit the website "Metaphorically Speaking" from the Annenberg Media Learner Interactive Workshops (http://www.learner.org/channel/workshops/nextmove/metaphor/). You may come up with several similes or metaphors that seem apt. As you choose them, explain why you think each is a good description of teaching.

goodness of fit A term generally used in descriptive statistics to describe the match between a theory and a particular set of observations; in this book, it means the match between a teacher candidate's personal attributes, values, and disposition and the demands of teaching.

begin this kind of thinking. Take a few moments to think about your own teachers.

1-1c A FAVORITE TEACHER

Does one teacher stand out in your mind as having influenced you in a positive way? How did this teacher make an impact, and what was the result of his or her connection to you? Answering these questions is another good way to reflect on your educational past. When I think about these questions I remember junior high school.

I had a seventh-grade teacher, Mrs. Fisher, in JHS 117 in the Bronx, in New York City. I was, as you read in the early part of my educational autobiography, really young for my grade; I was eleven years old. Mrs. Fisher was my science teacher, and, in those days, much of general science revolved around learning how the internal combustion engine of an automobile worked.

I really liked science, but I was shy, young, and from a poor neighborhood. I had little self-confidence. Mrs. Fisher took me aside one day and said, "You know, Janice, you are very good in science; you should go to the Bronx High School of Science." This high school is one of the specialized schools in New York City requiring that students pass an entrance exam. Mrs. Fisher gave me the application and helped me complete it.

I passed the exam, was admitted, and began attending the Bronx High School of Science at the age of twelve. My experience at this distinctive high school changed the course of my future education and career. Years later, I went to visit Mrs. Fisher and thanked her for having taken an interest in me. I determined that one day I, too, would make a difference for students.

1-1d WHAT QUALITIES ARE NEEDED TO BE A GOOD TEACHER?

After reflecting on your favorite teacher, you may want to compare the attributes of this teacher with a list of some general qualities of good teachers. Read "Qualities of Good Teachers." How do these qualities match up with the ones your favorite teacher had?

In making this comparison, think about to what extent you possess these qualities. As we proceed, we will often return to the concept of **goodness of fit**. This term refers to how good a match there may be between your personal qualities and the demands of teaching.

Do *not* be discouraged if you do not find a perfect match between yourself and the ideal characteristics listed. You are always growing and changing as a person, and you certainly may develop qualities you do not possess now. When you begin to think about a career in teaching, one of your responsibilities is to analyze your own strengths and weaknesses. Realizing your strengths allows you to use them to the fullest potential, whereas identifying your weaknesses allows you to work toward improving or overcoming them.

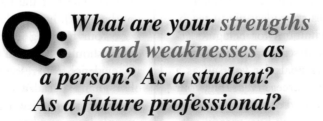

Q: *What are your strengths and weaknesses as a person? As a student? As a future professional?*

QUALITIES OF GOOD TEACHERS: 5 "Cs"

A good teacher needs to be:

Committed: Good teachers have a commitment to their own ongoing education as well as the learning experiences of the young people in their charge. They are committed to fostering a love of learning.

Caring: Teachers demonstrate their hopes for their students through the ways they nurture their development, encouraging students to achieve, and supporting them as they reach new heights of understanding.

Courageous: It requires courage to maintain a commitment over time, persisting in working on behalf of every student, regardless of ability.

Conscious: Good teachers are consistently aware of their interactions with their students. They consciously function to ensure respectful and meaningful discourse is the default mode in their classrooms.

Centered: Good teachers have a centered presence in the classroom. They command the students' attention by their own personal comfort with being at the center of responsibility. They communicate, through their body language and speech, their own readiness to work with their students.

1-2 Looking Forward: The Profession

Now it is time to begin looking forward. What is special about teaching as a career? What do you need to know about the profession you are considering?

1-2a AN ESSENTIAL PROFESSION

❝*Every child needs—and deserves—dedicated, outstanding teachers who know their subject matter, are effectively trained, and know how to teach to high standards and to make learning come alive for students.*❞
—President Bill Clinton, 1998

In a US Department of Education report, *Promising Practices: New Ways to Improve Teacher Quality* (1998), teaching is referred to as "the essential profession, the one that makes all other professions possible." What do you think that means?

The report further declares that without well-qualified, caring, and committed teachers, neither improved curricula and assessments nor safe schools—not even the highest standards in the world—will ensure that our children are prepared for the challenges and opportunities in this century. More than ever before in our history, education will make the difference between those who prosper in the new economy and those who are left behind. Teaching shapes education and therefore shapes the future of the United States—molding the skills of the future workforce and laying the foundation for good citizenship and full participation in community and civic life.

Hence, it is the teacher who will bring to life the ideals, attitudes, learning experiences, and joy that are possible

TEACHSOURCE VIDEO CASE

Advice from the Field

Find the TeachSource Video Case "Becoming a Teacher: Voices and Advice from the Field" on the student website, and you will meet several teachers, some new to the field and some who have been teaching for years. Also view the bonus video called "Essential Qualities That Teachers Must Possess." After watching the videos, consider the following question:

Which of my qualities match the attributes of good teachers?

Does this sound like a tall order? It is! Because what teachers know and are able to do has such a profound impact on the future of education, you need to understand how people come to learn. You need to become familiar with different contexts for teaching and the diversity of students in schools.

We would not expect that a future doctor would be able to examine a patient or perform surgery with just a few months' training. Yet we often expect students to become teachers after a period of only several weeks of in-classroom training. This is why many teacher education programs (and yours may be one) require early field experiences, during which you observe and participate in the life of a classroom at the grade level you are thinking about teaching.

People have debated for years whether teaching is technically a *profession* in the same sense that, say, medicine and law are. On one hand, teachers do not get paid as much as doctors and lawyers, nor is teachers' training as extensive. Also, to many people, the knowledge that teachers possess about teaching and learning does not seem as complicated and technical as what a neurologist knows about the nervous system. On the other hand, teaching does share a number of attributes with other professions. Look at Figure 1.2 and decide for yourself how many of the statements are true about teaching.

1-2b A CODE OF ETHICS

The **National Education Association (NEA)** is the nation's largest professional employee organization. It has 2.8 million members who work in educational settings from preschools to universities. With affiliate organizations in

in a classroom. The curriculum, which we will explore later in this text, is a lifeless document in itself. It is the classroom teacher who enables the curriculum materials to have personal meaning for each learner.

all fifty states and in more than 14,000 US communities, the NEA provides local services such as workshops and collective bargaining for teachers. On state and national scales, it acts as a lobbying group for educational issues.

Other chapters will have much more to say about professional organizations for teachers. I bring up the NEA here because, as far back as 1929, members adopted a code of ethics for the profession. The most recent revision of the code is shown in the "Code of Ethics of the Education Profession." Look at the first paragraph of the code's preamble. Let's take this statement apart and see what it means.

- **"Believing in the worth and dignity of each human being"** This phrase refers to a teacher's commitment to all of his or her students. A teacher's authentic desire to make a connection with every student and to consider each individual's needs is the essence of good teaching. For some further thoughts about the meaning of this clause in the NEA code of ethics, see "Honoring Diversity" on the next page.

Did You Know?

The NEA was founded in 1857 as the National Teachers Association. (It adopted its present name in 1870.)

Teaching requires a desire to help others by creating meaningful learning experiences.

© OJOImages/Photolibrary

- **"Recognizes the supreme importance of the pursuit of truth, devotion to excellence"** This phrase's meaning probably requires even more careful thought in the twenty-first century than it did in the past. We live in the context of an information technology revolution, a time when the amount of information available to us and to our students is exploding.

Teachers must encourage students to embrace the value of examining multiple viewpoints on a topic but also teach them how to evaluate the validity of information. Hence, our commitment might better be stated as recognizing the importance of *multiple* truths and *multiple expressions* of excellence.

FIGURE 1.2

Is Teaching a Profession?

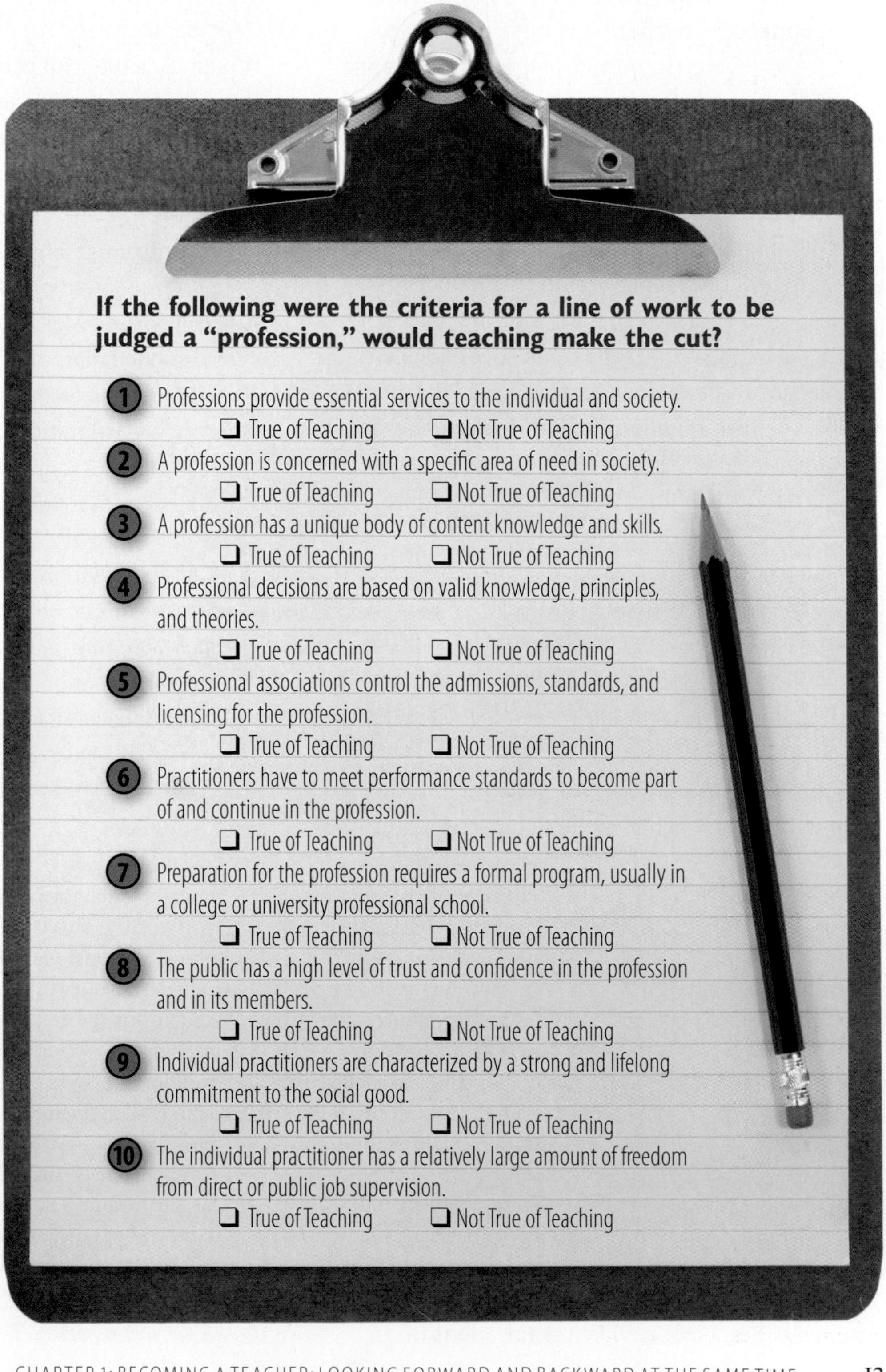

If the following were the criteria for a line of work to be judged a "profession," would teaching make the cut?

1. Professions provide essential services to the individual and society.
   ❑ True of Teaching   ❑ Not True of Teaching

2. A profession is concerned with a specific area of need in society.
   ❑ True of Teaching   ❑ Not True of Teaching

3. A profession has a unique body of content knowledge and skills.
   ❑ True of Teaching   ❑ Not True of Teaching

4. Professional decisions are based on valid knowledge, principles, and theories.
   ❑ True of Teaching   ❑ Not True of Teaching

5. Professional associations control the admissions, standards, and licensing for the profession.
   ❑ True of Teaching   ❑ Not True of Teaching

6. Practitioners have to meet performance standards to become part of and continue in the profession.
   ❑ True of Teaching   ❑ Not True of Teaching

7. Preparation for the profession requires a formal program, usually in a college or university professional school.
   ❑ True of Teaching   ❑ Not True of Teaching

8. The public has a high level of trust and confidence in the profession and in its members.
   ❑ True of Teaching   ❑ Not True of Teaching

9. Individual practitioners are characterized by a strong and lifelong commitment to the social good.
   ❑ True of Teaching   ❑ Not True of Teaching

10. The individual practitioner has a relatively large amount of freedom from direct or public job supervision.
    ❑ True of Teaching   ❑ Not True of Teaching

NEA CODE OF ETHICS OF THE EDUCATION PROFESSION

Preamble

The educator, believing in the worth and dignity of each human being, recognizes the supreme importance of the pursuit of truth, devotion to excellence, and the nurture of the democratic principles. Essential to these goals is the protection of freedom to learn and to teach and the guarantee of equal educational opportunity for all. The educator accepts the responsibility to adhere to the highest ethical standards.

The educator recognizes the magnitude of the responsibility inherent in the teaching process. The desire for the respect and confidence of one's colleagues, of students, of parents, and of the members of the community provides the incentive to attain and maintain the highest possible degree of ethical conduct. The Code of Ethics of the Education Profession indicates the aspiration of all educators and provides standards by which to judge conduct.

The remedies specified by the NEA and/or its affiliates for the violation of any provision of this Code shall be exclusive and no such provision shall be enforceable in any form other than the one specifically designated by the NEA or its affiliates.

PRINCIPLE I: Commitment to the Student

The educator strives to help each student realize his or her potential as a worthy and effective member of society. The educator therefore works to stimulate the spirit of inquiry, the acquisition of knowledge and understanding, and the thoughtful formulation of worthy goals.

In fulfillment of the obligation to the student, the educator—

1. Shall not unreasonably restrain the student from independent action in the pursuit of learning.
2. Shall not unreasonably deny the student's access to varying points of view.
3. Shall not deliberately suppress or distort subject matter relevant to the student's progress.
4. Shall make reasonable effort to protect the student from conditions harmful to learning or to health and safety.
5. Shall not intentionally expose the student to embarrassment or disparagement.
6. Shall not on the basis of race, color, creed, sex, national origin, marital status, political or religious beliefs, family, social or cultural background, or sexual orientation, unfairly

American Federation of Teachers (AFT)
An international union, affiliated with the American Federation of Labor and Congress of Industrial Organizations, representing teachers and other school personnel as well as many college faculty and staff members, healthcare workers, and public employees.

- **"Nurture of the democratic principles"** This phrase reminds us to honor individual expression, capitalize on special student interests, and expand students' abilities to explore and critique multiple ideas and values.
- **"Responsibility to adhere to the highest ethical standards"** Figure 1.3 shows statistics

indicating that the public considers teachers to be highly trustworthy. This is positive, as far as it goes. But your ethical responsibility as a teacher goes beyond telling the truth. Your responsibility is to place the needs of students at the center of your work and to give them priority over your own needs. Hence, your constant question is, "What is in the best interests of my students?" This is important as you consider a career in teaching. Many people enter the profession and discover that it is difficult to be as generous of spirit as the profession demands. That would not make you a bad person, but you need to consider how it relates to the "goodness of fit" between this profession and your personal attributes.

a. Exclude any student from participation in any program
b. Deny benefits to any student
c. Grant any advantage to any student

7. Shall not use professional relationships with students for private advantage.

8. Shall not disclose information about students obtained in the course of professional service unless disclosure serves a compelling professional purpose or is required by law.

PRINCIPLE II: Commitment to the Profession

The education profession is vested by the public with a trust and responsibility requiring the highest ideals of professional service.

In the belief that the quality of the services of the education profession directly influences the nation and its citizens, the educator shall exert every effort to raise professional standards, to promote a climate that encourages the exercise of professional judgment, to achieve conditions that attract persons worthy of the trust to careers in education, and to assist in preventing the practice of the profession by unqualified persons.

In fulfillment of the obligation to the profession, the educator—

1. Shall not in an application for a professional position deliberately make a false statement or fail to disclose a material fact related to competency and qualifications.

2. Shall not misrepresent his/her professional qualifications.

3. Shall not assist any entry into the profession of a person known to be unqualified in respect to character, education, or other relevant attribute.

4. Shall not knowingly make a false statement concerning the qualifications of a candidate for a professional position.

5. Shall not assist a noneducator in the unauthorized practice of teaching.

6. Shall not disclose information about colleagues obtained in the course of professional service unless disclosure serves a compelling professional purpose or is required by law.

7. Shall not knowingly make false or malicious statements about a colleague.

8. Shall not accept any gratuity, gift, or favor that might impair or appear to influence professional decisions or action.

SOURCE: National Education Association. (1975). Code of ethics of the education profession. http://www.nea.org/home/30442.htm; retrieved May 1, 2010.

1-2c AN ORGANIZED PROFESSION

Overall, teaching is a highly organized profession. In addition to the NEA, the **American Federation of Teachers (AFT),** created in 1916 and affiliated with the US labor movement, boasts more than 1.3 million members. Both the NEA and the AFT provide legal services and collective bargaining representation as well as a network of support for teachers, including professional development resources for your growth as a teacher. These large groups also wield a great deal of political influence on behalf of educators and schools.

When you enter the teaching profession, you may decide to join one or both of these organizations. We will visit them again in this book's final chapter, but it is not too early to think about becoming a member.

1-2d STARTING EARLY

The **National Association for the Education of Young Children (NAEYC)** is the nation's largest early-learning professional organization. Early-childhood education is recognized as the most critical stage for preparing future

National Association for the Education of Young Children (NAEYC) This professional organization is dedicated to improving the quality of education for all children birth to age eight.

learners. The NAEYC has standards for creating the first step in the "cradle-to-career" educational pipeline. High-quality early-learning programs are the foundation for future success in schools. The NAEYC focuses on the quality of education for all children, birth through age eight. A look at the position statement on student diversity developed by the NAEYC (see the sidebar on the next page) provides insight into the ways in which teaching very young children could never be considered an afterthought!

1-2e A NATIONAL BOARD

In 1987 the **National Board for Professional Teaching Standards (NBPTS)** was created to set forth a vision for what accomplished teachers might "look like." These principles were developed in response to the report *A Nation Prepared: Teachers for the 21st Century* (Carnegie Forum on Education and the Economy, 1986). Besides being an advocacy organization, the NBPTS sets standards for what accomplished teachers should know and be able to do and offers a national system to certify teachers who meet these standards.

© Ekaterina Monakhova/iStockphoto

FIGURE 1.3

Public Trust in Various Professions

Pollsters asked,

"Would you generally trust each of the following types of people to **tell the truth**, or not?"

The bars show the percentage of respondents who said they would trust each type of person.

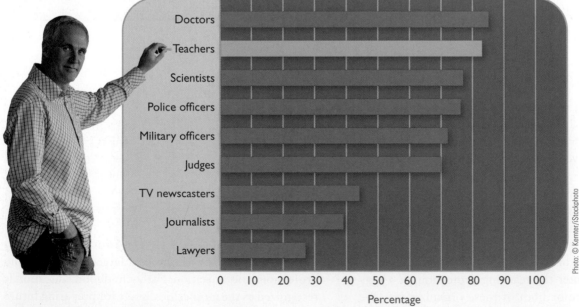

Photo: © Kemter/iStockphoto

SOURCE: Statistics from *The Harris Poll* #61, August 8, 2006; based on telephone interviews of 1,002 US adults, July 10–16, 2006.

HONORING DIVERSITY: POSITION STATEMENT

Young children and their families reflect a great and rapidly increasing diversity of language and culture. The National Association for the Education of Young Children's (NAEYC) recommendations emphasize that early childhood programs are responsible for creating a welcoming environment that respects diversity, supports children's ties to their families and community, and promotes both second language acquisition and preservation of children's home languages and cultural identities. Linguistic and cultural diversity is an asset, not a deficit, for young children.

Recommendations for working with families

- **Actively involve families in the early learning program.** Links between school, home, and community are important for all young children, but forging them can be challenging when families and program staff differ in culture and language. Ties to the community, respectful relationships with families, and encouragement of active, culturally meaningful family involvement are essential.

- **Help all families realize the cognitive advantages of a child knowing more than one language, and provide them with strategies to support, maintain, and preserve home language learning.** Families may think that speaking to their children only in English will help them learn the language faster. But home language preservation benefits children's cognitive development, and families with limited English proficiency provide stronger language models when they emphasize their home language.

- **Convince families that their home's cultural values and norms are honored.** Continuity between home and the early childhood setting supports children's social, emotional, cognitive, and language development. Though not always identical, practices at home and in school should be complementary.

Recommendations for working with young children

- **Ensure that children remain cognitively, linguistically, and emotionally connected to their home language and culture.** Children's positive development requires maintaining close ties to their family and community. If home language and culture are supported, children, families, and communities stay securely connected.

- **Encourage home language and literacy development, knowing that this contributes to children's ability to acquire English language proficiency.** Research confirms that bilingualism is an asset and an educational achievement. When children become proficient and literate in their home language, they transfer those skills to a second language.

- **Help develop essential concepts in the children's first language and within cultural contexts that they understand.** Although some children can seem superficially fluent in their second language, most children find it easier to learn new, complex concepts in a familiar language and cultural framework. Once established, these concepts readily transfer into a second language and contribute to later academic mastery.

Respect for diversity must become part of every classroom teacher's agenda, regardless of grade level and subject matter and of whether the teacher looks and sounds like his or her students.

Honoring diversity means accepting that we are all products of our own culture, our own biases, and our own beliefs. You must constantly ask, "Who are my students? What are their lives like? What are their stories? . . . and knowing these things, how can I help them learn?" This is all part of respecting the learner and ultimately respecting ourselves as learners. Chapter 5 addresses the issue of the wide diversity of students in today's schools and its implications for teaching and learning. If we think of diversity as an opportunity, we will grow from the challenge and become better teachers.

The NBPTS intends this certification to be a symbol of professional teaching excellence; it is entirely voluntary (National Board for Professional Teaching Standards, 2002). State licensing systems for teachers set entry-level standards, but NBPTS certification establishes more advanced standards. Out of approximately 2.9 million newly hired teachers in the United States, only about 50,000 will have achieved this certification.

Later in this book, we will review the standards set forth by the NBPTS as well as some of the components of the certification test. For now, the board and its work is yet another indication of the professionalism of teaching and the exciting prospects you have in entering the field.

1-2f MORE THAN A PROFESSION

We have been talking about teaching as a profession, but is that all it is? Carl Jung, the noted Swiss psychiatrist, said:

> An understanding heart is everything in a teacher. One looks back with appreciation at the brilliant teachers, but with gratitude to those who touched our human feeling. The curriculum is so much necessary raw material, but warmth is the vital element for the growing plant and for the soul of the child. (McGuire, 1954, paragraph 249)

So much is said about the skills and knowledge that are needed for teaching. The unspoken requirement, however, has to do with your dispositions, your own ability to understand your students, and to connect with them in ways that help them to become better learners.

More than in most other professions, your personality and your belief in yourself shine through the techniques and strategies you employ. Your authentic self—that part of you that wants to make a contribution to the social good—is evident in the way you address the students, in your smile, in your level of preparedness for class, in the questions you ask, and in the respect you demonstrate for students as individuals.

As you work with this text, be sure to explore your innermost hopes and dreams and keep asking yourself, "Is teaching really for me?"

WHY DO TEACHERS NEED A UNION?

Although teachers cannot be forced to join a union, both the NEA and the AFT have local affiliates all over the country, and there are more than 2.5 million people who belong to one or both of them. Because they are labor unions (the NEA became a union in the 1960s, and the AFT was founded as a union in 1912), many individuals challenge the professionalism of teaching, arguing that other professions do not have unions. In fact, many people see the unions' ability to call strikes as a potential means of victimizing the very people teachers serve, students.

Union advocates respond that teachers, unlike members of some of the wealthier professions, need collective bargaining to secure better working conditions and higher salaries. In negotiating contracts on teachers' behalf, unions have certainly helped teachers gain power over their workload expectations, class sizes, pay scales, and benefits.

The unions' role in school reform also provokes debate. As powerful national organizations, the NEA and AFT can lobby for educational improvements. But some people argue that teacher contracts can be so specifically written that it becomes difficult to enact meaningful school reform—that is, the contracts merely serve to maintain the current system.

You will need to form your own opinion about the role of teacher unions and their effect on teachers' professionalism. When you start your first teaching job, you should inquire about the local union affiliation of your school or district and the union's connection to the NEA, AFT, or both. Teachers' unions can provide tremendous support to the new teacher as well as resources for his or her professional development.

1-3 The Workplace: School Climate and School Culture

The day-to-day workings of a school influence how you enact your philosophy of teaching. Schools are constantly in flux, depending on student enrollment, collaboration among colleagues, pressures from the local community, and the vision of the school leader.

As you think about applying a teacher's professional commitments and values in a particular school setting, there are two terms you should know: **school climate** and **school culture.** These phrases refer to "the sum of the values, cultures, safety practices, and organizational structures within a school that cause it to function and react in particular ways" (McBrien & Brandt, 1997, p. 87).

Often the two terms are used interchangeably, but some educators make a distinction between them: *school climate* referring to the way students experience the school and *school culture* meaning the way teachers and administrators interact and collaborate.

Still other educators think about *school climate* as the general social atmosphere or environment in a school. This is my preferred way of using the term. The social environment in this sense includes the relationships among students, between students and teachers, among teachers themselves, and between teachers and administrators. Students experience their environment differently depending on the rules and protocols set up by school administrators and teachers. *School climate* also includes the orderliness of the environment, the clarity of the rules, and the strictness of the teachers in enforcing the rules (Moos, 1979, p. 96).

Think back to your educational autobiography. According to the definition of *school climate* as the general social atmosphere, how would you describe the climate of your elementary school, middle school, and high school? A school climate may be described as *nurturing, authoritarian,* or somewhere in between. For example, I experienced my high school as nurturing *and* strict, caring *and* rigorous. We can also ask whether a school has a *healthy* climate, one in which students are made aware of expectations for their behavior toward one another and their teachers. In your own elementary school, middle school, and high school, was the student body diverse in terms of ethnicity, race, and social class, and if so, was there evidence of

> **school climate** and **school culture** The values, cultures, practices, and organization of a school.

It is never too soon to consider yourself a reflective practitioner.

Some classroom climates can be experienced even by a casual observer.

CAN YOU FEEL THE SCHOOL CLIMATE?

Frequently, you can tell if a school's climate is nurturing by the feeling you get in the halls—if the principal and other administrators are readily visible, and if teachers smile and greet students by name. In such a school, students are treated as individuals.

At the other extreme, in a school with an authoritarian climate, the halls are very quiet, there are strict "no talking" rules, doors are closed tight, and there is a feeling of tension in the air.

Teaching practices, student and teacher diversity, and the relationships among administrators, teachers, parents, and students all contribute to *school climate*.

Although no single, universally accepted definition of *school culture* has been established, there is general agreement that it involves deep patterns of values, beliefs, and traditions formed over the course of the school's history (Deal & Peterson, 1990). A school culture may have, for instance, a reputation for being very academic. My high school did. The culture of my high school could be described as academically driven, college preparatory, nonathletic, and cerebral. We were thought of as "geeks" because we attended this serious-minded high school whose culture had been forged since its inception. Other high schools in my area had a culture that was more social, athletic, and active in the community, though also academic.

A school's culture is evident in its shared values, heroes, rituals, ceremonies, stories, and cultural networks. For example, if a school's leaders believe that motivation and academic achievement are a definitive part of the school's culture, they communicate and celebrate those values in as many ways as possible. A strong school culture flourishes with a clear set of values and norms that actively guide the way the school functions. In my high school, students were made to feel proud of the academic productivity of their classmates. Achievement was rewarded in the school newspaper and in organized assemblies.

When you think back to the ways in which the schools you attended functioned, how would you describe the school culture of your elementary, middle, and high schools? What did the schools stand for? How was that communicated?

---

prejudice or racism? How was that expressed? What did school officials do to make students feel like valued members of the educational community?

1-4 Concluding Thoughts

Although teaching is an important and essential profession, ideas about it are often oversimplified. Our memories of our teachers are sometimes selective and misleading. However, the interpersonal nature of teaching demands that those interested in the profession take stock of their own attributes and dispositions, their personal school experiences, and their future goals for themselves as teachers. It is never too soon to consider yourself a reflective practitioner.

STUDY TOOLS
CHAPTER 1

Located at back of the textbook
- Rip out Chapter Review Card
- Note-Taking Assistance

Located at CengageBrain.com
- Review Key Terms Flash Cards (Print or Online)
- Complete Practice Quizzes to prepare for tests
- Complete "Crossword Puzzle" to review key terms
- Watch the TeachSource Video Case "Becoming a Teacher: Voices and Advice from the Field"

USE THE TOOLS.

- Rip out the Review Cards in the back of your book to study.

Or Visit CourseMate for:

- Full, interactive eBook (search, highlight, take notes)
- Review Flashcards (Print or Online) to master key terms
- Test yourself with Auto-Graded Quizzes
- Bring concepts to life with Games, Videos, and Animations!

Go to CourseMate for (TEACH2) to begin using these tools.
Access at **www.cengagebrain.com**.

Complete the Speak Up survey in CourseMate at www.cengagebrain.com

f Follow us at **www.facebook.com/4ltrpress**

©iStockphoto.com/A-Digit

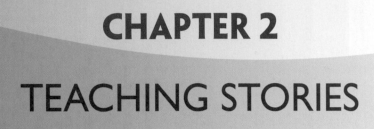

CHAPTER 2

TEACHING STORIES

© purestock/Photolibrary

This chapter gives you a glimpse into the ways teachers from grades pre-K–12 make their decisions to enter the field and what they consider the most exciting and challenging aspects of teaching. Their stories are designed to help you explore what Parker Palmer (1998) calls the "inner landscape of a teacher's life."

Being a teacher requires an emotional and intellectual commitment. By this I mean that, in a typical school day, teachers can experience excitement and frustration, pleasure and angst, great leaps of joy as well as sadness. How ready you are to navigate these emotions—while at the same time staying focused on your goals for the day—is something only you can know. The stories in this chapter may remind you of yourself or of a teacher you have had.

LEARNING OUTCOMES

After reading this chapter, you should be thinking about the following ideas:

2-1 Discuss common factors in individuals' decisions to become teachers.

2-2 Explain the idea "We teach who we are!"

2-3 Examine how the hidden curriculum may affect the climate in the classroom.

2-4 Explore the support systems that are in place for new teachers.

2-5 Compare the lifelong learning needs of teachers with those in other professions.

2-6 Create your own teaching story as you explore teaching as a career.

2-1 Who Are Our Teachers?

The National Education Association (NEA) that you read about in Chapter 1 conducts surveys every five years on the status of the US public school teacher. The results of those surveys give us a glimpse into the nature of the teaching workforce. Figure 2.1 presents various statistics about US public school teachers that give us insight into their ages, marital status, ethnicity, and education.

The majority of public school teachers in the US workforce are older than forty years of age, with the average age of forty-six. About 87 percent are white, which is a decline from 90 in 2001 (National Education Association, 2010). Given the increasing diversity of US students (see Chapter 5), many educators believe that US schools have an urgent need for young teachers from varied ethnic backgrounds.

One figure that has changed in recent decades is the proportion of males in the teaching force. It had declined from 31 percent in 1961 to about 21 percent in 2001, and then by 2006, it increased to 30 percent (Snyder, Tan, & Hoffman, 2006; National Education Association, 2010). Some researchers suspect that the declining number of male teachers had negative consequences for students and for the profession, so it is promising that more men are entering the profession.

Did You Know?

About 87 percent of US public school teachers are white. The majority are older than 40 years of age and female.

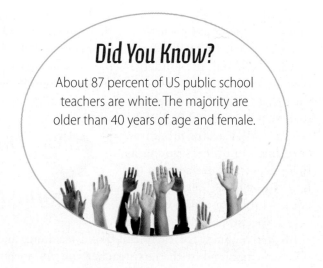

FIGURE 2.1

US Public School Teachers, by the Numbers

SOURCE: Data from National Education Association (2009), *Status of the American Public School Teacher 2005–2006*, Washington, D.C.: Author.

2-1a EARLY-CHILDHOOD EDUCATION

You may recall that we presented the National Association for the Education of Young Children's (NAEYC) code of ethics in Chapter 1. A national association dedicated to the early education of children highlights the significance of an auspicious beginning for a child's future learning. You may be wondering why so much attention is given to preschool and kindergarten through second grade.

Slightly more than one million children enrolled in public pre-kindergarten in 2008; that number is projected to reach 1,115,000 by 2012 (Snyder & Dillow, 2010). Preschool, pre-kindergarten, and kindergarten play a vital role in the development of children. What they learn and experience in their early years shapes their views of themselves and the world. Early-learning programs, enrolling children as young as three years old, are seen as the key to closing achievement gaps, which we will examine later. Special sensitivities and skills are required for early-childhood teaching, and they are embodied by the next teacher you will meet.

Q: *Do you have any memories of going to preschool?*

CAROL: Carol is in her eleventh year as an early-childhood teacher, specializing in young children at the pre-kindergarten level. I once had the opportunity to spend some time in her classroom and was struck by how competent her four-year-old students appeared. They understood the rules of the classroom environment and were encouraged to do things on their own, contributing to the life of the classroom by putting materials away in their proper places, managing their belongings in their cubbies, and much more. Carol's story that follows is a nontraditional path to early childhood education:

Carol spent her growing up years with a blackboard and chalk, playing school with her younger sister and her friends. But knowing she wanted to be a teacher was not enough, and life took her in other directions until, quite by chance, she was asked to assist in a pre-kindergarten classroom in a local private day school in her neighborhood. That was ten years ago, and she has since been a lead teacher for three-, four-, and five-year-olds in two different early-learning environments. Her college education and further courses enabled her to earn the proper early-childhood teaching credential, which she maintains annually by taking courses mandated by her state.

Carol described a major challenge for her work with young children as facilitating their social development. "The most rewarding part of the work is knowing that you are giving the children the tools to appropriately communicate with each other. The proper social development is essential for future learning. I have the opportunity to help the children to begin the process of communicating appropriately and effectively in social situations with other children. I spend a lot of time observing the children's interactions. You have to be able to sit with the child at eye level and discuss alternatives for non-judgmentally helping them to achieve their behavioral goals. It also requires that you understand that whatever the behavioral goals for the young child, they are not going to take place immediately (these are long-term goals that are seeded in the early-childhood classroom and are reinforced through the child's early education."

When asked what was most stressful about her work, Carol responded by describing the importance of being able to ascertain what acceptable and unacceptable developmental behavior is for a small child. "There are students who require special services that enter school having not been diagnosed; when this happens, the burden is on the early-childhood teacher who must be certain she or he can get the correct services for the child as research on early intervention reveals positive outcomes for children with social and emotional issues. These decisions are not rendered lightly and require thoughtful reflection and expert consultation."

When asked to share the most exciting aspects of her work, Carol responded, "When the kids get it and learn to become comfortable in the classroom—they have learned the routine and the sequence of activities—you can tell they feel safe and competent to carry out routines. These young children are on a journey of self-regulation. My classroom is one step in that journey. It is so exciting to see them grow in this area and see them functioning autonomously. Many people do not recognize how fragile young children are as they develop their own sense of themselves and how terribly important it is to have prepared, informed, and caring professionals with whom they can grow."

Often, early-childhood educators are dismissed by society as glorified "babysitters." This is both incorrect and damaging to the profession and to an understanding of the crucial role that early learning plays in the development of healthy children and productive students. There is consistent controversy over the role of play in early-learning environments. Watching Carol's children at play reminds us of the social skills the students develop through play, such as empathy, impulse control, capacity for sharing, communicating, and problem solving. Play-based activities also enhance children's capacity to think creatively, make choices, explore their environment, and develop prewriting skills and sequencing skills. Carol's emphasis on the children's development of appropriate social interactions is vitally important for how students learn. As we will see in later chapters, learning is an interactive, social experience that requires communication between the learners and their peers as well as their teachers. Perhaps the most dominant misconception about early-childhood education is that it is not as work intensive as teaching in the higher grades. In fact, preparing a curriculum and activities for young children requires many hours of research and careful planning. Like the teachers you will read about in the following section, Carol receives support from her colleagues and the director of the early-learning program.

2-1b Deciding to Become a Teacher

"In my entire life as a student, I remember only twice being given the opportunity to come up with my own ideas, a fact I consider typical and terrible."
—Eleanor Duckworth, educational researcher (1991)

© Wojciech Gajda/iStockphoto

Over the years, I have often asked elementary, middle, and high school teachers from all backgrounds to talk about themselves and their attitudes toward the profession. We begin with what some of them said about their reasons for becoming teachers.

KATHRYN: Kathryn is a high school biology and chemistry teacher, teaching grades nine and ten in a suburban northeastern school district. She teaches in two different schools in the same district and goes back and forth between them. Her students adore her and she works them really hard. She majored in the sciences in college and took a minor in secondary education. She just always knew that, as much as she loves scientific research, she always wanted to be a teacher:

When I was in elementary school, I loved being able to try new things and make new discoveries. I think I was initially taken with the idea of daily exploration in any way, shape, or form, and that trend continued well into middle and high school. Even simple things seemed magical in a classroom; tadpoles transformed in front of us, dissecting frogs became a lesson in the operating room; learning poetry turned me into John Donne. When considering college options, I knew my heart belonged in teaching. I spent much of my high school career forcing myself to master material, with the most effective method being through explanations to my peers. I had heard the saying multiple times, that if you want to prove you know a subject, try teaching it to someone else. Being in school exposed me to the teaching profession and I thrived in an environment that challenged me to adapt socially, intellectually, and emotionally on a daily basis. I knew that not every job had the potential to do that.

JESSICA: Jessica is an English teacher and literacy coordinator in a high school on a military base in the middle of the country. Her first love was dance, and she majored in it as an undergraduate student. She has been teaching for nine years. This is how she answers the question about deciding to become a teacher:

I had always wanted to be a teacher. When I was growing up, I loved to play school with the children I babysat, and I would give the neighborhood children free dance lessons. After college, I decided that I didn't want to be a dancer full time, so I turned to my other love—English. From the very first day of my very first graduate class in education, I knew I had chosen the right career.

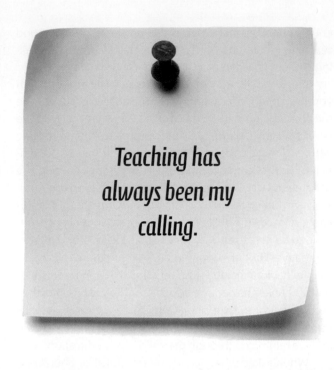

Teaching has always been my calling.

I attribute my interest in teaching to several things: (1) a lifelong love of learning; (2) I had always loved going to school, even when I wasn't the best student (I did better in school as I got older); and (3) the fact that my mother is also a teacher, and I grew up watching her grade papers and plan her instruction.

AMANDA: Amanda is a third-grade teacher in the northeast corner of the country. When I first entered her classroom, I was struck by how quiet it was. She apologized profusely for the silence, remarking that the students were usually noisier and more actively engaged in groups, but this time they were just finishing independent reading. She promised that soon I would see the real class! So often we think of good classes as silent, but learning often happens in social exchanges with others, as we will see in later chapters. When asked why she entered teaching, Amanda said:

Teaching has always been my calling. Ever since my first week of kindergarten, I knew that teaching would be my chosen path. That first day, I came home exclaiming to my mom, "I want to be a teacher just like Mrs. Seguin!" I spent the rest of my elementary school days playing teacher with my sister, my friends, and even my stuffed animals when no one was available. I had grade books, lesson plans, and homemade worksheets, and I made signs for my door that indicated my room was now "Miss Riggs's 1st grade class."

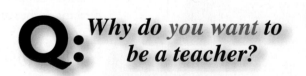

Q: *Why do you want to be a teacher?*

Even though I have always been drawn to the profession, it wasn't until my first year of college when I was taking an education course that I began to fully understand why I wanted to be a part of education. My dad was never what one might call a reader or a writer. The only book that I saw him read was the Bible, and I remember him asking me for help in spelling different words starting in second grade. Yet it was my dad who showed me the responsibility of being an educator. I was talking with him about a literacy lesson that I needed to prepare for class. I shared the many techniques that I had learned and how I was going to have the kids first participate in a hands-on activity and then draw the knowledge out from the activity. My father changed my outlook on education forever when he said, "I would have learned how to read and write if my teachers had taught like you." It was then that I realized I wanted to be a teacher to reach those kids who couldn't learn through traditional teaching methods. I wanted to find a way so that every student "clicked" with literacy and gained the skills to make his or her life one of continuous learning.

PEARL: Now semi-retired, Pearl was an elementary school teacher in an urban area of New York City. She has been both the mathematics specialist and the social studies specialist in her school as well as a mentor to countless student teachers. Her intellectual love is mathematics, and she is also committed to issues of social justice. She relentlessly celebrates women and people of color. Pearl's path to teaching went like this:

My parents were immigrants; my mom was born in Russia in 1905. In her little corner of the world, education for girls was not thought of as a necessity. She was never sent to school. When she came to the United States, she worked in sweatshops on the Lower East Side and cooked and cleaned for people to support herself. She cherished the educational opportunities that were afforded to children in this country—"God bless America," she would say. She especially cherished the opportunity afforded me, her daughter, to go to school. In my mother's eyes, teaching was ranked as the most highly important and respected profession.

My paternal grandfather was a theologian and a sought-after teacher in his town, known for his knowledge of religious texts. My father thought the world of him and respected him for his knowledge and ability to communicate ideas. So the teaching profession was well respected in my home.

Then there came Miss Rochford, my sixth-grade teacher. I loved Miss Rochford. She made math fun; she introduced us to musicals; she taught us how to write scripts and then we produced our own play; she showed us slides of her trips to Europe; and she exposed us to poetry. She introduced me to Mark Twain, Shakespeare, and Robert Frost. Miss Geraldine Rochford opened doors for me to a world beyond East New York, Brooklyn. I wanted to do the things she did. I wanted to travel, enjoy the arts, and share the wonders of learning with kids like myself. That is why I never wanted to leave the public school system. She was one of the people who made me into a lifelong learner. As early as the sixth grade, I knew that I wanted to teach.

Teachers are important role models for their students.

© Elizabeth Crews

JANE: Jane has been teaching eighth-grade mathematics in an urban area on the East Coast for ten years. Her decision to enter teaching came after her own children had gone off to college. The wife of a minister, she had taught religious classes in her church, and she wanted to choose a career she thought she would be good at. Jane is now a mentor teacher and very well thought of by students and faculty. Here's how Jane explains her career choice:

I feel like I entered teaching for all the wrong reasons. I wanted retirement benefits and good working hours, and I wanted to use skills that I believed I had developed as a mother and a minister's wife. I thought you should enter teaching because you had always wanted to be a teacher, but for me, it was really an afterthought that came later in life—that is why I think of it as being for the wrong reasons.

When I self-assessed, though, I recognized that I was a good listener and genuinely excited about math. I had majored in math in college, and I thought that was a good start. I also have a lot of self-knowledge, so I am able to recover from my mistakes. I have the ability to say "I'm sorry" when I have made a mistake, and I have a lot of respect for young people.

I knew when I entered my first education course that I had made the right decision since teaching would ensure that I was a lifelong learner. I am very focused on my own and my students' education. Teaching for me is like water walking; if you keep your eyes on the goals, you will not sink.

ADAM: Adam is in his fourteenth year of teaching history in a northeastern suburb. He was a perpetual student. He loved learning and loved the study of history, and he decided to get his PhD in history at the ripe old age of twenty-seven. Here is Adam's story:

I entered teaching when my university adviser told me I was ready to defend my dissertation. A perennial student, I realized I needed a job! My adviser told me of a local college that needed instructors in history, and I started my teaching career with no formal education training.

Once in the classroom, I immediately realized that I really liked making complex concepts understandable to students. I was excited about teaching. I knew that I had a lot to learn, so I entered a program to earn a teaching certificate. I wound up becoming a secondary school history

teacher. It gave me the opportunity to connect current events with the history curriculum and to join the faculty of a high-functioning, academically oriented school where we work hard and feel a lot of pressure to meet a high level of quality teaching.

I love it. I could not imagine becoming a high school teacher when I was younger, and now cannot imagine doing anything else with my life's work.

Did You Know?

Teachers work an average of fifty hours per week.

When teachers are asked why they decided to enter the profession, they often say, "I love children" or "I love kids." These answers echo the findings of many formal studies. Another burning reason for deciding to become a teacher is an individual's love of learning The most successful teachers I know—like the ones featured in this chapter—typically talk about how they "loved learning." That is not to say they do not also love children, but teaching is a complex activity. In the words of educational researcher Jackie Grennon Brooks (2002), from whom we will hear more in a later chapter,

Common thinking is that teaching is simple. But teaching isn't simple. It's a highly sophisticated intellectual activity that requires, among other things, a centered presence in the classroom, good negotiation skills, understandings of pedagogy and psychology that inform one another, and sensitivity to sociological factors in learning.

When beginning education students talk about entering teaching because they love kids, I learn from talking with them that they have been babysitters and camp counselors and that they have enjoyed these responsibilities. That is a fine start, but these informal experiences with children or adolescents are different from the more structured experiences found in classrooms and the demands of teaching. At this point in your reading, you may have already visited one or more classrooms and observed teaching in action, so you are aware of the vast differences between the formal and informal settings in which we interact with youngsters.

In addition to loving learning, people pursuing teaching careers often also loved school. That matches what we heard from Kathryn, Jessica, Amanda, Adam and Pearl, in this chapter as well as from Laura and Sharyn in Chapter 1. Notice especially what Kathryn said about the inspiration provided by daily exploration and experimentation.

"I LIKE THE HOURS"

Sam wakes up one morning and says, "I want to be teacher." When asked why, Sam answers, "I like the hours."

This is an uninspiring reason, and it is misguided as well. Did you know that teachers work much longer than the traditional 9:00-to-3:00 day? Look at the following data the NEA (2006a) gathered from its teacher members:

Twenty-first-century teachers:

- Spend an average of fifty hours per week on all teaching duties.
- Teach an average of twenty-one pupils in a class at the elementary level and twenty-eight pupils per class at the secondary level.
- Spend an average of $443 per year of their own money to meet the needs of their students.
- Enter the teaching profession to help shape the next generation.

Notice too, how Adam, who had never thought about teaching as a younger person, could not now imagine doing anything else! There are many researchers who believe that excellent male teachers have a strong positive impact on student achievement, especially, of male students (Dee, 2005, 2006).

Another major reason secondary teacher candidates cited for becoming educators was prior experiences as a high school tutor or peer teacher. Like Jane, some were motivated to teach because of positive experiences in informal teaching settings, and some had early religious training that affected their desire to serve others and teach.

What about Adam's story? His description of what we might call "falling into" teaching may resonate with you if you have just lately considered the idea of becoming a teacher. Not everyone who enters the field has had a lifelong calling to teach. Yet life as a teacher becomes fulfilling when there is a good match between the person and the demands of the profession. This is what I referred to as goodness of fit in Chapter 1. For Adam, teaching offered an excellent fit with his personality and his desire to share his love of history with his students while fostering his students' success.

2-2 Excitement and Challenges in Teaching

"Every September, every teacher proceeds into foreign territories." —Maxine Hong Kingston, distinguished writer and professor (1986)

When teachers are asked about the most exciting aspects of their work, invariably their answers relate to student learning. In this section we explore what some teachers say really excites them about their work, and then we examine some difficult challenges.

2-2a WHAT ARE THE MOST EXCITING ASPECTS OF TEACHING?

KATHRYN: When I started teaching, I lived for the light bulb moments—the times when difficult concepts finally clicked for a student. I liked being challenged to think of explanations and analogies that were outside of the box. As much as you plan and try to perfect your lesson, there will always be something that can totally derail a class. People are unpredictable, and the spontaneous moments show both the students' and the teacher's true colors. A lot of the profession is having the flexibility to handle whatever situation arises. I love being able to say that not a day goes by where I do the exact same thing. Good teachers change their lessons, try new techniques, master skills that work, but nothing is ever the same—guaranteeing that every day will be exciting.

The students in my building have a unique set of challenges, and I do the best I can to let them know they are safe and supported in my classroom. When students

© VisualField/iStockphoto

know you care, they are willing to go the extra mile for their teacher, and that's what makes my job so exciting. To have your "work" thank you is probably the most rewarding feeling ever.

AMANDA: Contrary to popular belief, I do not find it exciting when my students get 100 percent on their tests. It is the process that is exciting—the look on a student's face when he or she finally gets it, watching a student move from confusion to understanding, fielding a question you did not expect and do not know the answer to. It has been my greatest joy to see that student who struggled so much in an area work hard and become successful.

There are many times when I struggle with presenting difficult material so that all students can grasp the "big idea" of the lesson. I can go through four or five activities in my room, and sometimes there are a handful of kids who just cannot make sense of the material. Finally finding a way to reach those kids—now that is exciting.

The classroom is a complex roller-coaster ride in the dark; you never know what will happen next. From scheduling changes to student needs, environmental factors (try teaching about fractions in 90-degree weather!), and even your own moods, no plan is ever left in its original state. An educator must roll with the needs of his or her students, and those needs are ever changing, every day. I find that exciting.

JESSICA: The most exciting aspects of being a teacher are the possibilities that come with each new day. I teach adolescents, and they truly are different people every day. Watching them change and grow from the first day of the school year to the last is like watching a transformation right in front of your own eyes, and it is very exciting and challenging.

Though it seems like a cliché, the most rewarding part of the day is the "aha" that I see on students' faces when they understand something they didn't understand before.

Q: *What do you think will most excite you about teaching?*

JANE: To me, meeting a brand new group of students each year is the most exciting part of teaching. Because every group of students is unique, I am challenged to address my teaching strategies in an entirely new way than I did the previous year. It is like starting a new job every year. There is so much to learn from each new set of students. It is so exciting and challenging to understand each class's strengths and to tailor your teaching strategies to help them be all they can be in mathematics.

PEARL: Teaching has made me a lifelong learner. In order to keep things new and interesting, I am always reading, studying, and thinking of new ways to teach a concept.

As a classroom teacher, I had the opportunity to wear many hats: storyteller, dream weaver, mathematician, scientist, poet, author, playwright, producer, director, choreographer, historian, and social worker—you name it. A classroom teacher has to play each of those roles, and sometimes all in one day. Teaching makes you aware of process—for instance, coming up with a rubric for writing a good biographical report and teaching kids how to take notes, organize their materials, and pay attention to the editing and presentation. I get so immersed in my work very often that I forget to go to the bathroom until it is time to go home.

2-2b REWARDS OF A TEACHING LIFE

The following observations about teaching provide an overview of these teachers' beliefs based on their experiences and their hopes for the profession as they continue. You can think of these observations as the "teaching ideas behind their stories."

- For these teachers, the idea of meeting new students every year and, in Jessica's case, feeling like there are new students almost daily, is a stimulating aspect of being a teacher. Each day is different, requiring a sharp and attentive adult presence in the classroom. These teachers enjoy the challenge.
  - Kathryn loves that every day is a new challenge and that nothing is ever the same.
  - Amanda notes that the process of teaching is more exciting than the outcomes. Like Amanda, many teachers try different approaches to content material to make sure they reach the various types of learners in their classes.

- Kathryn, Pearl, Amanda, and Jessica talk about the excitement of reaching the children and recognizing that they "got it" as it related to new knowledge construction. Pearl gets so immersed in the activities with her students that she forgets to take a bathroom break.
- These teachers, typical of most, work actively on their teaching preparations and constantly challenge themselves to come up with novel ways to engage students in their own learning. They remind me that "to teach is to learn." Kathryn tells us that she really understands a concept when she has to decide how to teach it.

2-2c WHAT ARE THE MOST DIFFICULT CHALLENGES FOR TEACHERS?

KATHRYN: I've always prided myself on staying organized and on top of all responsibilities. Sometimes it's incredibly easy, and other times you don't know how you will make it through the day. There are just so many facets to being a good teacher that require all of your attention, that multitasking alone isn't possible. The paperwork, the grading, the extra help, the lesson planning, the phone calls, the make-up work, the list goes on and on, and it all adds up to an incredible amount of time. Finding time to complete everything to my personal level of satisfaction is hard. Not every new teacher is prepared for that when they walk in the door—I know I wasn't. I still give up Saturdays and end up having 13 hour Thursdays, but every minute is worth it when I know my students are becoming productive members of society and developing skills that will serve them throughout their life.

At first, I was intimidated by my colleagues and was afraid to ask for help. Your fellow teachers are your greatest allies. Any sports team will work better when they rely on each other, and teachers of any discipline learn that together they make better lessons. I could not have succeeded if my fellow science teachers had not been supportive and collaborative. Each person has a unique set of talents, and every student deserves access to that. We have found that, in collaborating, we have motivational, engaging, exciting lessons that reach all levels of learners. No man is an island, and teachers need not reinvent the wheel to be successful in the classroom.

AMANDA: I find that the most difficult challenge is staying focused on my purpose. I am not in the room to raise test scores, to be a child's best friend, or to follow every theory I learned in school. I am there to help students go beyond their potential and gain skill sets needed for a successful, learning life. Many distractions are found in the school environment—often created by those who are well meaning. Stick to what you know is best for your students despite what others around you might think.

One year, my room was across the hall from a teacher whom you might refer to as burned out. Every morning she arrived at the same time as the kids. By the time the children began to enter her room, my classroom was busy with morning learning activities. At least four times a week, our classroom was disrupted with her rants of "Why do Mrs. P's students get right to work and you are out here talking! I am tired of my class not being ready for the day!" These outbursts not only damaged her class but mine as well.

A good educator knows how to instruct students about expected behaviors and not shout about bad behaviors. No matter how frustrated, disappointed, or exhausted I become, I am here as a teacher and a learner, and learning happens mostly by my example—a good example or a poor one.

2-2d TEACHING, LEARNING, AND BURNOUT

By a "learning life," Amanda refers to a desire to know more and to have the skills to acquire new knowledge when the need and desire arises. Amanda herself has a "learning life," and, by example and through practice, she engages her students in what it means to be a learner. Previously in the chapter, the quote from Jackie Grennon Brooks introduced the concept of the teacher as a "centered presence" in the classroom. Amanda's understanding of her role in the classroom and her goals for her students helps her establish this centered presence. She is prepared and capable and has high expectations for her students. When Amanda says that learning happens by example, she means that she models to her students—demonstrates through her own behavior—what it looks like to be a learner. She learns about the content areas she teaches through her own research; she learns about her students through the interactions she has with them; and she learns about herself as she strives to refine her practice and to discover what works best for her students.

Amanda's teacher neighbor appears to be "burned out," meaning that she has lost the motivation to excel in her work and is no longer able to be an effective teacher. **Teacher burnout,** a reaction to prolonged high stress,

> **teacher burnout** The condition of teachers who have lost their motivation, desire, sense of purpose, and energy for being effective practitioners.

commonly results either in withdrawing and caring less, or in working harder, often mechanically, to the point of exhaustion (Farber, 1991). As in any other field, burnout can have serious consequences for the health and happiness of teachers, their students, and the families with which they interact. There are many causes of teacher burnout, the most common being working conditions that are unsupportive and stressful interactions with parents and students. New teachers may experience burnout when the work of teaching requires a different set of skills from what they had anticipated. Teachers who have been in the profession longer and have not taken advantage of opportunities to renew their skills through formal and informal professional development may also experience burnout.

Table 2.1 lists some symptoms of burnout and steps you can take to combat it. One of the most important protections from burnout is being reflective. Remember what Chapter 1 said about being a reflective practitioner. Often a teaching journal—an idea presented in the "Writing & Reflection" activity—is helpful in this respect. Writing in the journal is a way to monitor your work and your emotional availability for the tasks ahead of you.

In a remark not unconnected to the idea of burnout, Pearl complains about teachers' salaries. Many educators believe that the feminization of the teaching profession—the decline in the percentage of male teachers—has helped reduce the pressure for better pay and benefits. Yet teachers' salaries have, in fact, risen considerably over the past few decades. Elementary and secondary school teachers now make an average of about $51,000 per year. Starting salaries for new teachers average about $34,000 per year. These figures do vary considerably from district to district and state to state. It is important to note that more than half of US public school teachers feel satisfied with their salaries (National Education Association, 2009).

Did You Know?

Teachers in elementary and secondary schools have an average annual salary of about $51,000.

TABLE 2.1 — Recognizing and Dealing with Teacher Burnout

Signs of Burnout	What Teachers Can Do	What Schools Can Do
Your expectations for becoming a teacher and your experience are in conflict.	Consult with other teachers about your feelings and such matters as curriculum planning.	Create networks for new teachers and set up regular group meetings.
You do not feel like going to work.	Maintain a teacher journal in which you record your experiences and feelings.	Provide adequate resources and facilities to support teachers.
You have difficulty concentrating and feel inadequate in your role as a teacher.	Join new-teacher networks at your school or at the district level. Share your experiences, and keep journaling.	Provide clear job descriptions and expectations for new teachers.
You feel overwhelmed by the paperwork and the workload.	Find a mentor or seek the one to whom you have been assigned. Talk about your feelings!	Establish and maintain open communication between the school administration and the teachers.
You withdraw from your colleagues or enter into conflicts with them.	You may be emotionally exhausted. Find a professional to talk with.	Allow for and encourage professional development activities that help new teachers find mentors and become part of networks.

SOURCES: Adapted from Kyraciou (2001) and Wood & McCarthy (2002).

2-2e CHALLENGES AND OPPORTUNITIES

JESSICA: One of the most difficult challenges for teachers stems from paperwork! I had no idea going into the profession how much paperwork there is to manage. I assumed that lesson plans, student handouts, and student work would be all the paperwork I'd come into contact with. In addition to those items, there are constant requests for information from the office, the nurse, the psychologists, special education teachers, parents, administrators, and even people in the community that must be dealt with promptly and regularly. The amount of paperwork required for a classroom observation, or a field trip, or a school play, can be mind boggling.

Another major difficulty I didn't anticipate was dealing with parents. Although the majority of parents are on your side because both you and they are trying to achieve the goal of education for their children, there are parents who hold you responsible for things that are out of your control, who will blame you when a child fails even when you've done everything in your power to help the child. When parents see you as the adversary and not as their partner, it can be very painful.

These things shouldn't dissuade people from becoming teachers. You learn how to deal with them effectively and appropriately soon after you begin teaching. They represent difficulties I didn't know about before I entered teaching, but the benefits of this career far outweigh the challenges in the workplace.

Jessica's comment about paperwork excluded some other areas in the daily life of the classroom where paper needs to be managed. These include attendance reports, progress reports for each student, and evidence of student work. Elementary school teachers often keep work folders for each student, whereas in the middle and upper grades student work is often handled using computer software programs. Science teachers usually have lengthy lab reports to evaluate, and language arts and social studies teachers evaluate analytical essays, term reports, book responses, and creative writing. In a 2001 survey, "paperwork" combined with "heavy workload," "extra responsibilities," and "meetings" form the

WRITING & REFLECTION

Begin a Teaching Journal

Start now to keep a professional journal for yourself. If you have not had a lot of practice journaling, starting a reflective journal can be daunting. You may want to begin by inserting the writing activities from Chapter 1: drawing yourself as a teacher and your metaphor or simile for teaching, as well as your educational autobiography and a memory of a favorite teacher. You can keep your journal in a notebook, a blank book, a binder, or digitally on your computer or online—any method that is most comfortable and inspiring to you.

Being a reflective teacher is a theme we will return to again and again in this text. Reflective teachers take careful note of how their teaching practice is going and modify their methods accordingly. Because you are just embarking on teaching, your reflective journal should include how you are experiencing being an education student and what you are learning about teaching and yourself.

You can continue to fill your journal as you read this book, using as inspiration both the guided "Writing & Reflection" activities found in each chapter as well as your own thoughts and ideas on questions and topics presented. As you journal try to let your thoughts flow, without trying to edit them or get them down perfectly, and see where they take you. Your true feelings are more likely to surface this way.

Here are a few questions to help you begin your teaching journal:

- How are you experiencing the introductory education course you are taking?
- What are you discovering about the teaching profession that you did not know previously? Are there any surprises?
- At this point, how do you feel about a career in teaching?

Remember: You are on your own journey of growth and change, and the journal is a good record-keeping device for this process. Getting into the habit of journaling now can serve you well into your future career as a teacher.

Completing paperwork is one of many responsibilities as a teacher.

© Blend Images/Superstock

all jobs, the politics of the environment can affect each of the workers. It is a good idea to learn about the expectations and norms of the school environment in which you will be working. You may already have had jobs where the politics of the environment affected your work. Although workplace politics may annoy or sometimes discourage you, keep in mind how important it is that schools function as learning communities where all the professionals share a core set of common goals.

JANE: For me, the greatest challenge is having to implement the eighth-grade mathematics curriculum at a pace determined by the date of the standardized test. Instead of asking myself, "Should I linger longer on this topic since the students seem to need more time?" I speed along because I know there is so much to cover for the test.

This is a frustration in my teaching career since I am interested in how the students can make their math learning personal and relate it to their lives. This may take time, but it is important, and it always leaves me behind my colleagues in getting the curriculum done. I know that "teaching for the test" does not help the students make personal meaning for themselves.

Jane feels she is constantly challenged to cover math topics rapidly to prepare students for the standardized test they must take. With today's emphasis on standards—and on the tests that determine whether students meet those standards—many teachers feel similar pressures. A large number of educators, like Jane, believe that merely covering curriculum is the wrong approach. It leads to a shallow form of learning. Instead, these educators say, we need to uncover the curriculum by engaging students in exploring ideas and developing a deeper, more meaningful understanding. Remember what Jessica said previously in the chapter: "The best times are when students uncover new meaning for themselves."

PEARL: As a new elementary school teacher, I found one of the most difficult challenges was engaging with the curriculum. I had to familiarize myself with a lot of topics that I was not sure about. I spent hours each weekend

category that teachers said hurt them the most in their efforts to provide the best service in their teaching positions (National Education Association, 2003, Table 55). Fortunately, there are web-based software products that make handling data for especially large numbers of students much more manageable. We will visit those systems in Chapter 7.

Dealing with parents is part of a teacher's responsibility. We serve the children, but they are not ours. Jessica is conflicted about her communication with parents. Of course, parents are affected by what happens at their child's school and in their child's classroom. Communication between teachers and parents is important, and it is fostered through school practices that we will explore later in this text. Not only can parents influence decisions made about their child's education at school, but they can also contribute to the governance of the school though a parent teacher association (PTA) or

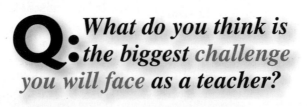

Q: *What do you think is the biggest challenge you will face as a teacher?*

similar group. It is always a good idea to reach out to parents and invite them to become part of your classroom community as helpers and contributors. In some school districts, parents are a frequent presence in classrooms. In other communities, parents are not available as often because of work responsibilities, but it is still important to invite them to contribute whenever possible.

Many people experience schools as "little villages," where the principal is the mayor and other individuals have varying amounts of importance or privilege. In

planning for the upcoming weeks by going to the library, finding the right books or the right motivational poems, leafing through magazines for the right pictures to support a lesson or illustrate a word, making visual aids, buying materials, and marking papers. As I became more experienced, I continued to plan on the weekends, but it became more a source of pleasure than of anxiety.

Pearl describes a major challenge for teachers at all levels: the preparation required to engage students in meaningful learning experiences. Many people, like Sam previously in this chapter, are unaware of the number of hours beyond the school day that teachers spend in preparation. Teachers can never be *over*prepared. The term *curriculum*, as we will explore later in this text, refers to a plan of studies that includes the ways in which the instructional content is organized and presented at each grade level. Even if you have studied a subject area extensively, you may need to deepen your knowledge of certain topics in the curriculum. Students know when a teacher is prepared for the school day. It is evident in the materials the teacher has assembled and the activities the teacher is ready to implement. It contributes to Brooks's centered presence in the classroom.

2-3 Teaching and Vision

Research has found that all teachers carry in their head a vision of what they want to be as a teacher (Hammerness, 2006). That is, all teachers have their own sense of what a classroom should "look like" and how it should function. Yet these visions of teaching are as variable as are the individuals who choose to teach.

Our beliefs and images concerning teaching are often difficult to enact; there is often a disconnect between what we imagine and what we can practice. For example, when I walked into a second-grade classroom early one morning, the teacher had the children in the center of the room and was engaging them in hand motions and movement routines to a popular rock song blasting from her boom box. The children were loving it! When the activity was done, Ms. Outerbridge said, "OK, girls and boys, we are now ready to work!" When I asked her about this activity, she said that (like Jessica) she had been a dancer, and her life in dance had taught her that releasing the energy in our

TEACHSOURCE VIDEO CASE

Surprises of the First Year

You can find another story about the excitement and challenges of teaching on the student website. Watch the TeachSource Video Case "The First Year of Teaching: One Colleague's Story," in which Will Starner talks about his initial year in a classroom. After watching the video, consider the following question:

What ways did Will find to cope with the challenges of his first year of teaching?

bodies was an important way to stimulate the thinking in our minds. She worried that when her students came to class, they were too docile, having already learned by grade 2 how to "be quiet." She wanted them to be active in their bodies so they could be active thinkers about the topics of study.

"How wonderful!" I thought. I knew, however, that try as I might, I could never get myself or my youngsters to learn and then enact this intricate movement routine. I do not have that set of skills. I admired Ms. Outerbridge's vision but could not enact it. It is in this way that who we are comes to bear upon what we do with children and how we engage them in learning.

Throughout your journey to become a teacher, you will be asked about your personal vision. It is a goal of teacher preparation programs that you develop a personal educational philosophy informed not only by the scholars and research you have learned about in your program but also by your own beliefs, metaphors, personal vision, and values. The combination of self-knowledge and scholarly knowledge will assist you in developing your own philosophy. You started to do this in Chapter 1 when you described your personal simile or metaphor for teaching.

The mantra that "we teach who we are" permeates this text. Ms. Outerbridge is a dancer; that background has served her as a learner, and she shares her passion with her second graders. Similarly, in the story that follows, my life as a scientist found its way into a third-grade classroom not long ago.

Every week, I was visiting a local elementary school classroom and exploring different topics in physical science with them. One weekend before a visit, I was in another state celebrating the seventh birthday of my first granddaughter. Her mother, my daughter, discovered that the batteries in her digital camera appeared to be dead and

A wide variety of classroom activities is necessary to engage students' minds and bodies.

© Michael Newman/PhotoEdit, Inc.

2-3a HIDDEN CURRICULUM

The stories we tell students about our lives and experiences outside of school are one small part of what may be considered the **hidden curriculum**: what students learn as they participate in the act of going to school, being part of a classroom community, and relating to their peers and their teachers. The phrase *hidden curriculum* was coined by the sociologist Phillip Jackson (1968), who described ways in which schools become arenas for socialization and transmit messages to students about how to be in the world. Long before that, educational philosopher John Dewey (1916) explored the hidden curriculum in schools as he examined the social values inherent in the experience of school. Hence, the hidden curriculum includes how we interact with students, how we enact the rules of the school culture, and how we communicate our expectations for student achievement and demeanor and our own passion for teaching and learning.

By telling the batteries-in-the-pocket story to my young students, I gave them a glimpse of what it is like to be an adult with a curious, scientific mind (and a family eager to make fun of my propensities). Perhaps the story helped some students in the class feel that science is fun, interesting, and relevant to daily life—and that certainly matches my vision of what I want to do in the classroom.

Every day, through countless similar incidents, teachers contribute positively to their school's hidden curriculum. However, teachers can also affect the hidden curriculum in negative ways. If you and other teachers are bored and cynical, for instance, you convey those feelings to your students. No matter how dutifully you slog through the subject matter, students will sense that it does not interest you, and they will absorb that message.

If you call on boys more than girls, for example, the hidden curriculum of your classroom might include the idea that boys are somehow more important. In early studies of gender and schooling in the 1980s, there were many instances in which teachers called on boys more frequently than girls as a way of exercising "control" in the classroom (Sadker & Sadker, 1994; Sadker & Zittleman, 2009). The

hidden curriculum
What students learn, beyond the academic content, from the experience of attending school.

asked if I had batteries in my camera that she could use. We made the switch; I handed the "dead" batteries to my husband, and my daughter was able to use her camera.

Some hours later, when we arrived back home after the party, my husband noticed that his right pocket was very warm—uncomfortably so. "What do you have in there?" I asked. "Just the batteries and my loose change," he replied. Delighted, I shrieked, "The batteries are not dead, and there is an electrical circuit in your pocket. It is generating all this heat!"

It is a family joke now that my thrill at finding "science in our daily life" seemed to overcome my empathy for his discomfort. However, I recognized that this was another opportunity to make the topic relevant to the third graders who were making circuits for an electricity unit. I told the story to them that week and stopped short of an explanation. "If my husband had the dead batteries and some loose coins in his pocket, why would it be warm? Can you draw a picture of the contents of his pocket?" Eagerly students drew coins and batteries and understood that the metal coins acted as a wire and conducted electricity.

This story illustrates how our personal lives meet our professional lives in the classroom. Your students will learn a lot about you, and you will also learn a lot about them.

© DNY59/iStockphoto

belief in the latter environment was that if you kept the boys engaged, they would not be apt to "act up." Today, we know that calling on boys and girls in equal numbers is of significant importance.

The hidden curriculum, not a part of public documents, includes messages that deal with attitudes, beliefs, values, and behavior. For example, since 2002, when the No Child Left Behind Act, which will be discussed in later chapters, was passed, regular assessment of mathematics and language arts prompted many elementary school administrators to allocate much more time to these subjects than to science, social studies, art, or music. The tacit message for children is that science is less important than math and reading, for example. A major purpose of the hidden curriculum has been to transmit the cultural and social norms of the school (how things are done, what routines matter, what dress is acceptable, who counts and who does not! When you visit schools and examine their routines and practices, ask yourself what matters to the leaders of this school. By exploring what is displayed in their showcases and on their walls, the hidden curriculum can be revealed.

Working with colleagues to plan curriculum and class projects and to bounce ideas off one another is an important part of the teaching profession.

© Elizabeth Crews

2-4 Support for Teachers

When asked who gave them the most support in their teaching careers, Kathryn, Jessica, Amanda, and Jane all agreed that their colleagues were the strongest source of support. This matches the findings of a survey in which teachers rated cooperative and competent colleagues and mentors as the factor that helped them most in their teaching positions (National Education Association, 2010, Table 52). The teachers I interviewed mentioned other sources of support as well. As you read the following stories, think about how these teachers interacted with their colleagues and others in the school and the community.

2-4a WHO PROVIDES THE MOST SUPPORT TO TEACHERS?

AMANDA: I have found it supportive to listen to fellow teachers and the administrators, students, parents, and community members. You can learn a vast amount from conversations with others. In a crowded teachers' room, I am the one who is content to sit alone and listen in on others' conversations. As you listen, you can learn so much about the expectations, the culture, the negatives and the positives, and ways to connect to the school and community in which you teach. I find keeping a teaching journal and jotting down what I discover about the students and the school to be very helpful. I try to make entries at least two or three times a week.

I jumped into school activities when I started and found that others who like to get involved were very supportive. My first year, I became a member of the Staff Development Committee, and I have never regretted that decision. I did not speak up as often as the other members, but I did listen and learn a great deal about the district that I was making my home. I am on various district-wide committees and involved in many school-based activities that have given me insight for understanding the context in which I teach.

JESSICA: In the first years of teaching, much of my support came from my fellow teachers in the building. They were the ones who knew the answers to difficult situations and who would give encouraging words. I have found that to be true even now that I am no longer a new teacher. Other educators can give you ideas, advice, and a sympathetic ear when needed, and this help can come from other new teachers as well as from veterans in the profession. I was assigned a mentor at school, and this teacher was very helpful in acclimating me to the routines and procedures that I needed to understand at the very beginning. As time went on, she became an important role model for me.

2-4b MENTORING NEW TEACHERS

Many schools and school districts are adopting mentor teacher programs. Mentor teachers are specially trained to work with new teachers and support them in understanding the school culture, the curriculum, and the resources available to them as professionals. You may want to ask if there is a mentor program where you begin teaching. Mentoring has been a trend over the past ten years as the teaching profession has recognized the need to develop a special transition period during which new teachers acclimate to their profession. This period as a whole is often called *induction*. Good mentors have a broad range of skills and are able to help new teachers apply their professional knowledge in the classroom. They are generally master teachers who have demonstrated a love of teaching and learning and are eager to share their experiences with others.

JANE: I gain the most support for my teaching from my colleagues, the school and district committees on which I serve, communication with my peers and my students, and my church.

Each Sunday, I teach a course in religion to adults, and I am struck by how much the enrollment in this class has increased over time. I employ teaching strategies similar to those I use with my eighth-grade mathematics students. I am organized and prepared, I respect their ideas and who they are, and I try to forge goals with them for our work together.

I also look inward for support. I evaluate my goals and reflect on my week in school and ask myself, "What should I change?"

From Jane's remarks we can see that, once again, teacher peers play an important role in supporting the work we do in schools. This kind of support, coupled

SUPPORT

professional development

professional organizations

mentors

colleagues

with Jane's capacity to articulate her teaching strategies, has contributed to her success. Notice the list of attributes that Jane uses to describe herself: organized, prepared, respectful of students, establishing goals with students collaboratively. The ability to be clear about your expectations for yourself and your students is essential to having a centered presence in the classroom. As Jane gains support from peers and weekend teaching experiences, she continues to reflect on her work and ask herself significant questions about her goals and practices. As mentioned previously, this is the best prevention against burnout.

2-5 Teachers as Lifelong Learners

We are living in a rapidly changing global environment in which youngsters' and adults' lives are drastically different than they were even ten years ago. We are all experiencing the information technology revolution, which has brought access to huge volumes of information—a degree of accessibility never before experienced in human history. This explosion of information, along with the continuous connectedness that we all feel as a result of Internet and cell phone technology, has changed the pace and progress of our daily lives.

In this ever-changing society, the activities that interest students today are necessarily different from the activities that interested you even just a few years ago. Teachers must constantly adapt and improve their skills as they respond to the recurring question: What works best in the classroom for these particular students at this period of time in our history?

Many educators today like to think of schools as **learning communities**, a term that emphasizes interaction and collaboration in the learning process. The phrase also conveys the idea that all the participants—teachers, students, and administrators—are always learning. Hence, teachers see their own continuing education as part of their work and their lives.

This need for this ongoing **professional development**, as it is called, actually makes many people excited about entering teaching. These individuals understand that to teach is to learn. To improve our practice requires targeted efforts at our own growth as teachers and learners. Professional development can take many forms. We will learn more about the many ways teachers extend their education in a later chapter. For now, let's hear from Amanda, Jessica, Jane, and others to learn how they are doing it.

2-5a HOW DO TEACHERS CONTINUE PROFESSIONAL DEVELOPMENT?

KATHRYN: Professional development is easy for teachers who know they still have a lot to learn. I'm still working on my master's degree for starters, so I'm definitely a long way off yet. The school I work in now consistently provides a variety of workshops focusing on literacy and technology. I attend a few seminars every year that are sponsored by a local science outreach institute. I've participated in a teacher program in Panama in association with the Smithsonian Institute to expose teachers to hands-on science. I've led workshops for my colleagues to show them how they can incorporate publications and inquiry based projects into everyday lessons. It is challenging, it is time consuming, but, when my students can apply skills because I took the time to learn them first, I know its worth the effort.

To teach is
to learn.

AMANDA: Alongside life experience, continued schooling is needed. Formal education presents important new ideas, strategies, and problems and helps your mind grow in the same way that you want your students' minds to grow. In addition, formal education puts you in contact with professors who are experts in their fields and classmates who have a wealth of knowledge to add to your own. Being in a formal learning environment gives you a community of peers with whom you can bounce around ideas. Formal education is a wonderful resource for a teacher.

JESSICA: I have taken courses on differentiated instruction, brain-based learning, and adolescent literacy. Whenever possible, I participate in local and national conferences, which enables me to meet teachers from all over the country. These conferences reaffirm my career

choice and reinvigorate me to try new ideas with students. I belong to a number of professional organizations that offer regular publications to read and ways to network with other educators. My district sponsors online educational book studies, and I try to participate in at least one per school year; there is a wealth of helpful, thought-provoking information that can be gleaned from the experiences of other teachers. I occasionally present at conferences, which requires a new level of understanding and preparation, so this furthers my professional knowledge.

JANE: I am always looking for conferences, classes, workshops, and news that can help me stay on top of the topics at hand. My master's program was extremely helpful in that I learned how to implement project-based learning activities in my class and how to do research on my own practice. It was very exciting, and each year I look for other opportunities to expand what I can offer myself and the students.

CAROL: I attend conferences of the NAEYC whenever possible and I participate in meetings arranged by the director of the program where guest speakers address a wide range of topics relevant to working with young children.

2-5b BENEFITS OF LIFELONG LEARNING

Teachers are expected to keep up with the latest developments in education. In many schools and districts, in fact, teachers are offered financial incentives to continue to learn though professional education courses at a college or university or through professional development courses, often referred to as in-service courses, offered by the school district itself. These incentives are based on how many formal graduate school credits or professional development credits a teacher earns in a given academic year. Obviously you'll appreciate the chance to earn a higher salary.

Yet, as the stories you have just read illustrate, there are other incentives for taking professional development courses. Amanda, Jessica, and Jane think of themselves as lifelong learners. They take a genuine interest in expanding their minds and improving their teaching. In fact, all of them have reached the stage of doing their own research or making their own presentations—contributing to the sum of knowledge in the field.

Professional organizations can play a major role in expanding your development as a teacher. The NEA, the American Federation of Teachers, and the NAEYC, discussed in Chapter 1, offer teachers the opportunity to attend conferences, read and contribute to journals, and access professional resources. So do many other organizations; here is just a partial list.

- The National Science Teachers Association (NSTA)
- The National Council of Teachers of Mathematics (NCTM)
- The National Council of Teachers of English (NCTE)
- The National Council for the Social Studies (NCSS)

Many teaching resources are available at no cost online through these professional organizations. Professional development takes place in informal settings as well, and this is often the most important kind. In one local school district where I have worked, teachers are encouraged to take field trips to local geological formations—by themselves, without their students—even if they do not teach science in a formal way. Imagine you are an elementary school teacher in this district. How might that type of field trip contribute to your professional development? How might it help you interest your young students in the world around them?

2-6 Concluding Thoughts

Learning about other teachers' hopes, dreams, and experiences, gives you a way to consider what teaching might be like for you. Teaching demands so much from the individual teacher. Our emotional sides have to be expressed to communicate a sense of warmth and congeniality, whereas our intellectual selves need to maintain a sense of order, continuity, and consistency. It is a complex endeavor, requiring self-reflection and good analytical skills. One cannot overemphasize the need for personal reflection and the desire to become a lifelong learner. Luckily, teachers receive support from organizations, mentors, preparatory institutions, and sometimes induction programs in their school districts.

Building a personal philosophy of teaching is an important starting point in your development as a teacher. Your teaching philosophy is a work in progress and will most likely change with time and exposure to new ideas about how people learn. In the next two chapters of this book, you will read about important educational philosophies that have influenced US education. Your own thinking should evolve as you engage with these ideas. What remains constant is the fact that teaching is hard work and requires that you be reflective, ever conscious, and well prepared—that you be a centered presence in the classroom and ask yourself, what kind of teacher would I like to be?

STUDY TOOLS
CHAPTER 2

Located at back of the textbook
- Rip out Chapter Review Card
- Note-Taking Assistance

Located at CengageBrain.com
- Review Key Terms Flash Cards (Print or Online)
- Complete Practice Quizzes to prepare for tests
- Complete "Crossword Puzzle" to review key terms
- Watch the TeachSource Video Case "The First Year of Teaching: One Colleague's Story"

Where did we come from? How did we get here? These are questions children often ask their parents about their backgrounds and their beginnings. We might ask similar questions about schools. How did they get here? Why are schools this way? How did elementary, middle, and high schools develop over time? When did schooling become mandatory in the United States? How is public schooling in the United States being challenged by reform movements?

In the same way, we might wonder about the thinking behind today's teaching practices. From where did we get our ideas about how to teach? What is really meant by words like *pedagogy* and *curriculum*? What does our understanding of how the brain works tells us about how people learn?

These are a few of the questions that the two chapters in Part 2 address as we go back in time to make more sense of the present. Teaching has a long and impassioned history in the United States. Knowing what and who came before us gives us a deeper understanding of our mission as we move forward.

Part Outline

CHAPTER 3

A HISTORY OF SCHOOLING IN AMERICA

> *Having a history is a prerequisite to claiming a right to shape the future.*
> —Sara Evans, a historian from the University of Minnesota (1989)

We are living at a time when many public and private figures espouse a quick fix for the problems that besiege public schooling in the United States. There are few who doubt that teachers make a huge difference—that it is better to be in a poorer school with a great teacher than a richer school with a terrible teacher. Still, amidst the fuss is the challenge how to evaluate a "terrific" teacher and what "terrific," "successful," or "great" look like. Reasonable doubts remain about effective school reform and even more doubts about the best way to educate future teachers like you.

This drama is set against a tapestry of experimental and traditional public schools, all designed to ensure a literate populace in a democratic society. Simultaneously, the digital revolution is transforming the meaning of teaching, and learning as "delivery systems" are designed to provide courses to students via the Internet. Many of you may have taken these courses; some of you may have even taken an online course or two in high school. There is so much information available online that it leaves one to ponder exactly what an educated woman or man needs to study and what delivery systems are most effective. Against this backdrop of rapid change and confusing options, this chapter provides an overview of the history of education in the United States. After reading this chapter, you should have a better perspective on how schools came to be the way they are today.

What do you picture in your mind when you think of an elementary school? A middle school? A high school? Did any of you attend a junior high school? The history of US public education reflects the changes that an emerging nation endures as it matures and ensures that all of its citizens become educated. Learning about the evolution of public schools in our country reminds us that free societies require an educated populace, one where people understand their choices in a diverse society. Like many other complex histories, the history of education reveals the changing belief systems of the times, and as the pendulum swings from more rigid governance of the schools to more flexible governance, the main goal and hope are that all its citizens will have access to, and participate in, the process of becoming educated through a public school system designed to meet their needs.

LEARNING OUTCOMES

After reading this chapter, you should be thinking about the following ideas:

3-1 Analyze the ways in which the early pioneers of public education shaped the way schools exist today in the United States.

3-2 Explain the dominant philosophies that influenced education.

3-3 Discuss the impact of federal government legislation, funding priorities, and court cases on the ways that public education has increased accountability in the twenty-first century.

3-4 Create a theme that would describe the period of educational history in which we currently find ourselves.

TO KNOW IS NOT ENOUGH

Although no one doubts the importance of "knowing" material to be an educated person, today, there is ready access to ideas, facts, and theories in all disciplines of knowledge on the Internet. So, what do we *do* after we "know" something? Although there is a lot of material presented in this text, it is the hope that that you, the reader, will act on what you know about schools, teaching, and learning to serve all learners in the best possible way.

dame schools Some colonial women transformed their homes into schools where they taught reading, writing, and computation. These schools became known as dame schools.

Latin grammar school A type of school that flourished in the New England colonies in the 1600s and 1700s. It emphasized Latin and Greek to prepare young men for college.

3-1 An Introduction to the History of US Public Education

We begin with a new nation emerging after the Revolutionary War in which the colonies won their independence and the wave of immigration in the nineteenth century. Notice the following themes as we move into the twentieth and twenty-first centuries:

- The meaning of education for a thriving democracy,
- The effect of geographic location on access to education,
- The roles that social capital, wealth, privilege, and poverty play in the success or failures of schools,
- The transmission of values and beliefs through public education, and
- Changes over time in the roles played by local communities, the states, and the federal government.

3-1a THE COLONIES

Colonial education in the 1600s began in the home when Puritans[1] established colonies in what is now the northeastern United States. In the early New England colonies, education was designed to further Puritan values and ensure that children were well versed in the Bible. The major thrust in early colonial education was the reading and understanding of scripture, so for many early colonists, religious education was synonymous with general education.

The primary responsibility for educating children was placed on the family. You may have heard about the homeschooling movement today in which parents educate their children directly, every day, in the home. We will discuss this current trend later in this text, but you can see that it has deep roots.

Many New England families could also opt to send their children to dame schools, which offered education to children six to eight years old. The dame school was like an informal day-care center. Parents would leave their children in the home of a neighborhood woman several days a week. The woman would go about her chores while teaching the children their letters, numbers, and prayers. Religious teachings, as you can see, were routinely woven into the daily lives of children. These women usually accepted a small fee for each child, and instruction often took place in the kitchen. For the most part, this was the only form of schooling offered to girls because education was not considered important for their life's work. Can you imagine that?

Another form of education in the colonies was apprenticeship. After young boys finished the dame school, they were sometimes apprenticed to craftsmen to learn a trade. Serving an apprenticeship allowed boys to learn a craft they could carry into adulthood. Girls, on the other hand, were usually taught domestic skills at home and learned to stitch letters and sayings onto embroidered samplers. Theirs was a second-rate education compared with what was available for boys.

Latin Grammar Schools

Realizing they needed a way to educate leaders for their communities, the Puritan colonists established Latin grammar schools, the first of which opened in Boston in 1635. Here, the sons of the upper social classes studied Latin and Greek language and literature as well as the Bible. To further extend the boys' education, the

---

[1]The Puritans were Protestant dissenters in England who opposed many practices of the established church. When Charles I took the English throne in 1625, government persecution of Puritans increased. Giving up hope of reforming the English church, many Puritans emigrated, among them the early settlers of the Massachusetts Bay Colony (Boston Historical Society and Museum, 2010).

SOCIAL CAPITAL

From the time of the early colonies to the present, Americans have frequently debated the relationship between schools and society and the best way for government to fulfill its responsibility to educate its citizens. Historically, various traditions and forms of schooling have been mediated by the political, economic, and cultural struggles of the people. This means that, for some people, access to education has been easier than for others.

The term *social capital* refers to connections among individuals that give them access to cultural and civic events and institutions. Hence, youngsters from families with social capital are familiar with libraries, museums, and travel. Moreover, parents with social capital know how to get the best education for their children. Social capital generally comes with wealth, privilege, and other marks of social status.

The concept of social capital helps us understand how social issues were addressed as US schools developed. Clearly, our systems of education have become more inclusive; but in the first 150 years of nationhood, high-quality education was readily available only if you were rich, white, and male.

Do you remember my story about Mrs. Fisher from Chapter 1? She encouraged me to apply to a special high school in my city. Information about special high schools was readily available to families with social capital, but my parents were working-class immigrants who did not fully understand how to negotiate the educational system in New York City. Fortunately, my teacher helped me through the process of applying to take the entrance exam.

The issue of social capital comes up often as we explore the history of schooling in the United States. There has always been pressure for schools to provide more and better services for an increasingly diverse array of students.

Puritans founded Harvard College in 1636. To enter this college, boys had to pass an entrance exam that required reading and speaking Latin and Greek.

In 1647, Massachusetts passed a law requiring formal education. Known as the Old Deluder Satan Act, it mandated that every town of fifty households must appoint and pay a teacher of reading and writing, and every town of one hundred households must provide a grammar school to prepare youths for university. With the passage of this law, new town schools were established for the youngest students and Latin grammar schools for older students spread through Massachusetts. Thus began the first education act in this country that ensured there would be public schools where children would learn to read and write.

Ultimately the Latin grammar school extended into the other New England colonies and to some extent into the mid-Atlantic colonies as well. These schools were run by an elected board of townspeople and financially supported by the families of the attendees.

Under this system, after finishing dame school or town school, wealthy boys could attend a Latin grammar school to prepare for college and a leadership role in society. Girls who finished the dame school or town school would continue to study their letters at home while learning domestic chores. The Latin grammar school is considered one of the forerunners of the US high school.

Geographical Differences in Colonial Education

Educational access in the early colonies was determined not only by wealth and privilege but by location. Where you lived had a great impact on the type of education that was available.

In the northern colonies, largely settled by Puritans, people lived in towns and relatively close to one another. Town schools, which principally taught the Bible, became readily available after 1647. In the mid-Atlantic colonies, however, a wide range of European ethnic and

academy A type of private secondary school that arose in the late colonial period and came to dominate American secondary education until the establishment of public high schools. Academies had a more practical curriculum than Latin grammar schools did, and students typically could choose subjects appropriate to their later careers.

religious groups established different types of schools, and various trades established apprenticeship programs. Local control was the norm. Though some Latin grammar schools existed, other private schools developed that were dedicated to job training and practical skills.

The southern colonies, where the population was more rural, had fewer schools during the colonial era. Wealthy plantation owners hired private tutors for their children. Many young gentlemen were sent to Europe for their education.

The Late Colonial Period

By the late colonial era, in addition to the types of schools described so far, options for parents included:

- Schools managed by private associations, often devoted to the skills needed for a specific type of job;
- Religious schools, sponsored by churches for their members; some churches also established charity schools for the urban poor;
- Boarding schools; and
- A few private academies offering secondary education with a broader curriculum than the early Latin grammar schools (academies are discussed in the next section).

Did You Know?

The Old Deluder Satan Act was so named because the Puritans believed in the presence of evil in the form of Satan; if children studied the Scriptures, they would resist Satan's temptations. Learning to read would thwart evil.

Q: *You had to be wealthy, white, and male to have access to the better forms of education in the early colonies. How has that changed and why?*

Several of these options required tuition, others were paid for by public funds, and some were funded by a combination of both.

It was still true that most girls received little schooling after the first few years. And if you were Native American or African American, you had practically no chance of formal education. The schools established for the poor typically required a family to sign a "Pauper's Oath"; so most poor children did not attend school. Consider how you would feel if, to send your child to school, you had to sign a public document admitting your poverty. Many families chose to leave their children illiterate rather than suffer the shame of this type of public admission.

3-1b A NEW NATION AND ITS EARLY PIONEERS OF EDUCATION

In the late 1700s, after the colonies gained their independence from Great Britain, efforts were made to consolidate schools and mandate education throughout the new nation. Congress enacted the Land Ordinance Act of 1785 and the Northwest Ordinance of 1787. These measures set aside land for public schools. Subsequently, as sending children to school, rather than teaching them at home, grew in popularity, formal schools were started wherever space could be found.

Schoolhouses of that day were practical shelters: one room with benches and a stove. Desks and blackboards did not appear until many years later. No grades were given in the beginning, and one teacher worked with several age levels at the same time. Children simply learned at their own pace.

The Academy

Thomas Jefferson and Benjamin Franklin, among other founders of the new nation, believed that schools should move beyond the education of wealthy men for the ministry to a more broadly based education. In 1751 Franklin established a new kind of secondary school, one that would eventually replace the Latin grammar school—the academy. The Franklin Academy in Philadelphia offered a variety of subjects, ranging from science and mathematics to athletics, navigation, and bookkeeping. It was open to both girls and boys—if their parents could afford the tuition.

Soon after the Declaration of Independence was signed, other private academies were established, most of them limited to boys. These included most notably Phillips Academy in Andover, Massachusetts (1778), and Phillips Exeter Academy in Exeter, New Hampshire (1781). Academies changed the model for secondary schools by offering elective as well as required courses. It was still the case, however, that the common denominator for attendance was wealth.

Rise of the Common School

At the turn of the nineteenth century, education in the new nation was a hodgepodge of schools for basic reading and writing and grammar schools or academies for college preparation and leadership. Many young people still learned through apprenticeships or private tutoring.

Jefferson, Franklin, and others believed that the new democracy required an educated citizenry for its survival. To work properly, they thought, a democracy needs informed citizens, as well as an educational system that allows people to succeed on the basis of their skills and dedication rather than inherited privilege.

These ideas gave rise to the movement for **common schools**—a system of tax-supported elementary schools. The common school is known today as the public elementary school. Horace Mann, an educational historian and reformer who championed the movement, saw common schools as promoting important civic virtues. He criticized private academies because they offered widely different curricula and perpetuated social differences between the privileged classes and ordinary citizens (Wisconsin Education Association Council, 2006).

From their beginnings in Massachusetts in the 1820s, common schools were gradually established in other New England, midwestern, western, and finally southern states. Their spread became more rapid after the Civil War.

Immigration played a key role in the thinking about public education. The 1830s and 1840s brought expansion in manufacturing and transportation. These decades also brought considerable immigration from Europe, especially in the Northeast. Immigrants were becoming an important part of the economy, and factory owners needed a trained, disciplined workforce. At the same time, as population grew in the cities, social tensions rose because of increased poverty, slums, and crime.

Prominent citizens worried about the morals of poor immigrant children and the influence their parents had on them. Many Protestant ministers looked at the rise of Catholic immigrant populations as a possible cause of social problems. Many people believed that schools could offer a way to address these concerns. By centralizing the control of public education, schools could be used to uplift the poor, spread dominant national values, and assimilate immigrant children into the English-speaking US culture. State authorities, not immigrant parents, would be in control.

However, even though public schools were at this point nonsectarian, they were not necessarily nonreligious. Because common schools were seen as responsible, in part, for the moral development of children, it was believed that religion could not be completely separated from the schools. There was much debate about curriculum. Although the main thrust in common schools was the study of the "three Rs" (reading, 'riting, and 'rithmetic), history, and science, some schools had regular readings of the King James version of the Bible. Catholic immigrants objected vehemently, and many church parishes in the late 1800s began their own church schools, known as **parochial schools**. Not until many years later, in 1963, did the Supreme Court rule that prayers and Bible readings would no longer be allowed in public schools.

With tax-supported public education in place, more and more children attended school on a regular basis (see Figure 3.1). However, because of the large size of many immigrant families, parents often needed to send their children into the workforce to help out economically. These poor working families viewed education for their children as a luxury they could not afford. To ensure that children went

common schools
A public, tax-supported elementary school. Begun in Massachusetts in the 1820s, common schools aimed to provide a common curriculum for children. Horace Mann, an advocate for the common school, is often considered the "father of the public school."

parochial schools
A school operated by a religious group. Today, in the United States, the term most often refers to a school governed by the local Catholic parish or diocese.

to school and not to work, compulsory attendance laws came into existence. These laws were adopted by each individual state, beginning with Massachusetts in 1852 and ending with Alaska (then a US territory) in 1929 (Information Please Database, 2006). Eventually, legislation restricting the employment of children in industrial settings was passed by the federal government.

Expansion of Public Schools

By the 1870s, there was broad attendance in US public elementary schools, but a large gap in available educational opportunities remained between those schools and universities. Only the wealthy continued their education at private preparatory schools for colleges and universities. Gradually, however, as society became more industrialized and laws were passed to discourage the hiring of teenage workers, parents came to view the high school as the pathway to better jobs for their children. Tax-supported public high schools slowly took hold and became the dominant form of secondary education by 1890.

The rise of the public high school led to the need for a bridge between elementary school and high school. In the early 1900s, the junior high school was established to bridge this gap, concentrating on the emotional and intellectual needs of students in grades 7, 8, and 9. In the 1950s, some middle schools were established for grades 5–8, and by the end of the twentieth century, the middle school was gradually replacing the junior high school (Manning, 2000). The emphasis in middle school was on interdisciplinary learning and team teaching, in which groups of students had the same teachers in common.

The timeline in Figure 3.2 summarizes many of the events we have discussed. It is remarkable to consider how many more children were educated as the common school movement took hold and public secondary schools began to flourish. In many areas of the United States in the early 1800s, school lasted only about seventy-five to eighty days a year because the entire family was needed to work the farm. By the 1830s, only about half of all children attended school, and then only for a short period of time. But as the industrial revolution drew people to the cities for work and common schools flourished, more children began attending school, and by the end of the 1890s, more than 70 percent of children were receiving schooling. There was such a great need for schools between 1890 and 1914 that a new high school was added every day in some part of the United States (Krug, 1964; Wisconsin Education Association Council, 2006).

Today we can celebrate the fact that, as our nation grew, more and more people attended public schools. This does not mean, however, that we have now achieved the goal of equal educational opportunity for everyone. Later in this text, as we compare the quality of education offered to students in poor urban and rural areas with the public education available in more affluent communities, you will see that challenges remain. Still, there is no question that more diverse students—including girls and women, people of color, and

Q: *Do you think today's schools still function as institutions for social control?*

Common schools, supported by taxes, marked the beginning of public education for all.

© Bettmann/Corbis

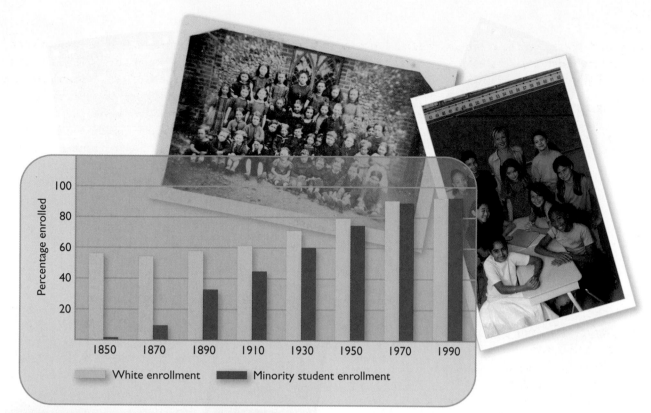

Photos: © Duncan Walker/iStockphoto (left); © Bonnie Jacobs/iStockphoto (right)

SOURCE: Data from Snyder, T. D., ed., *120 Years of American Education: A Statistical Portrait* (Washington, D.C.: National Center for Education Statistics, 1993), Table 2, p. 14.

FIGURE 3.1

Rising School Attendance in the 19th and 20th Centuries
This graph shows the percentage of US children (ages 5 to 19) enrolled in school, illustrating the dramatic growth that began in the second half of the 19th century as common schools became well established and compulsory attendance laws were enacted.

the poor—are graduating from high school today and going on to postsecondary education than ever before in this country.

3-1c TEACHER EDUCATION AND THE DEVELOPMENT OF NORMAL SCHOOLS

As the common school movement gained momentum, you may be wondering: Who were the teachers? Where did they come from and how were they prepared?

Once again, Horace Mann was a major influence. He promoted **normal schools**, which began shortly after the founding of the first common schools. These were two-year institutions designed to prepare teachers through courses in the history and philosophy of education and methods of teaching. Normal schools were intended to improve the quality of the growing common school system by producing more qualified teachers. The first of them, called simply the Normal School, opened in 1839 in Lexington, Massachusetts.

By the end of the 1800s, these schools became four-year colleges dedicated to teacher education. Many universities that are well known today, such as the University of California, Los Angeles, were founded as normal schools.

normal schools A type of teacher-education institution begun in the 1830s; forerunner of the teachers' college.

Normal Schools and Female Teachers

Normal schools played a major role in bringing women into the teaching profession. In the early days of US education, schoolmasters were almost always male. Women, who were mostly uneducated, were not considered suited for the job, even though the prerequisite for teaching consisted of little more than having attended school yourself. On the rare occasion that a woman did secure a job, it was with young children only. As the country expanded, common schools multiplied rapidly, but women still took a backseat in terms of employment. It was assumed that they were

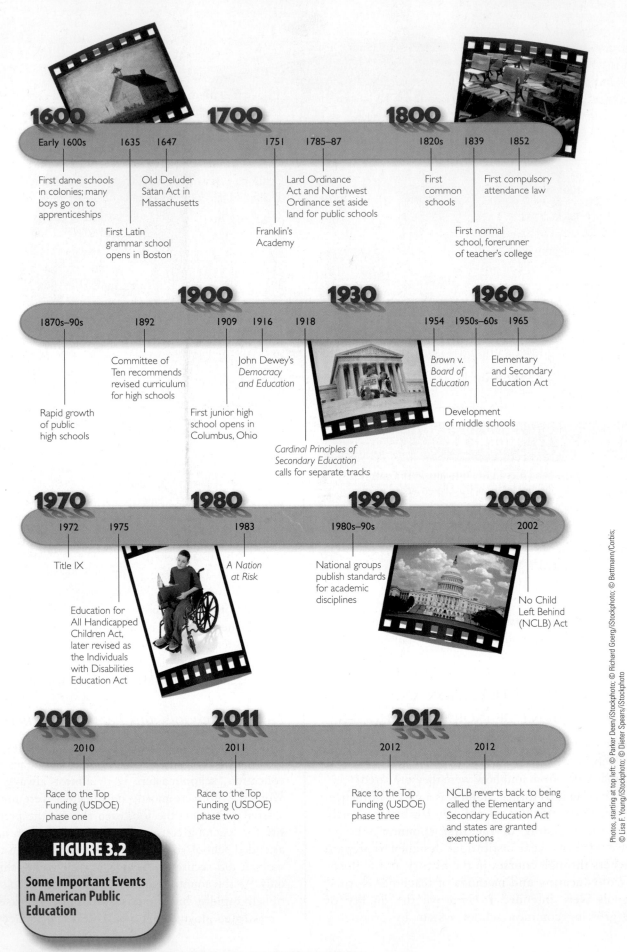

1600

Early 1600s — First dame schools in colonies; many boys go on to apprenticeships

1635 — First Latin grammar school opens in Boston

1647 — Old Deluder Satan Act in Massachusetts

1700

1751 — Franklin's Academy

1785–87 — Lard Ordinance Act and Northwest Ordinance set aside land for public schools

1800

1820s — First common schools

1839 — First normal school, forerunner of teacher's college

1852 — First compulsory attendance law

1900

1870s–90s — Rapid growth of public high schools

1892 — Committee of Ten recommends revised curriculum for high schools

1909 — First junior high school opens in Columbus, Ohio

1916 — John Dewey's *Democracy and Education*

1918 — *Cardinal Principles of Secondary Education* calls for separate tracks

1930

1960

1954 — *Brown v. Board of Education*

1950s–60s — Development of middle schools

1965 — Elementary and Secondary Education Act

1970

1972 — Title IX

1975 — Education for All Handicapped Children Act, later revised as the Individuals with Disabilities Education Act

1980

1983 — *A Nation at Risk*

1990

1980s–90s — National groups publish standards for academic disciplines

2000

2002 — No Child Left Behind (NCLB) Act

2010

2010 — Race to the Top Funding (USDOE) phase one

2011

2011 — Race to the Top Funding (USDOE) phase two

2012

2012 — Race to the Top Funding (USDOE) phase three

2012 — NCLB reverts back to being called the Elementary and Secondary Education Act and states are granted exemptions

FIGURE 3.2

Some Important Events in American Public Education

Photos, starting at top left: © Parker Deen/iStockphoto; © Richard Goerg/iStockphoto; © Bettmann/Corbis; © Lisa F. Young/iStockphoto; © Dieter Spears/iStockphoto

incapable of maintaining the discipline necessary to teach effectively.

Normal schools, however, welcomed female students and made elementary school teaching a career path for many women. By 1900, 71 percent of rural teachers were women (Hoffman, 1981).

Gender Roles in Teaching

After the Civil War and well into the 1900s, teaching became more attractive for women who wanted to find a place of employment outside the domestic sphere. Yet there were considerable constraints on women who became teachers, chief among them was that they were not allowed to marry. The stereotype of the "spinster" was often associated with schoolteachers. It was believed that women would have divided loyalties if they were allowed to marry while being employed as teachers. (Can you imagine that happening now?) It was not until after World War II that married women were allowed to enter the teaching profession.

By the 1950s, the teaching profession, once dominated entirely by men, had become a female-dominated, "feminized" profession in many people's eyes. However, young men were still attracted to educational administration as well as to secondary school jobs in mathematics and science. Here again, a stereotype persisted through the middle to late twentieth century: Women were seen as suited to teaching young children, whereas men taught math and science and ran the school.

In recent years, women have gained greater access to careers in educational administration and as teachers of mathematics and science. At the same time, however, the overall percentage of men in teaching has declined significantly since the 1960s, as we mentioned in Chapter 2. Just as it is important to have women teaching math, it is vital to have men represented in early-childhood and elementary education. Breaking down gender stereotypes in schools is important—not only for teachers themselves but also for the models they present to students. We will have more to say about gender and schooling later in this text.

> Breaking down gender stereotypes in schools is important—not only for teachers themselves but also for the models they present to students.

The Tuskegee Normal School and the Education of African Americans

Even after the Civil War, Reconstruction, and the Thirteenth Amendment which ended slavery in the United States, it took a long time for African Americans to achieve equal opportunity and access to a quality education. Some would argue that appropriate education remains unavailable to minority students today. As we will see in later chapters, our diverse culture and society pose many challenges and opportunities for teachers and students alike. In this respect, we can find inspiration in the story of Booker T. Washington, an African American teacher, who in 1881 became the first head of what was then called the Tuskegee Normal School for Colored Teachers in Tuskegee, Alabama. Later renamed the Tuskegee Institute, the institution today is Tuskegee University.

CATHERINE BEECHER

Catherine Beecher, who started the Hartford (Connecticut) Female Seminary in 1828, made a major contribution to the professional education of women. Beecher challenged accepted notions of femininity and the education of women in the nineteenth century.

Born in East Hampton, New York, in 1800, Beecher believed that education should prepare women to assume roles of high responsibility in society. In particular, she thought that women should train to become teachers, a profession that would be a natural extension of their family roles. Along with her famous contemporaries Elizabeth Cady Stanton and Susan B. Anthony, she promoted educational and political equality for women.

Under the leadership of Washington, the Tuskegee Normal School prepared African American teachers to be self-reliant and to acquire practical vocational skills, not only in teaching but also in agriculture and other occupations. By the early twentieth century, the African American scholar and advocate W. E. B. Du Bois, a graduate of Harvard College and a well-known intellectual, was criticizing Washington's emphasis on vocational training at Tuskegee. Du Bois insisted that formal education in an academically rich course of study was necessary for the African American people. Regardless of these later critiques, however, Washington did a great deal to advance the education of African Americans and their representation in the teaching profession.

Drawing African Americans and other minorities into the teaching force remains an issue today. African Americans make up more than 15 percent of US public school students; so do Hispanics. Yet only about 6 percent of teachers are African American, and only 5 percent are Hispanic. More than one-third of US public schools have no teacher of color on the faculty (National Collaborative on Diversity in the Teaching Force, 2004; Weaver, 2004). To improve this situation, state departments of education and many colleges and universities are offering financial incentives to minority students for becoming teachers. An example of such a program, in existence since 1985, is the Minority Teacher Recruitment Project (MTRP) at the University of Louisville (http://louisville.edu/education/research/centers/mtrp/).

Q: *What is the history of the college or university where you are studying? When did teacher education programs emerge in your institution?*

We are all a part of what we are trying to change. As teachers and future teachers, we seek a profession dedicated to student learning. As citizens we know that, as Thomas Jefferson observed, it is impossible for a nation to be both free and ignorant. But we are people of diverse regions, ethnicities, and social and economic backgrounds, and to be successful educators we need to make sense of (1) who we are in the world and (2) what conditions we believe are important for learning to occur.

At different periods in our history, different philosophies have dominated our thinking about teaching and learning and about the manner in which education should proceed. In this section, we look at several competing philosophies that have shaped efforts to reform US schools since late in the nineteenth century.

Many classrooms today are hybrids of several of these philosophies of education. As you read this section, think about what is happening in schools today and how the current phase of US public education will be viewed by others fifty years from now.

3-2a The High School Curriculum

From the end of the Civil War to the late 1800s, the high school curriculum kept expanding as the demand for new courses grew. There was no preset pattern for how the courses being offered should develop; hence the high school curriculum retained old subjects such as languages and mathematics and added new ones as demand arose. These new subjects included botany, physiology, anatomy, physics, and astronomy. For those students not

3-2 The Swinging Pendulum: Dominant Philosophies Influencing Education

The struggle to change or reform educational practices is as old as organized public schooling. From common school days to present times, the content and processes of education have been under continuous scrutiny. Schools, like other public institutions, are products of their times politically, socially, and economically. Schools both reflect and influence the societal events of their day.

© Andrzej Tokarski/iStockphoto

interested in pursuing a college education, courses such as commercial arithmetic, banking, business correspondence, stenography, and typewriting were added.

By the late 1800s, opinions about the purpose of high school were sharply divided. Some believed high school should groom students for college. Others thought high school should prepare students for more practical endeavors, serving those who saw high school as the termination of their formal education.

In 1892, the National Education Association (NEA) addressed this issue by appointing the Committee of Ten, which consisted of ten scholars led by Harvard University President Charles Eliot, to determine the proper curriculum for high schools. The Committee of Ten recommended eight years of elementary school and four years of high school and proposed a curriculum that was common to both college-bound and terminal students. The new curriculum featured fewer subjects, each of which would be studied for a longer period of time. The courses included foreign languages, history, mathematics, science, and English. Although these subjects offered an alternative to classical Latin and Greek courses, this was a rigorous academic curriculum, and the dominant belief was that the same subjects would be equally beneficial to academic and terminal students.

A generation later, in 1918, the NEA partly reversed course when its Commission on the Reorganization of Secondary Education issued a report called *Cardinal Principles of Secondary Education*. In this report, the commission recommended a differentiated curriculum for the comprehensive high school, offering four different tracks: college preparatory, commercial, industrial, and general academic. The commercial course of study included bookkeeping, shorthand, and typing. The industrial track included preparatory courses for domestic, agricultural, and trade endeavors.

Although high school curricula varied considerably during the rest of the twentieth century, some of the ideas set forth by the Committee of Ten and the *Cardinal Principles* continued to be dominant. The core courses—English, foreign language, science, mathematics, and history (which later evolved into social studies)—persisted in the comprehensive high school curriculum. So did the notion that high school should follow a **tracking** system, offering different courses or tracks for students with different academic aspirations.

3-2b THE EMERGENCE OF ESSENTIALISM

As you can see from the debate over the high school curriculum, educators in the early twentieth century were developing strong opinions about the proper sort of education for contemporary society. In the 1930s, the educator William Bagley coined the term **essentialism** as the name for a philosophy that had a strong impact then and continues to be influential today. According to this view, certain core kinds of knowledge are essential to a person's life in society. Essentialists believe that everyone can and should learn these key elements and therefore that the schools' primary mission is to teach them.

When you hear about teaching the "basics" or about rigorous training in the three Rs, you are listening to an essentialist view of education. The essentials are generally embodied in the standard, time-honored subjects; in other words, essentialists believe that students should take courses in algebra and history, not in ceramics and interpretive dance. In stressing that the curriculum should remain consistent, essentialists tend to assume that a common culture should exist for all Americans. Their vision of the classroom is teacher centered: Teachers are the dominant figures, transferring their knowledge and wisdom for the good of the students. An essentialist classroom is one in which the teacher knows best. Students listen to their teacher and learn what is taught.

To many educators in the early twentieth century, essentialism made good common sense. It was soon challenged, however, by the progressivism of thinkers like John Dewey.

3-2c PROGRESSIVISM AND JOHN DEWEY

Probably the most influential educator of the twentieth century, John Dewey (1859–1952) was an educational philosopher and a professor at the University of Chicago and Columbia University in New York. He participated in a variety of political causes, such as women's rights and the unionization of teachers, and he contributed

tracking The practice of placing students in different classes or courses based on achievement test scores or on perceived differences in abilities. Tracks can be identified by ability (high, average, or low) or by the kind of preparation they provide (academic, general, or vocational).

essentialism An educational philosophy holding that the purpose of education is to learn specific knowledge provided by core academic disciplines such as mathematics, science, literature, and history. Teachers must impart the key elements of these subjects so that all students have access to this basic or "essential" knowledge.

progressivism An educational philosophy that stresses active learning through problem solving, projects, and hands-on experiences.

perennialism An educational philosophy that emphasizes enduring ideas conveyed through the study of great works of literature and art. Perennialists believe in a single core curriculum for everyone.

frequently to popular magazines and journals in which he connected social action in democracy with educational principles.

In Dewey's view, students should be active participants in their own learning; they learn by doing, and their interests must be a driving force behind curriculum and classroom experiences. His educational philosophy has been referred to as **progressivism** and as *pragmatism*. It was progressive because it gave more responsibility to students and pragmatic (practical) because it embedded teaching and learning in the context of daily living. This approach contradicted the strict, top-down, authoritarian model of education that had thrived from colonial times into the nineteenth century and that continued to be reflected in essentialist approaches.

Dewey thought that schools should help children learn how to live and work cooperatively with others. Consequently, he believed that students needed to participate in decisions that affected their learning and that they should be guided by academically autonomous teachers—that is, teachers who were not bound by rigid rules about what and how to teach and who were able to build on students' strengths and talents. Dewey and his followers viewed the school as a laboratory in which the purpose of the curriculum was to integrate education with real-life experiences and a child's curiosity defined the process of learning just as much as the subject matter being taught.

Did You Know?

John Dewey (1859–1952), an educational philosopher and professor, was probably the most influential educator of the twentieth century.

Q: *What are some examples of Dewey's progressivism in classrooms today?*

Dewey, and the progressive movement that he helped found, had a profound influence on educational thought in the United States. Progressives advocated a vibrant school setting with a curriculum that followed the interests and needs of students, encouraged active learning and problem solving, fostered deep understanding of concepts through experimentation, and supported assessment of students through close observation by well-prepared and caring teachers.

Dewey's progressivism fell out of favor, however, when it was deemed necessary that the United States foster stricter teaching methods during the Cold War following World War II. The Soviet Union's launch of the satellite Sputnik in 1957—making that nation the first in space—became a symbol of what US public education had failed to achieve. Progressivism lost ground as US educators shifted again toward a more authoritarian approach and a strict adherence to lecture and rote learning. A new wave of essentialism took over, and schools focused on the task of preparing students for the technological and engineering challenges of the time.

Educational progressivism revived in the 1960s as the "child-centered" movement gained popularity in the United States. In the years since, various groups of educators have revisited the ideas of Dewey and his followers and revised them to address the changing needs of schools, children, and society. The philosophical influence of progressive ideas in education can be seen today in "whole language" reading programs, multiage approaches, experiential education, problem-based learning, and student-centered instruction.

3-2d ENDURING IDEAS: THE INFLUENCE OF PERENNIALISM

An educational philosophy related to essentialism, **perennialism** stresses the belief that all knowledge or wisdom has been accumulated over time and is represented by the great works of literature and art as well as religious texts. This educational philosophy found a strong expression in the 1980s with the *Paideia Proposal* by Mortimer Adler. In this influential call for school reform, Adler proposed one universal curriculum for elementary and secondary students, allowing for no electives. Everyone would take the same courses, and the curriculum would reflect the enduring ideas found in the works of history's finest thinkers and writers.

Like essentialism, perennialism holds that one type of education is good for all students. It differs from essentialism by placing greater emphasis on classic works of literature, history, art, and philosophy (including works of the ancient Greeks and Romans) and on the teaching of values and moral character. Essentialism can include practical, vocation-oriented courses—a class in computer skills, for instance—but perennialism leaves little room for such frivolity.

The perennialist approach has found a home at several US colleges, such as St. John's College in Maryland and in the state of New Mexico, and its influence shows in the core curricula at some larger universities, including the University of Chicago and Columbia University. Threads of the perennialist philosophy are present in many parochial schools as well. Whenever you hear about a program centered on "great ideas" or "great books," it most likely reflects perennialist ideas.

Adler emphasized the Socratic Method, a type of teaching based on extensive discussion with students. In this respect he was somewhat less teacher centered than many essentialists. His perennialism does, however, leave little room for flexibility in the curriculum and little opportunity to reflect the changing demographics of our times.

3-2e RADICAL REFORM PHILOSOPHIES: SOCIAL RECONSTRUCTIONISM, CRITICAL THEORY, AND EXISTENTIALISM

Alongside essentialism, perennialism, and progressivism, the twentieth century gave rise to some radical reform philosophies that proposed a fundamental rethinking of the nature of schooling. Among these are social reconstructionism, critical theory, and existentialism.

© Bettmann/Corbis

Progressivism asserted that students learned by doing and that their interests had to be a driving force of the learning experience.

Social reconstructionism is an educational philosophy that emphasizes social justice and a curriculum promoting social reform. Responding to the vast inequities in society and recognizing the plight of the poor, social reconstructionists believe that schools must produce an agenda for social change. Linked with social reconstructionism is critical theory or critical pedagogy, which stresses that students should learn to challenge oppression. In this view, education should tackle the real-world problems of hunger, violence, poverty, and inequality. Clearly, students are at the center of this curriculum with teachers advocating involvement in social reform. The focus of critical theorists and social reconstructionists is the transformation of systems of oppression through education to improve the human condition.

Among critical theorists, Paulo Freire (1921–1997), a Brazilian whose experiences living in poverty led him to champion education and literacy as the vehicle for social change, has had a particularly profound impact on the thinking of many educators. His most influential work was *Pedagogy of the Oppressed*, published in English in 1970.

Another philosophy that proposes fundamental changes in education is existentialism, which takes student-centered learning to an extreme. Rooted in the thinking of nineteenth-century philosophers like Søren Kierkegaard, existentialism gained popular notice in the mid-twentieth century through the works of Jean Paul Sartre and others. According to this philosophy, the only authoritative truth lies within the individual. Existentialism is defined by what it rejects—namely, the

TABLE 3.1 | Key Elements of Five Educational Philosophies

Philosophy	Focus of Study	Teacher's Role
Essentialism	Core knowledge that students need to be educated citizens; this knowledge is embodied in traditional academic disciplines such as history and mathematics	Teachers are the central figures in the classroom, transferring their knowledge to students
Perennialism	Enduring ideas found in the great works of literature and art	Teachers engage in extended dialogue with students, discussing and reasoning about the great ideas
Progressivism	Integration of study with real-life experiences through active learning, problem solving, and experimentation	Teachers structure the learning activities and encourage students to explore the ideas that arise; teachers can vary the curriculum to match the needs and interests of students
Social reconstructionism/ critical theory	Schooling promotes social and political reform by focusing on social problems and the need for change	Teachers guide students to think critically about social injustice and challenge oppression
Existentialism	Students choose their own course of study as part of their effort to figure out their place in the world and the meaning of their lives	Teachers support students in exploring their own interests

aesthetic education
Traditionally, this term referred merely to education in the fine arts, such as painting and music. In the broader view of Maxine Greene and other recent philosophers, however, it means education that enables students to use artistic forms and imagination to approach all fields of learning, including the sciences, and to share their perspectives with others.

existence of any source of objective truth other than the individual person, who must seek the meaning of his or her own existence.

Applied to education, existentialism proposes that students make all decisions about their choice of subject matter and activities as they seek to make meaning of their place in the world. This philosophy has not had as profound an impact on US schools as the other philosophies described in this chapter have, but you can find elements of it in classrooms where teachers insist that students make their own decisions about what is important for them to know. The best-known model of existentialism is Summerhill, a school founded in England by A. S. Neill in 1921. Clearly, students are at the center of this curriculum.

Table 3.1 summarizes some key features of the educational philosophies we have discussed.

3-2f AESTHETICS AND MAXINE GREENE

❝*We want to expand the range of literacy, offering the young new ways of symbolizing, new ways of structuring their experience, so they can see more, hear more, make more connections, embark on unfamiliar adventures into meaning.*❞
—**Maxine Greene (2002)**

In this era of global interdependence and multicultural diversity, educators continue to develop their ideas about the purposes of education and the best ways to reform schools. One influential contemporary thinker is Maxine Greene, a US philosopher, social activist, and teacher who has been an active scholar and educator at Teachers College, Columbia University, since 1965. Her belief is that the role of education is to create meaning in the lives of students and teachers through an interaction between knowledge and experience with the world.

Greene's educational philosophy is rooted in Dewey's ideas about art and aesthetics. Dewey's democratic view of education suggested that when children are able to approach problem solving artistically and imaginatively, they grow socially and culturally through their shared experiences, insights, and understandings. Therefore, the arts are an essential part of the human experience.

Building on Dewey, Greene has contributed to the growth of a paradigm known as **aesthetic education**.

She believes that the goal of education is to help students realize that they are responsible not merely for their own individual experiences, but they also have a deep connection to, and responsibility for, other human beings who share this world. Her philosophy asks us to consider how being able to express oneself in a number of different "languages"—including imagery, music, and dance—helps us make meaning of ideas (Greene, 1995). Greene also believes that education must lead students and teachers to the discovery of their own truths and that the arts promote a type of consciousness or "wide-awakeness" (1978) in service to this process. She stresses the importance of shared perspectives in looking at the world and a respect for differences in experience.

In connection with her work at the Lincoln Center Institute for the Arts in Education in New York City, of which she was a founding member, Greene began the Maxine Greene Foundation for Social Imagination, the Arts, and Education which prepares teachers to guide students in merging artistic expression with social justice. Its tenets focus on equity issues, quality of experiences in school, and the uses of imagination as a means of breaking down the barriers of diversity that children encounter in their daily lives. This perspective values the personal liberty of children and celebrates the imagination for its ability to open a child's mind to different possibilities and alternative solutions. An underlying assumption is that the humanities can serve as a catalyst enabling teachers and students to explore ideas more deeply and be more critically engaged with the world.

How do Maxine Greene's ideas work in an actual classroom? Consider this story:

In a sixth-grade class, Ms. Nelson is interested in her students' capacity for careful observation. She is a great admirer of many types of artists, and decorating her room are poster reproductions of famous paintings. The students move their chairs to position themselves by the poster of van Gogh's *The Starry Night* (see Figure 3.3), and Ms. Nelson asks, "What do you think van Gogh was thinking about when he painted this?"

"Circles" one student responds. Another says, "dreams," and still another student offers "motion." Then Ms. Nelson asks, "What do *you* think of when you look at this painting?" Students respond with phrases like "wind blowing," "scary dreams," "day and night," and "church spires." The students really seem to like the painting, and Ms. Nelson urges them on. She asks, "What is the organizing principle behind this painting?" (This is a question she asks often when the class looks at collections of objects: what principle did the collector use to gather these objects together?)

The Starry Night, June 1889 (oil on canvas) by Vincent van Gogh (1853–90) © Museum of Modern Art, New York, USA/The Bridgeman Art Library

FIGURE 3.3

The Starry Night (1889)
by Vincent van Gogh
Starry Night is one of the most well-known paintings in modern culture.

inquiry A multifaceted activity that involves making observations, posing questions about the subject matter, and conducting research or investigations to develop answers. Inquiry is common to scientific learning but also relevant to other fields.

Brown v. Board of Education of Topeka, Kansas A 1954 case in which the US Supreme Court outlawed segregation in public education.

The students decide that van Gogh was looking for images that used circles and pointy spires. Those were his organizing principles.

Asked about her goals for *The Starry Night* lesson, Ms. Nelson explains, "I am interested in getting students ready to make careful observations. We are doing a science unit on mystery powders, and I want them to think about properties that objects have in common."

Can you see how this lesson represents Maxine Greene's philosophy of integrating the arts into education?

The progressive philosophies of Dewey and Greene share a number of fundamental views:

- Making connections with social issues should be central to school curricula.
- The arts are creative tools that can expose children to new perspectives and new ways of communicating.
- Learning is an experiential process. Students learn by interacting with material in intellectual and sometimes manipulative ways; that is what "learning by doing" means.
- All forms of education should emphasize learning by **inquiry**—a process in which students ask meaningful questions and then seek their own answers.

Greene believes that people who choose to become teachers should ideally be "those who have learned the importance of becoming reflective enough to think about their own thinking and become conscious of their own consciousness" (Greene, 1995). What do you think that means?

3-3 Educational Reform: Funding, Priorities, and Standards

Although education of the citizenry was important to the founders of the United States, there is no mention of education for all in the Constitution. Hence, schooling became the domain and responsibility of the states, which left most of the control of schools to local communities.

Thus, US schools have traditionally been run by local school boards, and the bulk of the money they need has been raised through local taxes, especially the property tax. Many critics have argued that the reliance on local property taxes is unfair because it means that wealthier districts can raise more money for schools than poorer districts can. Yet Americans have long been reluctant to give up local funding and the control that goes with it.

As we noted previously, however, the Soviet Union's launch of Sputnik in 1957 prompted a rethinking of US educational priorities. Federal and state governments increasingly began to intervene in educational matters, setting priorities and (at least sometimes) providing funds to make sure those priorities were met. The overall result of these changes is that local school districts now supply less than half of the funding for public schools, as shown in Figure 3.4. Although local schools are happy to receive government money, they are not always pleased that the funds come with strings attached, reducing local control over the way schools operate.

The following sections introduce you to several ways in which government legislation, publications, and court cases have changed the course of US public education.

3-3a SEPARATE BUT EQUAL?

Previously in this chapter, we discussed the fact that African Americans were denied the right to an education when this country was new and evolving. Even after the Civil War, schools were slow to develop for African Americans, and, when they did, they were separate schools, only for black children. According to an 1896 Supreme Court ruling in *Plessy* v. *Ferguson*, "separate-but-equal" public facilities for different races were legal. But in time, during the first half of the 1900s, the schools serving African Americans were found *not* to be equal. They did not share equally in the resources available for public schooling; in most locations, they had fewer tax dollars and inferior conditions.

The situation came to a head in 1954 with the case of ***Brown v. Board of Education of Topeka, Kansas***. In this landmark case, the US Supreme Court ruled unanimously that separate schools for whites and blacks were inherently unequal because the effects of such separate schooling are likely to be different. Because of this inequality, the court decided, schools could not remain segregated.

© murat Sen/iStockphoto

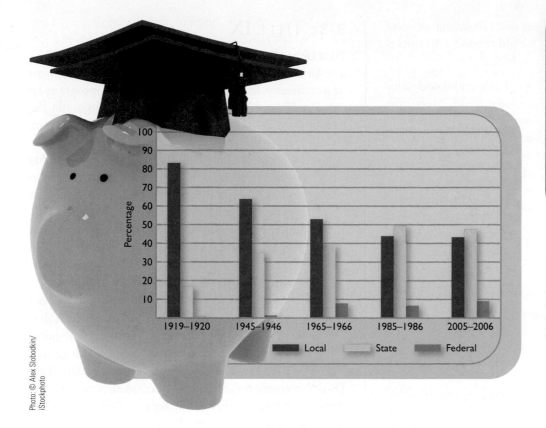

Photo: © Alex Slobodkin/
iStockphoto

FIGURE 3.4

Percentage of School Funds Derived from Local, State, and Federal Sources

Notice how the percentage of school funds raised by local governments has decreased since the early 1900s, while the proportion contributed by federal and state governments has grown.

Percentage

100 90 80 70 60 50 40 30 20 10

1919–1920   1945–1946   1965–1966   1985–1986   2005–2006

■ Local   □ State   ■ Federal

SOURCES: Data from National Center for Education Statistics. (2006). *The Condition of Education 2006* (NCES 2006-071). Washington, D.C.: U.S. Government Printing Office; National Education Association. (2006). *Rankings and Estimates: Rankings of the States 2005 and Estimates of School Statistics 2006.* Washington, D.C.: Author.

Initially, the *Brown* decision had particular impact in the South, where schools were segregated by law (de jure segregation). But many northern schools were segregated informally because of separate living patterns for whites and blacks (de facto segregation). Over the following decades, many school systems and various court cases dealt with the challenge of eliminating de facto segregation with mixed success. The efforts toward integration had a significant impact, but there was much turmoil and resistance. Numerous educators argue that de facto segregation still exists today in many cities and especially in suburban United States.

Federal legislation, including the Civil Rights Act (1964), reinforced the importance of creating educational opportunities for all Americans regardless of race, gender, or ethnicity. The Bilingual Education Acts of 1968 and 1974 provided supplemental funding for school districts to establish programs for large numbers of children with limited English-language ability. Similarly, the Equal Educational Opportunities Act of 1974 provided specific definitions of what constituted denial of equal educational opportunity. These included "failure to take the appropriate action to overcome language barriers that impede equal participation by all students in an instructional program."

3-3b THE ELEMENTARY AND SECONDARY EDUCATION ACT

Title 1 The section of federal education law that provides funds for compensatory education.

The most extensive federal financing of schools in the United States was made possible in 1965 when Congress passed the Elementary and Secondary Education Act (ESEA). At that time, this legislation was seen as part of President Lyndon Johnson's "War on Poverty" because it ensured that federal assistance would be sent to the poorest schools and communities in the nation. Its immediate impact was to provide $1 billion to improve the education of students from families living below the poverty line.

Every five years since its enactment, ESEA has been reauthorized; it is the single largest source of federal support for K–12 education. The federal government distributes the funds to the states, and it is the states' responsibility to identify the schools and districts to receive the funds. This legislation, particularly the section known as **Title 1**, has led to many important programs that fall into the general category of compensatory education—educational services designed specifically to create better opportunities for students with disadvantages, such as those from high-poverty neighborhoods. Examples include:

• Early-childhood education: Head Start, the most well-known national early-childhood program, helps prepare preschool children for school, focusing not just on academic skills but also on nutrition, health, and the family environment;

• Tutoring and other supplemental academic instruction;
• After-school centers;
• Computer labs for poor schools;
• Dropout prevention services;
• Job training;
• Parental education; and
• Professional development for teachers.

The No Child Left Behind (NCLB) Act of 2002 revised the ESEA and called for states to develop content-area standards and annual testing of math and reading in grades 3 to 8. Schools with poor test results face the possibility of being closed. This revision also gives parents greater choice about where their children go to school. We discuss the implications of this act at the end of this chapter and again in Chapter 6 where contemporary trends in education are explored.

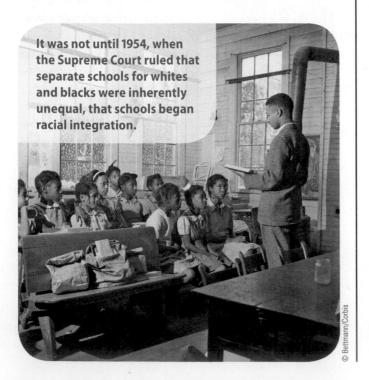

It was not until 1954, when the Supreme Court ruled that separate schools for whites and blacks were inherently unequal, that schools began racial integration.

© Bettmann/Corbis

3-3c TITLE IX

Title IX, part of the Education Amendments of 1972, is a federal law that prohibits discrimination on the basis of sex in any federally funded education program or activity. The main objective of Title IX is to avoid the use of federal money to support sexually discriminating practices.

Title IX was modeled on Title VI of the Civil Rights Act of 1964 which prohibits discrimination based on race, color, and national origin. However, unlike Title VI, which applies to all federal financial assistance, Title IX is limited to *education* programs or activities that receive federal financial assistance.

Title IX protects the rights of both males and females from pre-kindergarten through graduate school—in sports, financial aid, employment, counseling, and school regulations and policies. One impact of Title IX has been on girls' sports activities and facilities; it requires that schools provide equal opportunities, funding, and facilities for boys' and girls' teams. Unfortunately, Title IX enforcement has been fairly lax, so it is not entirely unusual to find schools in apparent violation of part of the regulation.

What has been your own experience of the effect of gender on educational opportunities? Many studies have explored the ways in which some girls and boys experience school differently. Many students, for example, who have attended single-sex private schools have had positive experiences. In fact, some public schools, for a wide range of reasons, have offered single-sex classes as well. In one public school I encountered, an all-girls physics class was thought to be a good way to engage more young women in physics. Success was measured by the achievement of the young women in the class. Similarly, in Queensland, Australia, several high schools are experimenting with all-boys English literature and writing classes. They also are meeting with successful outcomes in terms of achievement. Do these examples show that "separate but equal" can be a useful principle when it comes to segregation by sex? There is a great deal of controversy over this issue in education today.

Two other sections of the 1964 Civil Rights Act relate to education as well, and they can be used in conjunction with Title IX to challenge discriminatory practices:

• Title IV authorizes federal assistance to prohibit discrimination in education on the basis of sex, race, and national origin.
• Title VII prohibits sex discrimination and other types of employment discrimination both in and outside of education contexts (Klein et al., 2002).

3-3d A Nation at Risk

In 1983, the National Commission on Excellence in Education, a group of scholars and educators convened by the US Department of Education, issued a report in the form of an open letter to the US people. Called *A Nation at Risk: The Imperative for Educational Reform,* this document showed deep concern about the educational system in the United States:

> *Our society and its educational institutions seem to have lost sight of the basic purposes of schooling, and of the high expectations and disciplined effort needed to attain them. This report, the result of 18 months of study, seeks to generate reform of our educational system in fundamental ways and to renew the Nation's commitment to schools and colleges of high quality throughout the length and breadth of our land. (National Commission on Excellence in Education, 1983)*

The report called for tougher standards for graduation, increases in the required number of mathematics and science courses, higher college entrance requirements, and a return to what was called "academic basics." It also defined "computer skills" as a new basic.

The report further recommended an increase in the amount of homework given, a longer school day, more rigorous requirements for teachers, and updated textbooks. *A Nation at Risk* inaugurated a new period of academic rigor, with increased attention to skills and standards and less emphasis on progressive concerns such as schools' role in building social understanding. The "at risk" wording implied that the United States would lose its global competitive edge if the reforms were not carried out. Even though these recommendations came from the federal government, they were implemented (or sometimes ignored) in different ways at the local, state, and district levels.

3-3e The Individuals with Disabilities Education Act

In 1975, Congress passed the Education for All Handicapped Children Act (Public Law 94-142) to ensure that all children with disabilities could receive free, appropriate public education, just like other children. This law was revised in 1990, in 1997, and most recently in 2004. It is now known as the **Individuals with Disabilities Education Act (IDEA).**

What is so important about this act? Before 1975, there was no organized, equitable way of addressing the needs of disabled students in the public school system. Often they were marginalized, taught in separate classrooms, and provided with watered-down curricula.

As a result of the federal legislation, however, strong efforts have been made to include students with disabilities in regular classrooms. This reform, known as **inclusion**, has been implemented to greater or lesser degrees in different school districts. In some classrooms, students with learning disabilities are integrated with general education students as much as possible. In other classrooms, students with special educational needs are included in the general education classroom some of the time; this arrangement is called *partial inclusion*. Some districts have a self-contained class as well for students with special needs (who are often called *special education students*). Often, depending on the needs of the student population, all three models exist in the same school district. Reform movements on behalf of children with disabilities have dominated special education programs for the past thirty years. Much educational research suggests that inclusion benefits both special education students and students from the general population. We will return to the subject of inclusion in Chapter 6.

3-3f Standards-Based Reform and NCLB

As a response to *A Nation at Risk* and similar publications that followed, groups of scholars from content area associations developed standards for their

A Nation at Risk: The Imperative for Educational Reform A 1983 federal report that found US schools in serious trouble and inaugurated a new wave of school reform focused on academic basics and higher standards for student achievement.

Individuals with Disabilities Education Act (IDEA) The federal law that guarantees that all children with disabilities receive free, appropriate public education.

inclusion The practice of educating students with disabilities in regular classrooms alongside nondisabled students.

Q: *Do you remember ways in which your educational experience differed from that of your female or male peers?*

Strong efforts are made to include students with disabilities in regular classrooms.

National standards and the testing that assesses whether students are meeting those standards is a policy issue that has supporters and critics. This movement, supported in part by NCLB, is a model of considerable rigor, accountability, and strict benchmarks for student learning. Supporters of the movement contend that this reform movement encourages schools to set higher standards for their students and to find ways in which their students can meet those standards. Critics insist that curriculum needs to be connected to the students' lived experiences and that standards will stifle innovation and creativity in the classroom.

NCLB (actually signed by President George W. Bush in January 2002) was the most dramatic federal education legislation since ESEA. Although NCLB was a reauthorization and revision of ESEA, it went beyond the previous act in several important ways. It emphasized increased funding for less wealthy school districts and higher achievement for financially poor and minority students. It also introduced new measures for holding schools accountable for students' progress. Most controversially, NCLB set new rules for standardized testing, requiring that students in grades 3 through 8 be tested every year in mathematics and reading. This requirement had important implications for the way the curriculum was developed and implemented in many elementary schools across the country. Because of the initial push for statewide standardized tests in mathematics and reading, elementary students in the first decade of this century received less instruction in science and social studies. For many educators, the promise of the NCLB legislation became a massive testing movement, and there has not been substantial research to demonstrate that these standards-based assessments in each state actually improved student learning.

In 2012, President Barack Obama's administration recommended overhauling NCLB, and many of its features will change, including its name. It will revert back to the Elementary and Secondary Education Act, its original name. Currently, the Obama administration is providing states with flexibility from some of the NCLB requirements because a new education bill cannot meet approval in Congress. Hence, the President and Secretary of Education are creating a bridge to a new bill by giving states and districts more

disciplines, beginning with the National Council of Teachers of Mathematics. The first version of *Principles and Standards for School Mathematics* appeared in 1989. Language arts, science, social studies, and foreign languages followed in the 1990s, developing standards for what children at each grade level from pre-kindergarten to grade 12 should know and be able to do in each of the content areas. States were asked to prepare content standards based on these national guidelines and to create assessments to match the standards.

Hence the era in which we are presently living—and in which you are preparing to teach—is dominated by standards-based school reform and assessments. Many of you went to school as the standards-based movement was getting under way. Standards in the academic area were developed by professional organizations in concert with scholars and teachers in the field. Standards-based educational reform refers to clear, measurable, academic standards for all school students in all academic areas.

flexibility in how they raise standards and undertake essential reforms to improve teacher effectiveness. This flexibility means that a state can determine the assessment measures for student performance, and they do not have to rely on a single type of testing. They can use multiple measures to assess student learning while still maintaining a high level of accountability. Each state that was granted a waiver from the rigid requirements of NCLB had to develop specific approaches for raising standards and evaluating teachers. This provides relief from the rigid demands of NCLB, with many opponents arguing that classrooms were becoming test prep centers, while subjects that are not tested get too little attention. The waivers will allow local states and districts to make spending decisions and determine the best measures for assessing their learners. Clearly many feel that this one-size-fits-all formula for achievement and accountability cannot work in a society as diverse as ours. Based on standards set by NCLB, more schools were listed as failing in 2011 than in 2010. Many feel that the computations required to meet passing standards do not reflect the genuine progress made in many of these so-called failing districts and schools.

Since 2002, many teachers and school administrators have found that they have relatively little freedom to vary the curriculum or even the order in which topics are taught. Yet local control still predominates in some places, as the following story demonstrates:

Ms. Bennett is the principal of a public elementary school in Maryland, where children in grades 1 through 5 explore a different human-made artifact each year. The first grade studies bridges, the second grade studies elevators, the third grade investigates escalators, the fourth grade focuses on airplanes, and fifth-grade students explore the automobile. These various products of engineering design form themes that are addressed during the entire school year, regardless of what other topics are studied in that year.

How did this unusual curriculum come about? Few elementary schools have a mandate to teach students about such inventions in a formal way. When you meet Ms. Bennett, however, you learn that she entered the field of education after several years as a civil engineer. One of the first women in her college class to excel in civil engineering, she brought her passion for the work to her elementary school

Although there are many local and national academic standards, there is no standard student!

students. As a principal, Ms. Bennett enlisted her faculty's help to make learning about engineering design part of the school's curriculum. Many believe that the rigid testing that has dominated public education in the first decade of the twenty-first century has caused the more creative aspects of the curriculum to take a back seat to preparation for the exams.

3-3g COMMON CORE STATE STANDARDS AND RACE TO THE TOP

The Common Core State Standards Initiative is a state-led effort coordinated by the National Governors Association Center for Best Practices (NGA Center) and the Council of Chief State School Officers (CCSSO) to develop a clear and consistent framework to prepare students for

TEACHSOURCE VIDEO CASE

Find the TeachSource Video Case "Foundations: Aligning Instruction with Federal Legislation" on the Education CourseMate at CengageBrain.com to learn more about IDEA and NCLB. After watching the video, consider the following question:

How does this discussion help make sense of the NCLB revisions of 2012?

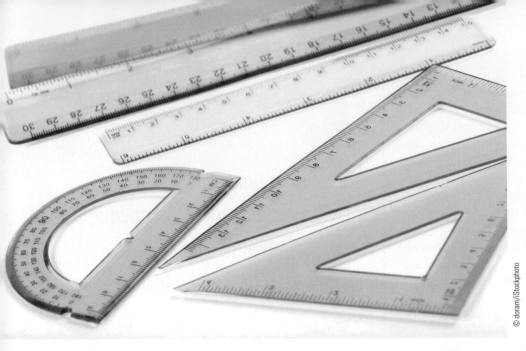
© doram/iStockphoto

student learning. It is a competition designed to provide states with extra funding for education if they can demonstrate a realistic, well-crafted plan to address criteria that include:

I. Improving teacher and principal effectiveness through creative preparation, mentoring, and support programs.
II. Creating a meaningful state education reform agenda and building capacity to scale up the implementation of programs designed to meet this agenda.
III. Adopting the Common Core Standards, improving upon them and developing high-quality assessments.
IV. Turning around the lowest achieving schools with an implementable plan.
V. Ensuring high performing charter schools and other innovative schools are successful.

These are some highlights of the criteria for states to receive this federal funding. The last point emphasizes the federal government's view that improvements in public schooling require experimentation and innovation in the design of the school. As we will see in later chapters, this has led to a proliferation of charter schools, supported by public funds and existing under a special state charter with its own set of standards. It is hoped that the RTTP Award winners will help trailblaze effective reforms and provide examples for states and local school districts throughout the country to follow. RTTP is in its third year of awarding large grants to successful state applicants. After the first two rounds of applications, states with a RTTP grant include Delaware, The District of Columbia, Florida, Georgia, Hawaii, Maryland, Massachusetts, New York, North Carolina, Ohio, Rhode Island, and Tennessee.

college and the workforce through the collaboration with teachers, school administrators, and experts. The standards are designed to provide teachers and parents with a common understanding of what students are expected to learn. Consistent standards will provide appropriate benchmarks for all students, regardless of where they live. These standards define the knowledge and skills students should have within their K–12 education careers so that they will graduate high school able to succeed in entry-level, credit-bearing academic college courses and in workforce training programs (http://www.corestandards.org/about-the-standards).

In 2009, the first official public draft of the college- and career-readiness standards in English language arts and mathematics were released. Care was taken to ensure that these standards in mathematics and English could be used broadly for every state in the country and are designed to influence the development of high-quality curricula in each state. These Common Core standards are a significant part of statewide initiatives for educational reform. State funding is largely dependent on their use as described by the Race to the Top (RTTP) initiative, a federal funding program that creates a statewide competition for education grants (http://www2.ed.gov/programs/racetothetop/index.html). RTTP, a heavily funded US Department of Education initiative, began in 2009 by the Obama administration and Secretary of Education Arne Duncan. This funding has been awarded to states that have submitted credible proposals with plans for implementing educational reforms that have the promise to help the lowest performing schools as well as provide blueprints for measuring teacher effectiveness and

3-4 Concluding Thoughts

As you think about the history of US public education, consider all the factors that contribute to the structure and design of schooling today. In addition to geography, acts of Congress, immigration, and educational movements, we now have international events, global challenges, an increased focus on accountability, and a digital revolution shaping and reshaping the landscape of public education.

Today we are faced with unprecedented cultural, ethnic, and racial diversity in our schools. Further, as young people spend more time online, texting, tweeting, and seeking information, the nature of teaching and learning in the classroom is undergoing a transformation, reflecting these modes of communication. Although there are many local and national academic standards, *there is no standard student!* In this respect, we live in an unusual period in US education. Yet our long educational history and the philosophies and debates that have emerged during that time continue to influence our choices.

CHAPTER 4

EXPLORING THE NATURE OF TEACHING AND LEARNING

© Liam Bailey/Photolibrary

If a doctor, lawyer, or dentist had 40 people in his office at one time, all of whom had different needs, and some of whom did not want to be there and were causing trouble, and the doctor, lawyer, or dentist, without assistance, had to treat them all with professional excellence for nine months, then he [or she] might have some conception of the classroom teacher's job.
—Donald D. Quinn

s you consider a teaching career, you will frequently hear the terms *pedagogy* and *instruction*. How do they relate to teaching and learning? What does Donald Quinn mean when he speaks of "different

needs"? How can we define professional excellence for ourselves as teachers?

In this chapter we examine the meaning of teaching and learning through an exploration of learning theories. Currently, the field of neuroscience—the study of the structure, function, development, and physiology of the brain and the nervous system—is at the forefront of understanding how people perceive and interact with the external world. Other important approaches have also contributed to the way educators think about learning today. We will explore what we teach—the school's curriculum—as well as how the content of a school's curriculum is shaped by not only national standards but also by states, local school districts, local school boards, school curriculum committees, and teachers themselves.

4-1 Anyone Can Teach?

Most people have spent much of their lives as students in classrooms. Add up the years of schooling you have had up to this time—the number is certainly considerable, is it not? Because people have been in classrooms for so much of their lives, there exists a common myth that anyone can teach.

As a new teacher just starting out, I confided my nervousness about my first day of teaching to a friend, and he said to me, "Teaching is easy. You just stand up there and talk—and you like to talk." For me, that was the first of several experiences with people who *think* they know what being a teacher is about.

As you are probably discovering for yourself, teaching and learning are complex activities. They are far from easy and automatic. As we explore the ways a teacher fosters learning, you will see that there is a lot to know about the principles behind what a teacher does. Remember, too, that the process is a dialectic. That is, it requires communication with your students, and it demands that you be an active listener, not just a talker. (My friend was right, however: I *do* like to talk.) As you will see, teaching is not "telling," and, in addition to what you have to *know* to be able to teach, there are many things you have to *do* to create the opportunities for students to learn.

LEARNING OUTCOMES

After reading this chapter, you should be thinking about the following ideas:

4-1 Explain why there exists the common myth that "anyone can teach."

4-2 Compare the art of teaching to the science of teaching.

4-3 Compare learning theories and examine how neuroscience has influenced current theories about how people learn.

4-4 Examine the ways in which curriculum is developed and the promised influence of the Common Core State Standards on mathematics and English curricula.

4-5 Analyze the statement that "we can teach our students but we cannot learn for them."

4-6 Discuss what it takes to learn to become a teacher.

4-7 Explain how understanding how your students learn and what their lives are like influence your role as their teacher.

Create: Compose a song, skit, poem, or rap to convey the Goldilocks story in a new form. (http://projects.coe.uga.edu/epltt/index.php?title=Bloom%27s_ Taxonomy January 2012)

As you examine the learning theories described in this chapter, examine the ways in which we now understand from neuroscience that learners are indeed active participants in their own concept construction.

4-3b BEHAVIORISM: A TEACHER-CENTERED APPROACH

In the mid-1900s, Harvard psychologist B. F. Skinner pioneered a theory of how people learn that still has followers today. Skinner's theory of *operant conditioning* viewed learning as a response to external stimuli in the environment. For Skinner, learning was a product

Learning about students requires that teachers be active listeners.

© Christina Kennedy/PhotoEdit, Inc.

that could be promoted by teachers who provided the right incentives and motivation. This general approach came to be known as **behaviorism**. Behaviorists believe that all learning is shaped by the stimuli in the environment and that free will plays no role in the process.

Using the behaviorist approach, teachers structured their lessons around clear objectives that stated what students would be able to do by the end of the lesson. The desired behaviors were regulated by carefully planned reinforcements and punishments. The external rewards could include good grades, increased privileges, or a special smile from the teacher. Students were seen as passive participants in the classroom who responded to the teacher's direct rewards and punishments.

Behaviorist ideas still form a backdrop for many techniques used to establish classroom discipline. For instance, teachers rely on behaviorist principles when they set up specific rewards for good behavior. Behaviorism asserts that students will modify their behavior in response to consistent delivery of rewards and punishments.

Yet there are many critics of behaviorist techniques today. Some argue that behaviorist teachers exercise too much control over their students, with the result that students tend to learn facts rather than deep concepts. Others remind teachers that rewards and punishments do not help students develop their own internal mechanisms for doing quality work and that students eventually lose interest in what they are essentially being "bribed" to do (Kohn, 1999). Today, in some areas, students are being paid to complete high school. Money for grades is an experimental approach to stimulate lower achieving students. It is, as you can imagine, quite controversial and most parents do not agree with cash-based incentives for achievement.

4-3c COGNITIVE LEARNING THEORIES: THE ROLE OF THE LEARNER

As behaviorists focused solely on students' observable behaviors as the indicators of learning, many educators and psychologists began to resist this view and suggested that the learner was not a passive recipient of new concepts but rather played a more active role in the learning process. **Cognitive learning theories** emerged to describe students' mental development. Cognitive learning theorists went "inside the head of the learner" to discover and model the thought processes that occur during learning.

A key figure in cognitive learning theory was the Swiss scholar and scientist Jean Piaget, who began conducting interviews and research studies with children in the 1920s. From these investigations, he developed the idea of stages of cognitive development. According to Piaget, at certain times in a child's intellectual growth, different mental structures begin to emerge. He believed that most children between birth and two years of age are in the sensorimotor stage, in which learning occurs mainly through sensory impressions and movement. The child learns that he or she is separate from the environment and that aspects of the environment—parents or a favorite toy—continue to exist even though they may be outside the reach of his or her senses.

Later, children begin to learn words and other symbols (the preoperational stage [ages two to seven]). In this stage, a child's thinking is influenced by fantasy—the way the child would like things to be—and he or she assumes that others see situations from his or her viewpoint. The child takes in information and then changes it in his or her mind to fit his or her ideas.

In the next stage, from age seven to eleven, the child develops the ability to generalize concepts from concrete experiences (the concrete operational stage). In this stage, the child makes rational judgments about concrete or observable phenomena, which in the past he or she needed to manipulate physically to understand.

Finally, the child develops the ability to manipulate abstractions (the formal operational stage [ages eleven and older]). In this stage, the learner no longer requires concrete objects to make rational judgments.

Piaget argued that at each of these stages of maturation, a child is ready for a different type of learning. The discrete boundaries of Piaget's stages of development came under scrutiny as researchers learned that children can be in several stages at once and that the stages cannot easily be linked to predetermined ages. In other words, as significant as Piaget's work is, we now understand that there are not clear demarcations of mental development from one stage to the next; as the learner progresses from one stage to the next, there is an overlap. For example, many children handle concrete operations earlier in their lives than Piaget thought.

At each stage, Piaget decided, knowledge is not passively received but is actively built up by the learner through a process of invention or creation, not reception. This gives a great deal of responsibility to the learner.

Piaget's Stages of Development

Formal operational (11+ years)

Concrete operational (7–11 years)

Preoperational (2–7 years)

Sensorimotor (birth–2 years)

Photo: © Petre Milevski/iStockphoto

Jerome Bruner (1960, 1966), another cognitive learning theorist, took Piaget's ideas a step further by arguing that at any stage of cognitive development, teachers should allow children to discover ideas for themselves. He was a leading supporter of Piaget's work, but he suggested that at *any* given stage of cognitive development, teaching should proceed in a way that allows children to discover ideas for themselves. His work became known as *discovery learning*. He differed from Piaget in one important respect. Whereas Piaget believed that readiness for a particular type of learning depended on a child's stage of cognitive development, Bruner noticed that children are always ready to learn a concept at *some level*. Realizing this, Bruner emphasized the importance of returning to curriculum topics at various ages, revisiting them at different stages of the child's development (1960). This produces a spiraling of curriculum topics, as the same broad topics are revisited at higher grade levels. This practice has become an important part of curriculum planning. Discovery learning remains influential today and has much in common with constructivism, which we will come to in a moment.

© Eugene Junying Sim/iStockphoto

4-3d SOCIAL COGNITIVE THEORIES: THE ROLE OF SOCIAL INTERACTIONS

Piaget's work was soon criticized for not taking into account the learner's social contexts. After all, when children develop their understanding of the world, they do not do so in a social or cultural vacuum. Some of Piaget's critics developed forms of social learning theory; these over time were extended into **social cognitive learning theories**, which take into account both the learner's own mental processes and the social environment in which the learning occurs.

One important social cognitive theorist, the Russian psychologist Lev Vygotsky (1962), showed how social contexts influence the ideas that people develop. As one example, the teacher and students in a classroom use language that is socially and culturally accepted in that specific environment. The ideas that children develop in the classroom conform to these socially accepted usages and meanings. When students work in groups and read each other's writing in order to critique it, for example, one student says of the other's work, "This is so cool." The meaning is that this student peer really liked the story, and the comment is readily understood. Clearly, different cultures, neighborhoods, and parts of the world would have different ways of expressing the same meaning. Because students do not learn in a cultural vacuum, studying how people learn requires consideration of the context.

Many social cognitivists stress the importance of modeling. For instance, if you were teaching young students how to add columns of numbers, you would probably model the process of exchanging ten ones for one ten. According to social cognitivists, students would learn, in part, by observing you; then they would learn more by doing a similar problem themselves; and they would be further served by using manipulative materials and working on exchanging units with their peers in a group.

Thinking about modeling reminds us that teachers are not the only important social influence on learning. Parents, other adults, siblings, and peers have major effects on a child's intellectual development as well. A young person learns a great deal by observing various other people, communicating with them, and solving problems with them.

4-3e CONSTRUCTIVISM: STUDENT-CENTERED LEARNING

The work of Piaget, Bruner, Vygotsky, and others have paved the way for understanding in greater depth how people learn. The accumulated research has shown that the essence of learning is the constant effort to assimilate new information. For real learning to occur, you also have to make that information your own so that it becomes significant to you and you can use it for your own purposes. These ideas form the basis of a group of learning theories called **constructivism**. The constructivist approach builds on cognitive and social cognitive theories but goes further by considering how new information becomes meaningful to the learner.

The Essence of Constructivism: Building Mental Schemes

Constructivism is the learning theory that most closely relates to what we currently understand about how people learn. Learners interact with people, objects, and ideas to construct their understanding of what is

Helping students work with others to meet common goals is an important part of teaching.

© Mark Garten/Corbis

FIGURE 4.2

The Role of Mental Schemes in Learning
In this *Peanuts* cartoon, Linus learns from Charlie Brown that his ambition to become a doctor requires eight extra years of school. Being admired is not sufficient compensation for this, and Linus revises his mental scheme.

happening around them. At the heart of this learning theory is the concept of "mental schemes." A mental scheme is a sort of organizer in the brain. As the result of all your experiences during your lifetime, you have formed these organizing structures in your mind that help you make sense of the world. When you encounter new information, you try to fit it into your existing schemes. Sometimes it fits easily, but when it does not fit, you have to revise your existing mental scheme. In Figure 4.2 Charlie Brown forces Linus to rethink his mental scheme about how long it takes to study to become a doctor. This changes Linus's thinking. When new information fails to match your existing schemes—when it does not fit your picture of the world—you have a choice. You can ignore the new information—in a sense, reject it. In that case, we can say that no new learning has occurred. Or you can remake your set of schemes to accommodate the new data—a process of truly making new information your own. That is what happens when we learn something.

The following story illustrates mental schemes at work. It is the story of my own personal mental scheme for how mail was delivered where I grew up.

Mental Schemes at Work

I grew up in an inner-city apartment building with six floors and twenty apartments on each floor. When I was six years old, I was allowed to use the small key to open the mailbox assigned to my family and "take out the mail." This was my daily job after school.

I had my own personal theory about mail delivery. I imagined that, when the envelope was dropped in the public mailbox on the corner, a tube carried it through underground chutes to its destination in my little mailbox. Even at the age of six, however, I was troubled by not being able to explain how the letter knew how to get to my mailbox.

One day, when walking with my mother, I bent down to look under the mailbox on the corner. "What are you looking for?" she asked. "I was wondering where the tubes were," I responded. "What tubes?" she asked, and I then proceeded to share my theory. Nodding, she said that she could not explain right then how the mail got to the mailbox but she would arrange a way for me to find out.

Shortly thereafter, I was home ill from school, in the care of my grandmother. My mother called from work and asked Grandma to take me down to the mailboxes at the precise time that Artie, our mailman, would arrive. She bundled me up and I was able to witness the mailman, with his special key, open the portal to all of the mailboxes in the building. One box at a time, he inserted the mail in the various boxes.

He allowed me to help him, thrilled with my curiosity about how mail "knows" where to go. He also invited me and my family to the local post office for a view of how the postal workers sort the mail for the various neighborhood routes.

I shall never forget this experience. It demonstrates, for me, what it means to reorganize my mental schemes as I set about understanding more of my external world.

It would have been easy for my mother to say, "No, Janice, mail does not travel through tubes in the ground." Instead, she honored my theory, found it quite interesting, and arranged for me to have an experience that would challenge my beliefs about underground tubes and mail delivery. By observing how the mailman opened all the mailboxes simultaneously with his large master key, I saw people as an intricate part of the mail delivery process. I began to expand my thinking and accommodate this new experience into my mental scheme.

TABLE 4.1	Learning Theories Compared
Learning Theory	**Key Elements**
Behaviorism	• Teacher-centered • Students respond to external stimuli and learn the correct responses through rewards and punishments, eventually internalizing rewards and punishments • Teachers are in absolute control through the stimuli they present in the classroom
Cognitive learning theories	• Somewhat learner-centered • Learning is active, not merely passive • Symbolic mental constructions in the minds of learners help them process information
Social cognitive learning theories	• Somewhat learner-centered • Internal mental processes are important, but we also learn through experiences shared with others; learning is as much social as it is individual
Constructivism	• Learner-centered • We all construct our own perspective of the world, based on individual experiences and personal schemes, which are internal knowledge structures • A person adjusts his or her mental model to incorporate new experiences and make sense of new information

Authentic instruction begins with close attention to students' existing ideas, knowledge, skills, and attitudes. Just as my mother realized, these are the foundation on which new learning builds (Bransford & Donovan, 2005). Learning as much as we can about students' existing mental schemes is important if we hope to help them learn. Effective teachers try to activate students' prior knowledge so that, in the course of the lesson, students can build on what they already know, challenge it, rethink it, and refine it.

Because teachers need to pay so much attention to students' preexisting ideas, they often face a situation similar to the one my mother encountered: the student reveals ideas that are plainly "wrong." What should a teacher do when a student has such misconceptions? Many educators believe that if a teacher merely corrects a student's erroneous ideas verbally, those ideas may go underground; they may linger in the student's mind, unrefuted. Instead, the teacher should treat the misconceptions with respect and guide the student in confronting new information that contradicts them. In wrestling with the contradiction, the teacher hopes, the student will modify old mental schemes or create new ones, and in this way genuine learning will occur.

There will be many times when you will be tempted to refute a student's idea or explanation. It is certainly true that you should not allow your student to harbor misconceptions for a long time. But try to find a way to provide convincing evidence for the alternative, more accurate explanation.

Perhaps you can remember a personal theory that you held onto when you were young. How did you eventually learn, through experience and interaction with the material, that you had to adjust your thinking?

Learning and Teaching

❝*A teacher's purpose is not to create students in his [or her] own image, but to develop students who can create their own image.***❞ — Anonymous**

The preceding quote refers to the need for teachers to help students build ideas for themselves. They can offer opportunities for students to work iteratively[1] on big concepts; the students can address those concepts over time until they can construct those concepts for themselves. One example is how understanding that

---

[1]*Iteratively* means repeatedly, on multiple occasions.

the order of the digits in a number tells you the value of the digits. Place value is a huge idea! Students cannot understand place value by having it explained, but when they have the opportunity to exchange bundles of units and bundle the bundles and then represent the bundles in some numerical form, then they can come to make sense of numbers. Representing numbers as numerals is part of the convention we establish. We talk in code to one another, and students need to reinvent that code for themselves. Then the ones, tens, and hundreds columns have meaning, and the number really represents a quantity.

This may seem like a radical idea—that individual students need to "reinvent" a basic operation we use for arithmetic. But think about what happens if students learn only the mechanical processes of mathematics. When young children are adding numbers, they can learn to "carry a 1" from one column to the next, but if they do not get the *meaning* of this procedure, they will have only a shallow and fragile understanding of what they are doing. Later on in their mathematical education, they will likely get confused because they do not fully grasp what is happening (Interview with Dr. Jacqueline Grennon Brooks, 2005).

Education is far broader than just schooling. All the experiences students have at home, on the playground, and in the environments of their lives bear on how they learn. The students' interests, sensibilities, and daily practices all contribute to their mental schemes. That is why the environment is so desperately important to learning. In an inner-city New York school, the second teacher takes her low-income students on sidewalk "field trips" to neighborhood places that her students never see (i.e., the subway, the neighborhood market, a municipal parking garage, local parking meters, and an auto repair shop). The teacher situates second-grade math around the parking meters and generates a list of vocabulary words based on their excursions. Students in this second-grade class get experiential exposure that, coupled with the formal classroom, gives context and meaning to learning (Winerip, NY Times, 2-12-12).

We base our practices of teaching on learning theories. The emerging relationship between neuroscience and teaching informs our pedagogy and helps us to guide instruction with meaningful context. The more we learn about how the brain cognitively processes, the more we realize that the way our mind works is dependent on how the neurons in our brain are fired, and that is dependent on the context that is created for learning. Actively engaged students have more neurons firing, allowing them to use more parts of the brain, connect with prior knowledge, and build on what they already know. John Dewey's progressive era had the right idea when it encouraged the active participation of students in their own learning. This simple story illustrates that type of engagement in the course of a simple lesson:

My teacher, Ms. Schultz, walked us outside our large brick building in an urban area into the schoolyard and asked us to feel the sun's warmth. It was an autumn day and the air was cool, but the sun felt warm against our faces. Then she asked us to move about and explore our shadows.

Something Ms. Schultz said in the midst of this experience has stayed with me forever: "Isn't it amazing, girls and boys, that this sun is 93 million miles away and it still has the power to warm us up?" I remember thinking that the sun must be very, very hot if, after traveling all those miles, it still warmed my skin. I have thought about the sun in that way ever since.

Using materials, conferring with peers, and asking questions are ways that students learn math.

curriculum A plan of studies that includes the ways instructional content is organized and presented at each grade level.

On the next sunny day, we returned early to the schoolyard and explored our shadows again, noticing how their length changed with the time of day. Experiencing the sunlight in the context of learning about shadows made a big difference to me. I was taken with how different the size of my shadow was at noon, compared with early morning. Experiencing myself in space, responding to the sun's warmth on my body, joining with my classmates in measuring our shadows—all these activities created a mental scheme on which my learning about the sun and shadows occurred. I have always remembered the distance of the sun from the Earth and that when the sun is overhead, around noon, my shadow is the shortest.

In these simple ways, Ms. Schultz helped create a context that shaped my learning.

Fish Is Fish

One of my favorite children's stories illustrates the role that prior and current knowledge plays in student learning. *Fish Is Fish*, by Leo Lionni (1970), is the story of a young minnow and a tadpole who become friends when they meet underwater in a pond. But the tadpole soon grows legs and explores the world beyond the pond and then returns to tell his fish friend about the new creatures he sees, such as birds, cows, and people. As the illustrations demonstrate, the fish imagines these creatures as bird-fish, cow-fish, and people-fish and is eager to join them. The minnow learns the limits of life beyond the safety of the water environment to which he is adapted, but not before we get to see the images of fish with wings as he hears about birds, fish with udders as he hears about cows, and fish walking on their tailfins as he hears about people. You may be wondering what this has to do with learning theories. In fact, it is a wonderful illustration of how learners process new material through their prior and current conceptions. Unless those ideas are acknowledged, learners create mental images that are quite different from those that are intended—in this case, by the minnow's friend, the frog. The implications for teaching are clear: Access students' existing understandings and experiences and draw attention to

the kinds of knowledge that help students to learn with understanding (Bransford et al., 2000).

Hence, if the frog had provided more details about birds, cows, and people, it would have helped the fish to understand that their body parts have functions that these animals need for survival. Of course, the fish in Lionni's story is endowed with human capacities for thought, but he does make a good illustration of why it is so important for teachers to understand how people learn.

4-4 What Is a Curriculum?

You have read in this chapter a lot about theories of learning and instruction, but what about the actual material you will be required to teach? Educators refer to this as the **curriculum**. Who determines the curriculum, and how can teachers express their personal and creative selves when handed a list of topics they must address? Think about these questions as you read the following sections.

4-4a FORMAL, INFORMAL, AND HIDDEN CURRICULA

The word *curriculum* derives from the Latin term meaning "running course." It is the overall plan that includes what you will teach and how the material should be arranged and presented. A curriculum may be thought of as an organizing tool for the myriad topics that are addressed at each grade level. Curricula are typically organized by content area. There are language arts, mathematics, social studies, foreign language, and science curricula. There is a curriculum associated with any subject matter taught at a given school.

Sometimes you will hear the official plan of studies referred to as the *formal curriculum*. There is also an

TEACHSOURCE VIDEO CASE

A High School Debate

Contemporary understanding of teaching places much responsibility for learning on the students by asking them to actively create meaning through their experiences. View the TeachSource Video Case "Constructivist Teaching in Action: A High School Classroom Debate" on the Education CourseMate at CengageBrain.com. After watching the video, consider the following question:

How are the students taking charge of their own learning?

informal curriculum, which includes all the things you do in the classroom that are not part of the official, prescribed plan. For example, you might use an important local event or news story to create a learning experience closely linked to the students' own lives. In a high school earth science class, the teacher might address an earthquake that was in the news that week and explore the causes for earthquakes, even if this was not the formal topic of study at that moment. Local news events often become the centerpiece of social studies lessons because of their relevance. Although not written into the preplanned curriculum, these informal events bring meaning to the formal curriculum and deepen students' understanding of the concepts they are learning.

In speaking of the informal curriculum, educators often include the concept of the hidden curriculum, mentioned previously in this book. The hidden curriculum consists of the social rules and values schools and teachers transmit to students. Hidden curricula are communicated through the rules of conduct, dress codes, social atmosphere, and relationships among teachers, administration, and students in a given school environment. They are hidden in the sense that they are not written down, or at least not presented as part of the subject matter to be learned; but they are very much part of the school experience for both students and teachers. For example, when I was growing up in the middle of the last century, it was customary for the girls in the elementary school that I attended to erase and wash the blackboards, also called chalkboards, which are not common in modern classrooms. It was also usual for boys to march in the assemblies carrying the flags in what was called a color guard. I always wanted to carry the flag; however, I knew that I dare not ask. The hidden curriculum dictated what girls and boys would and would not have permission to do in this school.

4-4b The Role of National Standards and Common Core State Standards

In the United States, the formal curriculum in public schools is established by each state, with individual school districts adjusting it to a greater or lesser degree. Each state, however, relies heavily on the input of national groups that have been actively involved in establishing standards for their discipline. For example, the National Council of Teachers of Mathematics has a great influence on mathematics curricula throughout the country. Today, the Common Core State Standards that you read about in Chapter 3 have great influence over the states in mathematics and English language curricula.

The standards movement has dominated public education since the early 1990s. This movement has prompted subject-area associations to state explicitly what students should know and be able to do at each grade level from kindergarten through twelfth grade, resulting in national standards for each subject. Hence, there are national standards for science, language arts, foreign languages, social studies, mathematics, technology, health, and physical education. Now, the National Governor's Association and the Council of Chief State School Officers used these documents and others to establish Common Core State Standards whose use is encouraged by each state in the criteria for the Race to the Top (RTTP) competition.

Local schools' control of their curricula in each area was quite broad until the federal No Child Left Behind (NCLB) Act was passed in 2002 and the RTTP competition was implemented in 2010. NCLB requires

informal curriculum
Learning experiences that go beyond the formal curriculum, such as activities the teacher introduces to connect academic concepts to the students' daily lives.

© Brian Santa Maria/iStockphoto

Did You Know?

The standards movement has dominated public education since the early 1990s, with the No Child Left Behind Act being passed in 2002.

that students be held accountable by means of statewide exams that assess their knowledge at various grade levels, often beginning in third grade. That change reduced local schools' control over their curricula. The statewide assessment is often thought of as a one-size-fits-all process because it demands a uniform statewide curriculum if students are to be successful on the tests. As stated in Chapter 3, the Obama administration is trying to exempt states from the rigid accountability of NCLB as long as those states can devise an assessment system that meets the criteria for RTTP Funding.

Curriculum and Standardized Assessment

Sometimes, local schools' curricula suffer as a result of the inflexibility imposed by standardized assessment. Consider this story of a project in an elementary school where the teachers and administrators had the idea and the funding to build a pond on the school property.

Several years ago, an elementary school in a northeastern suburb began an initiative to build a pond on its school property. The pond would attract birds and insects, the teachers and administrators thought, and they could build an elementary science curriculum around it. They had the pond installed and "seeded" it with a few small koi (similar to goldfish) and water plants.

Grade-level classes took responsibility for monitoring the temperature and turbidity of the pond as well as carefully noticing the life in and around it. The science curriculum in that school grew, with exploration of the properties of the pond being the centerpiece.

4-4c CURRICULUM AS WINDOW AND MIRROR

Ideally, curriculum should be both a window and a mirror. This metaphor, suggested by Emily Style in a 1996 essay (http://www.wcwonline.org/seed/curriculum.html), implies that:

1. Curriculum must provide windows for students into the worlds of others. That is, it should help students learn about other people, other cultures, and other realities.
2. Curriculum must also offer mirrors of students' own reality. It should be connected to their lives in ways that help them see the subject matter as meaningful.

Q: *Do you think a curriculum can be both innovative and standards-based?*

I am reminded of how I felt growing up in an inner-city environment and reading *Dick and Jane* basal readers. You are probably familiar with basal readers, which are textbooks used to teach reading. The *McGuffey Readers* are an early example; the *Alice and Jerry Books* are another. Typically, basal readers are published as a series of books with each book in the series designed for a particular reading level. Dick and Jane were the main characters in basal readers used to teach reading from the 1930s to the 1970s.

Dick and Jane lived in their own house with a white picket fence and a lawn sprinkler. They had a cute dog and a little red wagon. There is nothing wrong with those things, of course, but I used to ask my mother, "Where do Dick and Jane live?" I did not recognize the surroundings, and I wondered where they could be found. Certainly the private house and lawn sprinkler were not found on my block!

For me, the reading curriculum that relied on *Dick and Jane* may have been a window, but it was not at all a mirror. Many students in other areas of the United States had similar experiences with basal readers. The use of basal readers waned during the 1980s and 1990s because their stories and images did not reflect the diversity of students in classrooms across the country. Basal readers were also thought to be less authentic than other forms of writing, such as regular children's literature. Many states and local districts opted for authentic early-childhood literature as a way to teach reading. Students get a glimpse into many different kinds of worlds, and more types of students see themselves in the reading material.

In many places today, schools use basal readers *and* authentic children's literature, offering students a language arts curriculum that includes both formats. Often, local district committees select the required literature for each grade level, and this, in conjunction with a basal reader, forms the backbone of the language arts curriculum. Many of the newer basal readers include some combination of nonfiction, biographies, adaptations of original children's books, condensations of classic children's literature, and original stories. They also feature students of many origins, not only Caucasians.

In this way, the typical language arts curriculum has evolved to function better as both a window and a mirror. Students get a glimpse into many different kinds of worlds, and more types of students see themselves in the reading material.

4-4d ADAPTING THE CURRICULUM TO YOUR STUDENTS

One implication of what we have been saying is that you should evaluate the curriculum in light of who your students are. When presented with a curriculum in a subject area, ask yourself, "How can I make this curriculum more relevant to the students in this classroom at this time in their lives?" If we think of learning as a process of reforming mental schemes, then teachers need to begin to understand their students' mental schemes to be successful.

This is a challenging task. One way to accomplish it is to pay careful attention to the experiences of your students. Through discussion and writing assignments, you can invite the students' authentic selves into the classroom and learn much more about them. Table 4.2 lists some questions that can help you explore the world of your students.

4-5 Assessment: How Do We Know What They Know?

Closely linked to curriculum and instruction is **assessment**, the process of collecting information to find out what students are learning. As teachers, we are always asking, "What do my students know? How are they able to demonstrate that knowledge?"

Evidence of student learning, like learning itself, is complex and takes many forms. You are probably accustomed to traditional assessments, such as paper-and-pencil tests with multiple-choice, true/false, fill-in-the-blank, and essay questions, used to evaluate students' understanding of the subject matter being taught. Typically, except for the essay questions, these tests are thought of as a measure of what students can recall at the moment, not necessarily what they have incorporated into an existing or new mental scheme.

TABLE 4. 2	Questions to Ask about Your Students
Who are my students?	
What are their interests, concerns, hobbies, beliefs, and feelings about themselves and others?	
Where do they live? Do they have siblings? Do they have both parents at home? Do both parents work outside the home? What do the students do after school?	
How can I adapt the formal curriculum to the experiences that the students encounter every day? How can I provide students with a mirror so they will understand that their lives are part of the school curriculum?	

Many students think of assessments as tests of this traditional type, given at the end of a unit. However, the more we understand about how people learn, the more we realize that an assessment is like a good instructional task and should be part of every lesson, providing feedback to both the teacher and the students about how the students are developing their understanding of the concepts in a unit. Assessments of this type are often called **embedded assessments**.

Many of the questions in the "Writing & Reflection" sections of this text are examples of embedded assessments. These questions are tools for reflection on the current instruction, as you are reading the text. Embedded assessments feel like a natural part of the instruction, so you may not be aware you are being assessed!

When we ask students to maintain a journal, write a research report, engage in a debate, design a project, or write an essay explaining a phenomenon, we are using embedded assessments. When these assessments relate directly to tasks or examples in the "real world" outside the classroom, they are also thought of as **authentic assessments**. Activities of this type ask students to

assessment Collecting information to determine the progress of students' learning.

embedded assessments Classroom-based assessments that make use of the actual assignments that students are given as a unit is being taught. These can be used to evaluate developmental stages of student learning.

authentic assessment An assessment that asks students to perform a task relating what they have learned to some real-world problem or example.

"Cows," said the frog. "Cows! They have four legs, horns, eat grass, and carry pink bags of milk."

rubric A scoring guide for an authentic assessment or a performance assessment, with descriptions of performance characteristics corresponding to points on a rating scale.

perform tasks through which they can express their own ideas. You can see how different these are from tests in which students check true or false, circle a correct choice, or guess at a word for a fill-in question, relying on their recall abilities instead of demonstrating understanding.

Authentic assessment often involves some kind of student performance; hence, this type of assessment is also called *performance assessment*. One type of performance assessment was pioneered by a group of scholars at Harvard University's Graduate School of Education. In an effort called Project Zero, the educators and psychologists were interested in teaching for understanding and in designing assessment tasks called *understanding performances* or *performances of understanding* (Perkins, 1993). Understanding performances are activities that require students to use what they know in new ways or in ways that build their understanding of unit topics. In these performances, students publicly demonstrate their understanding by reshaping, expanding on, extrapolating from, and applying what they already know.

Q: *How did your teachers grade you in school?*

Your teaching portfolio is another example of an authentic or performance assessment. The "Building Your Portfolio" card in the back of the book guides you in developing your portfolio, using the information you are exploring in your course and in this text to present concepts and challenges that represent your view of teaching and learning. The portfolio reflects the sense-making in which you are engaged as you prepare to teach, and it also contains examples of plans and projects that you create for your students as you practice teaching in the schools.

Because of the open-ended nature of authentic assessments and performance-based assessments, guidelines for evaluating the final performance are important. These guidelines take the form of a checklist or rubric. A **rubric** defines the expected qualities of student performance and establishes a rating scale. Generally, rubrics specify the level of performance expected for several levels of quality. These levels of quality may be written as ratings (e.g., Excellent, Good, Needs Improvement) or as numerical scores (e.g., 4, 3, 2, 1). Numerical scores can be added up to form a total score, which is then associated with a grade (A, B, C, and so forth).

Imagine you are assessing student understanding of two sides of a contentious issue such as the trial of Dr. Jack Kevorkian, who was found guilty of assisting people in committing suicide. (This lesson is described in Chapter 6.) You decide to engage the students in a high

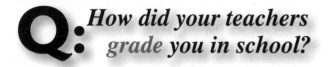

Your teaching portfolio is an example of an authentic or performance assessment.

Excerpt and illustration from FISH IS FISH. Copyright © 1970 by Leo Lionni. Used by permission of Dragonfly Books, an imprint of Alfred A. Knopf, Inc. New York, a division of Random House, Inc.

TWO EXAMPLES OF UNDERSTANDING PERFORMANCES

For a social studies unit with the understanding goal "Students will understand that history is always told from a particular perspective and that understanding a historical text means understanding who wrote it":

Students compare two accounts of the beginning of the Revolutionary War, one claiming the British fired the first shot and one claiming the colonists did. They then discuss why the two reports might be different and how they could find out what really happened. They use some of these strategies to figure out which (if either) of these accounts is the more plausible; then they present their explanation to the class.

For a mathematics unit with the understanding goals "Students will understand how percentages can be used to describe real-world happenings" and "Students will understand how to represent numerical information in clear graphs":

In small groups, students collect and compile data about school attendance over the course of two weeks. They calculate the percentage of students who fit various categories (percentage of students absent, percentage present, percentage tardy, and so on). They then create graphs to represent their data visually, collect feedback from the class, and revise their graphs in accordance with the feedback.

SOURCE: From Tina Blythe and Associates, *The Teaching for Understanding Guide*, Copyright ©1998 by Jossey-Bass, San Francisco.

school history class in a debate on the issue. Table 4.3 shows a rubric you might use. Notice that there are specific ways to describe student effectiveness and achievement. The highest score a student can achieve on this rubric is 24, indicating that she or he scored a 4 for each category described.

A student makes a presentation to her class, demonstrating her understanding of a particular topic. Then classmates ask questions.

© moodboard/Photolibrary

4-5a STANDARDIZED TESTING: A CHALLENGE FOR AUTHENTIC ASSESSMENT

As we noted previously, NCLB mandates large-scale, standardized assessments in each state and requires that they address mathematics and language arts at varying grade levels. These are traditional-style assessments that may not have any particular relevance to the nature of the instruction in a given class in a specific school. Because of this, critics argue that the data gathered from these large-scale assessments are not that reliable. In any case, these tests tell you only a little of what you need to know about your students' learning. Good teaching requires that we seek multiple ways to find out what students know and are able to do in a given area of content.

Because standardized tests are given to broad populations

TABLE 4.3   A Sample Rubric for a High School Class Debate

Category	Score			
	4	3	2	1
Understanding of topic	The team clearly understood the topic in depth and presented its information forcefully and convincingly.	The team clearly understood the topic in depth and presented its information with ease.	The team seemed to understand the main points of the topic and presented those with ease.	The team did not show an adequate understanding of the topic.
Presentation style	The team consistently used gestures, eye contact, tone of voice, and a level of enthusiasm in a way that kept the attention of the audience.	The team usually used gestures, eye contact, tone of voice, and a level of enthusiasm in a way that kept the attention of the audience.	The team sometimes used gestures, eye contact, tone of voice, and a level of enthusiasm in a way that kept the attention of the audience.	One or more members of the team had a presentation style that did not keep the attention of the audience.
Information	All information presented in the debate was clear, accurate, and thorough.	Most information presented in the debate was clear, accurate, and thorough.	Most information presented in the debate was clear and accurate, but usually was not thorough.	The information had several inaccuracies or was usually not clear.
Organization	All arguments were clearly tied to an idea (premise) and organized in a tight, logical fashion.	Most arguments were clearly tied to an idea (premise) and organized in a tight, logical fashion.	All arguments were clearly tied to an idea (premise), but the organization was sometimes not clear or logical.	The arguments were not clearly tied to an idea (premise).
Rebuttal	All counterarguments were accurate, relevant, and strong.	Most counterarguments were accurate, relevant, and strong.	Most counterarguments were accurate and relevant, but several were weak.	The counterarguments were not accurate and/or relevant.
Use of facts/ statistics	Every major point was well supported with several relevant facts, statistics, and/or examples.	Every major point was adequately supported with relevant facts, statistics, and/or examples.	Every major point was supported with facts, statistics, and/or examples, but the relevance of some was questionable.	Not every point was supported.

SOURCE: Developed with RubiStar, a free online rubric tool at http://rubistar.4teachers.org/. Reprinted by permission of Advanced Learning Technologies in Education Consortia.

of students, it is often difficult for test makers to consider the variations in students' geography and learning experiences. As a result, standardized tests, often criticized by educators because one size does not fit all, usually represent a small sample of what is important in a subject area. When you think about Bloom's Taxonomy, you can imagine how frequently the questions on these tests ask the students to "recall, remember, or repeat" what they know. Critics believe it is difficult for standardized tests to assess higher levels of cognitive function. As well, they often represent a single-assessment experience, which can result in getting an incomplete measure of students' understanding.

Many educators fear that teachers "teach to the test." This is because in many schools and districts, raising test scores has become the most important indicator of school improvement. As a result, teachers and administrators feel enormous pressure to ensure that test scores go up. Some schools narrow and change the curriculum to match the test. Teachers teach only what is covered on the test. Methods of teaching conform to the multiple-choice format of the many standardized tests. Teaching more and more resembles testing (http://fairtest.org/). If however, the standardized test had many modalities and offered different types of assessment formats, matching instruction to the assessment would not be as problematic. Previously in this chapter, you read the description of the beginnings of a pond curriculum for an elementary school in the northeast. If the standardized test did not address the science ideas behind freshwater ponds, it is doubtful that the students in that school would have that experience. This has serious implications for standardized curricula in all the subject areas.

4-6 Becoming a Teacher

There is often a disconnect between what we learn about teaching and what we are able to enact in an actual classroom. One reason is that teaching, like many other endeavors, requires practice. Another reason is that we need to examine our beliefs and become comfortable with ourselves as learners as we embark on becoming teachers.

There are no quick and easy ways to make the transition into teaching. But here are some ideas to keep in mind as you consider joining the profession:

- Be comfortable with yourself as a person and feel secure in who you are.
- Wherever possible, give students opportunities to express their own ideas and to be active thinkers.
- Interrogate your students about their thinking. That is, ask them where their ideas come from.
- Make connections between what you are teaching and the students' lived experiences.
- Gain an understanding *for yourself* of the material you will teach. Using that knowledge, construct activities and opportunities that lead students to engage with the materials *for themselves*.
- Preparation is a prerequisite for successful teaching!

4-7 Concluding Thoughts

Is your head spinning from all the theories, philosophies, and movements in US public education you have read about? If so, it is important to remember that your approach to teaching should never be "all or nothing." The boundaries between movements and learning theories can overlap and become blurred.

Understanding more about how people learn helps us know that exploring students' preconceived ideas is essential to planning for instruction. Your plan may borrow principles from learning theories other than constructivism. Naming your personal approach is less important than understanding that it is subject to revision as you grow and learn and enter classrooms in a more formal role. Your present style of teaching and learning is the result of all that came before you historically and all that you personally have experienced in school. Developing consciousness about the role of the teacher and the responsibilities you will have toward your students is important preparation for your future work. Education is broader than schooling experiences. Like you, students learn from formal and informal environments. Their interests are relevant to their abilities to learn. Remember learning is a complex process and there is a lot about what goes on in our brains as we learn that we still do not know.

By discussing how people learn, curriculum, instruction, and assessment, this chapter has provided perspective on part of a big question that all teachers face: Who are my students, and how can I best teach them? In the next chapter, we will explore in detail the nature and diversity of today's students. We will examine demographic trends in the country and consider the ways your pedagogy may be informed by who your students are.

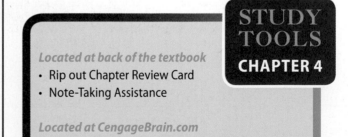

PART 3
LOOKING AT TODAY'S SCHOOLS

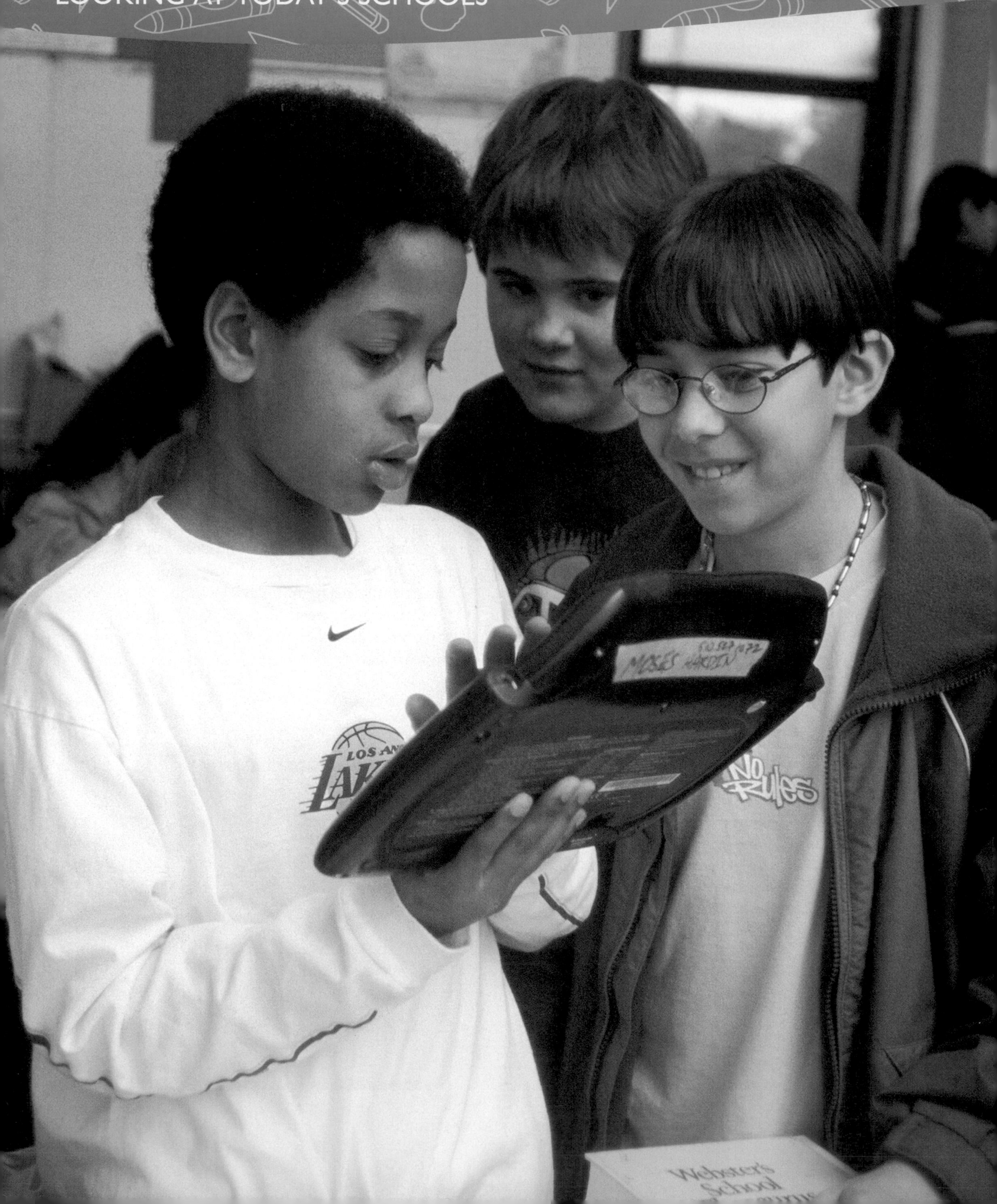

We are in the second decade of a new millennium, and the journey to become a teacher is embedded in social and economic policies and educational reforms. We know that teachers make all the difference for all kinds of students from all walks of life. This has prompted a teacher and student evaluation movement across the country that holds teachers accountable for students' academic progress by evaluating them based on their students' standardized test scores. Further, as schools reflect contemporary societal conditions, the proliferation of charter schools continues as a grand experiment in public schooling because of the thinking that we have not adequately educated the poorest students in our population.

The digital revolution enables us to communicate and access information in milliseconds through small handheld devices like smartphones, tablets such as iPads, and laptop computers. Although many students have access to these devices, there is often a digital divide between the economic haves and have-nots. Routine standardized testing has become embedded in the US's school culture, as has competition among states for available federal funding.

The following chapters look at phenomena such as the enormous influx of immigrant families from various parts of the world and the increased role of federal and state governments in setting standards to measure the performance of students and teachers. As you read, think about questions like these:

- What is the composition of the student body? In what ways does its great diversity pose both challenges and opportunities?
- What contemporary trends are visible in today's classrooms, and how has access to the Internet and social networking both enhanced and posed difficulties for education?
- In what ways has standards-based assessment affected the lives of teachers and students?

As you continue your journey toward becoming a teacher, I hope you will remember that goodness of fit remains an underlying principle of this text. Keep asking yourself: Am I selecting a career path for which I am uniquely well suited?

Part Outline

CHAPTER 5

WHO ARE TODAY'S STUDENTS?

© moodboard/Corbis

> *A person's a person no matter how small* . . .
> —Theodor Geisel (aka Dr. Seuss),
> *Horton Hears a Who!* (1954)

This chapter looks at the students in contemporary US schools—children between the ages of five and eighteen. As the quotation from Dr. Seuss indicates, our schoolchildren are important people; their education is vital not only to their own future but also to the future of our country.

You may be familiar with the Dr. Seuss books—the often silly, rhyming, outrageous stories that delight many children from preschool through graduation from high school. Often they have deep meaning. In a commentary on Dr. Seuss and his influence, A. O. Scott of the *New York Times* had the following to say:

> *Rather than describe the mental world of children, Seuss labored over his verses and sketches in the hopes of replicating it. His guiding insight was that some version of his words and stories was there to begin with, and that children, in discovering his work, would recognize in it what they already knew (Scott, 2000).*

The significance of these comments is that the students we meet and greet in the classroom come to us with their own stories, backgrounds, and experiences. It is your task to learn about your students; what their lives are like; and what hobbies, interests, talents, and challenges they bring to the classroom. Respecting and understanding them as people with their own ideas and experiences is the first step toward becoming an effective educator. In this chapter, we address the nature of the learner, today, in the second decade of the twenty-first century.

LEARNING OUTCOMES

After reading this chapter, you should be thinking about the following ideas:

5-1 Examine the ways in which students may differ from one another.

5-2 Examine factors that might hinder a child's success in school.

5-3 Explain why teachers must have an understanding of their students' lives through the lens of their ethnic, cultural, and daily life experiences.

5-4 Analyze how your students' intelligence profiles could explain their performance in your class.

5-5 Examine your own learning style or styles and relate that to the learning styles you may find among your students.

5-6 Assess the importance of knowing who your students are, what their lives are like, and how they learn best.

5-7 Examine the statement that "student diversity is a gift and not a barrier to overcome."

5-1 The Students: A Changing Landscape

Since the mid-1990s, student enrollment in US schools has mushroomed. In fact, when the estimated population of the country surpassed 300 million people in 2006, roughly one-quarter were children under the age of eighteen (Annie E. Casey Foundation, 2006a).

Total public school enrollment reached a peak in 1971, when the youngest members of the baby boom generation[1] arrived in school (Fry, 2006). Enrollment then dropped off considerably in the 1970s, but it began to climb again in the late 1980s and early 1990s. By the second half of the 1990s, enrollment passed the 1971 mark, and the number of students in school has continued to rise. Between 1985 and 2008, enrollment in public elementary and secondary schools increased by more than one-fifth, and by 2015 public school

---

[1] *Baby boom generation* refers to those Americans born in the quarter-century following World War II, roughly from 1946 to 1964. Some experts use slightly different dates.

TABLE 5.1 US Public and Private School Enrollment

ENROLLMENT IN ELEMENTARY AND SECONDARY SCHOOLS, BY CONTROL AND LEVEL OF INSTITUTION: SELECTED YEARS, FALL 1970 THROUGH FALL 2015 (THOUSANDS)

Year	Total	Public			Private		
		Total	Grades PreK–8	Grades 9–12	Total	Grades PreK–8	Grades 9–12
1970	51,257	45,894	32,558	13,336	5,363	4,052	1,311
1980	46,208	40,877	27,647	13,231	5,331	3,992	1,339
1985	44,979	39,422	27,034	12,388	5,557	4,195	1,362
1990	46,864	41,217	29,876	11,341	5,648	4,512	1,136
1995	50,759	44,840	32,338	12,502	5,918	4,756	1,163
2000	53,373	47,204	33,686	13,517	6,169	4,906	1,264
2005	55,187	49,113	34,204	14,909	6,073	4,724	1,349
2006	55,307	49,316	34,235	15,081	5,991	4,631	1,360
2007	55,203	49,293	34,205	15,087	5,910	4,546	1,364
2008	55,235	49,266	34,286	14,980	5,969	4,574	1,395
2009	55,282	49,312	34,505	14,807	5,970	4,580	1,389
2010	55,350	49,386	34,730	14,657	5,964	4,582	1,382
2015	56,859	50,827	35,881	14,946	6,031	4,757	1,275

NOTE: Elementary and secondary enrollment includes students in local public school systems and in most private schools (religiously affiliated and nonsectarian) but generally excludes homeschooled children and students in subcollegiate departments of colleges and in federal schools. Based on the National Household Education Survey, the homeschooled children numbered approximately 1.5 million in 2007 (and the trend is upward). Excludes preprimary pupils in private schools that do not offer kindergarten or higher. Detail may not sum to totals because of rounding.

SOURCE: US Department of Education, National Center for Education Statistics (2011). *Digest of Education Statistics, 2010* (National Center for Education Statistics 2011–015), Table 3.

enrollments are estimated to be more than 56 million students in grades preK–12 and more than 6 million students in preK–12 private schools, as shown in Table 5.1 (National Center for Education Statistics, 2011).

Clearly, the number of students in our schools has been rising rapidly. But who exactly are our students?

5-1a ETHNIC DIVERSITY

Our era of expanding school enrollment has been marked by a significant rise in minority students, driven mainly by an extraordinary influx of Hispanic[2] students, who account for more than 50 percent of the increase in student enrollment.

By 2012, 45 percent of public school students are considered to be part of a racial or ethnic minority group. The distribution of minority students in public schools differs across regions of the country, but minority enrollment grew in all regions between 1989 and 2009. In comparison, the number of Caucasians students decreased from 68 to55 percent of public school enrollment during this same period (US Department of Education, 2011).

Immigration accounts for a large part of the diversity among today's students. More than one-fifth of youngsters under the age of eighteen are part of immigrant families. States with the highest percentage of immigrant families are New York, New Jersey, California, Texas, and Nevada—states that attract the largest number of Hispanic immigrants (Annie E. Casey Foundation, 2011).

Although ethnic diversity is increasing overall, recent decades have seen a new rise in de facto segregation—that is, whites living in different neighborhoods than minorities. Neighborhoods that are primarily white naturally have a high concentration of white students in their schools, whereas neighborhoods that are predominantly minority have a high concentration of minority students in the schools. In some areas, this

[2]*Hispanic* refers to people whose origin is Spain or any of the Spanish-speaking countries of the Americas.

segregation has reduced the amount of diversity teachers encounter. Although most white students continue to attend schools populated primarily by other whites, and relatively few attend schools populated primarily by minorities, this leaves many schools predominantly minority populated.

As enrollment has expanded, so has the number of schools. About half of the students attending the newer schools are white, while the white enrollment in older schools has dropped. Most of the newer schools are being built in areas that are predominantly white, while the older school buildings are absorbing most of the Hispanic and other minority students, where neighborhoods are poorer and there is far less available taxpayer money for new schools.

5-1b LANGUAGE-MINORITY STUDENTS

Can you imagine going to school in a place where your own native language is not spoken? If your native language is English, that may seem inconceivable. However, for those of you who are reading these pages and who learned English as your second language, the challenge most likely was great and required understanding teachers and schools. By 2010, 22 percent of school age children spoke a language other than English at home (Annie E. Casey Foundation, 2011).

Among children who speak a language other than English at home, Spanish is the language most frequently spoken. About three-quarters of students who receive special assistance to learn English speak Spanish. Yet hundreds of thousands of students come from homes where other languages are spoken. These include Chinese, Vietnamese, Russian, Arabic, and French Creole. Various reports emphasize that, for most of these English-language learners (ELLs), success requires targeted and continuing intervention. As one report says,

Children who start school knowing little or no English can learn the basic skills of word recognition quickly—in about two years, if they are carefully taught. They need the same kind of reading instruction that works for native speakers, only more of it, and they need to be monitored carefully so they get help adapted to their language development needs as soon as they run into problems (American Educational Research Association, 2004).

Bilingual Education

There has been much debate over how best to boost the academic achievement of ELLs. **Bilingual education** programs support students with limited English proficiency by teaching them at least part of the time in their native language. Since the early 1970s, these programs have taken many forms. Some teach academic subjects in the students' native language and also provide English as a Second Language (ESL) classes to help the students learn English. Other models, known as two-way or dual-language programs, teach fluency in both languages, so that a class of both language-minority and native English-speaking students becomes fluent in both languages. These approaches have several variations and tend to vary from school district to school district. Other programs immerse language-minority students in English-only classes without any native-language communication.

> **bilingual education**
> Educating English-language learners by teaching them at least part of the time in their native language.

Did You Know?
By 2012, 45 percent of public school children were considered to be part of a racial or an ethnic minority group.

Non-native English-speaking students learn in both languages in bilingual classes.

© Elizabeth Crews

On a recent visit to an elementary school in Queens, New York, I encountered a large sign for parents that read, "We now have a dual-language program in Mandarin." I learned that 87 percent of the students in this K–5 school were from China and that those students who were native English speakers really wanted to learn Mandarin. Hence, the school began a dual-language immersion program with half of the instruction in Mandarin and the other half in English.

There are many other examples of schools that take pride in their bilingual programs. Yet, partly because of the large wave of Hispanic immigration during the past twenty-five years, the issue of bilingual education has become highly politicized. There are those who believe that only English should be spoken and taught in school. This has prompted some schools to adopt "English-only" programs in which language-minority students have no access to their native language in school. Criticizing this trend, many educators and linguists argue that valuing and

TEACHSOURCE VIDEO CASE

Bilingual Education in Fourth Grade

To see how a two-way language immersion program can function, find the TeachSource Video Case "Bilingual Education: An Elementary Two-Way Immersion Program" on the Education CourseMate at CengageBrain.com. As you begin watching the video, ask yourself if all the students are English-language learners. After watching the video, consider the following questions:

Would you have liked to be a student in this program? Why or why not?

honoring new immigrants' native languages enhances their self-esteem and their possibility for academic success.

Federal funding for bilingual education ended when the No Child Left Behind (NCLB) Act was adopted by Congress in 2002. Instead of continuing to fund bilingual initiatives at the federal level, the law turned most of the responsibility over to the states in the form of block grants to assist the academic achievement of language-minority students. The way these state funds are allocated is highly variable.

Teaching ELLs

You may find yourself in a classroom with ELLs, and it is important to use the most effective strategies to help your students grasp subject matter content while learning English. One current approach is called Specially Designed Academic Instruction in English (SDAIE). Many established teachers have taken workshops devoted to this approach—another example of how being a teacher is a commitment to lifelong learning. SDAIE is a method of teaching students in English in such a manner that they gain skills in both the subject material and in using English.

As we explored in Chapter 4, learning something new requires that the learner redesign his or her mental schemes. To do this, the student has to bring his or her existing knowledge into play. SDAIE pedagogy encourages this process by treating the ELL as a "knower," a student with lots of ideas that are temporarily inaccessible to the teacher because of the language barrier. Accessing the student's ideas involves teaching strategies like:

- Speaking clearly and at a slower pace,
- Using gestures and facial expressions,
- Using concrete materials and visuals,

Honoring diversity requires a respect for the learner and a genuine desire to bridge religious and cultural gaps.

© Bob Daemmrich/ImageWorks

- Avoiding idiomatic expressions that are peculiar to English,
- Engaging students in group work that is student centered (Kashen, 1994), and
- Finding "language buddies" wherever possible—that is, pairing ELLs with students who are more advanced in English but also fluent in the learner's native language.

If you teach a class with both ELLs and students who are already fluent in English, your task will be to plan for both populations in ways that enrich the environment. Imagine that two students are using a ruler for a lesson. The native English speaker says to the student who is new to this country, "How do you say 'ruler' in your language?" By sharing in this way, they both become learners. The challenge is to engage all students in helping their classmates overcome barriers to learning.

5-1c RELIGIOUS DIVERSITY

As we saw in Chapter 3, religion has always played a large role in American life and education. The Constitution of the United States guarantees religious freedom to all citizens, and we treasure that right. Yet Americans are divided about how the principle of "separation of church and state" (a phrase coined by Thomas Jefferson) should apply to public schools.

These matters have taken on more urgency in the past few decades as new strains of religious diversity have arisen in the United States. Christians account for 78.4 percent of the US population, with Protestants accounting for 51.3 percent of that total (http://religions.pewforum.org/reports). The total number of Americans who identified their religion as something other than Christian increased dramatically over the last two decades. Religions that barely registered in previous surveys, such as the Wiccan creed, now have a substantial number of adherents. Even the traditional affiliations of Protestant and Catholic contain many subgroups and differences.

With such diversity in the nation's religions, teachers have much to learn about the religious beliefs of their students. Religious beliefs bring with them various expectations for an individual's behavior, including observance of customs and traditions. Remember that culture and religion are linked. Understanding who your students are and the role that religion plays in their lives is significant in helping them to learn and in honoring their identities.

5-1d SEXUAL ORIENTATION

Like religion, language, and ethnicity, **sexual orientation** is an important component of a person's identity. Schools are often the places where teens develop social skills and begin to align with peer groups. For adolescents who do not identify as heterosexual in today's culture, this process of social acceptance and approval is fraught with danger and fear of rejection and even physical harm.

Categories applied to sexual orientation typically include heterosexual, homosexual (gay and lesbian), bisexual (sexual attraction toward both sexes), and transgender (having characteristics of the opposite sex). The acronym **LGBT** is sometimes used to refer to lesbian, gay, bisexual, and transgender people as a group. Because sexual orientations are often hidden from view, LGBT individuals are often thought of as the invisible minority. In schools, fear often prevents these students from revealing their sexual identities; it is therefore important that schools and classrooms provide safe havens for those of our students whose sexual orientation is not aligned with the majority.

Attitudes about sexual orientation are a product of individual family biases and beliefs. Students bring these to school, and LGBT youth often have to cope with prejudice and isolation. Lack of family support for these youngsters exacerbates the problem, and there is an enormous fear of stigmatization. These students are at greater risk than others for being harassed and bullied, experiencing depression, and attempting suicide. How widespread are these problems? The 2009 National School Climate Survey of 7,261 middle and high school students found that nearly nine out of ten LGBT students experienced harassment at school in the past year and nearly two-thirds felt

> **sexual orientation**
> An enduring emotional, romantic, sexual, or affectional attraction that a person feels toward people of one or both sexes.
>
> **LGBT** An acronym used to represent lesbian, gay, bisexual, and transgender individuals.

Q: *How does understanding the ways in which your own religious beliefs have influenced you help you to better serve your students?*

socioeconomic status (SES) A person's or family's status in society, usually based on a combination of income, occupation, and education. Though similar to social class, SES puts more emphasis on the way income affects status.

unsafe because of their sexual orientation (Gay, Lesbian and Straight Education Network, 2010). Nearly a third of LGBT students skipped at least one day of school in the past month because of safety concerns. An analysis of National School Climate Survey data over ten years showed that since 1999 there has been a decreasing trend in the frequency of hearing homophobic remarks; however, LGBT students' experiences with more severe forms of bullying and harassment have remained relatively constant. Teachers can create safe havens in their classrooms by interrupting statements of bias when they hear or see their occurrence. Safe havens also exist within schools that have clubs and assemblies for LGBT students and create a culture of caring.

Because all students deserve to work in an environment that is both friendly and supportive, student groups have emerged in high schools all over the country to combat LGBT bias and discrimination. These groups or clubs are often called Gay-Straight Alliances (GSAs); they are student-run organizations that provide a safe place for students to meet, support each other, talk about issues related to their sexual orientation, and work toward ending homophobia.

5-1e SOCIOECONOMIC DISPARITIES

Another way students differ from each other is in their **socioeconomic status (SES)**, a measure of their standard of living that relates to the family's income. According to recent census figures, more than one-fifth of young people under the age of eighteen live in poverty. In 2010 in the United States, 33 percent of children were living in homes where no parent has had full-time, year round employment (Annie E. Casey Foundation, 2011). The official poverty rate in 2010 was 15.1 percent—up from 14.3 percent in 2009. Since 2007, the poverty rate has increased by 2.6 percentage points, from 12.5 percent to 15.1 percent (http://www.census.gov).

Table 5.2 shows the official definition of poverty as related to family size. You may be surprised to see how much a family must earn to avoid being poor in the United States. Here is another important, related statistic: More than one-third of all children live in single-parent families (Annie E. Casey Foundation, 2011). In most cases, obviously, one parent has less earning power than two parents do.

SES relates to the concept of social capital that we mentioned previously. The point is that the students you encounter will come from various socioeconomic backgrounds. The more social capital a child's family has, the greater his or her intellectual and cultural advantages. A child with higher SES. and more social capital usually performs better than a student with little or no social capital does.

5-1f OVERLAPPING ATTRIBUTES: THE SOCIAL CONTEXT

The aspects of student diversity we have been considering are not isolated and independent. Often they overlap. Consider, for instance, what happens when poverty intersects with the need to learn a new language. The reality of many English-language learners is that they also represent our poorest children: They live in crowded housing environments where transportation and employment opportunities are limited and where schools are old and overcrowded. In fact, of all students who live in poverty, more than 32 percent are Hispanic

TABLE 5.2 — The Poverty Line: Annual Income Levels below which a Family is Considered Poor

Persons in Family	48 Contiguous states and District of Columbia ($)	Alaska ($)	Hawaii ($)
1	10,890	13,600	12,540
2	14,710	18,380	16,930
3	18,530	23,160	21,320
4	22,350	27,940	25,710
5	26,170	32,720	30,100
6	29,990	37,500	34,490
7	33,810	42,280	38,880
8	37,630	47,060	43,270
For each additional person, add	3,820	4,780	4,390

SOURCE: *Federal Register*, Vol. 76, No. 13, January 20, 2011, pp. 3637–3638.

or Latino (AECF, 2011). Conditions of this sort cannot help but affect the students' achievement in school, putting many of these students at risk for educational failure. In the next section we will consider the term *at risk* and its full implications.

Many analysts express concern that educational policy too often ignores such individual social contexts. One criticism of the former federal NCLB is that the law's mandated standards and assessments pay little attention to ethnic- and language-minority students.

Differences do not mean deficits; they just mean differences from the norms in public education that were once thought to be white and middle class. The norms are shifting, and it is important that we never think of students who are different in any way as lesser. As future teachers, the guiding question must be: How can I help each child feel successful in school?

5-2 Students Who Are at Risk

66*National research has shown that children living in poor, tough neighborhoods are much more likely to drop out of school, become pregnant as teens, get in trouble with the law as juveniles, and live in poverty as adults, with their own children struggling to succeed. They are much more likely to go to prison and suffer from debilitating health conditions that further limit their ability to provide support for their children.*99

— Annie E. Casey Foundation (2001)

When we examine all the ways our students can differ from each other, we need to ask ourselves what combination of factors might hinder a child's becoming a successful student, graduating from high school, and pursuing further education or vocational training. The term **students at risk** came into widespread use after the 1983 national report *A Nation at Risk*, described in Chapter 3. This report warned that US schools were becoming mediocre and that significant changes had to occur to keep the nation as a whole from declining.

Critics of this report noted that there was little mention of the role of poverty in the life of children. Many reacted to the report by citing glaring social inadequacies and saying that schools could not make up for these deficiencies. There was a "blame the victim" mentality, critics complained, in which students and parents were held to be the culprits. Indeed, schools cannot make up for many of the problems of poverty and degradation, but in turn educators must not blame their own inadequacies on the

students. Both points are at work when we examine who is at risk.

The precise definition of the term *student at risk* varies; however, the common attribute is that these students are judged to be seriously in danger of not succeeding in school and hence not completing school.

Failure to complete high school is a key attribute of at-risk students. The **dropout rate** in the United States represents the percentage of sixteen-through twenty-four-year olds who are not enrolled in school and have not earned a high school credential (either a diploma or an equivalency credential such as a General Educational Development [GED] certificate). It has declined from 14 percent in 1980 to 9 percent in 2009 (NCES, 2011). Despite the declining drop-out rate, there remains one in eleven students who fail to earn a high school credential. What puts a student at risk of dropping out or of not getting an adequate education? Social problems in our society make it difficult for even high-ability students to be successful. The greatest social risk factors include substance abuse, child abuse, poverty, homelessness, hunger, depression, and teen pregnancy. For teachers from stable homes and environments, it is often difficult to relate to these problems that affect the lives of some students every day. Therefore, it is essential to learn as much as possible about your students' lives.

To make the concept of risk more specific, a family risk index (Annie E. Casey Foundation, 2009b) identifies a "high-risk child" as one who lives in a family with four or more of these risk factors:

1. Child is not living with two parents.
2. Household head is a high school dropout.
3. Family income is below the poverty line.
4. Child is living with parent(s) who is (are) underemployed.
5. Family is receiving welfare benefits.
6. Child does not have health insurance.

Further statistics about risk factors come from the National Youth Risk Behavior Survey (YRBS), which monitors behaviors that contribute to death, disability, and social problems among youth and adults in the United States. Conducted every two years during the spring semester, the YRBS provides data representative of ninth- through twelfth-grade students in public and private schools throughout the United States. Factors that have been worrying educators and parents for several decades include drugs, sex, and violence. Recent surveys indicate that the percentage of students in grades 9 through 12 who have seriously considered suicide in the course of one year has gone down from more than 17 percent in 2005 to less than 15 percent in 2009. Rates for having sexual intercourse have remained steady at about 47 percent of ninth to twelfth graders. For the same group of students, alcohol use remains at 44 percent; marijuana use at 38 percent, and cocaine use at 8 percent of the student population. The percentage of students in this group who have been engaged in a physical fight on school grounds has remained the same at 12 percent (Centers for Disease Control and Prevention, 2010).

The US teen pregnancy rate has gone down in recent years, but it remains the highest of any industrialized nation in the world. For young women, teen pregnancy is the major contributor to high school dropout rates. Substance abuse is a serious problem that crosses all socioeconomic classes. The importance of sex education and drug abuse counseling programs in the schools cannot be overstated. Internet chat rooms, social networking sites, and informative websites have given teens better access to information on safe sex and the dangers of substance abuse. This has contributed to lowering the rate of teen pregnancy. Teachers and students can explore useful websites together.

Community and school collaborations including programs to prevent substance abuse targeted to parents of teens, family awareness projects, and parent-teacher associations can prevent students who are at risk from dropping out of school before completing high school:

Chana High School is a small "continuation" school in Auburn, California. A continuation school is designed to meet the needs of young adult students who were not successful in completing traditional high school; it has an enrollment of 250. In 2009, all of the students passed the California state exit exam, enabling them to earn a high school diploma. On its website (http://www.puhsd.k12. ca.us/chana/), Chana Continuation High School states that it is committed to developing individuals who value themselves, others, and the environment, and who possess the skills necessary to succeed in a changing world (2010). The school has a wealth of services to support these youngsters, including teen parenting classes, substance abuse counseling, anger management intervention, and mental health counseling. The dedicated teachers at Chana work diligently to bolster students' academic achievement while also supporting them emotionally. The school offers five vocational programs funded by the state (including computer technology and electronics), and partnerships with technical colleges and local community colleges allow the students to earn college credit while completing their high school work.

Q: *Do you identify with any of the risk factors that could lead to dropping out?*

5-3 Student Diversity: Challenges and Opportunities

As you might guess, the increasing diversity of US students has led to controversy about educational priorities. In this section, we focus on three areas that have provoked much recent discussion: multicultural education, gender-fair education, and the role of religion in the schools.

5-3a MULTICULTURAL EDUCATION

You may be feeling dizzy from all the data and statistics you have read in this chapter. Why are these details about students important? As we seek to become better teachers, we must understand the origins of our students and the ways their needs can be met in the classroom. If you are not of the same culture, race, ethnicity, or social class as your students, you should make a special effort to understand their needs. You can also turn the diversity of your students into an advantage—an opportunity to share identities and cultures as you create community in your classroom. It is a way to broaden our understanding of the human condition and reminds us that the informal curriculum can be both window and mirror!

If you pursue a career in teaching, you will hear a lot about **multicultural education**, a broad term for many approaches that recognize and celebrate the variety of cultures and ethnic backgrounds found in US schools. Students from groups that have traditionally been underrepresented in the school population—ethnic and racial minorities—have also been understudied. That is, until recently, most educators have not focused on what these students need to succeed in school. We now realize that these students will not be served well and will even become marginalized unless we seek answers to complex questions like the following:

- Whose stories are told in the classroom?
- How do we build community in a diverse setting?
- What is the role of identity formation in our work?

A diverse student body provides the opportunity to learn about other ways of being in the world.

- What can we learn by hearing the stories of those from traditionally marginalized groups? (Nelson & Wilson, 1998, p. xi)

For over 25 years, the Seeking Educational Equity and Diversity (SEED) project, begun by Dr. Peggy McIntosh at the Wellesley Centers for Research in Women, has offered teachers from all over the country the opportunity to participate in professional development workshops designed to broaden the possibilities for both curriculum and instruction, of teaching in environments rich with students from diverse backgrounds, cultures, and ethnicities. They are able to share strategies for appreciating that diverse learning environments offer a wonderful gift. Emily Style, a director of SEED offers the metaphor mentioned previously in the book . . . diverse learning environments provide "windows" into the worlds of people other than ourselves and create rich experiences for both students and teachers. As a result of these experiences, teachers are encouraged to develop culturally responsive teaching practices, also referred to as **culturally relevant pedagogy**. These teaching practices have several important attributes:

- They use cultural referents—from all the cultures represented in the classroom—to develop students' knowledge, skills, and attitudes.
- They honor the students' life stories and belief systems and find ways to incorporate them into the curriculum and learning context.
- They create classroom community by granting voice and legitimacy to the experiences of students from diverse backgrounds.
- They encourage all students to achieve academically by acknowledging the students' personal and cultural identities.

All of these strategies help us to honor the learner and create a classroom community in which each others' stories create the foundation for a caring community.

multicultural education Education that aims to create equal opportunities for students from diverse racial, ethnic, social class, and cultural groups.

culturally relevant pedagogy Teaching practices that place the culture of the learner at the center of instruction. Cultural referents become aspects of the formal curriculum.

© Elizabeth Crews

Culturally relevant pedagogy is one of many instructional strategies that seeks to answer the question, "How can the lived experiences of my students be reflected in the discourse of the classroom?" Consider planning a geometry unit in an eighth-grade math classroom in an urban area in the northeast. Ms. Petersen is in an old, overcrowded school building in an urban area. Ms. Peterson is exploring different types of symmetry that may be found in shapes using several patterns. About one-third of her students are Latino, and the rest are of many racial and ethnic origins.

This unit in geometry considers what happens to shapes when they are moved through space. Ms. Petersen has examined the basic concepts in many ways with her class, emphasizing that symmetry may be found in patterns in everyday life and having the students create symmetrical patterns with more than one shape. For instance, she brought in men's ties with many patterns on them and asked students to decide what type of symmetry each pattern represented. She then invited them to explore their native countries' flags. The classroom has three networked computers that students used to print pictures of their flags. The flag designs were examined for geometric shapes and symmetry (see Figure 5.1). It was a lesson that engaged all the students.

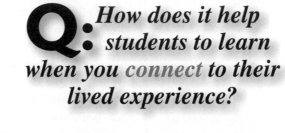

Q: *How does it help students to learn when you connect to their lived experience?*

After the students had experience with several types of symmetry, Ms. Petersen posed a challenge. In groups of two, the students were to design and create a classroom flag incorporating their room number. The flag had to be in the shape of a rectangle, include two types of symmetry, and appropriately represent the students in the classroom. Students were excited about designing patterns, and they selected the colors from the flags of their various countries of origin to represent themselves. Colors from the flags of Colombia, El Salvador, Mexico, Puerto Rico, Guatemala, South Korea, and the United States adorned the design of Room 303's classroom flags.

What do you think of Ms. Petersen's lesson? Can you imagine how excited the students were that their countries' flags were part of their study of mathematics? The concepts of rotation, reflection, and translation are quite complex in geometry, but by using materials her students could relate to, Ms. Petersen engaged them in a personal way.

We know from research in cognitive science that learning occurs best when students are fully invested in the process—when they can interact with the materials, "play" with them, explore and reexamine the concepts, and then individually make those concepts their own. You can see how culturally relevant pedagogy helps make this possible.

FIGURE 5.1

What Types of Symmetry Are Revealed in These Flags?

Your teaching should incorporate culturally relevant pedagogy

Flag of Mexico

Flag of Puerto Rico

Flag of South Korea

Flag of El Salvador

Flag of Guatemala

Flag of Colombia

5-3b Educating Girls and Boys: Separate or Together?

You may recall from Chapter 3 that Title IX, part of the education amendments of 1972, prohibits discrimination on the basis of sex in any federally funded education program or activity. That law might seem to discourage single-sex schooling—the practice of educating girls in separate schools from boys—on the grounds that separate is inherently unequal. In 2006, however, the US Education Department officially ruled that Title IX does not make single-sex schooling discriminatory as long as it is voluntary and takes place in an environment that also includes comparable coeducational schools and classes. As a result, single-sex schooling has become more prevalent in public schools and public-supported charter schools.

One model for quality single-sex schooling exists in a high-minority area of New York City—the Young Women's Leadership School of East Harlem sent all of its 2006 graduating class to college. Yet there is much debate about single-sex schooling. In the past, all-female schools were typically private schools for the wealthy, and their principles included giving females leadership roles and creating opportunities for them to excel. Many educators feel that if a gender-fair curriculum were commonplace—if it highlighted the lives and accomplishments of women as well as men and used teaching strategies that gave voice to female students as well as to males—the advantages of all-girl environments could be accessible in coeducational environments. That is, females would not need to be separate if indeed they were treated equitably.

Because more single-sex schools and single-sex classes in coeducational settings are now available to children from lower socioeconomic classes, many applaud the Department of Education's ruling. Advocates for single-sex schooling argue that girls in these separate schools will have opportunities for leadership and verbal expression often squelched in coeducational environments. Others worry, however, that single-sex environments may promote stereotyping and discrimination. In fact, many advocates for girls and young women believe that same-sex schools for females will be less authentically rigorous. There is some data that suggest that some single-sex environments designed for girls and young women actually cater to misguided stereotypes that girls need to be spoken to quietly, that they need classrooms free from harsh questions and competition, and that they should be analyzing cosmetics to study chemistry (Rivers & Barnett, 2011). Nothing could be further from the truth. A major National Science Foundation study of mathematics scores (2008) revealed that girls, primarily from coeducational settings in ten states did as well as boys in mathematics, at every grade level. Gender is not a predictor of mathematics ability! Many educators are perpetuating the myth that girls' brains and boys' brains are predictors of achievement in mathematics and science. Be wary of "science" that supports long held prejudices. Recent studies show that sex differences emerge and are not biological traits fixed at birth (Eliot, 2011). Explore single sex environments carefully to determine if the students in these classes are being educated in rich and demanding environments and not being taught through the lens of social stereotypes.

The intersection of gender, race, ethnicity, and social class poses challenges for teaching and learning that can be overcome and made into wonderful opportunities for your own and your students' growth. The movement for multicultural education also advocates **gender-fair education**, encouraging teachers to address the needs of females and males in their classrooms in ways that help both genders realize their full potential. With this concept in mind, consider the following story from Ms. Logan's sixth-grade classroom in an urban area in California:

The students are closing their eyes and thinking back to their earliest memories. Ms. Logan says, "To begin, step out of your body and see yourself at your desk with your head down. Now, travel back in time until you are in fourth grade, then third grade. What are you wearing? Who is your teacher? What are you doing? See yourself at home. What does your room look like? Who are your friends? What do you do after school? Now, see yourself as a kindergartner; see how you are playing. What do you love to do?

gender-fair education Teaching practices that help both females and males achieve their full potential. Gender-fair teachers address cultural and societal stereotypes and overcome them through classroom interactions.

Did You Know?

Title IX prohibits discrimination on the basis of sex in any federally funded education program but does not make voluntary single-sex schooling discriminatory.

equity The act of treating individuals and groups fairly and justly, free from bias or favoritism. Gender equity means the state of being fair and just toward both males and females, to show preference to neither and concern for both.

Travel back again until you are a baby. Look around your room. Notice things around you. Now travel back again and here you are—ready to be born! Everyone is so excited, so happy, waiting for your birth. But this time, imagine you are born as the opposite sex.

"Hence, if you are boy, pretend you are born a girl. If you are a girl, pretend you are born a boy. See yourself as a baby, coming home, learning to walk, starting school, attending elementary school. Look at your room and your friends and your activities. Without talking to anybody, create a list of how your life seems different since you were born a person of the opposite sex."

Ms. Logan really likes this activity because, as the students reveal their beliefs about their lives as a member of the opposite sex, they confront stereotypes. Ultimately they learn that they are really more similar to their classmates of the opposite sex than they are different. As students respond to this exercise, they find they hold various misconceptions: for example, about the paint colors girls or boys would have in their rooms, or how they would have to behave if they were of the opposite sex. The discussion gives students a chance to see the ways they are similar, dispelling stereotypes. *(Reprinted by permission of Kodansha America, Inc. Excerpted from* Teaching Stories *by Judy Logan, published by Kodansha America, Inc. [1999].)*

In Ms. Logan's class, boys said that if they were female, they would have to get up extra early to fix their hair. A few of the girls objected to that remark and pointed out that they never get up early to fuss over their hair. Girls felt that if they were male, they would be able to stay out later—only to learn that the boys in their class also had curfews. Some boys insisted that they would do better in writing if they were female, but other boys argued that they were good writers. In the end, these middle school girls and boys agreed that they both loved sports and a lot of different subjects, and that they were probably more the same than different; however, it was clear that the boys had more personal freedom and privileges than the girls.

It's important to remember that treating students *equitably* is not the same as treating them *equally*. **Equity** stands for being fair and just. Because students come from such diverse experiences, identities, and

backgrounds, you cannot be fair by treating everyone in exactly the same way. To ensure equality in the learning goals we hope to achieve for each student, we need to notice the differences among our students and use strategies to help each student reach maximum success in the classroom. In a science class, equity may mean asking how to encourage more females' interest. One of the many ways may be to post pictures of female as well as male scientists. In a language arts classroom, equity may mean asking how to engage the boys in more reading experiences. One way may be to integrate action heroes into the literature. In each case, the tacit message is: We are here to support all our students, and we will work to counter any stereotyping and biases in the classroom.

5-3c RELIGION AND SCHOOLS

In 1995, President Bill Clinton sent material containing guidelines on student religious expression to every school district in the United States. The letter accompanying these guidelines declared:

> *Nothing in the First Amendment converts our public schools into religion-free zones, or requires all religious expression to be left behind at the schoolhouse door. While the government may not use schools to coerce the consciences of our students, or to convey official endorsement of religion, the public schools also may not discriminate against private religious expression during the school day.... Religion is too important in our history and our heritage for us to keep it out of our schools.... [I]t shouldn't be demanded, but as long as it is not sponsored by school officials and doesn't interfere with other children's rights, it mustn't be denied.*

That message seems clear enough. Yet issues concerning religion and the schools continue to cause controversy. There have been many arguments regarding prayer, Bible readings, religious displays on school property, and similar matters. Many people want schools to promote religious values more openly, or at least allow students to do so; others, just as vehemently, demand that schools keep strictly out of religious affairs.

One conflict about religious beliefs and the school curriculum involves the teaching of evolution in science classes. A landmark court case (*Tammy Kitzmiller, et al. v. Dover Area School District, et al.*) occurred in the town of Dover, Pennsylvania, where the school board insisted that students be required to hear a statement about intelligent design before ninth-grade biology lessons on evolution. (Proponents of intelligent design believe that the diversity of living things can be explained as the work of a designing intelligence; they do not insist on calling that intelligence God.) The statement read to students said that Darwin's theory is "not a fact" and has inexplicable "gaps." Science teachers objected that science class is not the domain to discuss the presence of an all-powerful being, and some parents brought the case to federal court.

In his ruling in December 2005, Judge John E. Jones asserted that the school board's requirement was unconstitutional. The judge said: "We find that the secular purposes claimed by the board amount to a pretext for the board's real purpose, which was to promote religion in the public school classroom." He said that the policy "singles out the theory of evolution for special treatment, misrepresents its status in the scientific community, causes students to doubt its validity without scientific justification," and "presents students with a religious alternative masquerading as a scientific theory." Hence, he concluded, it was unconstitutional to teach intelligent design as an alternative to evolution in a public school science classroom.

In another case in a New Jersey public high school, an eleventh-grade history teacher told his students that evolution and the "Big Bang" theory of the universe's origin were not scientific, that dinosaurs were aboard Noah's Ark and that only Christians had a place in heaven. The teacher was audiotaped by a student, and the student's family considered a lawsuit on the grounds that the teacher promoted religious views in a public school history classroom. The incident divided and shocked this New Jersey community (Kelley, 2006), and no formal court case ensued.

In the midst of such controversies, teachers often receive conflicting messages about what they can and cannot teach regarding religion. The best understanding is to recognize that you cannot teach religion in public schools. Similarly, you *cannot* encourage or participate in student religious activity. However, you can teach *about* religion and can honor the privacy of religious ritual as long as it does not interfere with the functioning of the school or classroom and it is not forced on any other student. The following statement, posted on the

website of the First Amendment Center (http://www.firstamendmentcenter.org/), was agreed on by a broad range of religious and educational groups:

> *Public schools may not inculcate nor inhibit religion. They must be places where religion and religious conviction are treated with fairness and respect. Public schools uphold the First Amendment when they protect the religious liberty rights of students of all faiths and none. Schools demonstrate fairness when they ensure that the curriculum includes study about religion, where appropriate, as an important part of a complete education.*

5-4 Multiple Intelligences: What Does It Mean to Be "Smart"?

This section deals with another type of diversity: the variation in intelligence—or perhaps a better way of expressing it, *intelligences*. Until the 1980s, psychologists believed—and many still believe—that intelligence is a fixed and measurable attribute, calculated by an IQ test. Today, many educators draw on the work of psychologist and neuroscientist Howard Gardner and accept the **theory of multiple intelligences**. That is, instead of having a fixed, single intelligence, each of us is intelligent in several different ways.

From the research of Gardner and others, we now know that babies are born with many capacities. Their intelligences evolve and are expressed in multiple ways. These different ways, or different intelligences, may be more or less dominant in a particular individual. Each individual usually expresses several intelligences, to different degrees. Gardner posited a total of seven intelligences (1993, 2003). Table 5.3 describes Gardner's seven intelligences.

According to Gardner, each individual has all of the intelligences, but no two human beings have the same profiles of intelligence. In other words, we all have these different intelligences in differing strengths and capacities for expression. Each learner's **intelligence profile** consists of a combination of relative strengths and weaknesses among the different intelligences. Moreover, intelligences are not isolated; they interact with one another in an individual to yield many types of outcomes (Moran, Kornhaber, & Gardner, 2006).

Q: *In what ways do you learn best?*

Gardner's argument leaves educators with an important mission: finding out how to access all the types of intelligences so that all students can learn to their maximum potential. It is clear that schools traditionally have valued the first two of Gardner's categories—linguistic intelligence and logical-mathematical intelligence—and paid little attention to the others. As teachers, we need to change this emphasis; we need to explore topics in multiple ways to reach more students. When schools stress memorization of key terms without exposing students to other ways to learn about a subject. For example, students who are high in linguistic intelligence will grasp the material, but other students may lag behind and be labeled as underachieving—even though these low-achieving students would do much better if they were given the opportunity to learn and express themselves by other means.

One example of a teacher who organizes assignments that have the potential to express multiple learning styles is Mr. Slomin's sixth-grade science class. He includes a unit on the moon in which students study the moon's phases—how it appears from Earth at different times of the month. Here are Mr. Slomin's instructions for this unit:

The students are required to keep a moon-phase journal over a period of five weeks. Each day, they need to record the shape of the moon, the time that they see it, and other information about the moon that can include: how they felt watching the moon, moon poems (original or found), moon facts, or other relevant data about the moon. All these belong in the moon journal. There may be some days, due to weather or other reasons, when the students cannot see the moon. Then, they are asked to develop their own theory about why they cannot see it and keep observing until they see it again. Mr. Slomin's class is accustomed to receiving open-ended assignments. The students trust that he will examine their products as individual

© Aldo Murillo/iStockphoto

TABLE 5.3 The Multiple Intelligences Proposed by Howard Gardner

Intelligence	Explanation	Examples of People Who Display This Intelligence
Linguistic intelligence ("word smart")	Ability to use and manipulate languages	Poets, writers, lawyers, public speakers
Logical-mathematical intelligence ("math/ science smart")	Capacity to analyze problems, think logically, and carry out mathematical operations	Mathematicians, scientists
Musical intelligence ("music smart")	Ability to recognize and appreciate musical patterns, pitch, rhythm, and timbre; skill in performing and perhaps composing music	Musicians, composers
Bodily-kinesthetic intelligence ("body smart")	Ability to move one's body and its various parts in a coordinated way and to handle objects skillfully; capacity to use the body to create a performance or solve a problem	Athletes, dancers
Spatial intelligence ("art smart")	Ability to recognize patterns and relationships in physical space and manipulate them mentally	Architects, surgeons, artists
Interpersonal intelligence ("people smart")	Capacity to understand other people's moods, intentions, motivations, and desires	Educators, salespeople, counselors, religious and political leaders
Intrapersonal intelligence ("self smart")	Capacity to understand your own feelings, motivations, strengths, weaknesses	People who are good at regulating their own lives

SOURCE: Based on Gardner (2003).

Basketball: © Geoff Black/iStockphoto; Saxophone: © Izaokas Sapiro/iStockphoto; Paintbox: © Wintering/iStockphoto; Leaf: © Jill Kyle/iStockphoto

creations based on their own interests. At the end of the five weeks, the students are asked to present their moon journals and talk about how they felt during the experience of keeping them. To everyone's surprise and delight, Dan, a shy young man who does not participate much in class, created a beautiful painting on each of the nights he could see the moon. Neither his classmates nor his teacher knew how gifted he was. His entries included a relatively small number of words, but his pictures showed close and accurate observations. Dan's artistic talent was a well-kept secret. This assignment allowed him to express his observations through his artistic designs and keen observations.

Perhaps you have had interesting assignments like this one. Think about your own response to this type of experience and how it is meaningful to students.

5-5 Learning Styles

Gardner's theory of multiple intelligences has had a profound effect on how we think about the ways people perceive the world. A related idea is that people have various **learning styles**. In Chapter 4, we described learning something as a process of drawing it in from the outside and making it your own. *Learning style* refers to the particular way you take in the new idea, event, or concept.

Meeting the needs of students with a wide range of learning styles requires teachers to have more than one way to approach a topic.

© Jose Luis Pelaez/Getty Images

need to do something physical to make the concepts their own are kinesthetic learners. If you are one, quick—take notes on this chapter! There is so much to know.

Together, the research on learning styles and multiple intelligences has a strong message for teachers: Do not present activities, materials, ideas, and concepts in just one way! Because people learn in different ways and through different personal strengths, it is important to plan your lessons with multiple ways of knowing in mind.

5-6 Teaching the Broad Range of Diverse Students

❝_The prevailing question before us is not about what children need to succeed. The research is clear. They need supportive environments that nurture their social, emotional, physical, moral, civic, and cognitive development. Instead, the question becomes, who bears responsibility for creating this environment?_**❞**
—Gene Carter (2006)

New teachers often draw on their own experiences as learners, and those experiences become the default mode for what is presumed "normal" or "expected" in the regular classroom. As we have seen, however, students today bring to the classroom

Some people learn best by reading and writing—the traditional approach taken in schools. But researchers (Felder & Silverman, 1988, 2002; Felder & Brent, 2005) have identified other basic learning styles as well:

- _Auditory learners_ learn best through verbal lectures, discussions, talking things through, and listening to what others have to say. For these people, written information may have little meaning until it is heard. Such learners often benefit from reading text aloud and using a tape recorder.
- _Visual learners_ need to see the teacher's body language and facial expression to fully understand the content of a lesson. They may think in pictures and learn best from visual displays, including diagrams, illustrated textbooks, overhead transparencies, videos, flipcharts, and handouts.
- _Kinesthetic learners_ learn best through a hands-on approach, actively exploring the physical world around them. They may find it hard to sit still for long periods and may become distracted by their need for activity and exploration.

When you study for a test, is reading the book enough for you, or do you have to take notes on what you read to remember the ideas? Most people who

TEACHSOURCE VIDEO CASE

Teaching to Students' Strengths

To explore how one teacher accounts for his students' varying intelligence profiles and styles of learning, find the TeachSource Video Case "Multiple Intelligences: Elementary School Instruction" on the Education CourseMate at CengageBrain.com. The video examines a class writing assignment about the passengers' experience during the ocean voyage of the _Mayflower_. After watching the video, consider the following question:

In what ways is this lesson an example of teaching to multiple learning styles?

a wide range of ethnic backgrounds, languages, religions, sexual orientations, learning styles, and intelligences. All of these are embedded in their culture and upbringing. You also have your own identity, embedded in a particular culture with norms and traditions that are dear to you.

To be a successful teacher, you need to become a *student of your students*. Start to view "difference" from the point of view of a learner and ask yourself, "How am I enriched by learning more about my students? How does that contribute to my understanding of the human condition?" In this way, teaching becomes a never-ending story, a new adventure every year, just as Jane remarked in Chapter 2. Part of your job each year will be to learn about your students and the ways in which they and their backgrounds, languages, learning styles, sexual orientations, and lifestyles prepare them for your classroom.

5-7 Concluding Thoughts

The most important theme of this chapter is that differences among students are a gift to welcome in your classroom, not a barrier to overcome. They are a gift both for you and for your students. Unless we meet and interact with people from many walks of life and with different ways of being in the world, we run the risk of closing our minds to all that is possible in the human condition.

This chapter may leave you with more questions than answers, but you can "live into" the questions. Ask yourself: Can I do this? Can I examine my pedagogy and develop teaching strategies that help the young girl from the homeless shelter, the boy from Nicaragua with limited English, the suburban youngster who has more than she will ever need, the musically gifted eighth grader who hates history, the logical-mathematical young woman who wants to be a physicist? Can I learn from them and with them and help them be all they can be, as others have helped me?

That is the message of this chapter. In Chapter 6, we explore current trends in education. Some of these trends will feel like stumbling blocks, others like welcome boosts. The following anonymous quotation sums it up:

> **"***Teachers who inspire realize there will always be rocks in the road ahead of us. They will be stumbling blocks or stepping stones; it all depends on how we use them.***"**

CHAPTER 6

CONTEMPORARY TRENDS IN EDUCATION

© Image Source/Corbis

> *Education is not the piling on of learning, information, data, facts, skills, or abilities ... but is rather making visible what is hidden as a seed.*
> —Sir Thomas More, 1478–1535

ecause schools reflect the culture and politics of contemporary society, there are always many "trends" in education, and we could spend four or five entire books discussing current ones. By "trend" we are referring to a prevailing tendency that has impacted the lives of students and teachers in schools and that seems likely to remain around for the foreseeable future. In this chapter, we will concentrate on several major trends and issues affecting schools across the nation:

- Approaches to teaching students with special needs have expanded. Response to Intervention (RTI) is a multilevel teacher response system that identifies students at risk of underachieving and maximizes their chances for success with multiple strategies.

- The emphasis on standards-based testing has had an enormous impact on teaching practice, the construction of the curriculum, and teacher evaluations.

- The rising interest in alternative forms of schooling—specifically, public charter schools, homeschooling, and small urban high schools has changed the face of the "typical" school.

- The changing ideas about middle schools and the education of young adolescents have yielded school districts with "middle grades" in many configurations.

- The influence of students' social and emotional learning (SEL) on their attitudes, behavior, and performance in school has raised awareness of bullying and harassment in the hallways of the United States.

- Professional development has become more significant than ever before as teachers work to infuse creativity and imagination in classes where test preparation has become urgent.

LEARNING OUTCOMES

After reading this chapter, you should be thinking about the following ideas:

6-1 Explain why inclusion classrooms look no different from mainstream classrooms.

6-2 Analyze the ways in which students are labeled gifted and talented and how inclusion students may also be considered gifted or talented.

6-3 Examine how differentiated instruction meets the needs of *all* the students.

6-4 Evaluate the role of social and emotional learning for classroom teaching.

6-5 Compare problem- and project-based learning to each other and to the traditional class discussion.

6-6 Examine the affect of standardized testing on curriculum and instruction.

6-7 Analyze the results of experimental school design, initially encouraged by the passage of No Child Left Behind (NCLB) in 2002.

6-8 Debate the need for middle schools in today's school culture.

6-9 Examine the precautions that schools and teachers take to prevent violence in the classroom or the school.

6-10 Analyze the legislation ensuring students' rights as part of the US public school system.

6-11 Examine teachers' rights and their legal responsibilities as they perform their professional duties.

6-12 Debate the merits of standardized testing and the ways that today's contemporary trends pose challenges to teachers.

For you as a prospective teacher, the most significant question behind all these trends is "How can the needs of so many different types of learners be met in one classroom in one school?" As you can imagine, the answer lies in multiple approaches to implementing the curriculum. It is common to find teachers building a large repertoire of activities and experiences for a given topic. It is, therefore, important to remain professionally active and attend conferences, workshops, and professional development programs well after you have left the formal world of teacher education.

6-1 The Inclusion Classroom

> ❝*Inclusion involves all kinds of practices that are ultimately practices of good teaching. What good teachers do is to think thoughtfully about children and develop ways to reach all students.... Inclusion is providing more options for children as ways to learn. It's structuring schools as community where all children can learn.*❞
> —Chris Kliewer, Associate Professor of Special Education, University of Northern Iowa (quoted at http://www.uni.edu/coe/inclusion/philosophy/philosophy.html)

In the preceding chapter, we explored ethnic, social class, and learning profile diversity among students, but those are only a few of the ways students can be classified. In this chapter, we examine the extremes on the spectrum of learning—students with disabilities and students who are considered gifted and talented. Both of these groups of students are considered **exceptional learners**. Teaching exceptional learners

requires that teachers stretch themselves and their thinking to consider what works best for these students in their classroom settings.

Previously, you read about the Individuals with Disabilities Education Act (IDEA) and its various amendments. The law guarantees that children with disabilities receive a "free appropriate public education." But more than just providing access to education for students with disabilities, the law calls for improved results for these students and the implementation of programs to ensure their continuous progress. In fact, guidelines established by the US Department of Education's Office for Special Education Programs call for improved performance of students with disabilities, through an alignment with the No Child Left Behind Act (2002).

The question educators must answer for each student with a disability is: What does free and appropriate public education look like for this child? To comply with the law, this education must take place in the **least restrictive environment** appropriate for each particular student. Hence, to the greatest extent possible, students with disabilities must be educated with children who are not disabled.

Originally, this mandate led to the mainstreaming of students with disabilities. Generally, mainstreaming involved having those students with disabilities participate in general education classes for part of the school day and spend the remainder of the day in a separate, self-contained classroom for students with disabilities. Today, the prevailing concept is inclusion, which goes further than mainstreaming. **Inclusion** involves a

Inclusion classes give students with disabilities equitable access to an education.

© Realistic Reflections/Getty Images

commitment to educate students with disabilities in the general education classroom for the entire school day. Any special services the students need are brought to them in the regular classroom. Sometimes this arrangement is called *full inclusion* to emphasize that the students stay in the regular classroom full time. If students spend only part of the day in the regular classroom, the arrangement is called *partial inclusion*.

The field of **special education** focuses on the services and instructional practices needed by students with disabilities. You may be interested in becoming a special education teacher. Today, because of inclusion, that often means working in tandem with a general education teacher in the same classroom. In addition to having at least two teachers, an inclusion classroom may also have a teacher's aide, who may be specifically assigned to a student in the class with special needs.

The TeachSource Video Case features a general education class that uses the services of an inclusion specialist. Often, an inclusion specialist works with more than one teacher in a school.

There has been a great deal of controversy about inclusion. Parents of general education students worry that their child's education may be compromised by the presence of students with special needs. They fear, for instance, that the teacher may have to spend so much time with the "special" students that "regular" students get less attention. Other people, however, believe that inclusion helps general education students appreciate people who are different from themselves.

On the opposite side of the argument, there are many critiques of self-contained classrooms for students with disabilities. Many educators worry that students in such classrooms are "labeled" for life. Applied at an early age, the disability label persists over time and limits the students' potential. Other critics point out the disproportionate number of minority boys in self-contained special education classes, especially in urban areas. How do these children get placed in such settings? Why is there a larger number of students from one ethnic group and gender than from others? Who is advocating on behalf of students with special needs? These and other questions contribute to raging controversies surrounding special education and its implementation in public schools. Wherever you stand on this controversy, the chances are high that you will have an inclusion classroom at some stage in your teaching career.

6-1a TYPES OF DISABILITIES

Approximately half of all students with disabilities—more than 4 percent of US students as a whole—have **learning disabilities** (US Department of Education, 2005). These are students who have difficulty with reading, listening, speaking, writing, reasoning, or mathematical skills. Students with learning disabilities can be good in one subject area but perform poorly in other areas. For students with learning disabilities, hyperactivity and the inability to follow directions are typical problems.

In many cases, students with learning disabilities have social and behavioral problems. Sometimes the learning disability leads to behavioral distress, low self-esteem, and inappropriate behavior in the classroom.

Some other types of disabilities recognized under the IDEA are (in order from most to least frequent):

- Speech or language impairments
- Mental retardation
- Emotional disturbance
- Hearing impairments
- Orthopedic impairments
- Visual impairments
- Autism

(US Department of Education, 2005)

special education The branch of education that deals with services for students with disabilities or other special needs that cannot be met through traditional means.

learning disability A disorder in the basic psychological processes involved in learning and using language; it may lead to difficulties in listening, speaking, reading, writing, reasoning, or mathematical abilities.

▶❚❚ TEACHSOURCE VIDEO CASE

Teaching Strategies for the Inclusion Classroom

Find the TeachSource Video Case "Inclusion: Grouping Strategies for Inclusive Classrooms" on the Education CourseMate at CengageBrain.com. In this classroom, the students are studying the Caribbean, working in groups at different centers. After watching the video, consider the following question:

In what ways do the inclusion teacher and general education teacher function differently in this classroom?

6-1b INDIVIDUALIZED EDUCATION PROGRAMS

"After my son is out of public school, he'll be living and working with a diverse population of people. I want him to be accepted after he's out of school as much as when he's in school. For me, that is why inclusion is a key while he's in school."
—Parent of a child with disabilities, Waverly, IA (quoted at http://www.uni.edu/coe/inclusion/philosophy/philosophy.html)

Because there are so many types of disabilities with so many different representations among individual children, the IDEA legislation mandates that, for each student to have a free and appropriate public education, each student with disabilities must be provided with a learning plan. Known as the **individualized education program (IEP)**, this plan outlines long- and short-range goals for the individual student. It also includes a description of the instructional services that will be provided to meet the goals as well as the assessment techniques that will be used to understand the student's progress.

Figure 6.1 shows a few sections from a sample IEP form. This type of form is usually completed by the general education teacher and the inclusion teacher working together. In addition to these teachers, other people typically have input into the child's program, including the school psychologist, school administrators, and the student's parents or guardians. A successful inclusion model depends on the collaboration of all these people.

6-1c RESPONSE TO INTERVENTION

Response to Intervention (RTI) is a program that enables schools to identify the specific types of support that struggling students need and to provide this support when it is needed. It is a prevention model that intervenes to identify young students who may be at risk for poor learning outcomes. This organizational framework helps teachers screen all students to determine whether the curriculum and instruction they are implementing are meeting the needs of the majority of students. This screening typically happens for an entire grade and is a means for helping struggling students and preventing them from experiencing academic failure. The RTI program can also identify students with learning difficulties (Brown-Chidsey, 2007).

What makes RTI effective is the ways in which it can prevent academic failure and determine whether a student's underachievement is the result of an actual learning disability or the result of inadequate instruction. RTI is a systematic method for instruction and assessment of students that includes a three-tiered approach to intervening on behalf of students with varying instructional needs.

In Tier 1, all students are assessed to determine if they are meeting grade-level standards for the general curriculum. In Tier 2, students who are performing below grade level receive specific instructional activities to help their academic achievement. These are tailored to the individual and require collaboration between general education teachers and the special education teachers. In Tier 2, students are monitored weekly and, as their skills improve, receive less support until they are fully able to succeed with the general education curriculum as it is implemented in the school. If the students in Tier 2 do not make progress in a specified period of time, instruction is modified and they are further monitored. If they need additional support, the students are moved to Tier 3 services, in which the school conducts a comprehensive evaluation of a student's skills, including the data from Tiers 1 and 2, to determine why the student's performance is significantly different from that of other students in his or her grade and to decide what instructional support the student needs.

If this sounds complicated, that's because it is! However, outcomes from schools that have practiced RTI for years have shown that it raises the educational attainment of students in general and reduces the number of students who need special education services. One of the reasons for this is that the instructional interventions that are recommended have been validated by research and are not loosely constructed. Think about how wonderful it would

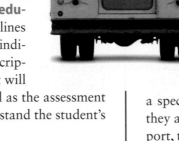

© Jon Patton/iStockphoto

FIGURE 6.1

Sections from a
Sample IEP Form

PRESENT LEVELS OF ACADEMIC ACHIEVEMENT, FUNCTIONAL PERFORMANCE AND INDIVIDUAL NEEDS

Current functioning and individual needs in consideration of:

- the results of the initial or most recent evaluation, the student's strengths, the concerns of the parents, the results of the student's performance on any state or districtwide assessment programs;

- the student's needs related to communication, behavior, use of Braille, assistive technology, limited English proficiency;

- how the student's disability affects involvement and progress in the general education curriculum; and

- the student's needs as they relate to transition from school to post-school activities for students beginning with the first IEP to be in effect when the student turns age 15 (and younger if deemed appropriate).

Academic Achievement, Functional Performance and Learning Characteristics:

Current levels of knowledge and development in subject and skill areas, including activities of daily living, level of intellectual functioning, adaptive behavior, expected rate of progress in acquiring skills and information and learning style.

Social Development:

The degree and quality of the student's relationships with peers and adults, feelings about self and social adjustment to school and community environments.

Adapted from Response to Intervention: Blueprints for Intervention. Reprinted with permission of National Association of State Directors of Special Education.

continued

Physical Development:

The degree or quality of the student's motor and sensory development, health, vitality and physical skills or limitations that pertain to the learning process.

Management Needs:

The nature of and degree to which environmental modifications and human or material resources are required to enable the student to benefit from instruction. Management needs are determined in accordance with the factors identified in the areas of academic achievement, functional performance and learning characteristics, social development and physical development.

MEASURABLE ANNUAL GOALS

Annual Goal: What the student will be expected to be able to do by the end of the year in which the IEP is in effect.

Evaluative Criteria: How well and over what period of time the student must demonstrate performance in order to consider the annual goal to have been met.

Procedures to Evaluate Goal: The method that will be used to measure progress and determine if the student has met the annual goal.

Evaluation Schedule: The dates or intervals of time by which evaluation procedures will be used to measure the student's progress.

Annual Goal:	
Evaluative Criteria:	
Procedures to Evaluate Goal:	
Evaluation Schedule:	

be to prevent a child's placement in special education simply because he or she needed specific early academic support to achieve success independently. RTI is a framework in which we think about organizing curriculum and instruction based on students' responses to screening, tiers of instruction, progress monitoring, and understanding of how the intervention was delivered. The National Center on Response to Intervention provides screening tools, case studies, and descriptions of tiered interventions (http://www.rti4success.org).

As we will see in this chapter, RTI is one form of differentiated instruction. In the next section we explore how instruction is differentiated for gifted students.

6-2 The Education of Gifted and Talented Students

> **"**A teacher asked a class what color apples are. Most of the children said 'Red'…a few answered 'Green,' and one child raised his hand with another answer: 'White.' The teacher patiently explained that apples were red or green or yellow but they were never white. The student persisted. Finally, he said, 'Look inside.'**"**
>
> —Adapted from Tara Bennett-Goleman (2001, p. 43)

This quotation reminds me of how students with "out-of-the-box" thinking often are not rewarded in school because their ideas are not aligned with conventional questioning or expected answers. Sometimes these thinkers are really gifted or talented students.

Most of us typically have less compassion for gifted and talented students than we do for students with disabilities. Conventional wisdom tells us that gifted students always land on their feet, and some of us even feel jealous of their exceptional skills and abilities. Research, however, indicates that gifted and talented learners are in as much need of special educational services as are students with disabilities (Davis & Rimm, 2004). Often their needs are not met in traditional school settings, and that situation frequently causes depression, lack of interest in school, and underachievement. Many people have an image of gifted students as well-behaved, high-performing, and compliant. Sometimes, however, they are failing, poorly behaved, and acting out because they are bored and underchallenged.

Additionally, fewer gifted and talented students from minority groups or groups of low socioeconomic status are identified than from white, middle- and upper middle-class populations. Part of this discrepancy stems from parent advocacy—parents of higher social status are more likely to push for their children to be included in gifted programs. The discrepancy also relates to the issue of social capital introduced previously in this book. Parents with social capital understand how to get their children into special programs. In addition, social capital exposes the learners themselves to a variety of educational and cultural experiences that poorer students often do not gain access to. That early and consistent cultural exposure outside of school contributes to a sense of "giftedness."

As you might guess, the attempt to define giftedness has led to controversy. For much of the twentieth century, giftedness was usually measured by IQ tests: people who scored in the upper 2 percent of the population were considered gifted. Critics pointed out, however, that those tests emphasized a narrow range of skills and tended to discriminate against minority groups. Today, giftedness is defined not so much by test scores as by consistently exceptional performance.

Federal legislation has generally referred to gifted and talented children as those who show high performance capability in specific academic fields or in areas such as creativity and leadership and who require special services by the school to develop these capabilities. The schools select students for such services using a variety of measures, including recommendations by teachers; test scores; and an understanding of certain identifying features of gifted and talented students, such as the pace at which they learn and the depth of their understanding (Maker & Nielson, 1996).

Services for the gifted and talented learner can provide enrichment (broadening the curriculum) or acceleration (speeding up the student's progress through the

© agencyby/iStockphoto

curriculum). Enrichment activities for the gifted are usually classroom based, whereas accelerated programs may allow students to skip grades or graduate early from high school. Accelerated programs range from segregated grade-level classes to high school programs such as the International Baccalaureate (IB) program and advanced placement (AP) courses. The IB program is a rigorous course of study concentrating on mathematics, science, and foreign language and is internationally recognized. AP courses offer college credit while students are still in high school.

There is no universally agreed-upon answer to the question of who is gifted. Many people believe that all children are gifted in different ways. The National Association for Gifted Children (NAGC) defines a gifted person as "someone who shows, or has the potential for showing, an exceptional level of performance in one or more areas of expression."

Some gifted people have general abilities such as leadership skills and the ability to think creatively. Other gifted people have more specific abilities, such as special aptitudes in mathematics, science, or music. By these standards, approximately 6 percent of the student population in the United States is considered gifted (NAGC, 2012).

Helen Keller (1880–1968) was deaf and blind; however, despite enormous odds against her, she was able, with the help of her teacher, Anne Sullivan, to graduate from college, become a prolific writer, and tour the world. It would have been infinitely easier for her today.

© Corbis

In many cases, gifted students learn differently from their classmates in at least five important ways:

- They learn new material in much less time.
- They tend to remember what they have learned, making reviews of previously mastered concepts a painful experience.
- They perceive ideas and concepts at more abstract and complex levels than do their peers.
- They become passionately interested in specific topics and have difficulty moving on to other learning tasks.
- They are able to operate on many levels of concentration simultaneously, so they can monitor classroom activities without paying direct or visual attention to them (Winebrenner, 2000, p. 54).

Finally, many people now recommend "gifted inclusion." That would prompt us to design regular classroom activities that offer gifted and talented students opportunities to expand on the unit of study. This is a common occurrence in classrooms of students with many different abilities. In the next section, we examine the importance of varying instructional strategies and adjusting your pedagogy to recognize the many types of learners with whom you may work.

6-3 Differentiated Instruction

Although there is great diversity among students, all learners want to be valued and need support, encouragement, kindness, and compassion. Examining student diversity provides teachers with the challenge of meeting the differing needs of students who may have exceptional learning needs, special learning profiles, language and ethnic differences, and cultural and socioeconomic differences. Sometimes, strategies for meeting the needs of these learners are developed through collaboration with a specialist, someone who has been trained in a field such as special education, gifted education, or bilingual education. The RTI model you read about previously is a good example of how instruction is specifically designed for students with special learning needs. This is a research-based model of differentiation. The various programs for gifted and talented students represent another model of differentiated instruction. As we noted in the previous section, gifted and talented students may require enrichment activities that are often classroom based and frequently designed with a specialist.

Whether in collaboration with a fellow teacher or not, you will be responsible for developing teaching strategies that can accommodate the learning experience to a wide range of student abilities. Teaching to diversity has a name. **Differentiated instruction** or **differentiation** has become an important educational philosophy recognizing students' varying background knowledge, learning profiles, abilities, interests, and language. It is the basis for developing instructional practices that engage all learners through multiple approaches, tasks, and activities.

Differentiated instruction contrasts with the notion that all children should be taught in the same manner. The movement for gender-fair education, for example, identified the different needs of girls and boys in the classroom resulting from the different ways they are socialized (Sadker & Zittleman, 2009). The movement first focused on the needs of girls but then went on to consider new ways to help boys succeed. Overall, the important message for teachers is that equality of treatment does not guarantee equity. Equity is what we should strive for because it provides equal opportunities for all students to succeed.

What teachers ask students to do on behalf of their own learning must be geared to their individual needs and strengths. Our approach must be designed to help them achieve to their fullest potential. In other words, one size does not fit all. One type of activity or lesson will probably not reach all of the students. When you approach teaching a topic, ask yourself questions such as:

- In how many different ways can I engage my students in this unit of study?
- How many different types of representations can I use for a concept?
- How can I support students with learning disabilities and challenge the gifted learner, while at the same time exciting all learners to find their inner confidence?
- What are the strengths of my students with disabilities? How can I teach to their strengths and not focus on what they cannot do?

Differentiated instruction is based on the following set of beliefs:

- Students who are the same age differ in their readiness to learn, their interests, their styles of learning, their experiences, and their life circumstances.
- The differences among students are significant enough to make a major impact on what students need to learn, the pace at which they need to learn it, and the support they need from teachers and others to learn it well.

- Students learn best when they can make a connection between the curriculum and their interests and life experiences.
- Students learn best when learning opportunities are natural.
- Students are more effective learners when classrooms and schools create a sense of community in which students feel significant and respected.
- The central job of schools is to maximize the capacity of each student (Tomlinson, 2012).

differentiated instruction or **differentiation**
The practice of using a variety of instructional strategies to address the different learning needs of students.

6-4 Social and Emotional Learning

Social and emotional learning (SEL) refers to individuals' abilities to manage their emotions, develop caring and concern for others, make responsible decisions, establish positive relationships, and handle challenging situations effectively. School programs that help students to develop these skills have been shown to be effective in preventing violence, substance abuse, and related problems, and in helping students succeed academically (Zins, et al., 2010). The Collaborative for Academic, Social, and Emotional Learning (CASEL) is a nonprofit organization that was founded by Daniel Goleman, author of *Emotional Intelligence* (2006). It works to advance the evidence-based practices for incorporating SEL into the curriculum in as many schools as possible nationwide.

It comes as no surprise that students' learning is influenced by social and emotional factors and that an anxious, afraid, or alienated student has a diminished capacity for learning. Helping students to communicate, make decisions, and solve problems increases the likelihood that they can develop a positive attachment to school and experience greater academic success (CASEL, 2010).

SEL skills are explicitly taught through planned, systematic, and evidence-based classroom instruction, and many of the activities that compose an SEL curriculum could be integrated with academic learning areas. These carefully structured learning programs engage students from pre-kindergarten through high school in experiences that build their self-awareness, self-management, social awareness, relationship skills, and responsible decision making. A related component to the SEL approach is the development and maintenance of caring classroom communities. We will explore those types of caring classroom communities further in Chapter 9. Well-managed learning environments are places where students feel safe, respected, and challenged, and where teachers are able to model and provide opportunities for students to practice their social and emotional skills. Teachers need to be in control of their own emotions and be confident that they will be able to interact with youngsters in a way that helps them to improve, feel good about themselves, and contribute to the classroom community. In the next sections, creative classroom experiences—that some experts think are the opposite of "teaching to the test"—will be examined. In the following sections we explore trends that have traction, that is, they hold the attention of students and of the educational community at large because they offer learners opportunities to think for themselves, create new designs, and solve compelling problems.

6-5 The Power of Projects and Problems for Student Learning

Looking for a history teacher, a suburban high school ran the following advertisement in the local newspaper:

Responsible for implementing curriculum specializing in the time period of 1500–1700 by designing lessons reflecting the theory of multiple intelligences, integrating with other domains using project-based learning and technology.

The phrase toward the end of the ad, "project-based learning," is one you will hear frequently. Both project- and problem-based learning are contemporary trends aimed at ensuring that students address content areas with depth and skill. Students with diverse needs and learning profiles have been shown to benefit from the use of these strategies.

One major characteristic of both these approaches is that students work in groups, with three to five students organized around a central learning task. This technique had its beginnings in the **cooperative learning** movement, which became popular in the 1990s. Every

member of each group is assigned a task, and each task is important for the goal to be reached. The students in the group are responsible for their individual learning as well as the group's learning. They work toward the common goal of promoting each other's and the group's success.

6-5a PROJECT-BASED LEARNING

To see what project-based learning looks like, consider a challenging project for a sixth-grade math class in the following story:

In Mr. Roberts's sixth-grade math class in an urban middle school, a visitor is immediately struck by what the students are doing. Students are working in groups of four to construct a model classroom, using cardboard boxes, glue guns, poster board, markers, and construction paper. Centimeter sticks and measuring tapes are scattered around each work station. When asked about their work, students eagerly show their sketches, which indicate the scale of their model and use principles of ratio and proportion. Clearly, this class is learning about mathematical concepts through a design project.

Mr. Roberts is convinced that the students will develop a deeper understanding of the concepts of ratio and proportion as a result of designing and constructing the model classroom. He is preparing a written assessment on this topic to more fully understand what the students know.

The *design challenge*, a term from engineering design, began with certain specifications. The ratio was stated in advance, using proportional units of 2 cm equal to 1 foot. The challenge also specified that the classroom contain (1) seating for eighteen students, (2) a teacher's desk, (3) a discussion area with a couch and arm chairs and an area rug, and (4) ample board space. Certain constraints were imposed as well: The students may not use materials other than those supplied by the teacher, and the final model should be no larger than 40 cm long × 40 cm wide × 18 cm high. The materials provided include foam board, cardboard, construction paper, markers, glue guns, cutting tools (handled by the teacher and other adults), and assorted recyclable materials, such as wooden spools from sewing thread, cardboard paper-towel tubes, cereal boxes, and other assorted containers.

Working in groups of four, the students present their designs to the entire class after completing their model. They demonstrate how they have met the specifications and constraints of their design challenge and explain why their model classroom contains objects that are in appropriate proportion to the rest of the room. They provide a rationale for the arrangement of the students' and teacher's desks. Throughout this performance, each member of the working group has the opportunity to present his or her understanding of the project and of ratio and proportion. All the students get feedback from their classmates.

This story demonstrates how **project-based learning** adds creativity and depth to a curriculum, promoting more meaningful learning than rote memorization or worksheet activities. Projects can be designed for any subject area, and they often embrace concepts from several disciplines. They also accommodate students with different learning profiles and abilities, helping students work from their own strengths. Everybody becomes engaged in completing the task or constructing the final product. As the newspaper advertisement indicated, projects typically reflect the theory of multiple intelligences and help students integrate knowledge from different domains.

Projects are challenging for teachers because they require more time and more materials than talking and doing worksheets, which is often the instructional device used when teachers are teaching to the test. A project is a carefully planned and organized experience involving thoughtfully selected groups. Although classrooms engaged in projects can be noisy at times, the students are usually self-directed and invested in their work.

6-5b PROBLEM-BASED LEARNING

Closely related to project-based learning is **problem-based learning**. Both strategies emphasize connections to real life, but project-based learning usually results in the construction of something, whereas problem-based learning focuses on a problem, the solutions to which may take many different forms. Problem-based learning is often more open-ended. The following story shows problem-based learning in action:

project-based learning
A teaching method that engages students in extended inquiry into complex, realistic questions as they work in teams and create presentations to share what they have learned. These presentations may take various forms: an oral or written report, a computer technology-based presentation, a video, the design of a product, and so on.

problem-based learning Focused, experiential learning (minds-on, hands-on) organized around the investigation and resolution of messy, real-world problems.

In Ms. Rhodes's fourth-grade Vermont classroom, a unit on recycling and conservation prompted the class to consider the amount of milk wasted in the school cafeteria during lunchtime. Ms. Rhodes introduced the problem by explaining to the class that the custodian had mentioned how many half-full milk cartons were tossed into the trash during lunch. "So many children—wasting so much milk," he said. Ms. Rhodes asked the class to consider the challenge of finding out just how much milk is wasted in a typical day in the cafeteria.

The students' problem was two-fold: (1) how to calculate the volume of milk wasted and (2) how to enlist the help of all the students in the school to curb this waste.

The class secured the help of the custodian, who brought discarded, but not empty, milk containers to the classroom each day for a week. Working in groups of four and using graduated cylinders, the students measured the amount of milk wasted each day. They constructed a huge bar graph

In project-based learning, students work together to meet shared learning goals.

© Elizabeth Crews

© Ryan Balderas/iStockphoto

titled "Milk Waste" outside their classroom, labeling the axes with "day of the week" and "liters of milk wasted." Under the graph, they posed the question, "What can YOU do about the amount of milk we waste in our school?"

The students also visited classrooms, talked about the problem, and gathered suggestions. By the end of the school term, there was a 70 percent decrease in the amount of milk wasted!

As this story demonstrates, problem-based learning can help students make connections between school subjects and the world outside of school. Conservation takes on new meaning when students relate it to their own lunchtime habits.

Notice, too, that that the problem the students faced was not a simple one. They were not told how to measure the amount of milk wasted. Instead, they faced an **ill-structured problem**, one for which they had to figure out their own approach to the question. With ill-structured problems, the solutions and the steps for reaching them are not clearly defined. In this way, they resemble real-life problems, which are usually complex and messy and require creative and critical thinking skills. To solve ill-structured problems, students need to make decisions based on the facts they gather and their beliefs about the best way to proceed. Solutions emerge from the process, and there may be more than one solution to a single problem.

Karen Rasmussen (1997) describes how a twelfth-grade geology teacher designed his entire course around six ill-structured problems. Each unit lasted six weeks. His goal was to teach students that scientific findings have a lot of relevance outside the school building. In one unit, for

example, students received a letter stating that a volcano in Yellowstone Park was showing signs of activity. If it erupted, the middle third of the United States could be wiped out. The students were asked what should be done. In response, they worked in groups to study volcanoes, determine the probability that such an event would occur, and describe the effect a major natural disaster would have on jobs and politics in the region. The teacher encouraged the students to locate information on the Internet. Students prepared a final paper for this unit and also presented oral reports. Their suggestions included:

- Drilling into the volcano to relieve the pressure.
- Developing evacuation plans.
- Not informing the public at all because, some students reasoned, the volcano was unlikely to erupt, there was no way to predict or prevent an eruption, and widespread panic would lower property values and scare industry away from the area.

None of these suggestions was right or wrong, but each had to be supported by the students' research (Rasmussen, 1997).

I want to emphasize that project- and problem-based learning can be applied in any subject area. The

© Michael Utech/iStockphoto

next story focuses on a high school course in government in which students consider a controversial social and political issue:

In a senior-level high school government course, students are shown a video of the trial of Jack Kevorkian, a doctor who was given a ten- to twenty-five-year prison sentence in Michigan for assisting in the suicide of a terminally ill patient. As is made clear in the video case, Dr. Kevorkian (now deceased) dismissed counsel and represented himself. He had been acquitted of similar charges several times previously, but in this case, he was found guilty of second-degree murder.

At the point when students are studying the case, Kevorkian is ill. After serving less than ten years in jail, he has appealed for parole to the governor of Michigan. The students are asked to make the case for or against granting Kevorkian parole, using data they collect from news reports, the video case, and their own research.

Students must present an argument with no fewer than five pieces of information to support their claim. Their teacher encourages them to learn as much background information about this case as possible, including the ways this case differs from previous cases in which Kevorkian was brought to trial. Students are also required to understand the parameters of second-degree murder and to decide why or why not they believe the verdict to be just and fair.

In this class of twenty-four high school seniors, opinions are almost evenly split. Three groups favor granting parole, and three favor refusing parole. Students' arguments cover a wide range of topics, from the techniques for assisted suicide to the actual poisonings Kevorkian helped perform. Although no one is clearly right or wrong in the conventional sense, the quality of the problem solving influences some students to reconsider their original decisions when they have heard all the arguments.

In a conversation with the teacher, Alex Winter, I was struck by the following remark: "When students are engaged in determining solutions to problems that exist in their real world, they use all of their mental resources to contribute to the solution. I find that I have to say very little. My role is that of a mediator—organizing presentations and moderating the conversations."

Have you ever thought of teaching in the way that Winter suggests? His technique reminds us, as mentioned previously in the book, that teachers may tell students many things in the classrooms, but teaching is *not* telling.

To sum up the discussion of project- and problem-based learning, note that these two approaches have several characteristics in common (Torp & Sage, 2002, pp. 15–16):

- Students are engaged problem solvers.
- Students work in groups and collaborate to find the best solution to a problem.
- Teachers are coaches and guides, modeling interest and enthusiasm for learning.
- Projects or problems deal with real-life issues that students care about.
- Students use interdisciplinary resources.
- Students acquire new skills as they work on different tasks.
- Students struggle with ambiguity, complexity, and unpredictability.

Whether project- or problem-based, however, students are given the opportunity to develop a set of concepts about the topic through their own explorations and collaboration with their peers. Each project- or problem-based experience has a set of "big ideas" or core concepts that will result from the experience. Those ideas become internalized in a much deeper and meaningful way through the journey the students take to reach those understandings.

6-6 Standardized Testing: From No Child Left Behind to Race to the Top

The No Child Left Behind Act (NCLB, 2002) was the most dramatic federal education legislation since the 1965 Elementary and Secondary Education Act (ESEA). Although NCLB was a reauthorization and revision of ESEA, it went beyond the previous act in several important ways. It emphasized increased funding for less wealthy school districts and higher achievement for financially poor and minority students. It also introduced new measures for holding schools accountable for students' progress. Most controversially, NCLB set new rules for standardized testing, requiring that students in grades 3 through 8 be tested every year in mathematics and reading. This requirement had important implications for the way the curriculum was developed and implemented in many elementary schools across the country. Because of the initial push for statewide standardized tests in mathematics and reading, elementary students in the first decade of this century received less instruction in science and social studies. The promise of the NCLB legislation became a massive testing movement, and there has not been substantial research to demonstrate that these standards-based assessments in each state actually improved student learning.

The next administration, under President Barack Obama, spent four years trying to overhaul the 2002 No Child Left Behind Act, and many things about NCLB are changing, including its name. It will revert back to the Elementary and Secondary Education Act, its original name. Whichever name it goes by, however, it will still maintain annual testing for reading and math for students because of the federally funded Race to the Top (RTTP) initiative described in Chapter 3. RTTP funding is an incentive project offered to states whose applications meet the criteria set forth by the US Department of Education.

6-6a TEACHING TO THE TEST AND RACE TO THE TOP

The most immediate effect of the NCLB legislation in 2001 was the emphasis on testing. Although President Obama proposed that teachers should stop "teaching to the test," his signature education program, RTTP, encourages states to award bonuses to teachers whose students attain higher test scores. Although accountability is necessary to assess student, school, and system progress, many argue that a single standardized test in mathematics and reading creates a culture of test preparation that often leaves little room for creative and in-depth teaching. Today's global education reform movement demands teaching to the test. The results of these tests are becoming the most important outcomes of education. Naturally, teachers who are being evaluated based on their students' test scores are resorting to teaching to the test as a pragmatic way to protect their jobs. A troubling outcome of the movement is to treat parents as consumers and students as products, with teachers treated as workers who are expected to obey orders (Ravitch, 2012). Fortunately, for teaching and learning, the country of Finland has confounded those in the corporate world who believe public education requires a corporate model. This is because Finland has a high-functioning system based on teachers' collaboration, professional development, and creating a culture of personal pride and intrinsic motivation, not by the hope of a bonus for high scores or by the fear of being fired for their students' lower scores.

Many argue that the rigid testing protocols established by NCLB and continued through RTTP further exacerbate the problem of teachers teaching to the test because in some states teachers' very jobs depend on the scores of their students. Assessment experts argue that there is more to evaluating student learning and teacher success than the students' performance on a single assessment event. Teachers who feel pressured to teach to the test—that is, to focus narrowly on the precise skills and information students need to do well on the exam, often resort to old-fashioned drill-and-practice exercises, trying to cram the knowledge into their students. There may be little time left for critical thinking, delving into a subject deeply, or exploring the students' own questions.

Some educators argue that teachers do not have to drill students for the tests. Strategies like problem- and project-based learning might produce equally good test results. At one middle school in Hahnville, Louisiana, that champions project-based learning, scores have indeed gone up. One teacher states: "Part of [the rise in scores] is probably due to project-based learning, because the knowledge does get across to them. I've had kids come back to me and tell me, 'Remember that project we did?' They have never, ever, come back to me and said, 'Remember that test we did?'" (Ball, 2004).

Unfortunately, few educational systems are willing to give up test-driven teaching in favor of more flexible and creative approaches to content. There is too much at stake when the scores of the students are tallied, summarized, and publicly reported. Many educators are

© Chris Schmidt/iStockphoto

concerned that if only what the tests measure are valued, then a standards-based movement is ignoring the importance of passion for learning and the celebration of individual talent.

6-6b DOES ONE SIZE FIT ALL?

In addition to the problem of teaching to the test, there is a big question about whether one size fits all in educational testing. Under mandated testing procedures, a single standardized test is administered to all students in the state, regardless of their individual learning contexts. Many educators believe that stripping away context denies the authenticity of the assessment—that is, it takes away any possible connection to the students' lived experiences. Therefore, many question if the test results that are unrelated to students' lives have any real meaning.

Many educators also object to the one-size-fits-all mandate based on what is known about cultural diversity and multiple intelligences. In this view, a single measure of progress is inadequate to evaluate students' understanding of content. Accurate assessments can be achieved only through multiple types of assessments and student performances. Many believe that schools and students are better off when local schools and districts have the "flexibility to create innovative solutions to meet their own unique situations" (Guilfoyle, 2006).

Consider Rhode Island, where annual assessments are only a small part of a student's graduation requirements. Students there demonstrate their proficiency in multiple ways:

- Portfolios, which include selected examples of student work.
- Capstone projects, which often involve in-depth research, reports, and oral presentations.
- Public exhibitions, such as posters showing the student's accomplishments in a given content area.

Hence, if testing were just *one* piece of an innovative, comprehensive assessment and accountability system, a more accurate picture of each school's strengths and weaknesses, as well as more information to help schools and individual students succeed, would be known (Guilfoyle, 2006).

6-6c VARIATION AMONG STATES: ARE THE STANDARDS REALLY STANDARD?

Within each state, the federal government mandates standardized tests. Yet, as states develop their own standards and tests for subject areas, there is enormous variability from one state to the next. In fact, students in some states perform better on the state standardized tests than they do on national math and reading tests. Some educators believe these states are setting the achievement bar too low. Because schools, administrators, and teachers—and the states responsible for them—face financial consequences if students fail to show adequate progress, there is some incentive to make the standards easy to meet. It is hoped that the Common Core Standards for language arts and mathematics will help level the playing field for all the states and that its widespread use would ensure that the standardized tests in all the states are compatible with each other.

6-6d THE ACHIEVEMENT GAP

❝*What might happen if we paid less attention to outcomes, as measured by test scores, and more attention to how children learn, which is one of the most important processes of education?... Studying the ways in which children learn could help us focus on cultural differences between and among the children who sit in the same classroom, and on how those cultural differences might be used to empower learning rather than to stand in its way.*❞

—Ellen Condliffe Lagemann (2007)

Perhaps the most discouraging effect of the NCLB legislation has been its effect on low-achieving schools and districts, precisely the constituents it had hoped to serve. After the first six years under the NCLB legislation, the gap between high- and low-achieving students had actually widened (NCES, 2008). Although accountability is terribly important, the implementation of one high-stakes test per grade level has forced many teachers to ignore the types of creative, problem-based teaching strategies that have been discussed in this chapter—strategies that engage students in their own learning. Consequently, the very students we are hoping to "hook" become discouraged by a lifeless curriculum.

Moreover, many teachers themselves are discouraged by the effects of high-stakes testing on their teaching. "In a study of 376 elementary and secondary teachers in New Jersey, teachers indicated that they tended to teach to the test, often neglected individual students' needs,... had little time to teach creatively, and bored themselves and their students with practice problems as they prepared for standardized testing" (quoted in Cawelti, 2006).

© Ryan Balderas/iStockphoto

A basic assumption of the US Department of Education is that maintaining high expectations is necessary for improving achievement. This is, however, only one part of a potential solution. Achievement gaps between ethnic groups and groups of differing socioeconomic status are not caused entirely by schools. They are caused by powerful social and family characteristics that affect children long before they start school and continue to operate as they enter school (Hart & Risley, 1995; Brooks-Gunn, et al., 2000; Lareau, 2003). This does not mean that social and economic disadvantages—the absence of social capital—cannot be overcome in schools. But substantial learning goals cannot be achieved by enforcing a standardized testing program that few low-income students can become invested in.

Did You Know?

Since the first charter school opened in Minnesota in 1991, the charter school movement has grown to more than four thousand schools with more than 1.4 million children enrolled.

6-7 Alternatives to Traditional Schools: More Choices in an Era of Accountability

In today's national school culture, schools that do not meet state standards for two consecutive years are subject to penalties by individual states. Depending on where you live, parents may move their children into other, higher-performing schools. Essentially, federal law obligates school districts to replace low-performing schools. Under the new legislation, schools that miss certain targets are required to provide students with tutoring or the option to transfer. This requirement has given a boost to charter schools, which are an alternative kind of public school. The new law will still emphasize parental choice in public schooling, however, but not as a punitive measure.

Another alternative to traditional schools is homeschooling. More and more parents dissatisfied with public schools have begun to investigate the options for teaching their children at home. What do you think is behind this movement?

As a teacher, you may end up working in a charter school, or you may teach children who have been homeschooled in the past. In this section, these two alternatives to traditional public and private schools will be discussed.

6-7a THE RISE OF CHARTER SCHOOLS

In 1999, charter schools represented 1 percent of public schools; today they are more than 5 percent of public schools. The number of students enrolled in public charter schools has nearly tripled, from 340,000 to 1.4 million (NCES, 2011). A **charter school** is a public school that has a specific, written charter from the school district, the state, or another governing agency. The charter typically exempts the school from selected rules and regulations that apply to other schools. In exchange for these exemptions, the school agrees to be accountable for producing certain results set forth in the charter in a specified period of time. Every three to five years, a school's status is reviewed; the school's right to exist can be revoked if the school has not met the standards promised in the charter.

By 2009, forty-five states, the District of Columbia, and Puerto Rico had established charter school laws. This means that concerned citizens, educators, or government officials can bring a plan for a charter school to the local or state education agency and, if the plan meets the established requirements there is a strong possibility that the school can be established.

The belief is that charter schools have the potential to develop new and creative teaching methods and that these innovations can thrive in a system that is not constrained by the usual rules and regulations. Many educators also hope that charter schools will foster a positive spirit of competition, encouraging traditional public schools to reform their practices.

Unfortunately, there is *no clear evidence* that charter schools are significantly more successful than traditional public schools. The National Assessment of Educational Progress, for example, found no significant advantages for charter schools in reading or math performance (National Assessment of Educational Progress, 2005). For low-performing students in particular—the focus of many reform efforts—no studies definitively suggest that the charter school system is more successful than what is already in place. One of the serious problems associated with charter schools in low-income areas is that they tend to enroll the highest-achieving students, leaving the traditional public schools with a less heterogeneous group of students. Consequently, the public schools from which the charter schools' students came usually experience a loss of academic standing. In some cities, those now-low-performing schools are being closed.

Because many different groups of concerned citizens can start charter schools, often without any prior training in education, professionals who do research in the area of learning and teaching are concerned about the charter school movement. Analyzing the success or failure of charter schools is complicated, however, because there are so many different types serving so many kinds of students. As one team of researchers explains:

> One of the most important difficulties in studying charter schools is that many of them are targeted specifically at particular student populations and thus serve dramatically different kinds of students than regular public schools do. Although most states require charter schools to have open enrollment policies, charter schools can still target specific populations by describing themselves as schools for a particular kind of student or by otherwise encouraging a certain kind of student to apply for admission (Greene, Forster, & Winters, 2003).

Similarly, the National Education Association (2007) comments:

> Because charter schools promise to improve student achievement as a condition of relief from some of the rules and regulations that apply to traditional public schools, it is appropriate to evaluate their effectiveness.

This is a reminder that teaching and learning are highly complex activities and that schools are complicated organizations functioning on behalf of diverse students with a broad range of differences.

Who Teaches in Charter Schools?

There are almost 4700 charter schools in the United States (NCES, 2011). Every state except for Montana has charter school laws, and half of them stipulate that charter school teachers must be state certified. For the remainder, the requirements vary. In some states, individuals may apply for a waiver to the certification requirement. In the District of Columbia, teachers do not have to be certified at all. In Illinois, charter schools may be able to employ noncertified teachers if they have a bachelor's degree, five years' experience in the area of degree, a passing score on state teacher tests, and evidence of professional growth; for all such noncertified teachers, mentoring must be provided (Education Commission of the States, 2007b).

Most professional educators, like the author of this book, believe that a formal program in learning to become a teacher is vital for anyone who wants to teach. For this reason, I hope that all charter schools will eventually require certification. This will ease some of the doubts about the value of charter schools for US education.

Types of Charter Schools

There is no "typical" charter school in the same way there is no typical public school. Be assured that charter schools vary in composition, curriculum, teacher preparation, administration, and philosophy. Some charter schools arise because of a desired focus or concentration. The Philadelphia Performing Arts Charter School (PPACS) was founded in 2000 as the only elementary performing arts school in the city of Philadelphia. Their mission is to integrate the developing mind and body of the child with academics and the performing arts. They seek to "preserve the spirit of our children through the visual arts, vocal arts, instrumental music, creative writing, classical ballet, French, and innovations in science, all intertwined with technology." This is similar to Maxine Greene's movement for aesthetic education when reading this part of their mission. There are 570 students enrolled in grades K–8 and their art-infused curriculum places a premium on academic excellence (www.ppacs. net). All the teachers at the PPACS are certified in the areas which they teach. There are more than fifty charter schools addressing elementary, middle, and high school grades. It should be noted that only 16 percent of these charter schools have high performance indexes. That being said, a major trend in urban education involves experimentation and seeking alternate routes to high school graduation. In the next section the small urban high school is detailed.

6-7b SMALL URBAN HIGH SCHOOLS

It was not just a culture of standardized testing that resulted from NCLB in 2002 but also a rise in re-imagining existing schools. Giving permission for cities and districts to experiment with school design and format, many large urban school districts began to deconstruct their massive overpopulated high schools and create smaller schools sometimes focused on an area of study or a theme and often coexisting on the same large campus. The pressing problem in education remains closing the achievement gap between low-income, predominantly students of color, in urban schools and their more advantaged, middle class peers, in predominantly white suburban schools. To that end, the Bill and Melinda Gates Foundation and other benefactors contributed funding to create high-performing high schools in urban areas. Often this meant the closing of large urban high schools where the population of students was more than four thousand students and creating smaller high schools of no more than one hundred students per grade. Small schools were formed to create and sustain a culture of achievement in inner-city schools.

Recent studies have shown that students who attend the new smaller urban high school have a better chance of graduating than those in larger urban high schools (MDRC, 2012). Creating this change for urban youth is not without its troublesome baggage. For example, those students who remain in schools that are in the process of closing by losing a grade each year

and not enrolling new students have been languishing in the "dying" schools and their graduation rates are abysmal. Disadvantaged urban teens often got "lost" in the anonymity of many large urban high schools and the study finds that small is better because it increases opportunities for achievement and graduation. Still, the debate is not over and many who support large urban high schools suggest that there are more course offerings and that certified personnel lead academic departments and promote professional development. Still, the small urban schools movement's success is about more than just size. New, smaller schools create specialized and rigorous curriculum and recruit teachers to their themes or dominant areas of study. In New York City, graduation rates from smaller high schools in the first decade of the twenty-first century were significantly higher than were the rates from their large urban counterparts. Clearly more research is needed before definitive answers are obtained. With all the experimentation in public school structure and design, there are more students than at any other time in the country's history who are being educated at home and not attending any school.

6-7c HOMESCHOOLING: ANOTHER NONTRADITIONAL OPTION

In 1997, a thirteen-year-old named Rebecca Sealfon won the Seventieth National Spelling Bee. What was remarkable about Rebecca's performance was that she had never gone to school! Having been taught at home exclusively, her performance turned a national spotlight on **homeschooling**.

A few decades ago, homeschooling represented a fringe element of the educational landscape, but currently it is a fast-growing trend. In 1999, an estimated 850,000 US students between the ages of five and seventeen were being homeschooled (Bielick, Chandler, & Broughman, 2001).

By 2012, according to some estimates, the number of homeschooled children was expected to have more than doubled as more families questioned the efficacy of traditional schools in preparing their children academically and socially for a global economy and a highly competitive marketplace. (In these statistics, students are considered to be homeschooled if their parents report them as being schooled at home

Did You Know?

At the current time, more than 2.5 million students are being homeschooled.

for at least part of their education and if their part-time enrollment in public or private schools does not exceed twenty-five hours a week.) At the current time, more than 2.5 million students are being homeschooled with a vast number of websites supporting curriculum construction for homeschooled children.

Although many different types of families homeschool their children, the majority tend to be white, middle or upper-middle class, religious, and well educated. Often they select homeschooling primarily for religious and cultural reasons, eager to protect their children from "a popular culture overflowing with images of sexual rebellion and promiscuity" (Anderson, 2000). Figure 6.2 shows statistics from a survey sponsored by the National Center for Education Statistics. In this survey, the most frequent reason parents gave for homeschooling their children was concern about schools' "environment," which included worries about safety, drug use, and peer pressure. More than one-third of parents mentioned this reason. A significant percentage of parents expressed dissatisfaction with academic instruction in schools (2009). (Clearly, some elements of homeschooling, including the lack of pressure to perform and a freedom of choice concerning the curriculum, are appealing alternatives to mandated curriculum that is based on standardized testing. Schooling children at home also keeps them out of harm's way and, for some parents, allows religious training that by law their children would not receive in public school.

Some critics of homeschooling worry that most parents cannot provide the academic support their children need to learn a wide range of subjects. After all, certified teachers are trained in educational methods and in curriculum content areas and most parents are not. However, a growing number of companies cater to parents who homeschool by providing curriculum materials. In addition, the Internet now offers an abundance of educational resources that were not available a decade ago. Many previously reluctant parents now choose to homeschool their children because of the wealth of materials available online.

Another worry about homeschooling is that students miss the socialization that occurs in schools. The entire experience of "going to school" is composed of much more than lessons, athletics, and theatrical and musical performances. It is a daily and annual ritual event that defines the growth and development of children. As we saw in previous chapters, many cultural beliefs and social values are transmitted through the "hidden curriculum" of schools. Students meet peers who represent a cross-section of their community—students with different learning styles, abilities, opinions, strengths, weaknesses, and ways of being in the world. So one must ask, are homeschooled children denied all these opportunities?

Proponents of homeschooling point out that parents have formed networks to engage their children in social and musical events outside the home. Homeschooling

FIGURE 6.2

Reasons Parents Give for Homeschooling Their Children

To provide religious or moral instruction

Concern about the school environment

Dissatisfaction with academic instruction

Other reasons

Desire to provide a nontraditional approach to education

Child has other special need or health problems

Percentage

Photo: © Barbara Sauder/iStockphoto

SOURCE: Princiotta, D. & Bielick, S. (2006). Homeschooling in the United States: 2003 (NCES 2006-042). Washington, D.C.: U.S. Department of Education, National Center for Education Statistics.

does not mean isolation. Some studies indicate that few homeschooled children are socially deprived and that homeschooled children in general have a a good self-concept. Most state governments regulate homeschooling to at least some degree. In some of these states, parents merely have to notify the educational authorities that they are schooling their children at home. In other states, parents must submit their children's test scores or other professional evaluations of academic progress. The strictest states have further conditions, such as requiring that parents file a plan or program of study before they can gain permission to homeschool their children.

6-8 Middle School: A Movement in Transition

In the early 1900s, the dominant school configuration was eight years of primary school followed by four years of secondary school. This "8–4" model was called into question as more and more students attended public school. In 1899, the National Education Association (NEA) issued a report calling for secondary school to begin in the seventh grade, citing that time—the beginning of adolescence—as a "natural turning point in a pupil's life" (NEA, 1899). Nevertheless, it was another fifteen to twenty years before the junior high school model of grades 7 through 9 emerged and began to proliferate.

Originally, junior high schools were thought of as preparatory grounds for the academic rigor of high school. By the late 1960s and early 1970s, however, various models for reorganization of school district grades were being considered to meet desegregation requirements. Further, many junior high schools were seen as focusing on content mastery rather than on the psychological and emotional needs of early adolescents.

By the 1980s, many school reformers endorsed a new "middle school" concept intended to create an educational experience more appropriate for young adolescents. The goal was to make the old junior high school more developmentally responsive by changing the grade configuration from grades 7–8 or 7–8–9 to grades 6–7–8 and designing new organizational structures such as interdisciplinary teams (Juvonen, et al., 2004). The teams would ensure that a group or cluster of students would be taught by the same four or five subject area teachers, thus creating a sense of community and closeness.

In the following decades, many school districts converted their junior highs to middle schools, but the process was far from uniform. There are several ways of organizing the middle grades, and, despite well-intentioned and committed educators, middle schools do not yet fully serve the needs of young teens. The history of the middle school movement suggests that the middle school became the norm because of societal and demographic pressures and not because of hard evidence to support the need for a separate school for young teens.

For these reasons, organization of the middle grades is still in flux. A comprehensive study of middle schools conducted by the Rand Corporation recommends that states and school districts seek alternatives to the now-typical 6–8 structure of middle school, for a number of significant reasons:

- National school-safety statistics suggest that physical conflict is especially problematic in middle schools.
- Social norms in middle school may foster antisocial behavior.
- Academic progress for middle schools is uneven and lackluster.
- Adequate state and federal supports to meet the new standards set federal legislation are unavailable for middle schools.

Middle schools are being assessed according to how well they meet the needs of preteens and young teens in transition.

© Elizabeth Crews

- Middle schools do not do enough to foster parental involvement.
- Many middle school teachers do not have certification in the subject areas they teach or specific training in the development of young adolescents (Juvonen, et al., 2004).

One example of the difficult problems of middle schools is the issue of school safety, which we have mentioned in passing several times in this chapter. When people talk about school safety today, they are referring to the outbreaks of violence that have become all too common in schools. This is the subject of the next section.

6-9 Creating a Safe School Climate: The Concern about Violence in Schools

Although the vast majority of the country's students will never be touched by peer violence in their K–12 school careers, serious isolated incidents of school violence have rocked the headlines and shaken confidence in schools. In 1999, the Littleton, Colorado, high school, Columbine, was the scene of a violent school attack by two students that claimed the lives of fourteen students and a teacher. This was the most violent school attack in US history until it was eclipsed by the 2007 rampage at Virginia Tech University in Blacksburg, Virginia, which claimed thirty-two lives, including twenty-seven students. In February of 2012, a teenager at Chardon High School in Ohio opened fire on classmates in the cafeteria, killing three students and injuring two others.

Although these incidents of targeted violence are rare, the highly publicized shootings of the last fifteen years have prompted educators to examine how, if at all, these incidents, and other less serious ones, could have been prevented.

Earlier in this text, we explored school climate and the ways it is evident when you enter a school as a student or teacher. It may even be evident to a regular visitor. The school climate is a result of the relationships that exist among the students, teachers, parents, and administrators within the school community. In a school with a climate of safety, adults and students respect each other and, importantly, students have a positive connection to at least one

© Ju-Lee/iStockphoto

adult in authority. When a climate of safety is created, it is sensed in a school; there is a feeling of emotional wellness. In this type of school climate, problems can be raised and addressed in peer groups and with counselors before they escalate. It becomes noticeable when a student is disturbed and in distress. If a member of the school community shows enormous personal pain that could lead to harm—to the student himself or herself or to others—it becomes a cry for help that is answered. The small schools movement in large urban areas, which was examined previously in this chapter, helps to ameliorate the potential for student violence, simply because the smaller number of students helps to ensure that one does not get "lost" in a crowded school environment.

The box "Creating a School Climate That Promotes Safety and Connectedness" lists some important factors that help establish a safe school climate. In Chapter 9, the classroom community and the ways to think about teaching as forging relationships with students is discussed. On a schoolwide basis, all the participants in the school community—the administrators, parents, school secretaries, custodians, grounds-keepers, as well as the teachers and students—must contribute to the establishment of a climate of safety.

Q: *Do you worry about violence in your school or classroom?*

6-10 Protecting the Rights of Students

Clearly, students have a right to be safe in school. That is one basic right that cannot be denied. What other rights do students have?

In most states, education of children has been compulsory for more than a century. Children must go to school or, as we discussed previously in this chapter, to a reasonable home-based alternative to school. Obviously, though, schools cannot do whatever they like with this captive audience. Along with schools' obligation to educate students, students deserve to have certain rights, but exactly what those rights should be is not always evident. A number of recent laws and court cases have raised serious questions about the subject. Some of the issues that have come to the fore will be explored.

Before reading further, stop a moment and think: What kinds of student rights do you suppose are covered by law? And how do you suppose the recent concern about school safety has affected students' rights?

6-10a THE RIGHT TO PRIVACY

Do you know where all of the information about your educational history is kept? Are your health records in the same place? Does the file contain records of your student loans and other information you might not like to share with everyone? What if you have a learning disability—is that documented in your file? Who has access to this file? What are your rights?

The **Family Educational Rights and Privacy Act (FERPA)** of 1974, also known as the **Buckley Amendment,** is a federal law that requires educational agencies and institutions to protect the confidentiality of students' educational records. It applies to all school systems and individual schools, including colleges and universities, receiving federal financial assistance or funding.

CREATING A SCHOOL CLIMATE THAT PROMOTES SAFETY AND CONNECTEDNESS

Working together, the US Department of Education and the Secret Service have produced a guide to help schools create a climate of school safety. According to this document, the major components and tasks for creating a safe school climate include:

Assessing the School's Emotional Climate

- How do the students and teachers experience the daily life of the school?
- Is there a culture of respect?
- Are students' emotional needs being met?
- Is everyday teasing and bullying dealt with immediately?

Creating Connections between Adults and Students

- Do students have a positive relationship with at least one adult?
- Does each student feel there is an adult he or she can talk to about problems and concerns?

Breaking the Code of Silence

- In many schools, students believe that revealing another student's pain or problems breaks a special peer code. This belief often forces troubled students to go it alone.
- In a safe school climate, students are willing to break the code of silence to get help for a peer.

Involving Everyone

- Are all members of the school community involved in creating policy and practices that help each member respond to stressful and potentially harmful events?

SOURCE: Fein, R. A., Vossekuil, B., Pollack, W. S., Borum, R., Modzeleski, W., & Reddy, M. (2002). *Threat Assessment in Schools: A Guide to Managing Threatening Situations and to Creating Safe School Climates.* Washington, D.C.: United States Secret Service and United States Department of Education.

FERPA allows students and their parents to have access to the student's records kept by educational institutions. The law also states that no one outside the institution may have access to a student's educational records, nor can the institution disclose any information from the records without the written consent of the student, or, for students under the age of eighteen, their parents. Congress passed this act in response to instances of parents or students being denied access to their records or information about students being improperly used.

FERPA clearly states that parents of students in attendance at a school have the right to inspect and review the education records of their children. Further, if the parents (or students older than eighteen) challenge the contents of the records, they must be given a hearing. At this hearing, the parents and student have the opportunity to insert their own written explanation into the record. The intent is to make sure the records are not inaccurate, misleading, or otherwise in violation of the student's privacy or other rights.

As a college or university undergraduate or graduate student, you should know what is in your personal records at your institution. Once you are eighteen years old, your parents have no inherent right to inspect your educational record; that right becomes yours alone. Parents may, however, gain access to so-called directory information, which includes simple facts that would not compromise a student's privacy, such as enrollment status, major field of study, degrees received, and so on.

Recent Challenges to FERPA

Until 2001, no cases involving violations to FERPA were brought to the US Supreme Court. In 2001, however, the court heard a case concerning the oral reporting by peers of student grades. In Oklahoma, in the Owassa Independent School District, a mother was disturbed when her son's teacher asked the class to grade each other's quizzes and then had students call out the grades so she could record them. This mother felt that the calling out of grades by her son's peers was a violation of his right to privacy. She lost the case; the Supreme Court ruled that peer grading did not violate FERPA.

A second case was brought to the Supreme Court by a college student at Gonzaga University in Washington State. The teacher certification officer at that university overheard a student discussing a teacher candidate's alleged sexual harassment of another student and

proceeded to conduct an investigation, place remarks about it in the student's record, and deny teacher certification to that student. The supposed victim of the sexual harassment denied that it occurred and never pressed charges. The alleged offender sued the university for violating FERPA. This case made its way through various levels of the state court system and finally reached the US Supreme Court in 2002. The justices ruled that FERPA did not give "enforceable rights" to individuals. Rather, it was up to the Department of Education to enforce FERPA by denying funding to educational institutions that violated the law.

Although this Supreme Court ruling may prevent individual students from collecting damages for violation of their privacy, FERPA still offers protection through the power of the purse. Because educational institutions do not want to lose their federal funding, they will be careful about allowing practices that infringe on rights established by FERPA.

Compromises on Privacy

In this age of readily accessible data, it often feels as though anyone can gain access to another person's information just by having Internet access and finding

Q: *Do you think that most teachers consider FERPA when making comments in students' permanent school files?*

STUDENTS' AND PARENTS' RIGHTS UNDER FERPA

- The right to inspect and review educational records.
- The right to request amendment of educational records.
- The right to exercise some control over the disclosure of information from educational records.
- The right to file a complaint with the US Department of Education if a school or other educational agency fails to comply with the act.

that person on Facebook. It is not quite that easy to get educational records. Unfortunately, however, since the Columbine High School shooting in 1999, educators and police agencies have felt an increased need to identify, collect, and share information in a coordinated effort to prevent a recurrence of this type of student violence. Events such as the terrorist attacks at the World Trade Center towers and the Pentagon on 9/11 have also made the sharing of information seem more imperative.

The scope of student data collected has expanded greatly since FERPA was passed in 1974. For example, student records now include data relating to the student's needs for specific educational services. Moreover, requests for student information now come from a growing number of sources inside school systems (including counselors, principals, school social workers, special education personnel, classroom teachers) and outside school systems (military recruiters, university researchers, law enforcement officers, the courts, college admissions personnel, the media, social services agencies, and others).

Some additional laws do help protect the new wealth of information. IEPs are protected under IDEA; parents must have ready access to student IEPs, but the information is considered confidential and schools are restricted from releasing it to people who do not have a legitimate educational interest in the child. Similarly, federal law ensures the right to privacy of individual students' scores. Nevertheless, the USA PATRIOT Act of 2001 created the possibility that, with a subpoena, authorities could gain access to a student's confidential information without the knowledge of the student or the parents (Vacca, 2004).

Clearly, educational institutions need to exercise careful monitoring of when and to whom student data are released. As a teacher, you, too, should be sensitive to your students' rights to privacy.

6-10b First Amendment Rights of Students

" *Congress shall make no law respecting an establishment of religion, or prohibiting the free exercise thereof; or abridging the freedom of speech, or of the press; or the right of the people peaceably to assemble, and to petition the Government for a redress of grievances.* **"**
—The First Amendment to the US Constitution

It is commonly accepted that, in schools and classrooms, the need for legitimate teaching and learning requires rules of behavior that, at times, restrict the speech of students. Yet the Supreme Court tells us in *Tinker* v. *Des Moines* that "students do not shed their constitutional rights when they enter the schoolhouse door." In this 1969 ruling, the Supreme Court upheld the First Amendment right of high school students to wear black armbands in a public high school as a form of protest against the Vietnam War. Wearing the armband was considered symbolic speech. According to the court, school administrators could prohibit the armbands only if the administrators showed that the protest would cause a substantial disruption of the school's educational mission. (Do you think the case would have come out differently if school administrators had demonstrated that the armbands caused loud debates to break out in class?)

Similarly, in the 1973 case of *Papish* v. *the Board of Curators of the University of Missouri*, the Supreme Court ruled in favor of the First Amendment rights of Barbara Papish, a graduate student, after the university expelled her for distributing a controversial leaflet containing profanity and a cartoon of policemen raping the Statue of Liberty.

Other court decisions, however, have supported schools in their attempts to restrict students' speech. In 1986, the court ruled in favor of the right of Washington state high school administrators when they disciplined a student for delivering a campaign speech that was full of sexual innuendo at a school assembly. In this case, *Bethel School District No. 403* v. *Fraser*, the court expressed the view that school administrators had the right to punish student speech that violated school rules and that interfered with legitimate educational objectives. As another example, in the 1988 case of the *Hazelwood School District* v. *Kuhlmeier*, the court upheld the right of school administrators to censor materials in a student-edited newspaper that concerned sensitive issues such as student pregnancy and that could be considered an invasion of privacy.

Also accepted is the school district's right to impose dress code restrictions on students—and teachers. Schools may require that students wear uniforms, and they may also impose reasonable grooming and dress codes for their teachers.

Overall, it seems that the Supreme Court has tried to strike a balance between the right to free expression and schools' need to maintain a productive learning atmosphere. In day-to-day terms, teachers and administrators make their own decisions on the basis of established school policies as well as common sense. Think back to the speech and dress policies of the schools you have attended. Do you think a reasonable balance was struck between individual rights and an orderly learning environment?

The right to express ideas and individual beliefs is fostered through responsible class activity.

© Elizabeth Crews

The First Amendment also addresses freedom of religion, and here the issues become even thornier and more confusing, as noted in Chapter 5. There are many legal questions surrounding the separation of church and state and the First Amendment's clause about free exercise of religion. In general terms, public schools must remain neutral about religious beliefs, but does this mean, for instance, that a student-led religious group cannot meet on school grounds? Does it mean that teachers cannot lead their students in reciting the Pledge of Allegiance, which includes the phrase "under God"?

The courts have been actively tackling these issues, and decisions made over the next few years may affect your classroom. Right now, to sum up the impact of various laws, court cases, and federal guidelines, it is fair to say that the following rules apply:

1. Prayer cannot be a regular part of the public school day.
2. Worship services, including Bible readings, may not be practiced in public school.
3. Public schools may not intrude on a family's religious beliefs.

4. Teachers and administrators in public schools may not advocate religious beliefs.
5. Extracurricular religious groups may meet on public school grounds as long as they are not led by a teacher or school official.
6. Many states require that schools include the Pledge of Allegiance in their daily schedules, but the practice remains the subject of court challenges. Individual students may not be forced to salute the flag if this conflicts with their religious beliefs.

> **due process** A formal process, such as a legal or administrative proceeding, that follows established rules designed to protect the rights of the people involved.
>
> **tenure** A status granted to a teacher, usually after a probationary period, that protects him or her from dismissal except for reasons of incompetence, gross misconduct, or other conditions stipulated by the state.

6-11 The Rights and Responsibilities of Teachers

Like students' rights, teachers' rights are protected by the Constitution. As agents of the government, public school teachers are protected by state constitutional provisions, statutes, and regulations as well. They are also held accountable to these regulations and may be dismissed if they are not meeting their obligations. This section gives a brief overview of the legal rights and responsibilities attached to the teaching profession.

6-11a TEACHERS' RIGHTS

Although private school teachers do not enjoy as much protection as public school teachers, both are protected by the Civil Rights Act of 1964, which prohibits racial, sexual, or religious discrimination in employment. Teachers' employment rights are further protected by the due process clause of the Fourteenth Amendment to the Constitution, which provides that no state may "deprive any person of life, liberty, or property, without due process of law." This **due process** requirement means that school boards and state agencies must follow established rules when deciding to dismiss or discipline a teacher.

In most states, teachers are also protected by **tenure** statutes. These statutes define a probationary period during which a teacher's performance is evaluated. If the performance is deemed acceptable, a teacher may receive tenure, and then his or her contract is automatically renewed each year unless there is a specified cause for dismissal. Legitimate causes for dismissal vary from state to state. In Illinois, for example, a teacher's certificate may be revoked or suspended for immorality, a health condition detrimental to students, incompetence, unprofessional conduct, neglect of duty, willful failure to report child abuse, or "other just cause" (Illinois School Code, section 21–23a). Many public policy officials protest that teachers' tenure status is too difficult to revoke once a teacher has earned tenure. This is the subject of much controversy today as teachers' unions are being challenged by state and federal policies mandating rigorous evaluation of teachers and, in some cases, the abolition of tenure.

Teachers have a number of other rights, such as freedom of expression and the right to personal privacy. The Civil Rights Act of 1964 prohibits racial, sexual, or religious discrimination in employment. By tradition, a teacher is reasonably free to teach according to his or her best understanding of subject matter and instructional methods. But the content taught by the teacher must be relevant to and consistent with the teacher's responsibilities; a teacher cannot promote personal or political agendas in the classroom.

Protected by the First Amendment, teachers can express their personal opinions; however, they must not use this freedom to undermine authority and adversely affect the working relationships in a school. Teachers enjoy limited rights to personal privacy. A teacher's personal life may lead to disciplinary action only if it affects the integrity of the school or district and hampers the teacher's effectiveness.

One important legal requirement is that teachers must report child abuse and negligence when they believe they have noticed it in one of their students. Child abuse is a state crime, and each state has specific reporting guidelines. Consider North Carolina's statute:

> *Any person or institution who has cause to suspect that any juvenile is abused, neglected,… or has died as a result of maltreatment, shall report the case of that juvenile to the director of the department of social services in the county where the juvenile resides or is found. The report may be made orally, by telephone, or in writing. The report shall include … the name and address of the juvenile …; the nature and extent of any injury or condition resulting from abuse [or] neglect …; and any other information which the reporter believes might be helpful in establishing the need for protective services or court intervention (quoted in Smith & Lambie, 2005).*

In some states, teacher candidates must complete child abuse seminars before they are allowed to have their own classrooms. In these seminars, they learn the symptoms of child abuse, sexual abuse, emotional abuse, and neglect. In many school systems across the country, there are support services to help teachers by providing in-service classes on child, sexual, and emotional abuse and neglect.

Many districts also have specific procedures for reporting bullying and sexual harassment among students. Teachers cannot sweep these incidents "under the rug"; they must report them in a timely fashion. In Chapter 9, this subject is discussed again because it is a crucial part of building classroom community.

6-11b Teachers' Legal Responsibilities

Teachers have many ethical and professional responsibilities to their students, the parents, the school, and the district. They also have certain legal responsibilities, established by state law or by court cases.

For example, teachers must take reasonable precautions to keep their students safe. If such precautions are neglected, the teacher or the school may be held legally responsible. Teachers and schools have been sued when students were injured in the classroom, on the playground, or on field trips.

TEACHSOURCE VIDEO CASE

Teachers Discuss Their Ethical and Legal Responsibilities

Find the TeachSource Video Case "Legal and Ethical Dimensions of Teaching: Reflections from Today's Educators" on the Education CourseMate at CengageBrain.com. Think about the discussion of rules and rights. After watching the video, consider the following question:

In what ways are the "rules of the classroom" meant to support students' First Amendment rights?

6-12 Concluding Thoughts

From inclusion to gifted education, and from problem-based learning to test preparation, public schools in the United States struggle to find the best way to educate all of their students. Complex, diverse, and challenging are good adjectives to describe students and the world in which they are educated. Pursuing a career in education requires that you consider all these factors, but it also holds the promise of making a difference for the most vulnerable of our citizens—our children.

There is a strong possibility that the school or district in which you teach will have inclusion classrooms because nearly 10 percent of all students in public schools have a disability. You will be exposed to approaches such as project- and problem-based learning that can make your students' school experience truly challenging and rewarding. At the same time, you will need to deal with the standards-based accountability movement, which is now a dominant trend in US education and is undergoing change as new data is examined. You will also be asked to protect the rights of your students as you seek to contribute to a climate of safety and equity.

You may be drawn to the charter school movement, which seeks alternative ways to educate students who are often ignored by traditional schools. You may be part of an antibullying task force in your school. You may be asked to teach to the test in your school or district. Wherever contemporary trends and pressing issues lead, there will be new ones to catch up to, especially as the technology revolution continues to challenge the way we think about teaching and learning.

There are contradictions here—forces pulling you in different directions. Being a teacher means finding your own way of reconciling these various demands. In the next chapter, information technology, no longer a trend but an integral way of life that must find its place in the world of teaching and learning, will be explored. It, too, brings both demands and significant benefits for you and your students.

STUDY TOOLS
CHAPTER 6

Located at back of the textbook
- Rip out Chapter Review Card
- Note-Taking Assistance

Located at CengageBrain.com
- Review Key Terms Flash Cards (Print or Online)
- Complete Practice Quizzes to prepare for tests
- Complete "Crossword Puzzle" to review key terms
- Watch the TeachSource Video Cases "Inclusion: Grouping Strategies for Inclusive Classrooms" and "Legal and Ethical Dimensions of Teaching: Reflections from Today's Educators"

CHAPTER 7

THE DIGITAL REVOLUTION AND EDUCATION

The information technology revolution has brought about a drastic and far-reaching change in our ways of thinking and behaving, leading us into a period that some are calling the "Digital Renaissance" (Jukes, 2006). When was the last time you went to a printed dictionary? How often do you send texts or tweets or look up product reviews on the Internet? Even your access to the web-based videos cited in this textbook is testimony to the ways in which communication and access to information have changed in the last fifteen years. Teenagers send, on average, twenty-three hundred text messages a month!

One big question for you as a future teacher—for all of us in education—is this: Although all aspects of daily life have changed so dramatically, why have the design and conditions of classroom learning and teaching remained somewhat unchanged? I say somewhat because we do now find networked and wireless laptop computers in many public and private school classrooms, and some teachers do seize the opportunity to engage their students in new learning experiences. Many schools have classrooms that are now using electronic whiteboards, and many teachers use portable wireless devices as part of their daily teaching routines. By and large, however, traditional instruction has lagged far behind the advances in technology.

This chapter addresses the ways information, knowledge, communication, and understanding can be redefined in this digital renaissance. It also underscores the fact that the same inequities that have dogged US education since its earliest days persist in the digital age. It is important to keep in mind that even though the Internet holds the promise of infinite knowledge, what gets delivered more often than not is infinite *information* (Orenstein, 2009). Sometimes, when we are inundated with data, it is difficult to make sense of it and connect to that which is most important. It falls to the classroom teacher, in any grade level and in any subject, to ask himself or herself, "What is the best way to make use of computers, iPads, netbooks, smart phones, streaming videos, and other communication tools that are available to my students?" For some teachers, it is overwhelming to answer this question, but to ignore what is available for teaching and learning in any area of the digital universe is to deny the way your students spend their time outside of school. That being said, it remains the teacher's responsibility to access and use the technology effectively, as we will explore in this chapter. Using technological devices to enhance teaching and learning is one way of connecting to many students' lived experiences. The technology connection, however, must make sense by providing the class with an experience, a challenge, or data it could otherwise not have access to.

© ARTappler/iStockphoto

7-1 What Does Technology Mean for the Classroom?

Most likely, your future students will spend a good deal of time online. In fact, they will be **digital natives**, a term that commentators like Marc Prensky (2001) coined to refer to people who have used digital technology all their lives. One educator explains the situation this way:

> Adults used to be able to ignore, resist, or fool ourselves about the realities going on in children's lives. Once they reached our classrooms, we paid attention to their engagement with our subject matter and their classmates—the world could and did, for the most part, stay out of school. But now, these digital natives . . . cannot keep their digital selves out of the classroom. . . . The one thing we cannot do is ignore the fact that many kids are playing around creatively, finding friends, watching videos, listening to music, communicating online whether we like it or not, whether we talk about it in school or not (Ganley, 2009).

Students, and, I suspect, many of you, are also creating content and posting it online. Technology is an integral part of our lives, and more and more, it is part of the work teachers do as educators in the twenty-first century. Do not confuse digital natives with digital learners. Technology does not necessarily "teach" material, but [it can] make learning more accessible and, if properly applied, more effective (Cowan, 2011).

7-1a The Flat Classroom

Despite the fact that many of today's students are digital natives, the structure of most classrooms remains unchanged. A shift has gradually begun, however, in the way we think about teaching and learning. To borrow an idea from Thomas Friedman's bestseller *The World Is Flat* (2006), this shift involves seeing the classroom as "flat."

The term **flat classroom** refers to the ways information access levels the playing field—or should I say learning field?—in the classroom. The teacher no longer must be seen as the keeper of the true truth, the source of all that is valuable to know. A typical student, through the Internet and other digital resources, has virtually limitless access to information on any topic.

If learners are accessing the Internet from home, at night, outside of the school buildings, then it stands to reason that those same learners will ultimately influence the direction of learning at school. Immediately we can see that, in a flat classroom, the teacher must be a filter, a guide, the one who directs the learning events and helps students develop their understanding as they gain access to more and more information. Because there is easy access to content, today's students often do not have much patience for step-by-step instructions or carefully writing things down. Because perseverance is important in learning, integrating technology in the classroom has to be gradual and purposeful so that students acquire new skills, not lose qualities necessary for learning. Remember, a teacher's skill, student motivation, and the context for using technology is what helps students learn, not the technology itself.

Did You Know?

Digital natives are not necessarily digital learners.

7-1b The Connected Classroom

Do you have a smartphone? Do you access the Internet daily? Do you check your e-mail and text friends? Do you access a weather site? Shop? Participate in an online discussion? Are you a blogger? Are you on Facebook? Do you have a Twitter account? Who do you follow? Because our lives have been transformed by the information technology revolution, the life of the classroom is sometimes transformed as well.

Although schools often resist change, the past twenty years have brought a significant increase in the use of technology in US schools. In the early 1990s, one networked computer was available for every twenty students. By 2010, US schools as a whole possessed more than one instructional computer with Internet access for every three students in primary and secondary schools (NCES, 2011). By 2013, the data is likely to be more like one networked computer for every two students; in many schools today, there is one laptop for each student. As will be seen later in this chapter, though, there are significant disparities in many urban and rural areas.

Imagine you are in a connected classroom—a room with high-speed Internet access for all the students—and your class is doing research in social studies on the causes of the Civil War. Or perhaps students are exploring a science problem related to global warming. Or they may be checking real-time weather all around the world in preparation for a report on climate trends. In a connected classroom, the ease with which students can access a wide variety of information—and the seamlessness with which this information gathering can be integrated into the rest of their work—makes it possible for you to be truly creative as a teacher.

7-1c THE PROBLEM OF INFORMATION OVERLOAD

Do you ever experience problems with the wealth of information available via the Internet? Is there simply too much of it out there?

Information used to be scarce, and having more of it was considered a good thing. Now it feels as though we are at a saturation point, with more information than we will ever need. One of the disadvantages of this overload is that it is easy for some students to get overwhelmed. Many teachers who use the Internet for project- and problem-based learning caution that students need to be taught how to use inquiry-based methods powered by technology. Technology use has to be suited to the content and based on a true understanding of how learning occurs. How do students make sense of what they find online? Researchers have found that there is a lot of "digital darting" when people are surfing the Internet or even seeking targeted information (Horgan, 2010). According to Nicholas Carr, "when we go online, we enter an environment that promotes cursory reading, hurried and distracted thinking, and superficial learning." Carr worries that people are losing their capacity for the kind of sustained, deep contemplation and reflection required to read serious works of fiction or nonfiction (2010). With that in mind, teachers cannot automatically assume that when their students read something online they "get it." Learning is about making the material your own, mulling it over, and being able to express it and apply it in a new context.

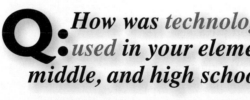

Q: How was technology used in your elementary, middle, and high schools?

Laptops have become commonplace in many classrooms. With Internet access, computers are a resource for research and a vehicle for expression.

© Ariel Skelley/Photolibrary

The following story gives a simple example of the benefits of a connected elementary school classroom; you can also see how the teacher avoids the problem of overloading her students with irrelevant information:

Ms. Frank's inner-city, third-grade class is studying China—a fact evident from the Chinese lanterns hanging along clotheslines overhead. In the current portion of the unit, the students are being challenged to design and construct a model of a Chinese hanging scroll. They must meet certain specifications; for instance, each scroll must provide three pieces of information about the inventions and customs of China. Today the students are beginning the research process for completing this design challenge, and Ms. Frank is discussing how to do research on the Internet.

The students sit at rapt attention and are visibly excited about beginning the project. They listen carefully to the directions for accessing three specific websites they will need to do their research. Ms. Frank has chosen these sites in advance because they provide easy access to the information the students need, they are at the right reading level for her class, and they do not include anything inappropriate or overly distracting.

Ms. Frank announces that students will work in groups of four, and she assigns group names based on the work students have already done on this unit. The groups are called Great Wall, Yeh-Shen, Chinese New Year, Red Envelope,

Chinese Lantern, and Dragon. The students nod and smile in recognition of the group names.

From a cabinet in the classroom, the students get their laptop computers, each of which is wirelessly connected to the Internet. There is one laptop for every two students. The groups work well together, carefully accessing the websites Ms. Frank has instructed them to go to. It is clear that they have done this kind of work before; using these laptops for research on the Internet is second nature to them. As they gather data, you can hear comments like, "The Chinese invented the compass!" and "Scroll down." Students read aloud statements about the invention of paper money and kites. In each group, the students jointly decide on the information to select from the websites, and they record their data in design portfolios.

Within a few minutes, they have collected plenty of information, and they move on to the next step in designing a hanging scroll.

Computer-based projects can include artifacts downloaded from the Web. The potential to expand upon student learning is part of technology integration.

© Patrick Olear/PhotoEdit, Inc.

When a class is researching a topic on the web, the teacher should filter the websites in advance, as Ms. Frank did, so that students do not waste their time on unproductive sources. In that way, teachers help students manage the information available and avoid problems of information overload. As you prepare units for your students, look for websites with useful links for many different topics or themes. That will make it easier for you to identify good resources for particular units. The sidebar "Guidelines for Internet Research" offers some additional hints for maximizing the web's potential as an information source for your students. In this example, the websites are a source of data that are used to complete an investigation, a design challenge. It makes it possible to have ready access to information.

7-2 Technology and Learning

In Chapter 4, we saw that learning requires the learner to be actively engaged with the material to be learned. Many educators believe that technology encourages this process. Others, like Mr. Carr, worry that students get "lost" online and lose focus.

How exactly does technology help get students involved in learning? Entire books have been written on this subject, but here is one important point: Because new technologies are *interactive*, it is easier

GUIDELINES FOR INTERNET RESEARCH

- Research is not simply a list of questions for which students find answers. Students' research should focus on finding the information they need to solve a problem or complete a project.
- As they use technology, students need to stay focused on the problem they are trying to solve or the area they are exploring.
- Guide students in interpreting and using the data they find.
- Guide students in finding creative and innovative ways to present their information.
- Encourage students to use the information they gather on the Internet to further other students' understanding of the topic.
- Invite students to collaborate with other students in designing a final product.

to create environments in which students can learn by doing, receive feedback, and continually refine their understanding. Through this process, students take charge of their own learning. By integrating technology into the classroom, you promote students' passionate involvement in their own learning, allowing them to be adaptable and flexible and to go beyond "education as usual" (Fisch, 2006). Most students are also familiar with the technologies being employed for classroom learning, and they can bring the skills of their real worlds into their classroom worlds. Today, school districts and individual schools are raising money to use iPads or other tablets in the classroom so that each student has easy access to interactive websites that allow for content to be read, listened to, observed, and experienced. The convergence of media elements such as text, audio, video, and animation into a seamless flow of content holds new promise for teaching and learning. There are more videos, for example, uploaded to YouTube in the last two months than all the television programming ever produced by the major networks since the mid-1900s (Fisch, 2011). Your role is to find the ones that have the most potential to be tools for student learning and focus the students' attention on how they will use the material and apply it to a new context.

7-2a WAYS THAT INTERNET TECHNOLOGY SUPPORTS LEARNING

The interactivity of digital technologies takes many forms, but most educators agree that, there are four major ways that it supports learning: (1) by allowing students to deal with real-world problems as part of the curriculum, (2) by expanding the possibilities for simulations and modeling, (3) by creating local and global communities of learners, and (4) by creating and uploading meaningful content.

Real-World Problems

Technology fosters the use of real-world, exciting problems in the classroom curriculum. Imagine you are working with middle school students on a unit about weather and global warming. Using the Internet, students can find real-time weather data about present conditions as well as archival data showing trends over time (see Figure 7.1). They can focus on a given part of the world or compare different areas. The learning occurs as the teacher helps the students to make sense of the data and its implications for global climate change.

Now imagine that a high school social studies class is exploring world population, comparing the number of births per day in China, India, and the United States. From the Internet, students gather the most current information related to population growth in these countries—data that have far-reaching implications for consumption of natural resources. This kind of real-world context makes the unit come alive for students. Yet the data retrieval

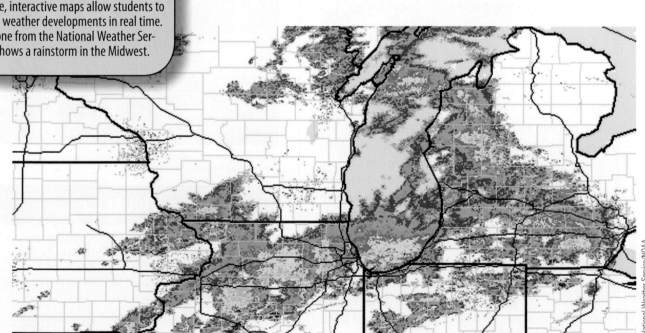

FIGURE 7.1

An Interactive Weather Map
Online, interactive maps allow students to study weather developments in real time. This one from the National Weather Service shows a rainstorm in the Midwest.

National Weather Service/NOAA

simulation A computer program or other procedure that imitates a real-world experience.

model A representation of a system or an object, such as a small physical structure that imitates a larger structure or a computer program that parallels the workings of a larger system.

augmented reality (AR) AR is a live, direct or indirect, view of a physical, real-world environment whose elements are augmented by computer-generated sensory input such as sound, video, graphics, or GPS data.

virtual reality Replaces the real world with a simulated one that has all the elements of the real world modeled by computer graphics and images.

requires only about as much time as it takes to read this paragraph! The learning occurs as the teachers helps students to analyze the data and draw conclusions about world demographics.

Simulations, Modeling, and Augmented Reality

Students can learn a great deal through **simulations**. Often these imitate real-world activities that would be impossible to bring into the classroom. Say you want your students to understand the movements of planets in the solar system. Obviously you cannot bring Mars and Venus to class, but you can use simulation software that shows the planets in motion and allows students to view the system from different positions. The story that follows is from the author's own experience using the WorldWide Telescope (WWT), available on the Internet (http://www.worldwidetelescope.org):

I have just returned from visiting the planets Mars, Jupiter, and Saturn. It was an exciting trip that revealed so many details of these planets—my, how huge Jupiter is! It took much longer to reach Jupiter from Earth than to reach Mars.

Okay, this was a virtual trip, but the views were breathtaking, and knowing I could "travel" anywhere in our solar system or the entire universe with my computer mouse was quite exciting. I was using the WorldWide Telescope available on the Internet. Replete with real images from the finest space and ground telescopes, this computer portal allows the viewer to visit real images in the solar system, the Milky Way galaxy, and beyond to other galaxies. I started on planet Earth, traveled to Mars, then Jupiter, and then on to Saturn and back to Earth. It was a quick trip in real time, but I began to get a feeling for celestial relationships: the planets that are closer to us and those

that are further; those that are much bigger than ours and those that are smaller.

The WWT is a Web 2.0 visualization software environment that enables your computer to function as a virtual telescope—bringing together imagery from the world's best ground- and space-based telescopes for the exploration of the universe. WWT blends images, information, and stories from multiple sources into a seamless, immersive, rich media experience delivered over the Internet. It allows students and adults to use its images and tell their own stories, make presentations, and share them with others. The software creates a realistic simulation with actual images taken from space. It is an extraordinary teaching tool.

Similarly, students often learn by creating **models**. For years, science students have created models of atoms and molecules, usually static ones made of plastic or Styrofoam™ pieces. With a computer, students can create atomic models in which the electrons move in cloudlike orbitals, and the software provides feedback about the correct number of protons and neutrons.

Do you suppose that simulations and models are useful mainly in the physical sciences? That is far from true. In social science, for example, simulations can model social dilemmas and engage students in finding their own creative solutions (see Figure 7.2).

SOURCE: http://www.tomsnyder.com/products/product.asp?SKU=DECCON. Permission authorized by Tom Snyder Productions.

FIGURE 7.2

Simulating the Writing of the U.S. Constitution
In this simulation from *The Constitution* (part of the *Decisions, Decisions* software series from Tom Snyder Productions), students prepare a constitution for a fictional republic that mimics the United States in the 1780s.

Extending one's perceptions of the environment belongs to a new class of images called **augmented reality (AR)**. AR is a live, direct or indirect, view of a physical, real-world environment whose elements are *augmented* by computer-generated sensory input such as sound, video, graphics, or GPS data. The view of reality is modified by a computer or even a smartphone application. As a result, the technology functions by enhancing one's current perception of reality. By contrast, **virtual reality** *replace*s the real world with a simulated one, as we saw in the prior section. AR uses the technology found in the gaming world and applies it to the real world by creating a way to infuse virtual images and events into real settings, For example, the yellow first down line on your television screen during football games is an example of AR at work. These kinds of virtual visualizations implanted onto real settings can create historical images for real buildings, demonstrate hidden sides of protected museum artifacts, or allow the user to write messages virtually on a real site. Many believe it is the future of interactivity for technology in education. Besides giving immediate feedback to users, many simulation, modeling, and AR technologies also provide opportunities for later reflection and discussion—and this point leads to a third key benefit of technology.

Communities of Learners

Many classes have their own web page, a site where teachers communicate with students and create an online extension of the classroom. The shared class web space has many uses; announcements and schedules can be posted, and areas for more informal communication can be created.

On any given topic, teachers can promote focused discussions online through the use of discussion boards or forums. You may already have participated in such reflective discussions using Blackboard courseware or a similar tool in your college classes. Later in this chapter, the rising use of blogs in educational settings will be discussed. Such technology-supported conversations can help students refine their thinking, and they help build a sense that everyone is working together in a learning community.

Technology easily extends the learning community beyond the immediate classroom. In Chapter 8, we examine the rise of global networks in which students from around the world collaborate to solve problems and share their cultures. Using technology, students from different places can work on the same projects with multiple solutions and collaborate via shared classroom websites, tweets, blogs, and e-mail. A deep sense of community is created as the groups work toward shared goals and communicate with one another about the strategies needed to solve a mutual problem.

2012 Digital Divide Infographic Highlights:

1. The Internet is responsible for 21% of economic growth in developed nations.
2. Over 6,000,000 students in the US are taking online classes.
3. 100,000,000 houses in the US still lack high-speed Internet access.
4. Almost *half* of the poorest households in the US do not own a computer.
5. Only 4% of the richest households in the US do not own a computer.
6. Minorities in the US have significantly lower rates of Internet access than whites.
7. Rural households are 2 times more likely to have dial-up Internet than urban households.
8. 96% of Americans have 2 or fewer Internet service provider (ISP) choices (lack of competition).

Adapted from http://ansonalex.com/infographics/2012-digital-divide-statistics-infographic/retrievedMarch 22, 2012.

The Flipped Classroom

Regardless of the subject area, many teachers, especially at the secondary level, use Power Point to present ideas to their classes. In 2007, software was produced that enables teachers to record a PowerPoint slide-show including voice and any annotations, and then convert the recording into a video file that could be easily distributed online. These were the tiny beginnings of a current technology movement called the "flipped classroom." Simply described, the flipped classroom gets its name from the distribution of classroom presentations as "homework"- what students need to examine before coming to class. Class time is then spent solving "homework" type problems or responding to in-depth questions as students wrestle with the content from the presentations they examined on their own.

Often, the class time is spent interacting with peers in small groups as teachers exchange ideas with students about their pressing questions and difficulties with the content.

Hence, the name, the "flipped" classroom: homework problem solving and question answering become class time and presentations by teachers using cutting edge technology become homework. The technology employed is referred to as "screencasting" and classes that employ this technology for instruction are often part of the "flipped model."

As we explore what can happen when students take more ownership of their learning by examining teacher presentations prior to coming to class, we begin to see the classroom as the hub of interaction with peers and teachers that represents teaching and learning as cognitive psychologists would describe it; a dialectic; a give and take; an interaction between peers and teachers that helps students to make meaning of content.

There are many versions of the flipped classroom, and there are educators who think of it more as an ideology than a methodology. That is, whatever it takes to interact with students and engage them in asking their own questions about the content and have them working in small groups to tease out meaning, is an important ideology about helping students to learn.

As you enter the teaching profession, look for its occurrence in the classrooms you observe and in which you participate. There may be several versions of the flipped classroom, but what is common to most is that interaction with students and students' interactions with each other are integral to the learning process and presentation time through screencasting is integral to the teaching time.

7-2b THE INTERACTIVE WEB

A surge of new technologies and social media innovations is altering the media landscape. Wikipedia, for example, was launched in 2001, and now features more than 13 million articles in more than 200 languages. A **wiki** is a website or other online resource that fosters collective authoring by allowing many users to add content or edit the existing content. Facebook is the most popular example of social media platforms that are constantly changing and new content is continuously uploaded by all who use it. These are examples of Web 2.0; some of the key aspects are:

- Data and software are continuously and seamlessly updated, often rapidly.
- User interfaces are rich and interactive.
- There is an "architecture of participation" that encourages user contributions.

To put it simply, a fundamental characteristic of Web 2.0 is this: a user can readily input information that then becomes an important source of content for other users.

Blogs

Most likely you're aware of the rapid proliferation of **blogs**, online journals on which a writer posts frequent observations and others respond with their own comments. It seems that everyone, from music fans to politicians, now has a blog. Blogs are becoming increasingly popular with teachers, too, because they offer a forum for expression for students as young as the second grade.

Blogging is not the same as using an online discussion board or discussion forum. Blogs are about "centered communication"—centered on the individual (Ganley, 2009). Blogs require a personal presence, unlike online discussion boards, which can be relatively impersonal as students respond to the questions posed by the teacher. Although discussion boards are directed and require specific, focused postings, blogging is open-ended, allowing users to add content through links called *tags*. Blogging also invites comments from online users outside of the immediate classroom community.

Blogs can be used for almost any subject. Students write about how they attacked a tough math problem, post observations about their science experiments, or display their latest art projects (Selingo, 2004). For teachers, blogs are attractive because they require little effort to maintain, unlike more elaborate classroom websites. Helped by templates found at a number of online sites, teachers can build a blog or start a new topic in an existing blog simply by typing text into a box and clicking a button.

TEACHSOURCE VIDEO CASE

Integrating Technology to Improve Student Learning

Find the TeachSource video case "Integrating Technology to Improve Student Learning: A High School Science Simulation" on the CourseMate website at www.cengagebrain.com. In this biology class, Mr. Bateman is using laptops for each student to create a simulation that relates genetic variation to appearance. After watching the video, consider the following question:

Would you consider the way Mr. Bateman integrates computer use an example of seamless integration in the science lesson? Why or why not?

Educational blogging, guided and monitored by the teacher, invites students to publish their work on the site. A related-comments link allows readers to post comments. Hence educational blogging gives students an opportunity not only to publish their writing but also to receive and respond to comments from their classmates and *the rest of the world!*

Wikis

For classroom teachers, wikis can provide a forum for student collaboration that even the shiest of students contributes to readily. Recently, a sixth-grade language arts teacher used a wiki, a collaborative website that allows students to post work, to comment on or critique the work of others, and to make revisions in a group setting. In traditional writing instruction, for example, a student writes only for the teacher or another small group of students. But when a student publishes on a wiki, "The audience includes not just the teacher but all of the other students, too, and each student can 'hear' every other student—now there is a symphony" (Bolton, 2009). The teacher expresses it this way: "The wiki is an equalizer in classroom participation; everyone has a role. It's a way to showcase their comments and their give-and-take in a medium they take to like a duck to water." This is because middle-school students are texting and using technology on a daily basis. The wiki used in this sixth-grade class requires correct grammar and spelling, a bit different from the "texting language" to which many students are accustomed.

Twitter

Twitter is an online social networking service that enables its users to send and read text-based posts of up to 140 characters, known as "tweets." It was created in March 2006 by Jack Dorsey and launched that July. A simple form of social media, Twitter makes communication among communities quick and easy because Twitter messages have a finite number of possible characters. The service rapidly gained worldwide popularity, with more than 300 million users as of 2012. Using Twitter is a handy way to be connected to other people with similar interests with whom you share ideas, ask questions, and gather data. For educators, Twitter has professional communities that link users to educational resources and to other teachers who share your ideas and questions. For classroom uses, teachers and students can share tweets and even write a story as a collaborative community. Students can create a story taking turns to contribute one line each.

The Twitter application is available on smart phones as well as all different types of computers and tablets. Teachers use Twitter to remind students of homework and assignments and provide relevant information for their next class. In a classroom setting, Twitter can be used to contribute to a discussion and also gives students and teachers a way to keep the conversation going long after the class is over.

Social media can make a useful educational tool, giving students and teachers an easy way to communicate that goes beyond the classroom. **Facebook** sites are often used in public schools to create classroom communities, which will be discussed more in Chapter 9, and to communicate to parents about classroom news.

Facebook

Facebook is a social networking service and website that by 2012 had more than 845 million users worldwide. Many of you, I suspect, have your own Facebook page as do I. Users must register before using the site, after which they may create a personal profile, add other users as friends, and exchange messages, including automatic notifications when they update their profile. Additionally, users may join common-interest user groups, organized by workplace, school or college, or other characteristics, and categorize their friends into lists such as "People from Work" or "Close Friends."

You can use Facebook as a communications hub. Create a public page or smaller closed group for your classes to keep parents informed, distribute homework or permission slips, and share photos or videos from classroom activities or field trips. Anyone can "like" a page on Facebook, and students who do will see updates in their News Feed. Groups, on the other hand, allow you to limit membership to only those you approve. You can also e-mail all the members of a group. Maintaining a page or group is also a useful way to establish a presence as a teacher without blurring the line between your personal and professional lives. You can interact with parents, students and colleagues via your page or group, called

Twitter An online social networking service that enables its users to send and read text-based posts of up to 140 characters, known as "tweets."

Facebook A social networking service and website that, by 2012, had more than 845 million users worldwide. Users must register before using the site, after which they may create personal profiles, add other users as friends, and exchange messages, including automatic notifications when they update their profiles.

something like "Ms. Smith's 9th Grade English Class." It is important that you understand and comply with your school's social media policies (http://www.facebook.com/safety/groups/teachers/, retrieved March 19, 2012).

Engaging with students online through Facebook is one way to model appropriate communication online as well as offline. Facebook publishes tips for teachers as they use this platform with their students.

Implications of Web 2.0

Think about the implications of Facebook, Twitter, blogs, wikis, and similar developments. In the current wave of wireless communication, handheld devices have implications for teaching and learning and for assessment. The end user of the content or information is also an author of content, along with everyone else who is interested in a given topic. This situation challenges our thinking about information and its reliability and veracity. With Web 2.0 technology, not only "experts" have access to cutting-edge information; there is increasing reliance on communities of experts that are redefined to include us all.

Did You Know?

The number of text messages sent and received by the average teenager monthly is over 2300.

This is the flat classroom on a global scale, and it has important implications for the way we teach and learn. Again we are reminded that the most meaningful learning involves inquiry processes, reflection, and active, committed participation by the learner.

7-3 Parents, Teachers, and Students Online

Parents have new tools with which to track student progress at school. Several companies have developed software products that allow parents to view a password protected web-based grade book that tracks student attendance, homework completion, and grades on tests and projects. The site may also be like a class web page or Facebook page and indicate what the homework assignment is for each class, the due dates, and the criteria for the assignment. Many parents and teachers have embraced the use of these software tools because it fosters consistent communication between parents and teachers. Although teachers have used e-mail as a form of communication to parents, these secure websites allow parents to intervene early if students need guidance because they can be updated daily on their child's performance. It allows teachers to communicate with parents on a timely basis.

It should be noted that software companies have specialized in services for schools, teachers, students, and parents. Often, a school, district or county hires a software company to meet the needs of their locale providing electronic services to teachers, parents, and students and enhancing communication. As recently as five to ten years ago, parents had to wait for written progress reports to learn how their children were doing in school. Now, those data may be readily available on their smartphones! Paper grade books are a thing of the past for most teachers in most schools and districts across the country. Opinion is mixed on whether the web-based record keeping is more or less work for the classroom teacher. What do *you* think?

7-4 Internet Safety

So far in this chapter, the many advantages that students can reap from ready access to the Internet and ease of connectivity have been discussed. But teachers must also consider students' safety in online communication.

Experts agree on several areas of concern (National School Boards Foundation, 2007):

1. Young people may accidentally stumble onto websites that are violent, pornographic, or objectionable because of inappropriate language and content.
2. "Cyberstalking" and threats from online predators pose threats to children's and teenagers' safety. Drawn to social networking, students may reveal personal, identifying information to predators without realizing it.

3. Online marketing aimed directly at children and teens influences young people's decisions about products and brands. This can undermine parental authority in much the same way that television advertising can. The difference is that Internet advertising is not regulated by the government, and exposure is often more intense.
4. The interactive, two-way nature of the web gives marketers the ability to collect data about individual computer users. Companies collect personal information about children and teens as their websites encourage youngsters to share their hobbies, interests, and other personal preferences. This invasion of privacy is commonplace on the Internet.

Chapter 9 addresses an additional concern, "cyberbullying," which can have devastating consequences for individual students and for which some school districts are held liable. Cyberbullying refers to willful and repeated harm inflicted through the use of computers, cell phones, and other electronic devices. It occurs when a child, preteen, or teen is tormented, threatened, harassed, humiliated, embarrassed, or otherwise targeted by another child, preteen, or teen using the Internet, interactive and digital technologies, or mobile phones. It has to have a minor on both sides, or at least have been instigated by a minor against another minor (http://www.stopcyberbullying.org/what_is_cyberbullying_exactly.html, retrieved March 23, 2012). Cyberbullying has become more prevalent as teens' use of texting on cell phones and posting on Facebook pages and Twitter accounts on their smartphones has skyrocketed in the last five years.

All of these are important issues, and school districts have taken steps to address them. Most school districts and libraries have installed blocking and filtering technologies to safeguard against offensive websites. Schools and districts are also implementing "Net safety" workshops and discussions. As a teacher, you need to be aware of the potential problems in students' Internet and wireless electronics use and make sure sufficient safeguards are in place.

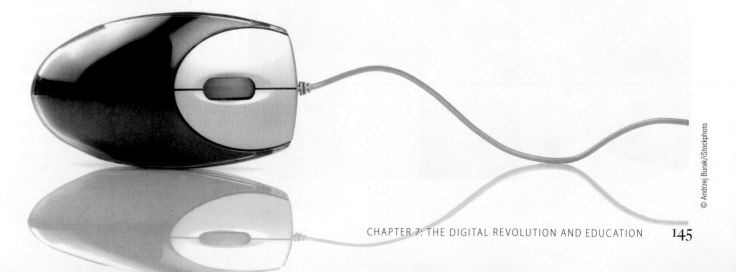

Chapter 9 addresses how to create community in the classroom and provides more information on cyberbullying.

7-5 The Digital Divide

Although all students are expected to develop **technological fluency**, some struggle if they come from schools and home backgrounds in which technology is not widely accessible. Later in life, they will be at a disadvantage for technology-based tasks, and they may even miss out on educational opportunities that involve technological resources (Kim & Bagaka, 2005, p. 319). In a world that is so information-rich, we have to remember that technology access is not equal.

According to Wikipedia, the **digital divide**, a term coined by David Bolt in 2000 in a book of the same name, is "the gap between those with regular, effective access to digital technologies and those

without." On one side of the divide, people have easy access to technological resources and know how to use them. On the other side, people have substantially less access, less experience, and correspondingly less knowledge. It was the US Department of Commerce that first coined the term *digital divide*. The distinction is not only between those who have computer access at home and those who do not. The digital divide also refers to the *quality* of hardware, software, and connectivity that is available to users across social classes.

Who are those with less technological access and experience? Families living below the poverty line rarely have computers and broadband connections in their homes. Students living in poverty are twice as likely as other students to access the Internet at school only. Although instructional computers have become commonplace in high-needs, high-poverty schools, the existence of the computers and the broadband connections does not fully make up for the lack of mobile technology access outside of school and the absence of computers in the home.

Access to computers at home has been found to be an important factor in students' ability to use computer resources for word processing, information processing and presenting, and other types of communication, including connecting through social media platforms. For many students in poor urban areas, public libraries provide a free option for Internet access, and Internet cafés may be nearby as well. Still, people are more likely to make regular use of an Internet connection at home than anywhere else. And for students in poor rural areas, Internet-enabled public libraries and coffee shops are rare. Rarer still is the student from rural or poor urban areas who has access to smartphone technology or other portable, mobile web devices.

To help underserved populations develop technological fluency, a means of closing this technology gap caused by lack of access at home and in informal learning environments where young people are increasingly using small mobile devices to access the Internet must be found.

Q: *In your view, what are the most important reasons for integrating technology in schools?*

Students with Internet access at home have an advantage over those whose families are not able to afford it. This creates a digital divide.

© Elizabeth Crews

7-6 Assistive Technology

A chapter on digital technology would not be complete without a brief discussion of assistive technology. The term **assistive technology (AT)** refers to devices that promote greater independence for people with disabilities by enabling them to perform tasks that would otherwise be difficult or impossible. AT can take many forms, from simple to complex. For students with visual impairments, for example, a simple type of AT is a keyboard with large symbols that makes it easier for the students to type. A more complex form is speech recognition software that converts the student's spoken words into text on the screen. Similarly, screen reader software can read aloud the information displayed on a computer screen.

In the past, for blind students who read by means of Braille (a writing system that uses raised dots identifiable by touch), curriculum materials were usually converted through a lengthy process that required two to four weeks' lead time. Now, with computer technology, relevant materials can be converted at the time they are needed. With a computer program, text that the teacher types into a word-processing document is transformed into Braille and printed on a Braille printer within seconds. This technology makes it possible for the teacher to include blind students in the same activity as the rest of the class at the same moment.

For disabled students whose fine motor skills do not allow them to write easily and without pain, note taking is an arduous task. Teachers with interactive whiteboards in their classrooms can save the notes written on the board and print them for these students. An **interactive whiteboard**, typically the size of a regular chalkboard, is linked to a computer. Teachers can project images from the computer onto the board. When a student or the teacher writes on the board with a special marker, the notes can be saved as text in the computer.

In the following story, students with a wide range of learning disabilities experience a lesson on maps using a SMART Board, one brand of interactive whiteboard:

On the day that I visit their classroom, the ten students in Ms. Mandel's self-contained special education second-grade class are learning about maps.

Seated on a carpeted area in front of a SMART Board, they tell me that a map is a bird's-eye view of the earth from above.

Ms. Mandel chats with the children about maps that are found on the subway, on trains, in the mall, and at a major sports complex. She uses the SMART Board to display different types of maps. One map has roads, street names, stores, gas stations, and houses. There is a produce map with images relating to fruits and vegetables grown in New York, where the school is located. Still other maps show weather changes, vacation spots, and geographic features.

The children can manipulate a pointer and direct it to different images on the map. By manipulating the image of a car or a plane, they can take a ride from one destination to another. Taking turns with the pointer, the students respond to questions on cards located in a wall "pocket" next to the SMART Board. Each card has a number corresponding to the map type and a question like, "How would you get from Amy's house to The Home Depot?" or "What is the name of the town closest to the dairy farm?"

Deeply engaged in this activity, the students do well manipulating objects and moving them to destinations on the SMART Board. They are using the technology creatively. One student tells me, "We are having a great time." The questions on the cards involve the class in interpreting symbols,

> **assistive technology (AT)** A device or service that increases the capabilities of people with disabilities.
>
> **interactive whiteboard** A whiteboard that works together with a computer to display and save information.

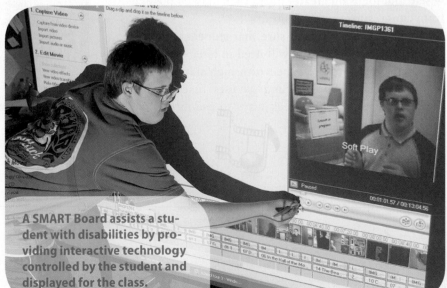

A SMART Board assists a student with disabilities by providing interactive technology controlled by the student and displayed for the class.

© John Birdsall/Image Works

locations, and directions, and I am struck by the way these students with various learning disabilities are making sense of the maps and are developing higher-order thinking skills.

This story highlights ways technology can reduce or eliminate the barriers to learning experienced by students with disabilities. But do not suppose that only "special" technology is suitable for these students. The technology you use with all your other students—the same technology that enhances meaningful learning, reflection, and discussion—also provides benefits for those who are disabled. For instance, a student who struggles to write with pen or pencil may find it much easier to write on a computer.

7-7 Concluding Thoughts

Although teachers look forward to new ways of teaching students, they face many challenges imagining how the traditional classroom is becoming transformed to reflect the high-tech world around us. Remember that as exciting the new technologies are, they are tools for learning and teaching, not the end in itself.

In the flat classroom, the traditional hierarchy is broken down. Many students can find information as quickly as teachers can and that means our role as teachers must change accordingly. Teachers should take full advantage of the ways technology can promote independent learning through real-world projects, simulations, and collaborative investigations. At the same time, teachers have to guide students in negotiating the overload of information so that they use their time wisely and focus on greater depth than may be possible from casual surfing of websites.

Teachers should make sure that students gain the technological fluency they will need in later life. To do so, teachers need to meet their own high standards for understanding technology and its uses in education. Further, teachers need to seek ways to use technology to "level the learning field," so that all of the students are served equitably by our schools.

Finally, a study from the Kaiser Family Foundation (2010) revealed that the average young American now spends nearly every waking minute, *except for the time in school*, using a smartphone, computer, tablet, netbook, television, or other electronic device. Those ages eight to eighteen spend more than seven hours and thirty-eight minutes a day with such devices, and that does not count the hour and a half that youths spend texting or the half-hour they talk on their cell phones. It is significant to note that most teachers in most schools in the country ask students to "shut down" their devices when they enter the classroom. Although that is certainly appropriate from the standpoint of socializing during teaching and learning time, just think about how empowering it would be for educators and students to use these devices for the very purpose of teaching and learning. Teachers must acknowledge the students' lived experiences and use them as tools for learning.

STUDY TOOLS
CHAPTER 7

Located at back of the textbook
- Rip out Chapter Review Card
- Note-Taking Assistance

Located at CengageBrain.com
- Review Key Terms Flash Cards (Print or Online)
- Complete Practice Quizzes to prepare for tests
- Complete "Crossword Puzzle" to review key terms
- Watch the TeachSource Video Case "Integrating Technology to Improve Student Learning: A High School Science Simulation"

WHY CHOOSE?

Every 4LTR Press solution comes complete with a visually engaging textbook in addition to an interactive eBook. Go to CourseMate for (TEACH2) to begin using the eBook. Access at **www.cengagebrain.com**

Complete the Speak Up survey in CourseMate at **www.cengagebrain.com**

 Follow us at **www.facebook.com/4ltrpress**

CHAPTER 8

GLOBALIZATION AND EDUCATION

© Tanya Constantine/Blend Images/Photolibrary

> *More people collaborate and connect on more stuff than in any other time in the history of the world.*
> —Thomas Friedman, *The World Is Flat* (2006)

In this chapter, several ways that education is changing in the digital age are examined. As a result of seamless and portable access to the Internet, students and teachers from all over the world can communicate electronically, sharing their cultures, their school lives, and their larger world. Students can work side by side even if they live thousands of miles apart. Students can now take courses online from anywhere in the world, and online high schools are emerging as the line between virtual and classroom-based learning continues to blur. Currently, about 275,000 students are said to be enrolled full-time in online programs (Schwartz, 2011).

Let us explore how this interaction occurs and what it means for students.

8-1 Online Education in the Knowledge Economy

Teachers are educating students to become part of an information society in which the creation, distribution, and manipulation of information is a significant economic and cultural activity. The **knowledge**

LEARNING OUTCOMES

After reading this chapter, you should be thinking about the following ideas:

8-1 Explain how online high schools can foster critical thinking and collaboration in the global marketplace of ideas.

8-2 Explain why globalization can enhance the learning experiences and the lives of today's students.

8-3 Describe how the language of the digital age helps students to take control of their own learning.

economy is this society's economic counterpart. In the knowledge economy, businesses operate through the collaboration and shared problem solving of people across the globe, transforming information into creative innovations for an ever-changing technological world.

In June 2012, thirty students graduated from a little known high school: Stanford Online High school, begun by the elite university of the same name. The University of Nebraska, George Washington University, and the University of Missouri are among the many other colleges and universities that are awarding high school diplomas while charging private school tuition and offering financial aid. In addition, thousands of other students, enrolled in concrete schools, take one or more online courses per year from the many offerings available through new online high schools, sponsored both by universities and for-profit online schools that are proliferating rapidly. More than 1.5 million students were enrolled in online courses in 2010 (Queen and Lewis, 2011)

The term **online learning** can be used to refer to a wide range of programs that use the Internet to provide instructional materials and facilitate interactions between teachers and students and in some cases among students as well. Online learning can be *fully online*, with all instruction taking place through the Internet, or online elements can be combined with face-to-face interactions in what is known as *blended learning* (Horn and Staker, 2011). Although there is little research examining the impact of online learning on educational productivity for secondary school students at this time, the International Association for Online Learning (iNACOL), a nonprofit advocacy group, has several reports related to effective online teaching and learning that you will find useful should you be asked as a new teacher to teach an online course.

knowledge economy
An economic system in which the use and exchange of knowledge plays a dominant role. In this kind of economy, knowledge is both an economic asset and a key product.

online learning The use of the Internet to provide programs of study or individual courses that offer instructional materials and interactions between teachers and students.

What do you think it would be like to be a student in an online high school? Thirty states, as well as Washington, D.C., have full-time, state-wide online schools (Watson, et al., 2011). The typical online high school student lives in a remote area, was previously home-schooled, or is deeply involved in an extracurricular activity that is incompatible with a traditional brick-and-mortar school setting. The students in a typical class session at Stanford Online High simultaneously watch a streamed lecture with video clips, diagrams, and animations. When they have comments or questions, students click into a queue and teachers call on them by choosing their audio stream, which can be heard by all. If any of you have participated in an interactive Webinar, it is similar. Another instant-messaging window allows for constant discussion among students, so there are frequent interactions (Schwartz, 2011). In many cases, you are seeing the students' faces in the online class and responding to them as you would in person. The students who are taking a full five-course load at Stanford Online High must be present for ten seminars a week, sixty to ninety minutes, and an additional fifteen to twenty minutes that are recorded by the teachers and viewable asynchronously. If you are wondering how students are assessed, those at Stanford must find a Stanford-approved proctor to oversee their exams.

Because the world is a global marketplace, some states require online learning for high school graduation. Michigan was the first to do so in 2006. Educators and policy makers want to ensure that high school graduates are proficient with information communication technologies. As well, the top reasons why school districts make online learning opportunities available to their students is to provide courses not otherwise available at their schools and to provide opportunities for students to recover course credits from classes missed or failed (Watson, et al., 2011). As we will discuss in this chapter, community, state, national, and global collaborations are part of functioning in the twenty-first-century marketplace. This challenges teachers to think about how to create learning opportunities online because many schools offer blended courses and most students engaged in online courses work from their schools.

APPLICATIONS OF ONLINE LEARNING FOR INCREASING EDUCATIONAL PRODUCTIVITY

Adapted from the US Department of Education. Office of Educational Technology Report, January 2012. http://www.ed.gov/technology

1) **Broadening access** in ways that dramatically reduce the cost of providing access to quality educational resources and experiences, particularly for students in remote locations or other situations where challenges such as low student enrollments make the traditional school model impractical;

2) **Engaging students in active learning** with instructional materials and access to a wealth of resources that can facilitate the adoption of research-based principles and best practices from the learning sciences, an application that might improve student outcomes without substantially increasing costs;

3) **Individualizing and differentiating instruction** based on student performance on diagnostic assessments and preferred pace of learning, thereby improving the efficiency with which students move through a learning progression;

4) **Personalizing learning** by building on student interests, which can result in increased student motivation, time on task, and, ultimately, better learning outcomes;

5) **Making better use of teacher and student time** by automating routine tasks and enabling teacher time to focus on high-value activities;

6) **Reducing school-based facilities costs** by leveraging home and community spaces in addition to traditional school buildings.

8-1a THE FLAT WORLD

In his best-selling book *The World Is Flat*, Thomas Friedman (2006) uses the metaphor of a flat world to describe the leveling of the playing field on which industrialized and emerging-market countries compete. Friedman recounts many examples of **globalization** in which companies in India and China are becoming part of global supply chains that extend across oceans, providing everything from service representatives and X-ray interpretation to component manufacturing. He also describes how these changes are made possible through intersecting technologies, particularly the Internet.

In a flat world, Friedman explains, the work done by corporations is no longer conducted vertically—that is, in a structure of workers and supervisors with each person at each level having different specific tasks. Rather, much of the work has gone horizontal: corporate analysts examine each step in a process and ask whether the firm is a leader in that step; if not, they determine who in the world can best do that work at the appropriate level of quality and the lowest possible cost. The firm then contracts with providers for each service; the firm itself performs only those functions it does best. This arrangement is known as *outsourcing*, and many functions formerly performed by US workers are now being outsourced to workers in other countries who can do these jobs better, more cheaply, and faster. Remember, one does not have to be in the same geographical location to be a coworker in a company.

Like the flat classroom described in Chapter 7, the flat world creates significant challenges for teaching and learning. We are facing educational decisions that will "ultimately determine not merely whether some of our children get 'left behind' but also whether an entire generation of kids will fail to make the grade in a global economy because they can't think their way through abstract problems, work in teams, distinguish good information from bad or speak a language other than English" (Wallis & Steptoe, 2006). Yet there are still school classrooms that resemble the ones our grandparents attended—with the teacher front and center and the students listening and writing at their desks. Clearly, our educational system has a lot of adapting to do.

> **globalization** The increase of global connectivity, integration, and interdependence in economic, cultural, social, and technological spheres.

8-1b THE GLOBAL STUDENT: HAVING INFORMATION VERSUS CONSTRUCTING KNOWLEDGE

One of the first steps in preparing ourselves and our students to function in a data-rich global knowledge economy is to explore the ways in which having a lot of information is different from gaining a lot of knowledge.

In today's digital age, *learning how to learn* becomes more important than *what* we learn. Thus, it is the individual with curiosity, imagination, and a passion for learning who will be most successful in the global knowledge economy. Curious students work hard at learning and eagerly find new opportunities to learn. Hence, when we gather information, we reflect on it, apply it to different contexts, examine its meaning, and try to communicate it to others . . . and then we are starting to be knowledgeable. Finally, we can create something new and innovative out of what we have learned and we then reach the apex of Bloom's Taxonomy, discussed in Chapter 4.

Working together to accomplish a task can be face-to-face or virtual.

© Michael Newman/PhotoEdit, Inc.

Learning How to Learn

The kind of information teachers used to ask students to memorize is now available on the Internet, usually just a few keystrokes or taps on the touch screen away. Consider this memorable anecdote:

> Learn the names of the rivers in South America. That was the assignment given to Deborah Stipek's daughter Meredith in school, and her mom, who's Dean of the Stanford University School of Education, was not impressed. "That's silly," Stipek told her daughter. "Tell your teacher that if you need to know anything besides the Amazon, you can look it up on Google" (Wallis and Steptoe, 2006).

Because simple facts are easy to locate, today's students require what educators refer to as more *depth* of understanding and less *breadth*. In other words, key ideas and topics should dominate the curriculum, not lists of facts that can be found easily enough on the Web.

Educators also talk about the importance of **metacognition**, the understanding of one's own learning processes. Students with metacognitive skills know how to approach a learning task. They have good learning strategies. In other words, they have learned how to learn.

The projects and problems described in Chapters 6 and 7 illustrate some ways of developing metacognitive skills and depth of understanding. As students work in teams, both in their classrooms and online, they risk making mistakes on their journey to finding solutions and consensus. They develop critical thinking, making connections between ideas and events, and they learn how to keep on learning.

Worldwide Collaboration

Knowing how to work with others to solve a problem is an essential skill, but knowing how to collaborate across a digital learning environment adds another dimension. Around the world, teachers are using online education tools to bring a global perspective to their students by developing cross-cultural education projects to bring the diverse cultures of the world into their classrooms.

A growing number of schools are using Skype videoconferencing to collaborate nationally and globally. Skype is free communication software that allows you to make calls, instant message, and video conference online. Imagine your class is reading a book by a favorite author and the author is your Skype guest where the students communicate through the class SMART Board in real time! Mike Artnell, an author and artist, virtually visits elementary school classrooms thousands of miles from where he lives and the students engage with him about his stories and his illustrations. He demonstrates his drawing techniques and engages students in the wonders of his creativity (http://www.teachhub.com/using-skype-classroom).

Teachers and students can Skype with partner classrooms across the country or across the world. Imagine taking your class on an "around-the-world" field trip. Collaborative project-based learning is easily accomplished through Skype for educators' website (http://education.skype.com). There are projects listed that invite collaborating classes from all over the world. In one project students from Iran, Taiwan, and Delaware planned the autumn week in which they would plant daffodil bulbs. They then looked for their emergence in the spring, carefully observing when they started to bloom and taking the air temperature each day. Each class kept a record of the weather indicators and their latitude and longitude; the photos of the daffodils and their weather data were shared on a project website (https://sites.google.com/site/daffodilandtulip/). Students got to experience what latitude and longitude really meant when they located their partner schools on a world map. Climate patterns and global climate change became a topic of conversation.

Another collaborative project site has been around for more than twenty years. The International Education and Resource Network, iEARN is a nonprofit organization made up of more than thirty thousand schools and youth organizations in more than 130 countries. iEARN empowers teachers and young people to work together online using the Internet and other new communications technologies. More than 2 million students each day are engaged in collaborative project work worldwide (http://www.iearn.org/). There are more than 150 projects in iEARN, all designed and facilitated by teachers and students to fit their curriculum and classroom needs and schedules. Projects take place in the iEARN Collaboration Centre. To join, participants select an online project and look at how they can integrate it into their classroom. With the project selected, teachers and students enter online forum spaces to meet one another and get involved in ongoing projects with classrooms around the world who are working on the same project.

Collaborative projects not only help teach content but also help students to develop twenty-first-century skills such as communication, time management, teamwork, and facilitation. These are essential skills, as will be explored in the following section. These skills enable students to function globally and cooperatively, sharing information and ideas and learning how to "to think outside the box"—a necessary skill for promoting innovation.

Skills for the Twenty-First Century

Jean Pennycook is a science educator who studies Adelie penguins on Cape Royds in Antarctica. Each year she travels there to observe the penguins and the shrinking polar ice and communicate, through her web cam, with classrooms all over the world. Her work is one example of the ways that our global reach has shrunk the size and scope of our world, making accessible to students a vast array of experiences that would otherwise remain hidden from them. What types of skills do our students need to navigate these virtual terrains? Twenty-first century skills include:

Knowing More about the World. Kids are global citizens now. They need to understand the world economy, be able to identify the nations in the developed and developing world, become sensitive to foreign cultures, and learn foreign languages.

Thinking Outside the Box. Students need to think creatively to solve problems, seeing patterns where others may see chaos. As the report confirms, it is interdisciplinary combinations—such as design and technology, mathematics and art, music and science—that spawn really innovative ideas and products for the global economy. Creativity expert Ken Robinson (2006) believes that "we get educated out of creativity" in school. It is essential, therefore, to foster creative problem solving by providing students with challenging problems and guiding them to find solutions.

Managing New Sources of Information. Students need to develop skills that help them manage the vast amount of information to which they are exposed. For one thing, they must learn to distinguish between reliable and unreliable information.

Developing Good People Skills. With so much being accomplished online, we can get the mistaken notion that good people-to-people communication is unnecessary in today's marketplace. However, as noted previously, most recent innovations involve collaboration among teams of people. The ability to work and communicate with others—often people from different cultures—is essential.

8-2 Teaching in the Global Classroom

After all that has been said so far about the flat world, the global student, and the needs of a technology-driven world, you must be wondering, "What does this mean for teaching?"

First of all, it means that your job as a teacher is to demonstrate a love and a passion for learning. In the words of Thomas Friedman (2006), "You can't light the fire of passion in someone else if it does not burn in you to begin with" (p. 305). You can not expect your students to become curious and inventive if you do not display those qualities yourself.

Second, it means that you should help students develop the necessary areas of understanding and skills we have mentioned: knowledge of the world; the ability to collaborate; metacognitive skills; the skills of managing, interpreting, validating, and acting on information; and the willingness to think outside the box to come up with new solutions.

It is an exciting time to be a teacher if you imagine how much you are learning from your status as a digitally connected adult and then imagine what is possible for your soon-to-be-global students.

For example, an ambitious global communication project engaged sixth-grade students from several countries in collaborating to design a website that provides information about artificial intelligence:

"Good evening, Earthling!" says the greeting on a website called Artificial Intelligence: Manufactured Minds. This site provides links and animations that address the history and uses of artificial intelligence as well as the ethical questions involved. Its topics range from neural networks to the meaning of consciousness. The site is an impressive achievement, especially when you realize that it was designed by high school students—and that the students are from New Hampshire, South Australia, and India.

You can find this site in the library at ThinkQuest.org (http://library.thinkquest.org/05aug/01158/index.html). For a window into the world of global high school

Students are learning over a large distance through videoconferencing. Technology makes virtual classrooms possible.

© Syracuse Newpapers/Dick Blume/The Image Works

corporations have developed websites dedicated to this kind of networked project-based learning

8-2a TEACHING WITH DIGITAL MEDIA

In the project space of the Skype for Education website (http://education.skype.com/projects), a teacher from Japan posted the following suggestion for a collaborative project:

My high school and jr. high is in Hiroshima prefecture in Japan. We are interested in using Skype to help our students practice their English, learn about foreign cultures, and basically have a "window to the world."

High School or Jr. High School classes who want to participate in some form of cultural exchange, comparing and contrasting different foods, clothing, music, pop culture, customs—you know, nothing too heavy—using simple English, come together once in a while with prepared questions and something that they want to present—and hopefully gain understanding and respect for others while practicing English.

A teacher from Oklahoma, not far from Tulsa, responded to this teacher's request and a conversation between the classes occurred. Exploring the projects can offer a sense of the scope and magnitude of teaching in a digital world. There are so many possibilities!

Gaming

gaming Used in this context, gaming refers to playing computer and video games. Video game culture is a form of new media that has enormous potential for teaching and learning.

collaboration, look at the Colophon section of the website, where the creators describe their backgrounds and their process of teamwork. I loved reading about the creators and discovering how they learned from each other as they worked on this project. You will, too.

In addition to being an amazing example of cross-cultural collaboration, this story demonstrates the use of project-based learning to foster the type of creative thinking students need in a knowledge economy. ThinkQuest (http://www.thinkquest.org), sponsored by the Oracle Education Foundation, offers a project-based learning experience to students and teachers around the world. It is a competition in which nobody loses. The challenge is for students, grades 4 through 12, to work in teams to design and build innovative and educational websites to share with the world. Teachers and students select from a broad range of educational categories and topics. The teams that work on the website collaborate via Skype, Internet chat, and online forums. Global perspectives are encouraged.

Collaboration of this sort—students from diverse areas of the world working on a project that requires multiple ways of thinking and knowing—can become cumbersome and complex without a well-organized structure. Luckily, in addition to ThinkQuest, other educational foundations, organizations, and

Gaming has the potential to change education as video games permeate our culture and schools use them for learning. When developed correctly, games can engage players in learning that is specifically applicable to school curriculum (Klopfer, et al., 2009). PBS offers educational games for young learners in content areas including math, reading, science, social studies, music, and art. Trends in serious gaming for education suggest that video games can enhance classroom learning by having a positive effect on a broad range of learning outcomes including engagement, motivation, content mastery, and sustained interest in the subject area (Young, et al., 2012). It should be noted, however, that careful research studies of video games and their affect on achievement is complicated by research measures that are not yet perfected.

So, what can we say about the benefits of gaming for learning? First, the type of games being explored should be defined. Serious games are those that are designed for a primary purpose other than our entertainment; examples are **digital learning games**. They are those that target the acquisition of knowledge as its own end and foster habits of mind and understanding that are generally useful or used within an academic context (Klopfer, et al., 2009, p. 21). Learning games are associated with formal or informal learning environments or with self-learners interested in acquiring new knowledge or understanding. Although there is little hard and fast research to correlate video gaming with student achievement, there are promising findings (Young, et al., 2012): (1) Digital learning games for language learning show evidence of enhancing student learning, not only by the users, but by those watching the games played as well; and (2) deep understanding of content takes time, reflection, and active engagement, which are strengths of video games. Although, studies in language learning, for example, point to promising impacts that video gaming can have on student achievement, there needs to be further study of the pedagogical benefits of particular game mechanics that can then be integrated into other content area games.

Other research suggests that in addition to being motivating, playing video games affects brain function and plasticity (Bavelier, 2009). Some research indicates that playing action video games on a regular basis can alter a player's attention skills. These include low-level vision, monitoring several objects at once, or searching through a cluttered scene; multitasking; task-switching; and a general speeding up of perceptual processing. Exploring video games from PBS for primary-grade learners reveals a host of choices where the learners are problem solvers. They acquire understanding through the multistep processes of solving the problems as they play the games. An art education game downloaded from one site contains paintings from great masters belonging to various periods of artistic creation, from the early Renaissance to Surrealism and beyond. As the game unfolds, the paintings are reorganized and some are missing—students need to find the missing works of art and place them in their proper period. All this happens quickly, with fifth graders manipulating the mouse and discovering how to make the best display. Players today are often using tablets to engage with the games, eliminating the need for a mouse.

"Business Education" is a set of online high school games that tests students' knowledge of business strategies. Users create their own company and product and participate in simulations, including the Business Game, the Entrepreneurship Game, and the Finance Game. In this high school program, simulations approach reality as students need to apply the principles they have learned in their business education classes. The Business Game gives students the chance to experience a business scenario in which they develop and market a new product. This provides training in pricing issues, product positioning, sales and marketing budgets, stock levels, and production versus demand. Students build relationships with simulated mentors and coworkers through daily interaction using e-mail and video phone calls (Schaffhauser, 2010). According to contemporary data, today's high school students take simulations seriously and do not see them as "second-best" to the real thing. Although different from learning games, simulations offer a somewhat risk-free environment, one where learners are free to experiment, make mistakes, and rethink and redesign without fear of destroying something that cannot be easily replenished in a traditional setting. A report from MIT suggests that, although gaming and simulations can not single-handedly change the way a subject matter is taught, they can promote deeper understanding through active engagement. "Games [promote] understanding, motivation, and enjoyment and are terrific at immersing players in complex, feedback-rich problem spaces. And while they are most often not sufficient in and of themselves for a course of study, they can help many students advance beyond the temporary memorization of facts and procedures, attainments that are usually lost when classes stop" (Klopfer, et al., 2009).

8-2b DIGITALLY INCLINED

Teachers report that their students prefer **digital media** over other types of instruction and that digital media increases student motivation and stimulates discussions. According to this study, teachers also believe digital

digital learning games These games target the acquisition of knowledge as its own end and foster habits of mind and understanding that are generally useful or used within an academic context.

digital media Web-interactive video games, podcasts, and lesson plans downloaded to digital devices such as laptops, mobile devices, DVDs, and CDs.

virtual school An institution that exists in cyberspace, teaching all of its classes online.

media supports their own creativity and student creativity. What is really significant here is acknowledging the many types of digital media to which students are exposed and then asking ourselves, "How can these media serve teaching and learning and extend our understanding of the world?" As you are well aware, ever-increasing numbers of teachers are joining virtual professional communities and many use social networking tools in their personal and professional lives. These technologies, available globally, hold the promise of exciting changes in K–12 education. These include using digital media to foster more engaging, creative, and collaborative learning environments; engaging students in using new tools to produce content and take charge of their learning; and creating more possibilities for real-time cross-cultural conversations with students from all over the world.

Precollege students who take online courses to supplement traditional courses offered at their brick-and-mortar schools are changing the face of US public education. These virtual classes are becoming more and more popular. In *synchronous* distance learning, students are virtually present through the Internet at the same point in time. More commonly, though, the learning environment is *asynchronous*—that is, students from different geographical areas work at different times.

As we mentioned previously in this chapter, one of the significant advantages of **virtual schools** is that they can provide courses otherwise unavailable to a local student. This is especially important in rural areas, where one school often serves all students from prekindergarten to twelfth grade and the financial resources for extensive enrichment courses are unavailable. Some school districts form partnerships with a distance learning firm that tracks open seats in distance learning courses and offers them to school districts at discounted rates.

In the typical arrangement, similar to the one described at Stanford Online High School, students who take courses online communicate daily with the teacher, who may be in some other part of the country or even in another nation. Yet students do much of their course work independently on their own schedule. Usually a school guidance counselor

QUESTIONS FOR TEACHING AN ONLINE COURSE

To prepare for teaching an online course, you need to ask yourself questions like these:

- What do I hope the online students will get out of this course?
- Why have I been teaching this course in this particular way?
- What needs to change for the online environment? Which elements of my lesson plans do I keep? Which do I leave out?
- How do I substitute an online activity for something I have done face-to-face?
- How can I foster group work and collaboration among students who are physically far apart?
- How can I improve the way I communicate with students?

SOURCE: Adapted from Pape, et al. (2005).

stays in touch to make sure students are keeping pace with the work required from the online course. Naturally, some students are better at independent work than others; for some students, online courses at the precollege level are not the best choice. The value of an online course depends in part on the individual's maturity, work habits, and motivation.

Online courses can enroll students from many localities and even from many countries. Learning to work with such a diverse group enhances precollege students' abilities to be team problem solvers and to appreciate the contributions of people from radically different environments.

What does an online environment mean for teaching? When teachers are asked to develop an online course from a

© geopaul/iStockphoto

A teacher addresses several groups of students separated by large distances in a virtual classroom.

course they are used to teaching face-to-face, the challenge is often transformative. Imagine that you have developed lesson plans for a unit of study and now you are going to use these lessons online with fifteen to twenty students who are working at different paces and at different times around the globe. To make this leap, you have to ask some soul-searching questions, like the ones listed in the box "Questions for Teaching an Online Course." In fact, research shows that teaching an online course leads many teachers to reexamine some of their beliefs about teaching and learning. The concepts of teacher-student and student-student communication, as well as student accountability and assessment, change in the online environment. Many teachers improve their skills as they think more deeply about their subject area as well as the nature of communication with and among their students (Lowes, 2005).

Perhaps you will be asked to be part of a virtual high school when you are teaching a face-to-face classroom. You may find it challenging to do both—teach face-to-face and teach online. The intellectual "space" of the online class requires a different type of preparation. You will be happy to know, however, that most

students who take online courses feel like they are part of a learning community and value the experience. Most teachers who teach online find valuable suggestions and resources on the Internet.

8-2c THE TEACHER'S ROLE IN A GLOBAL CLASSROOM

At this point in the chapter you may be wondering, "Why am I going into teaching if students can get so much information elsewhere and connect so readily to the rest of the world?" That is a legitimate question. The answer lies in the importance of your passion, your curiosity, your capacity to listen to and accept students, to gently challenge their ideas and guide them—these are the qualities that will make you a successful teacher.

Your expertise in your content area must be apparent, but it is less important than your ability to help students navigate the flood waters of information available to them. Your challenge is to become a teacher who helps students become discriminating consumers of information, capable of validating data by doing research and formulating well-supported opinions. In other words, your message to students is, "Now that you know what the raw information says, how do you process it?" As a teacher, you will help students make meaning from the data they find; you will help them draw out the big ideas or core concepts in ways that connect to the real world.

Remember as well that you are your students' guide through group learning, collaboration, conflict resolution, and socially acceptable communication. You can help them become lifelong creative learners by challenging them with problems and projects that require them to collaborate and share in this new, open-source world. That sounds like a tall order, but more and more it is how we live our lives.

Did You Know?

When many of today's college-aged students were born, there were hardly any cell phones or digital cameras, no iPods or MP3 players, no iPads, very few Internet sites, no GPS devices in cars, and no TiVo or Google.

8-3 Concluding Thoughts

❝Why do some things take root and grow while others barely break the surface? How long does something have to be around before we can declare that it's here to stay? What has to happen in order to transform an oasis of change into an entire landscape?**❞**
—Ronald Thorpe (2003)

The twenty-first century challenges us to understand more about how people learn, communicate, and do business in a global environment or what Friedman calls the "flat world." Who we become as teachers will reflect the times in which we live—our global interconnectivity and our unending access to information and media.

It is difficult to predict the world in which your students will take part as adults. Think about this: in the years many of today's college-aged students were born, there were hardly any cell phones or digital cameras, no iPods or MP3 players, no iPads, very few Internet sites, no GPS devices in cars, and no TiVo or Google. Now try to think twenty years into the future. Can you even begin to imagine what further changes will occur?

Connectivity, communication, and collaboration have become this century's reading, 'riting, and 'rithmetic; three Cs to replace the traditional three Rs of the twentieth century. Of course, we need the three Rs to become adept at the three Cs. Yet the world into which you must guide your students is more complex and demanding than ever before.

Clearly, to teach in this environment, teachers must be students of history and of current affairs and able to keep pace with constant change. Further, the global community challenges teachers to see beyond our own world and into the worlds of others as a way to make the planet a more tolerant, more sustainable, and safer place. As teachers, our personas are revealed in the classroom: how generous of spirit we become and how capable we are of listening to and learning with our students.

With so much information available through such a large variety of media, today's students have become masters of the art of multitasking. Barbara Kurshan, executive director of Curriki, a community of educators, learners, and education experts who are working together to create high-quality online materials for teachers and students, refers to a recent experience she had with a group of middle-school students she encountered in a friend's basement. Some students were on the computer, some were sending text messages via their mobile phones, and others were on Facebook. She asked them what they were doing, and they responded, "Studying." They had been given a problem set and were collaborating on how to find the answers, working together, and reaching out to other friends to see who had the knowledge they needed.

"That's exactly what goes on in the work world when solving a problem," she says—and too often, "it doesn't go on in the classroom."

Some people believe that when students are multitasking, they are not learning as well. "I disagree," Kurshan says. "I think they're learning the way we work in the business space. If there's something you don't know, you're finding it, and you're doing a lot more critical thinking and problem solving. At the moment, kids may be learning more outside of schools than they are [inside them]" (http://www.eschoolnews.com/2010/01/01/esn-special-report-convergent-education/, retrieved April 2, 2010).

Clearly, the experience that students are having in many schools is linear and disconnected, starting from page one and continuing to the end of the book and then being tested on the material. Students must disconnect from the electronic communities that keep them anchored and keep them learning within their own communities. A gap is growing between the way students have begun to learn and the way schools continue to teach. It is the wired, connected, and tech-savvy teacher who can use the language of the digital information age to help students to take charge of their own learning.

STUDY TOOLS
CHAPTER 8

Located at back of the textbook
- Rip out Chapter Review Card
- Note-Taking Assistance

Located at CengageBrain.com
- Review Key Terms Flash Cards (Print or Online)
- Complete Practice Quizzes to prepare for tests
- Complete "Crossword Puzzle" to review key terms

PART 4
CLASSROOMS, COMMUNITIES, AND YOU

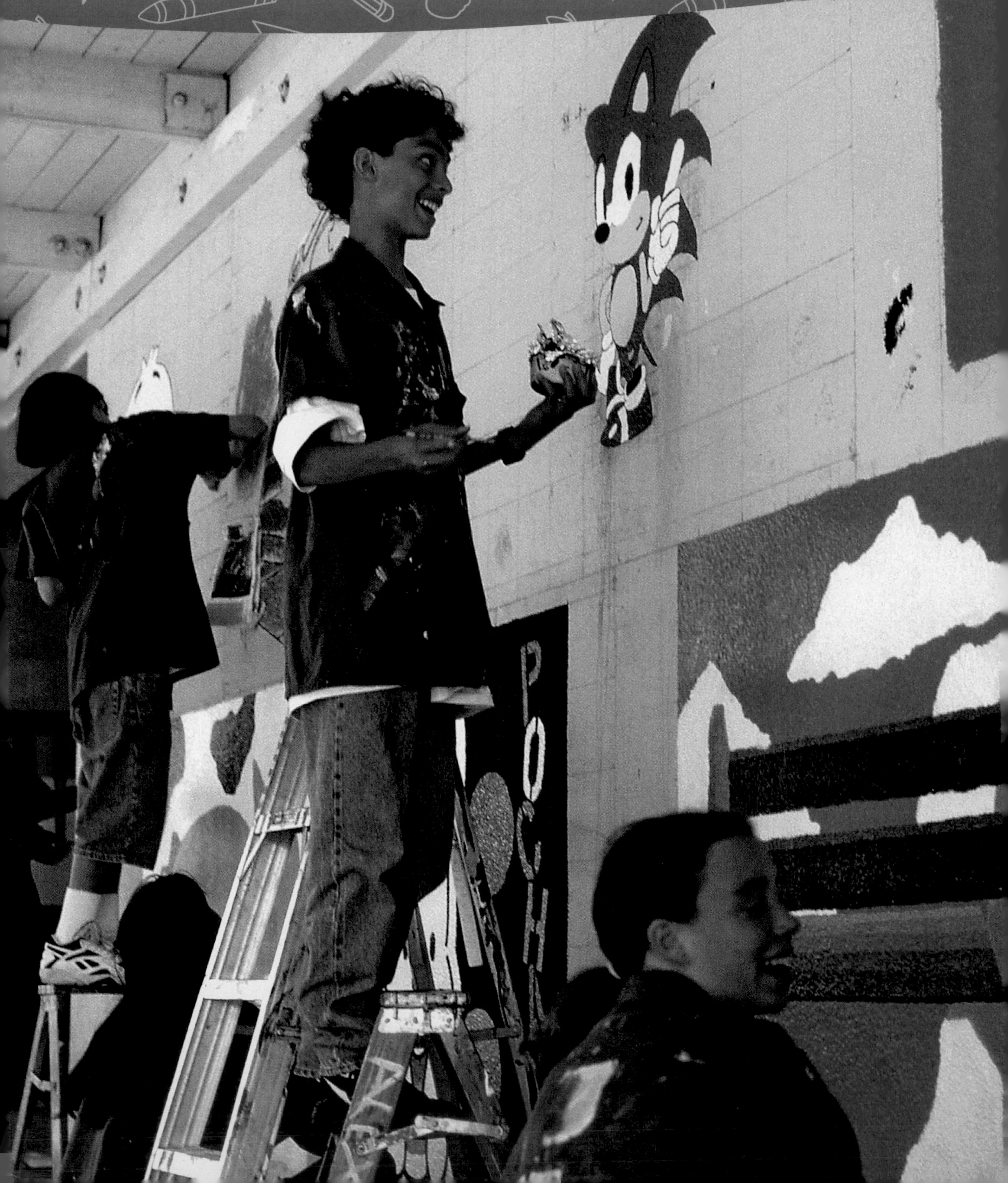

Part 4 addresses the pressing question of how to create classroom environments—real or virtual—that are welcoming, caring, and ultimately effective for teaching and learning. The personal nature of teaching distinguishes it from many other professions. Teaching keeps you on your toes and requires self-awareness and a special mindfulness of your actions and intentions. You need this level of consciousness to become an effective teacher. Remember, teaching is about building relationships.

In this part of the book, we also explore the importance of instilling a sense of belonging among your students—a feeling that everyone in the classroom belongs to a shared community. This sense of community not only enhances students' learning experiences; it also acts as a buffer against some of the problems in today's schools, such as bullying and sexual harassment.

Finally, Part 4 offers several tools to assist you in analyzing—once again—whether teaching is the right career for you. Thinking about the "goodness of fit" between yourself and the profession is a crucial step in preparing for a fulfilling and successful teaching life.

Part Outline

CHAPTER 9

THE CLASSROOM AS COMMUNITY

This chapter considers the issue of community" in conventional classrooms—where students are gathered, physically face-to-face, with a teacher for a specified period of time. Many of the principles described here also relate to online or virtual classrooms, such as those that were discussed in the previous chapter. Whatever the domain in which you teach, your primary function is to ask, "How do I create an environment in which students have respect for themselves and for the other members of the classroom community?"

In the current era, in which schools focus intensely on the academic proficiency of their students as recorded by standards-based tests, it is important to recognize that academic proficiency is only one of the major goals of education. There are social and emotional goals as well. Students should become learners with the capacity to love, work, and be active community members (Cohen, 2006). Along these lines, the philosopher John Dewey (1916–2004) urged educators to have a sympathetic understanding of learners as individuals to have an idea of what is actually going on in their minds (1938, p. 39). To show that you care about your students, you must *listen* to them. Teaching depends on understanding what the twenty to thirty different minds in your class are thinking. How do they feel about being in school? About themselves? About you?

> **classroom management**
> The ways teachers create an effective classroom environment for learning, including all the rules and conditions they establish.

9-1 Building Community in the Classroom

Dewey asserted that the aim of education is to support the development of the skills and knowledge needed for responsible and caring participation in a democracy. In a sense, then, the question this chapter seeks to answer is, "How do students become engaged, responsible participants in a democracy, and how does that process start with the environment created in your classrooms?"

9-1a CLASSROOM MANAGEMENT AND CLASSROOM COMMUNITY

New teachers often seek to understand more about what is typically called **classroom management**. By *management*, they mean the ways the teacher can get students to do what the teacher wants them to. Classroom management refers to "the actions teachers take to create an environment that is respectful, caring, orderly and productive. It supports both academic learning and socio-emotional learning" (Ryan & Cooper, 2013, p. 183). Other educators believe that "if a teacher's notion is to manage, his or her style becomes domineering. This results in resistance from students and an adversarial relationship" (Tomlinson, 2011).

As a result, the term *classroom management* is frowned upon because it can imply that teachers use the power differential between themselves and their students to force students to follow a certain set of rules. Recently, educators interested in classroom management have

---

LEARNING OUTCOMES

After reading this chapter, you should be thinking about the following ideas:

9-1 Explain how classrooms with diverse students can share a common set of beliefs, values, and goals.

9-2 Examine the role of personal power in the abusive behaviors of bullying and sexual harassment.

9-3 Explain how being fully conscious in the classroom can promote a sense of community.

9-4 Describe the roles of communication and collaboration for classroom communities.

begun to focus instead on the creation, through various strategies, of a **classroom community** in which each participant is invested in the smooth operation of the whole and all participants have an interest in outcomes. In this viewpoint, rules and conditions are not established by the teacher alone, but by the group as a whole.

Although structures, routines, and class rules are needed to guide the teaching and learning in classrooms, the way these guidelines are arrived at is crucial. Different teachers have different ways of establishing classroom expectations. When I was chatting with Meredith, who has been in the classroom for two years, we explored her experiences as a first-year teacher in an urban school known for its discipline problems. She taught a second-grade class of thirty students, and she felt her first year had been successful and satisfying. I asked her how she felt before the first day of school.

I was scared. I wanted to meet the children, and I was excited, but before the first day of school, I was told that I had behavior problems in my class. But, after the first five minutes with the class, I was fine. My classroom management skills kicked in, and I was on my way.

When I asked Meredith where she got those skills, she said, "From my mother." I was stunned because I know there are many teaching courses with the title "Classroom Management." Was her mother wiser than professional educators? She elaborated on what she had learned from her mother:

My mother always expected the best from me, and she was strict and demanding, but I knew she really cared about me and had my best interests at heart. Still, she was a "no-nonsense mom" who set goals with me and had clear expectations. She checked with me to see how I felt about

how I was meeting my goals. I do the same thing with the children in my classroom.

I ask them what type of classroom will help them learn. I have strict policies, but we discuss each policy and why it makes sense for their learning environment. I hold out the expectation that they will abide by the rules, and I keep my door open. I explain to them that anyone passing our classroom should be able to see a model of students busy with their work and their class discussions. Of course, when they work in pairs or groups, there is some noise, but that is necessary for them to collaborate with their classmates.

When asked if she used any little tricks to keep students focused and productive, Meredith said that she had hand signals to get their attention when they were working in pairs or groups; she introduced those signals on the first day of school. Also, during a group conversation, she would quietly walk over to students who were not paying attention, and her body language helped amend their behavior.

Mostly, Meredith explained, she genuinely cares about her students and expects them to be successful. She wants a classroom that works for both the students and the teacher, and sometimes that means she has to alter her plans. For example, if she notices that the second graders are engaged in a topic and working diligently on task, she extends her lesson, altering her own routine to allow them to go further in an area of study that *they* find compelling:

Everything is a collaboration; there is no such thing as "teaching" separate from "learning." It is not always possible to know what curriculum areas will set an entire class on fire—and when one comes up, I hate to let it go just because my plan book says I should.

Good teachers live for those moments when the students are "on fire" (Intrator, 2003), carried away and enthused by a topic, a project, an experience, or a story. It is at these times, when students are fully communicating with each other, responding to peers and to you, that you think, "Wow, this is why I came to this work!" These experiences engage students' thinking and enthusiasm so completely that they "forget" they are supposed to resist school, and they get carried away by the excitement of the moment.

> # Q: *Can you remember a time when you were truly excited by learning as a student?*

© Lisa Thornberg/iStockphoto

At these moments, you understand that the classroom is "managed" by the quality of the learning experience, the engagement of the students, and the appreciation of the teacher for the intellectual work that is happening. This is a learning community. It is managed by everyone in it. Let us look at another story about one of my experiences that can tell us more about the foundations of a classroom community:

In an old school building in the east Bronx in New York City, I am trying to bring eighth-grade physical science to life. As part of a unit on the properties of mixtures, we are studying solutions. For this lesson, I want to show the students that, in a solution with water, even though the particles of a solute (the substance that dissolves) seem to disappear, they can be reclaimed. If you boil off the water, the original solute remains at the bottom of the flask. In fact, if you collect the steam and condense it back into water, you can end up with the solute and the water in separate containers—exactly the way they started before the solution was made.

To do this, I set up an apparatus called a Liebig condenser, made popular by the German chemist Justus Baron von Liebig, which makes it possible to collect vapors and turn them back into a liquid. The condenser has an inner tube and an outer tube. The entire apparatus connects to the lab sink in my classroom.

We start with blue crystals of copper sulfate. We stir them into water, making a copper sulfate solution. Then we try to reverse the process. We place the flask containing the solution on a tripod over a Bunsen burner, connecting the open end of the flask to the Liebig condenser with rubber tubing. When the copper sulfate solution boils, the water vapor is collected in the condenser's inner tube, and cold water from the lab sink swirls around the outer tube. Slowly, clear water—the steam turned back into liquid—drips from the condenser into a collecting beaker. The students sit in rapt attention, enthralled.

I ask the class if this process would work if the tube were hooked up to the hot water faucet. All the students shout, "No, it's the cold water that does it!" They seem to understand that the cold turns the steam back into water

by removing the heat from the vapor. I do not mind that they are shouting: "Mrs. Koch—look inside the flask—look—the blue crystals are coming back!"

"Yes," I remark, "and how many thought they were gone for good?" Many students raise their hands. They are smiling; they "get it."

They ask if we can try another solution tomorrow. "Sure," I reply, and tomorrow we will try it with salt water. When the students file out at the end of class, some of them call out, "That was so cool, Mrs. K."

I leave the school building elated. I know the students have had a learning experience. They now know more about evaporation, condensation, and the entire process of distillation. As I drive home with a big smile on my face, I am reminded that it is just for days like this that I keep teaching. I say to myself, "It's worth all the preparation!"

> The classroom is "managed" by the quality of the learning experience, the engagement of the students, and the appreciation of the teacher for the intellectual work that is happening.

Think about what is happening behind the scenes in this eighth-grade classroom. For one thing, the students have learned that I go to a good deal of trouble on their behalf. I have taken the time to set up this complex apparatus and have it ready for their class. They appear to understand that I am deeply invested in their learning and in providing a good science experience. Today will tide us over other days that may not be as exciting, but the students will expect a similarly exciting lab demonstration at some future date.

Over time, as I continued to show my commitment to these students, they never cut science. They were interested. They were well behaved. They managed themselves.

But there are other factors at work here as well. By saying that the students managed themselves, I do not mean that we had no classroom rules. We did in fact have rules in which everyone was invested. This leads us to our next topic.

9-1b RULES, PROCEDURES, AND ROUTINES: A COLLABORATIVE EFFORT

To create classroom community, teachers must provide opportunities and structures that can encourage students to help and support one another. To do so, teachers need to offer explicit instruction so that students learn *how* to support one another (Hittie, 2000).

Rules, procedures, and routines are a good example. Effective teachers use these to manage their classrooms. Too often, however, the decisions are solely in the hands of the teacher, and the students have no voice in, and hence no responsibility for, the way their classroom is managed. To build classroom community, a teacher needs to involve the students in establishing the rules and procedures. Remember what Meredith said: "I ask [my students] what type of classroom will help them learn. I have strict policies, but we discuss each policy and why it makes sense for their learning environment."

Now think about my eighth-grade science classroom. The students were all fired up about the distillation experiment, but their behavior stayed well within the limits of appropriate classroom decorum. What rules do you think the class and I developed?

The students and I developed a chart guiding behavior for watching complex demonstrations. As we made up the chart, the students were creative and inventive, and the result was a true collaborative effort. Rules for observing demonstrations included no crowding around the lab desk; no blocking other students' views; respecting everyone's right to see the demo; and so on. As the story reveals, there *was* some calling out, and it was a fitting expression of the students' excitement.

The point is clear. A classroom that functions well allows students to provide input about the ways it should be run. Classroom rules and procedures result from a collaborative effort. Building a community honors all the participants, and the value of creating community is that each participant is invested in the outcomes. Some strategies to start thinking about include:

- Take the time to get to know your students and enlist them in their own success.
- Collaborate with your class to create guidelines for appropriate behavior.
- Establish a signal that indicates when students should give you their full attention.
- Give clear directions and create a strategy for the students to seek help.

- Find creative ways to set the mood as the students enter the room. Be consistent.
- Plan a high-quality, exciting, and engaging lesson!

Adapted from Jennifer Salopek, "Manage Your Classroom Effectively," *ASCD Update* Vol 53 (11), November 2011.

9-1c IS A WELL-MANAGED CLASSROOM SILENT?

Many new teachers, and veteran teachers as well, confuse a well-run classroom with pervasive silence. As the distillation experiment reveals, appropriate noise related to the activity or experience in which the students are engaged is a healthy aspect of a well-managed classroom.

At times, the classroom needs to be quiet with students listening or studying attentively.

© Elizabeth Crews

Good classroom management allows time for the active engagement of students, encouraging the thinking process, and creating engaged learners.

© Michael Newman/PhotoEdit, Inc.

In fact, classrooms in which teachers insist on quiet all the time run the risk of students becoming disengaged and not really present in the social and emotional ways required for learning.

In Chapter 4 and throughout this text, teaching and learning are described as active processes requiring thoughtful reflection on challenging ideas and concepts as we make them our own. The best ways to facilitate the process of learning is to engage students in projects and problems related to the conceptual understanding you are hoping to achieve and then invite students to work in small groups to reach consensus. With all that going on, a classroom can be a noisy, not a silent place. This is productive "noise"—communication in the service of learning.

The stereotype of the teacher in the front of a room full of rows of silent children runs counter to everything we now know about how people learn. Today, classrooms have many configurations: students may be seated at tables, in groups of desks, or, yes, even in rows. But, however the classroom is arranged, learning cannot happen in silence. The well-managed classroom usually has groups of students communicating, collaborating with other students, working online, and, yes, making comments that pierce the silence.

9-1d BEING FULLY CONSCIOUS

As a teacher, you are "on" from the moment your school day begins. Everything you say and do may have an effect on your students. For that reason, it is impossible to overstate the importance of being fully aware and in control of your own behavior. As an example, I share the story, as a parent, of an experience my daughter had some years ago. Note the reactions of the student, the teacher, and the parent. What was the effect on classroom community?

TEACHSOURCE VIDEO CASE

Teachers Building Community
To see more examples of how teachers conduct their classrooms, find the TeachSource Video Case "Classroom Management: Best Practices" on the student website. After watching the video, consider the following questions:

In what ways does the elementary teacher's management approach differ from that of the middle school teacher? Why do these different approaches work?

At the end of a school day in third grade, my nine-year-old daughter Robin came off the school bus, made eye contact with me, and started to sob. She had held back tears all afternoon and had to struggle to compose herself to tell me about her humiliation by her third-grade teacher.

Q: *Has there been a time when you hurt somebody's feelings without realizing it?*

It appears that left-handed Robin was holding her pencil in an awkward way. Mrs. Owens held her hand up to the class and said, "Class, do you all see the way Robin is holding her pencil? You must never hold your pencil that way." Well, that was it for Robin for the rest of the school day. Humiliated, she retreated quietly into herself and returned home bruised by this criticism in front of her peers.

I visited Mrs. Owens the following day, and before I could recount the episode, she showered me with compliments about Robin. When I shared my concern about the pencil incident with her, she said, "Oh, that was nothing. I didn't mean anything by it. I just want her to hold her pencil correctly."

The teacher reacted impulsively, without regard for how her words and actions could have affected her student. In fact, her student's feelings were hurt by the exchange, and she did not even recognize it. Teachers cannot afford to "shoot from the hip." They must be careful to explore ways to change students' habits by engaging in constructive and caring dialogue.

© Rasmus Rasmussen/iStockphoto

Among the essential qualities teachers need to be successful, one is a clear sense of their own adulthood and a grounded sense of who they are. When you teach, your personality and needs are on display at all times. If you are needy, your students will sense that. You should make certain that your students' needs come before your own needs.

Teachers have different personalities, but what they have in common is that the teacher is usually the responsible adult in the classroom. As the adult, the teacher is obligated to create a safe, secure, and organized learning environment in which routines and expectations are consistent and respectful.

9-1e The Classroom as a Safe Place

In Chapter 6, the importance of creating a safe school climate was discussed. In many ways, a classroom community is a microcosm of the larger school climate. You may not be able to control the climate elsewhere in the school, but you can do a lot in your own classroom.

To foster a sense of community in the classroom, teachers must ensure that the classroom is a safe place—not just a physically safe environment but also an emotionally safe place where students are treated with respect, both by the teacher and by each other. In such a place, everyone is held accountable for what happens. Students come to rely on the teacher's sense of fairness and the consistency with which he or she upholds classroom rules and guidelines.

Some teachers establish a classroom meeting time to help build the sense of community. Teachers may have a "Morning Meeting" every day, or they may have class meetings as needed to discuss a particular event or to handle a problem. Each type of meeting serves a different purpose and contributes to the shared sense of community. The following teaching story illustrates how the meetings work in one fifth-grade classroom:

In a fifth-grade inclusion classroom, Ms. Sanders, who has been teaching for five years, has established the practice of daily Morning Meetings. This is a critical part of the day that fosters relationships among the students. The inclusion students, in particular, comment that this is their favorite part of the day.

The four parts of the Morning Meeting are the greeting, the share, announcements, and the news. The meeting takes place at the beginning of each school day on a rug at the rear of the classroom, where students sit on pillows in a circle facing each other, with the teacher positioned in a prominent spot in the circle.

Ms. Sanders views Morning Meeting as a critical event of the day, a time when students are recognized, life stories are heard, and all individuals are valued. She explains, "I make sure I greet each child, even if he or she is going out to a band lesson or early math. I make sure that I talk to them all, and they are greeted by name. I look at Morning Meeting as a place to talk about what is on the kids' minds and what is going on in their lives. Morning Meeting gives the students a place to share with the whole class, not just me. I love it! It really brings us together as a community, and I learn so much about the students as people from this daily exchange."

The students regard Morning Meeting as an important opportunity to share their life outside of school, learn about their classmates, and celebrate their differences. One boy remarks, "We do Morning Meeting, and I especially like the sharing part when you get to bring in something and share it with the class. I always like to see what other people bring in, and when I bring in something, people always come up to me at snack and want to see it. Then when I have a play date they will ask to see the thing I shared, like my arrowhead or rock collection. It makes me feel good inside and kind of special."

Another student says, "I like Morning Meeting the best because you get to hear about current events and what is going on in the world. You also get to hear what is going on in other people's lives during sharing. I really like that."

Ms. Sanders explains: "I think that the personality of the teacher helps the classroom become a warm and caring atmosphere. I think that I am very easygoing and laid back. I am always happy and smiling, and I try really hard to make the class a fun place for all kids. If I come in and I tell the kids a story that happened to me yesterday or a story about my life, then they will share with me. That creates a nice warm environment in which to learn. I try to make the class like a community. I stress that from day one. I promote an environment where they are free to take risks. They can treat each other like friends, and they can count on each other for help."

> To foster a sense of community in the classroom, teachers must ensure the classroom is a safe place.

The students in this class are aware that they are a part of a special classroom community. Their sense of belongingness is not necessarily the norm outside of their classroom. They talk about bullying, ridicule, and aggressive behavior by students from other classes—experiences that occur regularly on the playground, in the lunchroom, and on the bus. Some express outrage at the social injustice experienced by their peers. The students in this class feel a sense of responsibility toward each other, reflecting the care and concern embodied by their teacher, Ms. Sanders.

In this classroom, clearly, the management is handled by everyone. (Reprinted from an unpublished paper by doctoral student Christine Schroder, 2006, Hofstra University, NY).

Sanders is quite aware of the various ways she encourages a sense of community. She mentions her easygoing personality; her storytelling, which connects her life experiences with those of the students; and her vigilance in promoting a risk-free environment and a safe place for friendships to grow. All of these are critical components in developing a caring classroom.

Morning Meeting in itself is a structure that can build a sense of community and acceptance among the members of a classroom. The daily exchanges among students allow them (1) to feel validated and an important part of the classroom community, (2) to make meaning out of new concepts, (3) to assist themselves and others in the learning process, and (4) to celebrate personal differences. If you establish a Morning Meeting in your classroom, you may find that students rush to the rug each morning to engage in this community-building ritual.

In this era of high-stakes testing many teachers are preoccupied with students' academic achievements as recorded on standardized tests. This preoccupation sometimes leaves little room for sensing the emotional climate of the class. Research studies have discovered, however, that if students do not feel emotionally and socially safe, the opportunities for them to learn are limited. According to research, a sense of belongingness—of being connected in important ways to others—is one of three basic psychological needs essential to human growth and development, along with autonomy and competence (Osterman, 2000, p. 325). In simple terms, students' learning improves when teachers *integrate* academic and social learning in the classroom (Bickart et al., 2000; Rimm-Kaufman, 2006). Building classroom community is an intrinsic part of creating academically competent students.

9-1f THE RESPONSIVE CLASSROOM APPROACH TO COMMUNITY BUILDING

A group of educators from the Northeast Foundation for Children (NEFC) has developed a program called the **Responsive Classroom**, which introduces teachers to the theory and practice of sound classroom management through democratic principles and practices. The Responsive Classroom approach rests on principles such as (Northeast Foundation for Children, 2007; Rimm-Kaufman, 2006):

- The social curriculum and the academic curriculum are equally important.
- How children learn is as important as what they learn.
- Social interaction facilitates cognitive growth.

A Morning Meeting is one effective way to create community in the classroom.

© Elizabeth Crews

- Children need to learn cooperation, assertion, responsibility, empathy, and self-control if they are to be successful socially and academically.
- Knowing children individually, culturally, and developmentally is essential to good teaching.
- Knowing children's families is essential to good teaching.
- The working relationships among the adults in a school are critically important to students' learning.

Notice that many of these principles align with what we have said previously in this book. These ideas rest heavily on the understanding that teaching and learning are about building and fostering relationships—relationships among teachers and students; among students and their peers; and among teachers and other teachers, administrators, and the community at large.

Following these principles, the developers of the Responsive Classroom model recommend a number of specific teaching strategies. They advocate Morning Meeting, for instance. They also recommend "academic choice," a term that highlights the importance of activities in which students make their own choices, solve problems, and work collaboratively. They even propose

strategies for arranging materials, furniture, and displays to encourage independence, promote caring, and maximize learning. You can read more about Responsive Classrooms at http://www.responsiveclassroom.org/.

9-1g Tips for Creating a Classroom Community

From what you have read in this chapter, you should already have some good ideas for creating community in your classroom. The most basic suggestion I can offer is to take a genuine interest in your students. Authenticity outs itself. Students can sense when you are honestly interested in them as people as well as learners. Remember, it is often the little things you do that build a sense of trust among your students. For example, elementary school teachers learn quickly that their young students, even in first and second grade, are capable of managing many of the classroom routines—and that doing so gives them a sense of community and responsibility. Giving students classroom jobs facilitates the classroom routines while allowing the students to feel important to the community. These jobs include plant monitor, lunch menu reporter, library helper, whiteboard cleaner, pencil sharpener, and many others. A great deal of psychological research indicates that people, even young children, experience feelings of well-being and happiness when they have a sense of purpose and are of use. Psychologists suggest that this sense of well-being rests on individuals' ability to use their strengths and virtues in the service of something larger than themselves (Seligman et al., 2005).

Enlisting your students in service to the classroom community gives them a sense of purpose and allows them to make a contribution to the whole. Even in middle and high school, when your time with the students is of shorter duration, you can make this happen.

Beyond the classroom, your students may have the opportunity to engage in **service learning**—that is, community service done in collaboration with a larger project at the

When students have specific jobs, they feel more responsible to the class.

© Somos Images/Photolibrary

school. This type of learning not only connects students with the larger community, but it also forges bonds among the students as they collaborate to make a difference in their own neighborhoods.

9-1h COMMUNITY BUILDING IN THE SECONDARY CLASSROOM

Think about a middle school in an urban area like Los Angeles. In one classroom, students file in, take their seats and immediately begin working on a language arts warm-up exercise. While the teacher takes attendance, the eighth graders silently work. When the short exercise has been completed, students raise their hands and wait for the teacher to call on them as they go over the answers together.

Down the corridor, seventh graders stream into another classroom and take over. Some sit on table tops; others wander around the room. As the teacher takes attendance, one boy brushes his hair, three girls suck on lollipops, one girl sings, and a boy in the last row unleashes a barrage of spitballs. The day's warm-up is quickly forgotten. Same school, same day, similar students, similar teachers—yet profoundly different behavior (adapted from Mehta, *Los Angeles Times*, December 14, 2009). Educators remind us that the ability to calmly control student behavior so learning can flourish has a huge impact on a teacher's ability to be successful.

Teachers who have good skills in creating an organized classroom community in middle and high school agree on several factors. Most important, an organized teacher who

CLASSROOM COMMUNITIES: TIPS FOR TEACHERS

- Teachers can never be overprepared. The first key to a successful teaching experience is to plan, plan, and plan!
- Understand your expectations for students' behavior, and share those with them. Show them and tell them what you are hoping for.
- To build a sense of community, develop rules collaboratively with your students, and be clear about these.
- Be consistent. Have clear consequences when rules are broken, and follow through!
- Be prepared to admit your mistakes. And use humor when appropriate.
- Make respect central to your classroom culture. Make it clear that you care about your students and that your class will lead to real learning that will benefit them.
- Minimize the power differential in everyday communication. Keep calm in all situations. Whenever possible, connect your classroom discussions and curriculum to students' lives, communities, and culture.
- Learn as much as you can about your students and make connections to their lived experiences.

- Build students' confidence in their own intelligence and creativity.
- Talk about multiple intelligences, if appropriate, and how people can be smart and creative in many ways.
- Have engaging activities prepared for the students when they walk into the classroom. Keep lecturing to a minimum.
- Engage students in group projects, centers, presentations, discussions, or role plays.
- Place the students at the center of the learning experience. Make the classroom about them.
- Remember, the best and most appropriate consequences for students are positive ones—the intrinsic joy that comes from success, accomplishment, social approval, good academic performance, and recognition. Create experiences that enable all students to feel good about themselves.

Sources: Adapted from Miller, L. (2004). "12 tips for new teachers." In K. D. Salas, R. Tenorio, S. Walters, & D. Weiss (Eds.), *The New Teacher Book: Finding Purpose, Balance, and Hope during Your First Years in the Classroom*. Milwaukee, WI: Rethinking Schools, Ltd.; and from "Tips for creating a peaceful classroom," *Teacher Talk*. http://education.indiana .edu/cas/tt/v2i3/peaceful.html, retrieved May 29, 2007.

Foresight

Map out your class in advance with your students. Spend the first few days of class discussing an overview of what you hope to accomplish as far as content, skill development, student behavior, and class format. If students do not abide by class expectations, they know in advance what repercussions they will face.

sexual harassment
Unwelcome sexual advances, requests for sexual favors, or other physical and expressive behavior of a sexual nature that interferes with a person's life.

has good communication skills and cares deeply about the students will be able to earn their respect and hence their cooperation. Routines are important, whether in kindergarten or twelfth grade. Students feel safe when they know what to expect. The following attributes are helpful but so is practice! Learn as much about your students as possible, and demonstrate that you are interested in them as people.

Consistency

Teachers should tell students what to expect and then deliver. This applies to all aspects of the secondary classroom, ranging from identifying test days to delivering instruction. Starting every English class, for example, by posing a question for discussion or written response, helps establish a routine that students can expect.

Clarity

Teachers must clearly explicate their learning objectives for the course as well their expectations for student behavior. Discuss these topics with students during the first week of class and provide specific examples of what students are expected to accomplish and how they are expected to behave. Practicing classroom rules is not solely reserved for elementary school. By illustrating through role play with students what is considered appropriate and inappropriate behavior, teachers leave no room for student interpretation on these important points.

Fairness

This relates to showing respect for your students by setting realistic expectations and offering guidance and support to help students achieve those goals.

Q: *Do you recall having a classroom job?*

9-2 Preventing Harassment and Bullying

Successful teachers invite their students' lives, languages, and cultures into the classroom. They start building a classroom community on the first day of school. They care about their students, and they create an environment where social justice is both a goal and a reality.

> **"**If you say the next person who talks in class will be set on fire and rolled down the hallway, you're in trouble if someone talks and you don't set them on fire and roll them down the hallway.**"**
> —Kendra Wallace, Middle School Principal, Los Angeles, 2009
> (Source: http://classroom-organization.suite101.com/article.cfm/ develop_classroom_management_plan, retrieved March 25, 2010.)

In this type of environment, injustices toward individuals or groups of students become readily apparent. Two prominent examples of social injustice in today's schools are sexual harassment and bullying. This section explores these topics and discusses how you can help prevent them from endangering your classroom community.

9-2a SEXUAL HARASSMENT IN SCHOOL

Under the guidelines established by the federal Office for Civil Rights, sexual harassment is considered a form of sex discrimination and is therefore prohibited by Title IX of the Education Amendments of 1972. Generally speaking, **sexual harassment** is any "unwanted and unwelcome sexual behavior" that interferes with a person's life. Sexual harassment does not include "behaviors that you like or want (e.g., wanted kissing, touching, or flirting)" (AAUW Educational Foundation, 2004, p. 11).

Sexually harassing behaviors happen in school hallways, stairwells, and classrooms, and they have a negative effect on the emotional and educational lives of students. In a 2000 federal survey, more than 36 percent of US public schools reported at least one incident of sexual harassment (Dinkes et al., 2007, p. 84). Eight in ten students experience some form of sexual harassment during their school lives. Eighty-five percent of students in grades eight through eleven say that students harass other students at their schools, and almost 40 percent of students report that teachers and other school employees sexually harass students in their schools (AAUW Educational Foundation, 2011, 2004, 2001).

On May 24, 1999, the Supreme Court ruled that school districts can be liable for damages under federal law for failing to stop a student from subjecting another student to severe and pervasive sexual harassment (Koch, 2002, p. 262). Title IX also guarantees that hostility and ridicule toward gay and lesbian students that is not immediately acted upon by the school or district may be grounds for a lawsuit against that district. See Table 9.1 for a simple checklist to determine what has been done to prevent harassment in the school or district.

As a teacher, you need to learn about your school or district's policies concerning sexual harassment and teach them openly to your students. Make sure students know the sanctioned procedures for reporting abuse so they do not needlessly suffer victimization by others. Many schools use role-playing scenarios or videos to prompt student discussion of sexual harassment issues. Teachers and schools are responsible for creating a harassment-free environment in which all students are safe to learn.

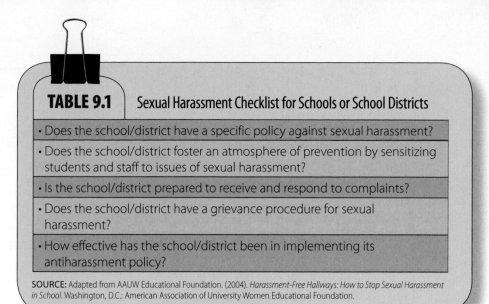

TABLE 9.1	Sexual Harassment Checklist for Schools or School Districts
• Does the school/district have a specific policy against sexual harassment?
• Does the school/district foster an atmosphere of prevention by sensitizing students and staff to issues of sexual harassment?
• Is the school/district prepared to receive and respond to complaints?
• Does the school/district have a grievance procedure for sexual harassment?
• How effective has the school/district been in implementing its antiharassment policy?

SOURCE: Adapted from AAUW Educational Foundation. (2004). *Harassment-Free Hallways: How to Stop Sexual Harassment in School*. Washington, D.C.: American Association of University Women Educational Foundation.

Establishing a sense of community with your students is a vital means of preventing harassment in school. When students feel responsible for one another and care about their learning community, harassing behaviors are less likely to occur; and when they do, they are less likely to persist. If your classroom community fosters an atmosphere of risk-free communication, your students will be better able to talk about alleged harassment and determine what to do.

Beyond the general principle of making respect central to your classroom culture, you should consider specific guidelines for student behavior that will help prevent sexual harassment. Often, well-meaning teachers ignore certain behaviors, especially in middle and high school, as long as they seem socially acceptable to the students themselves. For instance, teachers may decide that name calling and excessive flirting are "normal" for the students' age, when in fact these behaviors can be disruptive to the victim's well-being. It is important to know how to respond to this type of occurrence. There are many surveys and checklists that help teachers and students recognize sexually harassing behavior. A checklist for teens might suggest, for example, that acceptable flirting makes you feel flattered, whereas harassment makes you feel unattractive or ashamed. The particular guidelines you adopt should take into account your students' age, the cultures represented in your classroom, and your school and district policies.

Did You Know?

Eight in ten students experience some form of sexual harassment during their school lives.

bullying Repeated cruelty, physical or psychological, by a powerful person toward a less powerful person.

9-2b BULLYING AND TEASING

Although creating community in the classroom is an important deterrent to negative student behaviors, teachers cannot be everywhere. Let us go back to Ms. Sanders's classroom, described earlier in this chapter. Despite the warm and caring environment promoted by her use of Morning Meeting, one of the students reported bullying and teasing on the playground at lunchtime. Because there is a longstanding tradition of the classroom or school bully, this problem is often overlooked. In fact, half of schoolchildren report being bullied at least once a week in the United States, and ten thousand children nationwide report staying home from school once a month because of a bully (Corcoran, 2002).

Bullying implies repeated harmful acts and an imbalance of power. It can involve physical, verbal, or psychological attacks or intimidation directed against a victim who cannot properly defend himself or herself because of size or strength or because of being outnumbered or less psychologically resilient. Bullying includes assault, tripping, intimidation, rumor spreading and isolation, demands for money, destruction of property, theft of valued possessions, destruction of another's work, and name calling (Sampson, 2002). Figure 9.1, which focuses on teenagers, shows statistics about some of the prevalent types of bullying.

The most likely targets of bullies are gay students or students who are perceived to be gay (Corcoran, 2002). As teenagers' sexual identities are beginning to emerge, homophobia, the fear of and intolerance toward homosexuals, is, unfortunately, part of the culture of many secondary schools.

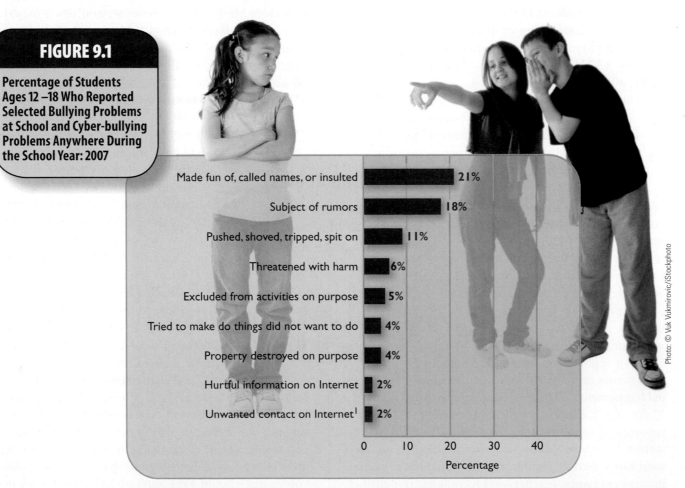

FIGURE 9.1

Percentage of Students Ages 12 –18 Who Reported Selected Bullying Problems at School and Cyber-bullying Problems Anywhere During the School Year: 2007

Made fun of, called names, or insulted	21%
Subject of rumors	18%
Pushed, shoved, tripped, spit on	11%
Threatened with harm	6%
Excluded from activities on purpose	5%
Tried to make do things did not want to do	4%
Property destroyed on purpose	4%
Hurtful information on Internet	2%
Unwanted contact on Internet[1]	2%

Percentage

Photo: © Vuk Vukmirovic/iStockphoto

[1] Unwanted contact on Internet was defined as another student making "unwanted contact, for example, threatened or insulted [the respondent] via instant messaging." **NOTE:** "At school" includes the school building, on school property, on a school bus, or going to and from school. SOURCE: U.S. Department of Justice, Bureau of Justice Statistics, School Crime Supplement (SCS) to the National Crime Victimization Survey, 2007.

SOURCE: Dinkes, R., Cataldi, E. F., Kena, G., Baum, K., & Snyder, T. D. (2006). *Indicators of School Crime and Safety: 2006.* NCES 2007-003/NCJ 214262. Washington, D.C.: U.S. Government Printing Office.]

TYPES OF SEXUAL HARASSMENT

According to the Office for Civil Rights of the US Department of Education, sexual harassment falls into two basic categories.

Quid pro quo sexual harassment occurs when a school employee causes a student to believe that he or she must submit to unwelcome sexual conduct to participate in a school program or activity. It can also occur when a teacher suggests to a student that educational decisions such as grades will be based on whether the student submits to unwelcome sexual conduct.

Hostile environment harassment occurs when unwelcome verbal or physical conduct is sufficiently severe, persistent, or pervasive that it creates an abusive or hostile environment for the affected student (Office for Civil Rights, 2001, 1997).

Many antibullying programs have been put in place, including procedures that students can follow if they feel they are being bullied. Most of the time, however, students do not reveal that they are being bullied, and witnesses tend not to come forward. Although there are more male bullies and male victims, the numbers of female bullies and victims are on the rise (Olweus, 2003). Victimization by bullying has been linked to student depression, eating disorders, and even suicidal tendencies (Sears, 1991).

In classes where a strong sense of community has been created, not only is bullying less likely to occur in the first place, but if it does, the bullying victim is more likely to come forward, as are the witnesses. The emphasis is on the common good and on care and respect for one another.

9-2c CYBERBULLYING

Social networking is a way of life for our nation's youth. They are part of myriad online communities, and with all these opportunities to communicate online, there are hidden dangers. On Facebook and other social media websites, Twitter, and in chat rooms, people can pretend to be someone they are not and entice unknowing children and teenagers to meet them. This is a major source of Internet child and teen abuse, and many schools are adopting programs to warn their students about online sexual predators and establishing ways to report online solicitations. Internet crime is a crime like any other and should be reported to proper local, state, or federal authorities.

Cyberbullying is a prevalent phenomenon that refers to hurtful texts, e-mails or Facebook posts about an individual student. It can be a computer crime if it reaches a level of causing serious harm to the intended victim. It is a federal crime to anonymously annoy, harass, threaten, or abuse any person via the Internet or a telecommunications system. Cyber bullying, although not causing physical harm, can lead to effects as damaging and traumatic as physical harassment. There are several forms of cyber bullying. Among the most common are: spreading mean or malicious rumors through online posts or cell phone texts. Additionally, a person's e-mail account or cell phone can be the receptacle for hurtful messages and their accounts can be broken into, allowing the victim to appear to be sending damaging messages to others. Sexting has become popular among teens and leads to the circulation of sexually suggestive photos on the Internet. Cyber bullying can be very painful for adolescents, leading to states of anxiety and depression and even suicide. (adapted from http://www.bullyingstatistics.org/content/cyberbullying-statistics.html, March 25, 2012).

cyberbullying Bullying or harassment through electronic means such as e-mail, website postings, instant messaging, text messaging, blogs, mobile phones, or chatrooms; also called *online bullying*.

Q: *How would you recognize sexual harassment or bullying in your own classroom?*

Bullying is all about power. The bully has it; the victim does not. Technology accelerates bullying as social media make it easy for bullies to enlist large, usually anonymous groups to carry out relentless attacks with text messages, Facebook posts, e-mails, and sometimes compromising digital photos. Adults are removed from this assault and are not present electronically to intervene. Victims often feel ashamed, powerless, and fearful of retaliation if they report the bully or bullies.

Facebook has a stop cyberbullying page (https://www.facebook.com/stopcyberbullying); however, most students who are on Facebook continue to post the most personal items on their pages. Many students are not aware of the ways in which they are compromising their privacy. Unless users are extremely careful about their Facebook privacy settings, just about everything that is posted becomes public knowledge to anyone accessing their page. School communities are now raising awareness of how to select privacy settings on social media sites and thus, add a layer of personal protection for today's students. There are many who are concerned that the openness and ease of electronic communication has inured many young people to the concept of privacy and personal boundaries. In cyberbullying, these boundaries are consistently violated and the victim often feels powerless to respond effectively. Cyberbullying is a serious, behind-the-scenes event that often occurs not only during, but also, after school time. It is essential that this type of bullying be addressed openly in schools and that all students understand what each of them can do to report bullying they have witnessed or bullying where they are a victim or an unwitting collaborator. All cyberbullying interventions require a school climate of trust and caring that ensures all communications with school personnel are confidential.

The most important action a student can initiate if he or she is experiencing cyberbullying is to tell someone immediately. Many schools are promoting Internet safety programs, and a number of websites offer helpful tips for students that teachers can use to educate their students on preventing cyberbullying (see the box "Tips for Students Who Are Cyberbullied"). Creating a safe and trusting classroom community extends to protecting your students from online abuse.

9-3 Classroom Community and Goodness of Fit

As we mentioned previously, good classroom management requires that you be fully conscious in the classroom. It requires what Jacob Kounin (1970) called "withitness," a concept sometimes interpreted as having "eyes in the back of your head" to ward off any undesirable behavior. I prefer to think of withitness as a broad awareness that you have about yourself and your students together. Do you have a centered presence in the classroom? Are you aware of the students' dispositions on any given day as they enter your room? At any moment, do you know whether the principles of classroom community that you and the students have developed are working?

TIPS FOR STUDENTS WHO ARE CYBERBULLIED

Teachers can help students who experience cyberbullying by advising them of ways to prevent and stop the harassing behavior:

- Tell a trusted adult.
- Never open, read, or respond to messages from people you know to be cyberbullies.
- If the problem is school-related, tell a school teacher or administrator. All schools have bullying solutions.
- Do not erase the messages. They may be needed to take action.
- Block those who are using chat or instant messaging to bully.
- Think carefully before giving out private information online such as passwords, PINs, addresses, or phone numbers. This information can be used by bullies.
- Be polite online, and others will tend to do the same. If someone gets angry or bullies you, ignore him or her—cyberbullies want a reaction just like other bullies.
- If you are threatened with harm, call the police.

Source: Adapted from "Beware of the Cyber Bully," iSAFE, Inc. http://www.isafe.org/imgs/pdf/education/CyberBullying.pdf, accessed April 2, 2010.

These are important matters to take into consideration when deciding on the "goodness of fit" between yourself and the teaching profession. Think about the following concepts:

- Good teachers are usually interested in learning as much as they can about their students.
- Effective teachers are organized and plan ahead.
- New teachers frequently imagine how they will speak and act in front of a class.
- Good teachers care deeply about listening to and valuing their students' ideas.

- Teachers need to be fully conscious or "with it" at all times, and especially in a large group of students.
- Effective teachers are often role models for their younger, less empowered students.

9-4 Concluding Thoughts

Clearly, good communication and collaboration with your students are vital for creating a classroom in which everyone feels responsible for managing the environment and working toward the common good. As a teacher, you should identify the most effective rules for your classroom and seek the students' assistance in establishing these as classroom priorities. When you involve your students in setting guidelines for everyone to follow, you help them buy into an environment where everyone can learn and occurrences like bullying and sexual harassment are stopped in their tracks.

Classroom community relates to the principles of teaching and learning we have discussed throughout this book. When you have your students work in groups, develop their own strategies for solving problems, and apply their concepts to meaningful real-world projects, you not only help them learn individually, but you also foster their sense of the classroom as a learning community. When you honor diversity and use culturally relevant pedagogy, you create the same effect. All of these practices are good teaching methods *and* good classroom management strategies.

Finally, your ability to be honest with your students and to show your interest in their lives will go a long way toward earning their trust and turning the classroom into a safe place and a genuine learning community.

STUDY TOOLS
CHAPTER 9

Located at back of the textbook
- Rip out Chapter Review Card
- Note-Taking Assistance

Located at CengageBrain.com
- Review Key Terms Flash Cards (Print or Online)
- Complete Practice Quizzes to prepare for tests
- Complete "Crossword Puzzle" to review key terms
- Watch the TeachSource Video Case "Classroom Management: Best Practices"

CHAPTER 10

MAKING THE DECISION TO BECOME A TEACHER

© Jack Hollingsworth/photodisc/Getty Images

> *Most good teachers leave the classroom in June and ask how they can do it better in September. They spend their summers taking workshops, going to conferences, and seeking professional development on a variety of topics....*
> — Judy Logan, 2011

At this point in your journey, you would be correct to conclude that modern classrooms are complex places, that teaching is a highly sophisticated activity, and that a career in education requires careful planning, the capacity for spontaneous decision making, and actions based on careful personal reflection.

In this final chapter, some ways of thinking about teaching as a profession are examined in the hopes that it will inform your decision-making process. Moments of absolute certainty are rare, but there are signs that can help you make your choice.

LEARNING OUTCOMES

After reading this chapter, you should be thinking about the following ideas:

10-1 Explain how teachers in the twenty-first century are challenged in ways that their predecessors were not.

10-2 Examine the requirements of your state for earning a teaching certificate.

10-3 Analyze the roles of the American Federation of Teachers (AFT) and the National Education Association (NEA) for beginning teachers.

10-4 Discuss how a teaching portfolio can demonstrate your talents for teaching.

10-5 Analyze the self reflections that lead you to believe that teaching is for you.

10-1 Goodness of Fit

> *You have to love kids and want to connect with them—because if you don't connect with the kids, you will never be able to convey the materials; if you cannot feel the music, you cannot play the music....I can teach anyone about pedagogical strategies but I cannot teach a person to love kids. And you can feel it in a classroom as soon as you walk in.* —Day, C. (2004). A Passion for Teaching. New York: Routledge.

As you learned in Chapter 1, *goodness of fit* is a term used in descriptive statistics to mean a match between a theory and a set of observations. By using the term to refer to the match between a teacher candidate's attributes and the job of a teacher, this book has invited you to consider your own suitability for the teaching profession.

Think about what you have learned about teaching and what you have recognized about your personal attributes. Remember that there is no one definition of a "good" or a "successful" teacher. The power of a teacher cannot be overestimated. You will be responsible for the education of tomorrow's thinkers and leaders, and you will learn the joy of making a contribution to other people's growth and development.

Research has found that people are often happier when they are making a contribution to others (Seligman, 2002), and that is certainly true of teaching. But considerable evidence also shows that people are more successful when they are engaged in work that plays to their strengths. If teaching does not play to your own strengths, perhaps it is not the best profession for you. An article written for the *New Yorker* magazine (2008) discussed how difficult it was for professional sports scouts to determine, based on observing college athletes at play, who would be the best draft pick for particular positions, in this case, in football. Titled "Most Likely to Succeed," the article emphasized how difficult it is to predict how someone will do in a position once he or she is hired, no matter how much you learn about the person beforehand (Gladwell, 2008). Nowhere is this as serious an issue as when hiring a new teacher.

This is mainly because research tells us that really good teachers have profound effects on student learning and, unfortunately, the converse is true. In fact, some research indicates that a student would be more likely to succeed with a terrific teacher in a lower-performing school than with a terrible teacher in a high-performing school (Hanushek et al., 2005).

This is a good time to consider how you may be able to tell if you are a good fit for teaching. These are some attributes of good teachers that form only the beginning of a list. You probably have others and can make this list even longer. Many individuals who succeed as teachers have:

- A centered presence in the classroom.
- A sensitivity to the classroom setting.
- An ability to respond thoughtfully to each student.
- A personal capacity for juggling many tasks at once.
- An appreciation of how children and young adults grow and change.
- An understanding of the ways our students bring their outside worlds into the classroom.
- A desire to help students feel capable and competent.
- An ability to listen to others.

10-1a The Importance of Observing in the Field

As we mentioned in Chapter 1, visiting a school and spending time in classrooms can provide a sense of the school culture and the school climate. This is important to gain a real-time, current look at the life of teachers and students. Your first formal experience in a classroom will probably be through your field placement. The field placement is an opportunity for you to serve as an apprentice and learn from the regular classroom teacher and from your own experience of working with the students.

In some formal field experiences, you begin by making observations. Keep some of the attributes just mentioned in mind as you observe in the classroom setting. In other placements, you may be considered a *participant-observer*. While participating in the life of the classroom, you make careful observations and study the classroom environment to learn about child and adolescent development and teaching methods. Usually, participant-observers are not required to spend the entire school day in the field placement; rather, they must be immersed in the school for a specific number of hours each week.

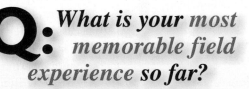

Q: *What is your most memorable field experience so far?*

In other field placements, you are considered a *student teacher*. In this arrangement, you are assigned to a teacher, usually called the "cooperating teacher," on a daily basis for a specified period of time, such as ten to twelve weeks. Student teachers at the secondary level often receive two placements, one in a middle school and the other in a high school. At the elementary level, depending on your state's requirements, you may receive one placement in grades K–2 and another in grades 3–5.

As a student teacher, you will be expected to teach the class at prearranged times. During some of these teaching experiences, you will be formally observed by a supervisor assigned by your institution. Student teaching is a special time when you develop a clear idea of what the life of a classroom teacher is all about. It is an important part of your professional preparation.

Before you start your field experience, it is important to learn as much as possible about the school and classroom to which you have been assigned. Be certain that you understand your role in the classroom and that you are aware of the dress code for teachers in the school. Ask questions. Be gracious, and be sure to thank the teacher in whose classroom you are gaining experience.

10-1b The Purposes of Public Education and the Role of the Teacher

❝*Above all things, I hope that the education of the common people will be attended to, convinced that on their good sense we may rely with the most security for the preservation of a due degree of liberty.*❞ —Thomas Jefferson, in a letter to James Madison, 1787

Chapter 3 described the vital role public education has played in American democratic society since the early days of the nation. As the preceding quotation from Thomas Jefferson indicates, US public schools have always been expected to fulfill certain public missions that go beyond the purely academic.

Today, as you have seen throughout this book, **public education** serves the basic function of preparing young people to lead productive lives by increasing their academic achievement and improving their readiness to secure jobs in an increasingly global economy.

In addition, however, public education helps equip our youth to become responsible and active citizens in a democratic society. In other words, it prepares them to participate in decisions that contribute to the social good (Center on Education Policy, 2007).

Although the current era of standards-based assessments emphasizes quantifiable academic achievement, it is useful to envision your career in education as serving a broader purpose. The Center for Education Policy (2007) describes the mission of public education in terms of six main themes:

1. To provide universal access to free education.
2. To guarantee equal opportunities for all children.
3. To unify a diverse population.
4. To prepare people for citizenship in a democratic society.
5. To prepare people to become economically self-sufficient.
6. To improve social conditions.

In Chapter 9, we explored how classrooms can create a sense of community, a social group mindful of the needs of each of its members. In this sense, creating a classroom community becomes more than a tool for effective teaching and learning; it becomes a model for social justice and social participation in the microcosm of the classroom. Clearly, the important goals of education include helping students develop their abilities to think critically, appreciate diverse cultures, maintain curiosity about the world, and show confidence in expressing their own ideas.

In Chapter 1, teaching as an essential profession was described and a code of ethics developed by the National Education Association (NEA) was reviewed. Now that we have come to the end of this text, I invite you to think about the profession of teaching as requiring an overriding commitment by its members to the well-being of their students. Teaching is not an ordinary job. It is a profession that establishes our identities and reveals our values.

Most important, the functions and responsibilities of teachers are not confined to the classroom. Central to your work as a teacher is devoting time and energy to professional communities, activities, conferences, and workshops. Teaching is an opportunity for intellectual development, both through professional teacher development courses and through your own intimate contact with new books, ideas, and technologies. Actually, few teachers who are not also intellectually curious are successful.

Further, as you have seen in this text, teaching in the twenty-first century requires guiding students through the huge quantity of information that enters their lives daily. It is your job to help them understand what is valid and what needs to be discarded. All this has to be accomplished as you prepare your students for this era of standardized testing and find creative ways to help them to be successful. The ways in which teacher performance is evaluated is now starting to include your students' test scores. For better or worse, this reality means you want a prepared class but not a class that has suffered from test preparation! These contemporary teaching needs make the teacher's role more complex and ever-changing as compared to any previous era. Luckily, you can find support through various professional organizations and on many online sites, in chat rooms, and on blogs.

public education
Education that is publicly financed, tuition-free, accountable to public authorities, and accessible to all students. The term covers various types of public schools, including traditional schools, charter and magnet schools, vocational schools, and alternative schools.

Communication, collaboration, and connection are the hallmarks of twenty-first-century teaching and learning.

10-1c ONE SIZE DOES NOT FIT ALL

In Chapter 3, when we explored the history of US public education and the many reform movements that have dotted the landscape of teaching and learning, we saw that public education is a large mosaic. Methods are varied, and successes and failures weave their way through each successive period of history. There is no one right way to teach; there are many right ways—and many incorrect ways as well. Just as there are multiple learning styles and learning profiles, teaching is as variable as the types and personalities of teachers.

The challenge is to imagine you are on a journey of both inward and outward exploration. You will explore your own personality traits, subject areas of expertise, capacity for generosity, and school stories. Try to remember the special moments that made you feel like school was the best place in the world. Also recall those times when being a student was painful or you were victimized by a teacher, knowingly or unknowingly.

One of your most useful tools is your capacity for reflection, along with your humility. It is profoundly moving to affect the lives of young people; it is also an extraordinary responsibility.

Find a way to connect with colleagues or classmates with whom you can have a conversation about teaching. Learning to teach is very much about having conversations and exchanging stories with willing colleagues. These discussions will help you discover the ways teaching will be a personal expression of yourself.

10-1d CREATING A CULTURE OF CARING

Many teachers talk about the importance of caring about students so that they see themselves as valuable and capable of learning. Creating a caring environment has a deep affect on you as well. Katy Ridnouer tells the following story, illustrating how an ethic of caring contributes to the life of a middle school teacher:

Although the United States trains more than enough teachers to meet its needs, the attrition rate for educators is higher than for any other professional occupation. According to a report from the National Commission for Teaching and America's Future, up to one-third of new US teachers leave the profession within the first few years. I was one of them. In my second year, I taught eighth-grade language arts in a school full of challenges. I felt isolated, unsafe, and incapable, but I trudged on. I met with parents, I brainstormed with colleagues, and I discussed issues with members of the administration. Nothing changed. At the end of the year, I decided to leave teaching for the quiet solitude of the bookseller's life.

For six months or so, I convinced myself that I had made a good choice. Then the dreams about my classroom started. I was in front of my eighth graders, leading a grammar lesson. I saw their willing faces. I saw *them*. I then realized that I had expected everyone else to change while I remained the same. I expected the surly child to be pleasant, but I did nothing to encourage this behavior. I expected the underachieving child to work to his potential, but I did nothing to bring this about. I even expected the motivated child to stay motivated but did nothing to contribute to that end. My eyes opened, I returned to teaching, and I have never looked back.

I identify as a teacher. It's what I am meant to do, and it is as rewarding to me as art is to the artist, a great play is to the athlete, and the correct diagnosis is to the doctor. When I see students grapple with a concept and come away with new understanding of the material and a new respect for themselves, the long hours I invest hardly matter.

Today, my guiding maxim as a teacher is to create a learning community within the four walls of the classroom. I define a learning community as a group of people who come together with a willing spirit to learn and support one another despite racial, economic, religious, and achievement differences. Learning communities promote curiosity, higher-level thinking, enhanced interpersonal skills, and confidence in both students and teachers. I have found that the key to creating a learning community is to *manage your classroom with heart*—and, by that, I mean permeate the classroom atmosphere with caring concern. This involves

Did You Know?

Up to one-third of new US teachers leave the profession within the first few years.

care in interactions with students, lesson planning, seating chart decisions, discipline concerns, grading, and more. Putting care for your students first creates a learning community that inspires them to be their best selves, both in school and out in the world.

When I went back to the classroom, I changed the way I perceived my job....Most significantly, I had to care about my students, which was something I hadn't really allowed myself to do before. Sure, I was friendly to them and I wanted them to succeed, but I can't say I was a caring teacher. Frankly, I saw caring as a risky venture. I worried that my feelings might be hurt if my students mocked my concern for them or if they didn't reciprocate it. I worried that I might get caught up in my students' personal concerns and neglect their academic achievement. I worried that the administration would think I had "gone soft." But on my second go-round, I decided to take the risk: to allow myself to care about my students—to nurture them and their learning. I am a happier teacher, a better teacher, and a richer human being because of it. My great hope is that by welcoming my students into my heart, I have enriched their lives.

Source: From *Managing Your Classroom with Heart: A Guide for Nurturing Adolescent Learners* (pp. 1–3), by Katy Ridnouer, Alexandria, VA: ASCD. © 2006 by ASCD. Reprinted with permission. Learn more about ASCD at www.ascd.org.

Ridnouer's story is one of hope and resolve. She returned to the middle school classroom because she instinctively knew that was where she was meant to be. That intangible quality, that inner knowing, cannot be taught; it must be felt. She needed to revisit her desire to teach because on the first go-around she was not meeting with a sense of personal success.

Her story is a reminder that the early years of teaching confront us with many challenges. Working with young people is often unpredictable and can shake one's confidence. Feelings of frustration are not uncommon; however, they are often counterbalanced by a sense of profound accomplishment when students have that "aha" moment and demonstrate that they really "get it." This story reminds us that becoming proficient in our chosen profession takes time. Being patient with yourself as you begin is an important attribute.

The next story offers another perspective on a new teacher and the culture of caring she has created:

Jaime Barron started teaching the fourth grade in an urban area where poverty is commonplace, most children are from minority backgrounds, and more than

90 percent have lived all or some of their lives in homeless shelters. The students come to school with little social capital. Many are from single-parent families where their responsibilities include the care of younger siblings. All of the students receive free breakfast and lunch daily.

Because Jaime's experience with these fourth-grade students was very positive, she asked if she could "loop" with this class to fifth grade. (*Looping* is the process of sending an entire class together into the next grade level with the same teacher. In some school districts, it requires parental approval.) When I visited her and her class, it was the middle of the fifth grade, and the twenty-nine students were working in seven groups on projects that involved designing model ecosystems for different animals around the world.

Jaime's room is covered with print; student work hangs everywhere. There are posters hanging from clotheslines strung across the room. The posters explain group-work rules that include taking turns, listening to others, and offering ideas. For these students, working independently is a challenge, but they enjoy working on projects and accessing information on the computer, and they tell me they really like Ms. Barron.

The classroom is small and crowded, and there are not enough resources. The students have little knowledge about environments beyond their urban apartments and shelters. Doing group projects that construct environments far beyond their streets is a new experience for them. To aid their imagination, a world map hangs in the classroom. Their city is circled in red.

All the students, who range in age from ten to thirteen, appear to have a fundamental understanding that Ms. Barron cares about them. They respond to this. Each morning they bring her enormous plan book to her and ask, "What are we doing today?" They understand that she prepares for them. She is calm and firm; she never yells; she never takes unacceptable behavior personally. Jaime knows that the students with whom she works struggle in their environment. She reminds them of rules and structures they have developed to keep the class running smoothly and to maximize learning. The students tell me they feel safe in her class and are lucky to be with her. "She never yells." Jaime tells me there is little truancy in her class.

I ask Jaime if she will remain in this school next year, when her current students move on to middle school. Yes, she will stay, she explains, because she feels she is making a difference and she is needed here.

> She is very calm and very firm; she never yells; she never takes unacceptable behavior personally.

It will come as no surprise to you that, to Barron, teaching is much more than a job. It is an authentic commitment to working on behalf of her students. Her clarity about her purpose finds its way into the classroom community that she and her students have created. The students trust her and know she will not harm them, demean them, scream at them, or use her power over them. Her calm voice and caring manner are accompanied by classroom structures that keep the students productive and safe.

Jaime is extremely well prepared all the time. She consistently has a creative, activity-oriented experience in which to engage the class. She takes the students on field trips, monitors their homework, and works with them one-on-one during lunchtime.

Jaime also actively reflects on her teaching. She has some days that are worse than others, some days that are better, but throughout the ups and downs she loves her work and cannot imagine doing anything else.

10-1e Looking Again at Multiple Ways of Teaching and Learning

"Now that my five-year-old niece, Maren, has entered kindergarten, we have an ongoing philosophical discussion about education. 'Teachers know everything,' she says. 'No,' I say. 'Teachers know some things. Nobody knows everything. There are some things you know that your teacher doesn't know.' 'Like what?' 'Like what it feels like to be your Mommy and Daddy's oldest child, to be Gary's good friend, to be my five-year-old niece.'**"**
—Logan, J. (1999). Teaching Stories. New York: Kodansha America.

Throughout this text, we have visited different types of classrooms with varying approaches to teaching. As we have seen, studies in neuroscience show that, for a concept to get hooked into their prior knowledge, individuals need to construct meaning for themselves. We have explored project- and problem-based learning as ways to place the students' own construction of knowledge at the center of their learning experience.

Many educators see "student-centered learning" as an "anything goes" method. On the contrary, student-centered environments seek to draw out students' ideas to deal with the misconceptions that often accompany the learning of something new. Unless we understand what students are thinking about the material in which we engage them, we cannot know if they "get it."

Do remember, however, that student-centered environments use multiple teaching strategies, ranging from direct explanations to project- and problem-based

Student projects become part of the fabric of the classroom.

learning. The successful teacher learns how to adapt the materials to the class in a way that reaches the individual students and asks them to do something to demonstrate their understanding. Hence, student-centered classrooms invite learners to create explanations, demonstrate meaning, and come up with their own ideas and questions related to the content area.

10-1f USING CURRENT TECHNOLOGIES

Today, making connections to students' lived experiences means accessing the wired world of cyberspace in ways that enhance students' critical thinking and their abilities to understand a concept. In previous chapters, we emphasized the growing effect of technology on education. Connect, communicate, and collaborate—these are the three Cs of the newest wave of technology use in the classroom. Teaching can involve creating a class website for which all of the students collaborate to determine the content. Students may use the website to publish digital videos related to a topic of study. With Web 2.0 technology, such as Twitter, blogs, Facebook, and YouTube videos, the user can readily add to the content.

Technology offers two more benefits that are not always appreciated:

1. Learning is more powerful when students are prompted to take information presented to them in one form and "represent" it in an alternative way. The technology now available for teaching and learning helps students do just that. When students create their own representations of information, they provide clues about their thinking and give teachers a view of the accuracy of their conceptions.
2. You have seen the importance of recognizing that there are multiple intelligences and different learning styles. Media convergence on the Internet can help students integrate information from multiple modalities, ensuring that all students, no matter what their learning style, have the opportunity to grasp key concepts.

Consider your teaching role in a "flat" world and take an interest in other languages and the global community. Explore possibilities for linking your class with classes in different regions of the country or in foreign countries. The opportunity to engage your students in communication on a global scale is one of the most exciting teaching challenges of the twenty-first century.

The technology revolution has made possible collaboration across classroom, state, and country borders.

© Ed Kashi/Corbis

Google sponsors a site called Google for Educators (http://www.google.com/educators/) that includes a number of online tools such as blog software and collaborative word-processing applications. The section on Google Earth, a satellite-mapping resource, includes suggestions for use in the classroom. Get a head start and investigate the technological capacities of the schools or districts in which you find yourself observing and practice teaching—and do the same when you get your first teaching job. Remember that your students will be deluged with data and that one of your critical roles will be helping them assess the value of the information to which they are exposed.

10-2 Getting Started in the Teaching Profession

If you follow a traditional path toward becoming a teacher, you will receive guidance along the way and help in finding the full list of requirements for your state. As mentioned

10-2a CERTIFICATION AND STANDARDS

Becoming a teacher in the public schools requires **certification** by your state. A state teaching certificate or license shows that you have met the state's requirements for becoming a teacher at specific grade levels and (especially for higher grades) in a certain subject area. For instance, your certificate might be for elementary education (grades K–6), for middle school social studies, or for middle school and high school biology.

Your state's Department of Education (DOE) website will describe the range of areas for which you can be licensed. Requirements for teacher certificates or licenses vary from state to state. Some states are relatively compatible with other states in their certification requirements; some states are more individualistic. Of course, your teacher education program will go a long way toward preparing you for state certification, but it is important to understand the certification requirements *beyond* completing your program.

The Praxis Tests

> **"**Praxis is the doctrine that when actions are based on sound theory and values, they can make a real difference in the world.**"** —Freire, P. (1970). Pedagogy of the Oppressed. M. B. Ramos (Trans.). New York: Continuum.

Most states require that future teachers pass a state exam or series of exams. The Educational Testing Service has developed **The Praxis Series** of professional assessments for beginning teachers. (As used by social scientists, the term *praxis* relates to action based on principles and theories that have a sound basis in research and experience.) A large number of states use this

previously, field experiences play an important role in teacher preparation. Many states require professional certification, and although the exact process for becoming a teacher varies from state to state, there are some common requirements.

series of tests to assess your knowledge of subject matter and pedagogy.

The Praxis Series consists of three separate kinds of tests:

1. The Praxis I tests measure basic academic skills in reading, mathematics, and writing. Usually you take these tests before entering your teacher education program or before your student teaching or internship.
2. The Praxis II tests measure knowledge about specific subject areas and about principles of learning and teaching. Generally you take these tests when you complete your teacher preparation program.
3. The Praxis III assessment focuses on actual classroom performance. If your state requires Praxis III, the assessment usually takes place in your first year of teaching and leads to a higher level of certification. It includes direct observation of your classroom practice, review of a video or other documentation you send in, and interviews.

Several states offer their own assessments for certification and licensing, but these tests are typically similar to the Praxis tests. See the Review Card at the back of the book for sample test questions, and visit the Praxis website (http://www.ets.org/praxis/) to find out whether the state in which you hope to teach requires the Praxis tests.

The InTASC Standards

Many of the requirements for certification are based on standards and principles called the Interstate New

Learning to teach requires observing, participating, and practicing in real classrooms.

© Elizabeth Crews

Teacher Assessment and Support Consortium (InTASC). They are developed by a national organization, the Council of Chief State School Officers (CCSSO). Established in 1987, InTASC represents a combined effort by numerous state education agencies and national educational organizations to reform the preparation, licensing, and professional development of teachers. The CCSSO is a nonpartisan, nationwide, nonprofit organization of public officials who head departments of elementary and secondary education in the states, the District of Columbia, the Department of Defense Education Activity, and five US extra-state jurisdictions. The CCSSO provides leadership, advocacy, and technical assistance on major educational issues. In 2011, the CCSSO issued the InTASC Model Core Teaching Standards that outline what teachers should know and be able to do to ensure every K–12 student reaches the goal of being ready to enter college or the workforce in today's world. These standards address what effective teaching and learning looks like in our contemporary public education system. The recent update of these standards is designed to address the fact that teachers are now being held to new levels of accountability. The purpose of these standards is to describe a new model of teaching that matches today's public school culture. The broad standards topics listed here can be accessed in greater detail on the InTASC website.

Standard #1: Learner Development.
Standard #2: Learning Differences.
Standard #3: Learning Environments.
Standard #4: Content Knowledge.
Standard #5: Application of Content.
Standard #6: Assessment.
Standard #7: Planning for Instruction.
Standard #8: Instructional Strategies.
Standard #9: Professional Learning and Ethical Practice.
Standard #10: Leadership and Collaboration.
Available at http://www.csso.org/InTASC_Model_Core_Teaching_Standards_2011.

Each of these standards relates to teaching practices and dispositions that have been addressed in this text including: understanding how people learn, differentiation, school climate and culture, knowing and applying content, assessment, and professional development and team work with colleagues, students, and families in your teaching life.

For each of these standards, InTASC has performance expectations that match what the CCSSO is hoping excellent teaching performance may look like.

The National Board for Professional Teaching Standards

As mentioned in Chapter 1, the National Board for Professional Teaching Standards (http://www.nbpts.org/) offers a national system for certifying teachers who meet rigorous standards. These standards are relevant to what you have already explored about teaching and learning. It is an advanced teaching credential but does not replace a state's teaching certificate or license. National Board Certified Teachers (NBCTs) embody these "Five Core Propositions":

- **Proposition 1:** Teachers are committed to students and learning.
- **Proposition 2:** Teachers know the subjects they teach and how to teach those subjects to students.
- **Proposition 3:** Teachers are responsible for managing and monitoring student learning.
- **Proposition 4:** Teachers think systematically about their practice and learn from experience.
- **Proposition 5:** Teachers are members of learning communities. (National Board for Professional Teaching Standards, 2012)

These are themes familiar to all those who are preparing to become teachers. The National Board has used these general propositions to establish standards for certification in many areas of teaching, from early-childhood education through middle-childhood education to the various academic specialties in secondary education. National Board standards are created by committees of educators who are accomplished professionals in their fields.

The process of becoming a NBCT is arduous and has many steps. To seek this certification, you must:

- Hold a bachelor's degree.
- Have three full years of teaching or counseling experience.
- Possess a valid state teaching or counseling license for that period of time, or, if you are teaching where a license is not required, have taught in schools recognized and approved to operate by the state.

Compared with an ordinary teaching certificate, National Board Certification is recognized in all states as a higher level of achievement. To obtain this certification, you must meet the requirements of a portfolio assessment that includes videotapes of your teaching, student work, and your accomplishments outside of your school experience. In addition, you must take an exam that assesses your content knowledge in your certificate area; test centers are located across the country.

10-2b TEACHING POSITIONS HERE AND ABROAD

Teachers are in demand throughout the United States and all over the world. In the United States, the teaching areas in shortest supply include, but are not limited to, special education, bilingual education, earth science, chemistry, physics, mathematics and computer science, and foreign languages. Of course, these shortages vary by particular location and with population trends.

As Chapter 8 indicated, though, the world has shrunk tremendously because of technology. You may want to challenge your thinking by going to a foreign country and gaining firsthand experience teaching there. If you decide to do this, it is wise to find others who have traveled this path before you and learn from them what the experience was like. There are groups of teachers who have taught abroad and can serve as resources for you. You can access these groups through teaching-abroad websites, blogs, Facebook pages, and Twitter feeds.

What kinds of positions are available in foreign countries? Although there are teaching opportunities in all disciplines and languages, the majority of positions available are for native English speakers teaching English as a foreign language. To be eligible for these positions, you usually must hold a certificate for Teaching English as a Foreign Language (TEFL). Native English speakers may take an online course to become certified in TEFL. A number of websites, such as the one shown in Figure 10.1, list opportunities for teaching abroad and offer information about TEFL courses.

In addition, there are more than three hundred American International Schools overseas. These are typically private, nonprofit schools based on a US or British model. Often, the schooling they provide leads to the International Baccalaureate diploma, an international credential that is offered at some schools in this country as well. To explore US International Schools, visit the International Schools Services website (http://www.iss.edu/). Half of the staff members at these schools are from North America. Before signing up for a position at an international school, be certain to follow the reviews of others who have had this experience. Those reviews and contacts are readily available over the Internet.

10-2c TIPS FOR NEW TEACHERS

As you begin your field work or your work in your own classroom, remember that as a teacher you are an educational leader. Your teaching is as much a product of *who you are* as of how you implement strategies. The following list offers some tips as you get started.

- **Learn as much as you can about your school environment.** Learn everything you can about the school in which you will be doing your field placement work or getting your first teaching job. Do your homework. Be prepared.
  - How long has the school been in this community?
  - How many students and teachers are there?
  - How many administrators are there?
  - Who are the students? What types of homes, apartments, or other forms of housing arrangements do they live in?
  - Can you expect a student body that is diverse ethnically? Socially? Economically? How many inclusion classrooms are there?
  - What is the technological capacity of the school? How many SMART Boards are in the school?
  - What does the school website have to say? Is this school or district known for any particular achievements?
  - Do classes have their own websites?
  - How do the students perform on mandated assessments? These scores are a matter of public record.
  - If this is your field placement, from whom do you need permission?
  - Are visitors and invited guests required to sign in? What is the correct protocol?

Figure 10.1

Part of a Screen from the Teach Abroad Website
Teach Abroad is one of a number of websites that offer information about overseas teaching positions and certification.

WHAT COUNTRY DO YOU WANT TO TEACH IN?
any country   GO
text list of countries
POPULAR SEARCHES: China, South Korea, Taiwan, Thailand, Mexico, Japan, England, Spain, United Arab Emirates, India

Begin your search for a TEFL Certification Program

Most Recent Teach Abroad Opportunities

Most recent World Wide postings
Most recent Korean postings
Most recent Taiwanese postings
Most recent Chinese postings

RSS Feeds

SOURCE: From http://www.teachabroad.com/. Reprinted by permission of GoAbroad.com.

Your teaching is as much a product of who you are as of how you implement strategies.

- **Keep a journal.**
  - Record your experiences as you begin. Include your fears and your questions. If you have a smartphone, an iPad, a netbook, or another small electronic device, save these journal entries and look back on them as you continue.
  - Be fully conscious in the classroom. Journaling can help you stay conscious so you do not "shoot from the hip."
- **Join a collegial group, and find a friend.** Become part of a new-teacher group, either in your school or college or in your community. If you cannot find one that meets face-to-face, check for responsible groups online. In the most trying of times, it is often your colleagues who offer the most support and help you move forward. This point was made clearly by the teachers who shared their stories in Chapter 2.

  If you are lucky, you will find one particular person in your new school with whom you can connect and share your experiences of teaching. This kind of relationship often builds into a lasting friendship.

- **Find a mentor.** Connect with an experienced teacher whom you trust, and communicate your hopes and fears to this person. Being a teacher means you are always a learner: learning about yourself, your content area, and your students. There is much to learn from mentors, so seek out a person who can fill this role for you.
- **Remember that teaching is not telling.** Teaching is not about you; it is about the students. Your focus should be on them. How will you engage them? What will

you do on behalf of their learning? *Listen* to them and really hear what they have to say.

- **Plan for creative experiences and activities.** Prepare lessons in which the students' active engagement is at the center, and listen to their ideas. Showing your students that you value what they think is priceless.
- **To create a safe environment, show that you are human.** Do not believe that you have to know everything and do everything right. Model vulnerability for your students; show them that you can laugh at your own mistakes. Students will feel more comfortable when you show that you are learning as well. This does not mean that you are not credible; it simply means that as humans we all make mistakes.
- **Be passionate.** Teachers express their passion for teaching in different ways, but being delighted to be with your students, coming in well prepared, and having a specific plan in mind are all ways to show the students that you care.
- **Differentiate instruction.** Remember that treating all students equally does not ensure equality of outcomes. Equitable and fair-minded teaching considers the ways all of our students, in all their diversity, learn best.

10-3 Educational Associations

Dozens of professional organizations provide continuing support of one kind or another for teachers. These range from national associations that offer professional development resources to local union affiliates that may negotiate your next contract with the school district.

Professional organizations have the potential to create learning communities among their members. They offer rich resources for you to use in planning lessons and expanding your professional knowledge. Some of them also help improve your salary and working conditions and protect your professional rights.

Two of the most prominent organizations are the American Federation of Teachers (AFT) and the National Education Association (NEA). There are also many subject- and grade-level–specific groups that provide resources, grants, and guidance for you as you begin your professional career.

10-3a THE AMERICAN FEDERATION OF TEACHERS

The AFT, a union affiliated with the American Federation of Labor and Congress of Industrial Organizations (AFL-CIO), was founded in 1916 to represent the interests of classroom teachers. Its first member, John Dewey, recognized the importance of teachers' having their own organization. Today, one visit to the organization's website (http://www.aft.org/) reveals a wealth of resources for the classroom teacher and for other education personnel as well. For example, the site provides information about professional development opportunities and grants.

In addition to being a valuable resource, the AFT directly represents teachers in many school districts around the country. The organization has forty-three state affiliates, more than three thousand local affiliates, and more than 1.5 million members. You may find, particularly if you teach in a large urban school system, that the AFT negotiates contracts for the teachers and other school employees in your district. If so, you will probably become a member of the union, and you may want to take an active role in the local affiliate.

You may keep a personal journal . . .

. . . and use it to create an online portfolio!

© Dar Yang Yan/iStockphoto

10-3b THE NATIONAL EDUCATION ASSOCIATION

The NEA, founded in 1857, now has more than 3 million members and more than fourteen thousand local affiliates. In addition to its Code of Ethics, the NEA provides job searches, teaching tips and tools, important resources for your professional development, and activities and workshops of interest in your state. The organization's website (http://www.nea.org/) is a valuable point of entry to these resources.

Since the 1960s, the NEA has functioned as a union, conducting collective bargaining on behalf of teachers and working to protect teachers' rights as employees of a school district. It also acts as a lobbying organization on educational issues, and it helps set professional standards for the teaching profession.

Most teachers belong to either the AFT or the NEA, and some belong to both. Your decision about membership may be governed in part by local conditions, such as which organization represents the teachers at your school. Remember that an important benefit of membership is that it provides links to other teachers for professional collaboration.

10-4 Build Your Teaching Portfolio

Developing a portfolio is an excellent way to organize your thinking about teaching and to display some of your accomplishments on this journey. You should continue to update the portfolio each year you teach. It is your professional and personal record, and it demonstrates your knowledge and beliefs as well as your accomplishments. What you choose to include in your portfolio is a statement of what you think is important.

When you begin to look for a job, you will need a version of your portfolio to present to prospective employers, either on a CD, a thumb or "jump" drive, or in the form of a personal website. The portfolio you show others should be concise, clear, readable, and well organized.

Here are some suggestions for preparing your portfolio:

- Your portfolio should be easily accessible online.
- Include a table of contents so that viewers can skip to parts that particularly concern them.
- Begin with a short essay introducing yourself. In a few paragraphs, describe your interest in teaching and learning and what you have accomplished. See the box for a sample introductory essay.
- Describe your educational philosophy, what you believe a good teacher needs to understand about teaching and learning.

- Discuss your classroom management theory. If your focus is on building community in the classroom, be specific about how you plan to do that.
- Become familiar with the new Common Core State Standards for mathematics and English. (See videocase.)
- Describe your student teaching experience with specific mention of the grade levels you taught and the lessons and activities you prepared. If you have copies of supervisors' observations that attest to your abilities, include them.
- Include photos or electronic files of a few samples of student work from your field experience.

TEACHSOURCE VIDEO CASE

Find the TeachSource Video Case on the CourseMate website, "Common Core Standards: A New Lesson Plan for America." A seventh-grade math teacher in Atlanta shares her thinking about the new Common Core State Standards in mathematics. These standards place all students K–12 on the same track in mathematics and reading. Consider the following question:

Some educators are worried that Common Core Standards will "dumb down" the curriculum... how could that happen?

- If you have approved photos of yourself and a class in action, or even a brief video (no more than three minutes long), include them. ("Approved" means that you have received consent forms from the other people shown in the photos or video.)
- Include your resume, certifications, awards, and letters of reference.
- Do not overdo it. We live in a fast-paced culture, and people do not have a great deal of time to read your portfolio. Be concise and to the point.

A SAMPLE INTRODUCTORY ESSAY FOR A PORTFOLIO

I have just graduated from Hofstra University, where I majored in biology and secondary education. I have always loved science and enjoy sharing it with others. I have had experience student teaching in grades 7–9 and 10–11. My certification area in biology and general science prepares me to teach grades 7–12 in New York State. I have passed all the exams and requirements for this initial certification.

For my field experience, I have been a participant-observer in grades 8 and 11, and I feel equally comfortable in the middle school and the high school. I have also spent two summers as a counselor at an environmental education camp in Maine, where I enjoyed working with teenagers in a natural setting. I believe my organizational skills, my ability to plan, my understanding of the content area, and my passion for teaching will enable me to be a successful new teacher.

10-5 Concluding Thoughts

10-5a TURNING TO TEACHING

As we explored in Chapter 1, people often think that because of their many years as students in classrooms, they can also teach. Such was the case for actor Tony Danza who expressed a desire to teach after many years working as an actor. With a college education and a major in English, he began teaching in a Philadelphia inner-city high school, and his experiences were being documented for an A&E television show called, coincidentally, "TEACH."

While the cameras roll, Danza quickly learns that being an effective teacher requires many skills, and he professes to wanting to do "right" by the students, maintain their attention, and instill in them a desire to learn. He loves teaching but admits that as a first-year teacher he was unprepared for how complicated it gets and how much he has to do. The experience he had revealed the joys and the frustrations of helping students learn and how much work is needed to prepare adequately. Because he is not certified, a mentor teacher sits in the class with him. He certainly seems to have some of the attributes described in the beginning of the chapter—a centered

Actor-turned-teacher Tony Danza discovers the challenges and joys of teaching.

© Bonnie Weller/MCT/newscom

forget to pick it up at the main office of the junior high where I taught science. The school secretary used to tease me, but one day she gave me a wonderful compliment. She said, "Judging by the smile I always see on your face, I can tell that you get paid for this job in other ways." I was touched by this statement (although my landlord, of course, needed payment in cash).

Becoming a teacher is a commitment to a life of service that has the potential to bring you great joy and personal satisfaction. My best wishes to you on this journey.

presence in the classroom, a sensitivity to the classroom setting, an ability to respond thoughtfully to each student, and a desire to help students feel capable and competent. He also learned that preparation is the key and you cannot just "wing" it with the students. Excellent preparation, guidelines, and expectations for the students count!

10-3b PASSION QUOTIENT

A noted author (Friedman, 2006) talks about something he calls the "passion quotient" for teaching. He tells the story of a young child who receives his or her first fire truck or doctor's kit and wants to be a fireman or a doctor. That innocent passion for a certain job, without knowing the salary or the working hours or the preparation required, is what you need to get back in touch with. You need to discover your inner passion, and when you find it, you will know it.

You may already know that your passion is teaching, in which case you will be eager to explore the professional organizations described in this chapter. Or you may still be searching and wondering. If we are going to be successful, what we select as our life's work must bring us joy, especially if it is teaching. Remember, it is fine to change your mind and say, "I thought this was for me, but now I see I'm better suited to another career."

I want to remind you, though, that teaching is wonderfully satisfying work. The feeling you get when you realize that you have made a contribution on behalf of someone else's development is indescribable. I remember my first year of teaching like it was yesterday. I was nervous, overprepared, and in the end overjoyed. Although I needed the paycheck (which in 1966 was quite meager), I would

© RonTech2000/iStockphoto

STUDY TOOLS
CHAPTER 10

Located at back of the textbook
- Rip out Chapter Review Card
- Note-Taking Assistance

Located at CengageBrain.com
- Review Key Terms Flash Cards (Print or Online)
- Complete Practice Quizzes to prepare for tests
- Complete "Crossword Puzzle" to review key terms
- Watch the TeachSource Video Case "Common Core Standards: A New Lesson Plan for America"

References

AAUW Educational Foundation. (2001). *Hostile Hallways: Bullying, Teasing, and Sexual Harassment in School.* Washington, DC: American Association of University Women Educational Foundation.

———. (2004). *Harassment-Free Hallways: How to Stop Sexual Harassment in School.* Washington, DC: American Association of University Women Educational Foundation.

Aleman, A. M. (2006). Latino demographic, democratic individuality, and educational accountability: A pragmatist's view. *Educational Researcher,* 35(7): 25–35.

American Educational Research Association. (2004). English language learners: Boosting academic achievement. *Research Points,* 2:1 (Winter).

American Federation of Teachers. (2003). *Where We Stand: Teacher Quality.* AFT Teachers Educational Issues Department, Item Number 39–0230. Washington, DC: Author.

———. (2007). A vision that endures. http://www.aft.org /about/vision.htm; retrieved February 7, 2007.

Anderson, B. C. (2000). An A for home schooling. *City Journal,* 10(3), Summer. New York: Manhattan Institute for Policy Research.

Annie E. Casey Foundation. (2001). *Where Kids Count, Place Matters: Trends in the Well-Being of Iowa Children.* Des Moines: Iowa Kids Count.

———. (2006a). 2000 Census data: Key facts for United States. Kids Count Census Data Online, http://www.aecf .org/; retrieved February 10, 2010.

———. (2006b). *2006 Kids Count Data Book: State Profiles of Child Well-Being.* Washington, DC: Author.

———. (2007). Children in immigrant families: Percent: 2005. Kids Count State-Level Data Online. http://www .kidscount.org/sld/compare_results.jsp?i=750; retrieved March 20, 2010.

———. (2009a). Children in single-parent families: Percent: 2008. Kids Count State-Level Data Online, http://www .kidscount.org/sld/compare_results.jsp?i=721; retrieved April 20, 2010.

———. (2009b). *Kids Count Indicator Brief: Reducing the High School Dropout Rate.* Baltimore, MD: Author. Available: http://www.aecf.org/KnowledgeCenter /Publications.aspx.

———. (2011). *Kids Count Data Book* Online, http ://datacenter.kidscount.org/databook/2011/; retrieved February 23, 2012.

Ashford, E. (2009). Technology facilitates learning in small groups. *eSchool News,* November 1. Available: http ://www.eschoolnews.com/2009/11/01/esn-special-report -small-group-collaboration/.

Ball, A. (2003). Geo-literacy: Forging new ground. Edutopia-online, http://www.edutopia.org/geo-literacy-forging-new -ground; retrieved May 11, 2010.

———. (2004). Innovative techniques provide a well rounded education. Edutopia-online, http://www .edutopia.org/landry; retrieved April 5, 2010.

Bavelier, D. & Green, C. S. (2009). Increasing speed of processing with action video games. *Current Directions in Psychological Science* 18(6): 321–326.

Bennett-Goleman, T. (2001). *Emotional Alchemy: How the Mind Can Heal the Heart.* London: Harmony Books.

Bickart, T., Jablon, J., & Dodge, D. T. (2000). *Building the Primary Classroom: A Complete Guide to Teaching and Learning.* Washington, DC: Teaching Strategies, Inc.

Bielick, S., Chandler, K., & Broughman, S. P. (2001). *Homeschooling in the United States: 1999* (NCES 2001–033). Washington, DC: US Department of Education, National Center for Education Statistics.

Bloom, B. S., Englehart, M. D., Furst, E. J., Hill, W. H. & Krathwohl, D. R. (1956). *Taxonomy of Educational Objectives: Cognitive Domain.* New York: Longmans, Green & Co.

Blythe, Tina. (1998). *The Teaching for Understanding Guide.* San Francisco: Jossey-Bass.

Bolton, M. M. (2009). Their words, unleashed by wiki: Web tool opens brave new world for young writers. *The Boston Globe,* December 3. Available: http://www.boston .com/news/local/articles/2009/12/03/young_writers_in _westwood_unleash_their_best_words_with_web_tool /?page=2.

The Boston Historical Society and Museum. (2010). Who were the Puritans? http://www.bostonhistory.org/?s =librarymuseum&p=researchguide; retrieved July 10, 2010.

Bransford, J., Brown, A. L., & Cocking, R. (Eds.). (2000). *How People Learn: Brain, Mind, Experience, and School.* Washington, DC: National Academy Press.

Bransford, J. & Donovan, S. (2004). *How Students Learn.* Washington, DC: National Academy Press.

Braun, H., Jenkins, F., & Grigg, W. (2006). *A Closer Look at Charter Schools Using Hierarchical Linear Modeling* (NCES 2006–460). Washington, DC: US Department of Education.

Brooks, J. G. (2002). *Schooling for Life: Reclaiming the Essence of Learning.* Reston, VA: Association for Supervision and Curriculum Development.

———. (2005). One-to-one interview with Janice Koch. Hempstead, NY: Hofstra University.

Brooks, J. G. & Brooks, M. (1999). *In Search of Understanding: The Case for Constructivist Classrooms.* Reston, VA: Association for Supervision and Curriculum Development.

Brooks-Gunn, J., Duncan, G. J., & Aber, J. L. (Eds.). (2000). *Neighborhood Poverty. Volume 1: Context and Consequences for Children.* New York: Russell Sage Foundation.

Brown, J. (2000). *The Sea Accepts All Rivers and Other Poems.* Alexandria, VA: Miles River Press.

Brown-Chidsey, R. (2007). No more "waiting to fail." *Educational Leadership* 65(2): 40–46.

Bruner, J. S. (1960). *The Process of Education.* Cambridge, MA: Harvard University Press.

———. (1966). *Toward a Theory of Instruction.* Cambridge, MA: Harvard University Press.

Bullough, R. V. & Gitlin, A. D. (2001). *Becoming a Student: Linking Knowledge Production and Practice of Teaching.* New York: Routledge Falmer.

Carnegie Forum on Education and the Economy. (1986). *A Nation Prepared: Teachers for the 21st Century.* New York: Carnegie Corporation.

Carr, N. (2010). *The Shallows: What the Internet is doing to our Brain.* New York: WW Norton & Co.

Carter, G. (2006). Supporting the whole child. *ASCD Education Update* 48(12): 2, 8. Alexandria, VA: Association for Supervision and Curriculum Development.

Cawelti, G. (2006). The side effects of NCLB. *Educational Leadership* 64(3): 64–88.

Center on Education Policy. (2007). *Why We Still Need Public Schools: Public Education for the Common Good.* Washington, DC: Nancy Kober. http://www.cep-D.C.org/; retrieved February 1, 2010.

Center for Education Reform. (2005). *All about Charter Schools.* Washington, DC: Center for Education Reform.

Centers for Disease Control and Prevention (CDC). (2010). Youth risk behavior surveillance—United States, 2009. *Morbidity and Mortality Weekly Report* 59(SS-05), June 4.

Chana High School. (2010). A California model continuation high school. http://www.puhsd.k12.ca.us/chana/; retrieved January 25, 2010.

Christenson, S. L. & Thurlow, M. L. (2004). Keeping kids in school: Efficacy of check and connect for dropout prevention. *NASP Communiqué* 32(6): 37–40.

Cohen, J. (2006). Social, emotional, ethical, and academic education: Creating a climate for learning, participation in democracy, and well-being. *Harvard Educational Review* 76(2): 201–237.

Collaborative for Academic, Social, and Emotional Learning (CASEL). (2010). http://www.casel.org/; retrieved April 9, 2010.

Condliffe Lagemann, E. (2007). Public rhetoric, public responsibility, and the public schools. *Education Week* 26(37): 30, 40.

Corcoran, K. (2002). Bullying slurs are rampant, nationwide survey finds. *San Jose Mercury News*, December 13.

Council of Chief State School Officers. (2007). Interstate New Teacher Assessment and Support Consortium (INTASC). http://www.ccsso.org/Projects/interstate_new_teacher_assessment_and_support _consortium/780.cfm; retrieved February 13, 2007.

Cowan, Brian (2011). Digital natives are not necessarily digital learners. *The Chronicle of Higher Education*, Nov 6, 2011. http://chronicle.com/article/Why-Digital-Natives-Arent/129606/.

Davis, G. A. & Rimm, S. B. (2004). *Education of the Gifted and Talented.* (5th ed.) Boston: Allyn & Bacon.

Day, C. (2004). *A Passion for Teaching.* New York: Routledge.

DeBell, M. & Chapman, C. (2003). *Computer and Internet Use by Children and Adolescents in 2001 (NCES 2004–014).* Washington, DC: US Department of Education, National Center for Education Statistics.

Deal, T. & Peterson, K. (1999). *Shaping School Culture.* San Francisco: Jossey-Bass.

Dee, T. S. (2005). A teacher like me: Does race, ethnicity, or gender matter? *American Economic Review* 95(2): 158–165.

———. (2006). The why chromosome. *Education Next,* No. 4 (Fall): 68–75.

Dewey, J. (1916/2004). *Democracy and Education.* New York: Dover.

———. (1938). *Experience and Education.* New York: Collier Macmillan.

Dinkes, R., Cataldi, E. F., & Lin-Kelly, W. (2007). *Indicators of School Crime and Safety: 2007 (NCES 2008-021/NCJ 219553).* Washington, DC: US Department of Education, National Center for Education Statistics.

Downes, S. (2004). Educational blogging. *Educause Review,* September/October: 14–26.

Duckworth, E. (1991). Twenty-four, forty-two, and I love you: Keeping it complex. *Harvard Educational Review* 61:1 (February): 1–24.

Eccles, J. S., Lord, S., & Midgley, C. (1991). What are we doing to adolescents? The impact of educational contexts on early adolescents. *American Journal of Education* 99: 521–542.

Eccles, J. S. & Midgley, C. (1989). Stage/environment fit: Developmentally appropriate classrooms for early adolescents. In R. Ames & C. Ames (Eds.), *Research on Motivation in Education*, Vol. 3. San Diego, CA: Academic, pp. 139–186.

Education Commission of the States. (2007a). Charter schools: Quick facts. http://www.ecs.org/clearinghouse/76/44/7644.pdf; retrieved May 13, 2010.

———. (2007b). StateNotes: Charter school teacher certification. http://mb2.ecs.org/reports/Report.aspx?id=93; retrieved November 13, 2009.

Eliot, Lise (2009). *Pink Brains, Blue Brains: How Small Differences Grow into Troublesome Gaps and What We Can Do about It.* New York: Houghton Mifflin, Harcourt.

Evans, S. (1989). *Born for Liberty: A History of Women in America.* New York: Free Press Publications.

Farber, B. A. (1991). *Crisis in Education: Stress and Burnout in the American Teacher.* San Francisco: Jossey-Bass.

Fein, R. A., Vossekuil, B., Pollack, W. S., Borum, R., Modzeleski, W., & Reddy, M. (2002). *Threat Assessment in Schools: A Guide to Managing Threatening Situations and to Creating Safe School Climates.* Washington, DC: United States Secret Service and United States Department of Education.

Felder, R. M. & Brent, R. (2005). Understanding student differences. *Journal of Engineering Education* 94(1): 57–72.

Felder, R. M. & Silverman, L. K. (1988, 2002). Learning and teaching styles in engineering education. *Journal of Engineering Education* 78(7): 674–681. Author's Preface by R. M. Felder, written in 2002, http://www4.ncsu.edu /unity/lockers/users/f/felder/public/Papers/LS-1988.pdf; retrieved June 30, 2010.

Fisch, K. (2006). This is not education as usual. http://the fischbowl.blogspot.com/2006/12/this-is-not-education-as-usual.html; posted December 15, 2006, retrieved December 18, 2006.

———. (2009). The Fischbowl: Did you know? http ://thefischbowl.blogspot.com/2009/09/did-you-know-40 -economist-media.html; retrieved March 29, 2010.

———. (2011). Did you know? (shift happens) version 4.0. http://thefischbowl.blogspot.com/2011/01/ahs-faculty -dance-2011.html.

Freire, P. (1970). *Pedagogy of the Oppressed.* M. B. Ramos (Trans.). New York: Continuum.

Friedman, T. (2006). *The World Is Flat: A Brief History of the Twenty-First Century.* (Updated and expanded ed.) New York: Farrar, Straus and Giroux.

Fry, R. (2006). *The Changing Landscape of American Public Education: New Students, New Schools.* Washington, DC: Pew Hispanic Center Research Report.

Ganley, B. (2009). Teaching and learning with technology. Presentation at the University of British Columbia. http ://vimeo.com/3008955/; retrieved June 12, 2010.

Gardner, H. (1993). *Frames of Mind: The Theory of Multiple Intelligences.* New York: Basic Books.

———. (2003). *Intelligence Reframed: Multiple Intelligences for the 21st Century.* New York: Basic Books.

———. (2006). *Multiple Intelligences: New Horizons.* New York: Basic Books.

Gay, Lesbian and Straight Education Network (GLSEN). National School Climate Survey. http://www.glsen.org /cgi-bin/iowa/all/home/index.html; retrieved February 2, 2010.

Gladwell, M. (2008). Most likely to succeed: How can we hire when we can't tell who is right for the job? *The New Yorker Magazine,* December 15. Available: http://www .newyorker.com/reporting/2008/12/15/081215fa_fact _gladwell?currentPage=all.

Goleman, D. (2006). *Emotional Intelligence: Why It Can Matter More Than IQ.* New York: Bantam.

Graham, K. A. (2010). Tony Danza goes back to school. *Los Angeles Times,* March 31. Available: http://articles.latimes .com/2010/mar/31/entertainment/la-et-danza31-2010 mar31.

Greene, J. P., Forster, G., & Winters, M. (2003, July). Education Working Paper No. 1. New York: The Manhattan Institute for Policy Research.

Greene, M. (1978). *Landscapes of Learning.* New York: Teachers College Press.

———. (1995). *Releasing the Imagination: Essays on Education, the Arts, and Social Change.* San Francisco: Jossey-Bass.

Guilfoyle, C. (2006). NCLB: Is there life beyond testing? *Educational Leadership* 64(3): 8–13.

Hammerness, K. (2006). *Seeing Through Teachers' Eyes: Professional Ideals and Classroom Practices.* New York: Teachers College Press.

Hanushek, E., Kain, J. F., O'Brien, D. M., & Rivkin, S. G. (2005). The market for teacher quality. NBER Working Paper Series, Vol. w11154. Available: http://ssrn.com /abstract=669453.

Hart, B. & Risley, T. R. (1995). *Meaningful Differences in the Everyday Experience of Young American Children.* Baltimore: Brookes Publishing Co.

Hinchcliffe, D. (2006). The state of Web 2.0. http://web2 .wsj2.com/the_ state_of_web_20.htm; retrieved December 10, 2006.

Hittie, M. (2000). Building community in the classroom. Paper presented at the International Education Summit, Detroit, Michigan, June 26, 2006.

Hoffman, N. (1981). *Woman's True Profession: Voices from the History of Teaching.* New York: The Feminist Press and McGraw Hill.

Horgan, J. (2010). So many links, so little time. *Wall Street Journal,* June 4, 2010. http://online.wsj.com/article /SB10001424052748703559004575256790495393722. html.

Horn, M. & Stark, H. (2011). *The Rise of K-12 Blended Learning.* Innosight Institute. http://www .innosightinstitute.org/innosight/wp-content/uploads /2011/01/The-Rise-of-K-12-Blended-Learning.pdf.

Humphreys, T. (1998). *A Different Kind of Discipline.* Dublin, Ireland: Gill & Macmillan, Ltd.

Information Please Database. (2006). State compulsory school attendance laws. http://www.infoplease.com/ipa /A0112617.html; retrieved February 22, 2010.

Initiative on Educational Excellence for Hispanic Americans. (2002). Ten reasons to become a teacher. http://www.yic .gov/publications/tenreasons/; retrieved January 25, 2010.

International Society for Technology in Education. (2002). *National Educational Technology Standards for Teachers: Preparing Teachers to Use Technology.* Washington, DC: Author.

Intrator, S. (2003). *Tuned in and Fired Up: How Teaching Can Inspire Real Learning in the Classroom.* New Haven, CT: Yale University Press.

Jackson, P. (1968). *Life in Classrooms.* New York: Holt, Rinehart & Winston.

Jackson, P., Corey, S., Kleibard, H., & Gage, N. L. (1968). *The Way Teaching Is.* Reston, VA: Association for Supervision and Curriculum Development.

Joubert, J. (2005). *The Notebooks of Joseph Joubert.* Paul Auster (Trans.). New York: The New York Review of Books.

Jukes, I. (2006). From Gutenberg to Gates to Google (and beyond . . .): Education for the online world. http://ibo .org/ibap/conference/documents/IanJukes-From GutenbergtoGatestoGoogleandBeyond1.pdf; retrieved December 2, 2009.

Juvonen, J., Le, V., Kaganoff, T., Augustine, C. H., & Constant, L. (2004). *Focus on the Wonder Years: Challenges Facing the American Middle School.* Santa Monica, CA: Rand Corporation.

Kaiser Family Foundation. (2010). Generation M2: Media in the lives of 8- to 18-year-olds. http://www.kff.org/entmedia/upload/8010.pdf; retrieved February 1, 2010.

Kashen, S. (1994). Bilingual education and second-language acquisition theory. In C. F. Lebya (Ed.), *Schooling and Language Minority Students*. Los Angeles: California State University, pp. 61–63.

Kelley, T. (2006). Talk in class turns to God, setting off public debate on rights. *New York Times*, December 18. Available: http://www.nytimes.com/2006/12/18/nyregion.

Kim, S. H. & Bagaka, J. (2005). The digital divide in students' usage of technology tools: A multilevel analysis of the role of teacher practices and classroom characteristics. *Contemporary Issues in Technology and Teacher Education* 5(3/4): 318–329.

Klein, S., Ortman, P., & Friedman, B. (2002). What is the field of gender equity in education? In J. Koch & B. Irby (Eds.), *Defining and Redefining Gender Equity in Education*. Greenwich, CT: Information Age Publishing.

Kliewer, C. (1998). The meaning of inclusion. *Mental Retardation* 36: 317.

Klopfer, E., Osterweil, S., & Salen, K. (2009). Moving learning games forward. An MIT Education Arcade paper. Available: http://education.mit.edu/papers/Moving-LearningGamesForward_EdArcade.pdf.

Koch, J. (2002). Gender issues in the classroom. In W. R. Reynolds & G. E. Miller (Eds.), *Educational Psychology*. Volume 7 of the *Comprehensive Handbook of Psychology*. Editor-in-Chief: I. B. Weiner. New York: Wiley.

Kohn, A. (1999). *Punished by Rewards: The Trouble with Gold Stars, Incentive Plans, A's, Praise, and Other Bribes*. Boston: Houghton Mifflin.

Kosciw, J. G., Diaz, E. M., & Greytak, E. A. (2008). *The 2007 National School Climate Survey: The Experiences of Lesbian, Gay, Bisexual and Transgender Youth in Our Nation's Schools*. New York: Gay, Lesbian and Straight Education Network.

Kounin, J. S. (1970). *Discipline and Group Management in Classrooms*. New York: Holt, Rinehart and Winston.

Krug, E. A. (1964). *The Shaping of the American High School, 1880–1920*. New York: Harper & Row.

Kyraciou, C. (2001). *Essential Teaching Skills*. Cheltenham, United Kingdom: Nelson Thornes LTD.

Lareau, A. (2003). *Unequal Childhoods: Class, Race, and Family Life*. Berkeley and Los Angeles: University of California Press.

Levine, M. (2007). The essential cognitive backpack. *Educational Leadership* 64(7): 16–22.

Lionni, L. (1970). *Fish Is Fish*. New York: Scholastic Books.

Lofing, N. (2007). Chana named model school. *Sacramento Bee*, April 5. Available: http://www.sacbee.com/293/v-print/story/148899.html.

Logan, J. (1999). *Teaching Stories*. New York: Kodansha America.

Lowe, C. (2002). Why weblogs? http://kairosnews.org/why-weblogs; posted July 27, 2002, retrieved December 20, 2009.

Lowes, S. (2005). Online teaching and classroom change: The impact of virtual high school on its teachers and their schools. Teachers College, Columbia University: Institute for Learning Technologies. http://www.ilt.columbia.edu/publications/lowes_final.pdf; retrieved January 16, 2010.

Maker, J. & Nielson, A. (1996). *Curriculum Development and Teaching Strategies for Gifted Learners*. (2nd ed.) Austin, TX: PRO-ED.

Manning, M. L. (2000). A brief history of the middle school. *The Clearing House* 73(4): 288–301.

Markoff, J. (2006). For $150, third-world laptop stirs big debate. *The New York Times*, November 30.

McBrien, J. L. & Brandt, R. S. (1997). *The Language of Learning: A Guide to Education Terms*. Alexandria, VA: Association for Supervision and Curriculum Development.

McGuire, W., Ed. (1954). *Collected Works of C. J. Jung*, Vol. 17. Princeton, NJ: Princeton University Press.

McGuirk, J. (2001). "Youth at risk": Is technology the answer? Brisbane, AU: Australian National Training Authority. Available: http://www.eric.ed.gov/PDFS/ED480395.pdf.

Mehta, S. (2009). Controlling a classroom isn't as easy as ABC. *Los Angeles Times*, December 14, p. A1.

Miller, L. (2004). 12 tips for new teachers. In K. D. Salas, R. Tenorio, S. Walters, & D. Weiss (Eds.), *The New Teacher Book: Finding Purpose, Balance, and Hope During Your First Years in the Classroom*. Milwaukee, WI: Rethinking Schools, Ltd.

Minority Teacher Recruitment Project. (2010). University of Louisville College of Education and Human Development. http://louisville.edu/education/research/special-projects/mtrp/; retrieved March 3, 2010.

Mitchell, S. (2004). *Charter Schools, Still Making Waves*. Washington, DC: Center for Education Reform.

Moe, T. M. (2001). *A Primer on America's Schools*. Stanford: Hoover Institution Press.

Moos, R. H. (1979). *Evaluating Educational Environments: Procedures, Measures, Findings, and Policy Implications*. San Francisco: Jossey-Bass.

Moran, S., Kornhaber, M., & Gardner, H. (2006). Orchestrating multiple intelligences. *Educational Leadership* 64(1): 23–27.

National Assessment of Educational Progress. (2005). *America's Charter Schools: Results from the NAEP 2003 Pilot Study* (NCES 2005–456). Washington, DC: US Department of Education.

National Association for Gifted Children. (2010). What is gifted? http://www.nagc.org; retrieved October 14, 2010.

National Association for Gifted Children. (2012). How many gifted children are there in the US? http://www.nagc.org/index2.aspx?id=548; retrieved January 8, 2012.

National Board for Professional Teaching Standards. (2002). What teachers should know and be able to do. Arlington, VA: Author. http://www.nbpts.org/UserFiles/File/what_teachers.pdf; retrieved January 5, 2010.

National Center for Education Statistics. (2006). *The Condition of Education 2006* (NCES 2006–071). Washington, DC: US Government Printing Office.

———. (2009). Fast facts: Enrollment trends. http://nces.ed.gov/fastfacts/; retrieved February 17, 2010.

National Center on Education and the Economy. (2006). *Tough Choices or Tough Times: The Report of the New Commission on the Skills of the American Workforce.* San Francisco: Jossey-Bass.

National Collaborative on Diversity in the Teaching Force. (2004). *Assessment of Diversity in America's Teaching Force: A Call to Action.* Washington, DC: National Education Association.

National Commission on Excellence in Education. (1983). *A Nation at Risk: The Imperative for Educational Reform.* Washington, DC: US Department of Education.

National Education Association. (1899). Report of the Committee on College Entrance Requirements. *Journal of the Proceedings and Addresses of the Thirty-Eighth Annual Meeting, Los Angeles,* pp. 632–817.

———. (1975). Code of ethics of the education profession. http://www.nea.org/aboutnea/code.html; retrieved July 14, 2006.

———. (2003). *Status of the American Public School Teacher 2000–2001.* Washington, DC: Author.

———. (2006a, May 2). National Teacher Day spotlights key issues facing profession. http://www.nea.org/newsreleases/2006/nr060502.html; retrieved July 14, 2006.

———. (2006b). *Rankings and Estimates: Rankings of the States 2005 and Estimates of School Statistics 2006.* Washington, DC: Author.

———. (2007). Issues in education: Charter schools. http://www.nea.org/charter/index.html; retrieved May 13, 2007.

———. (2009). *Status of the American Public School Teacher 2005–2006.* Washington, DC: Author.

National School Boards Foundation. (2007). Safe and smart: Research and guidelines for children's use of the Internet. http://www.nsbf.org/safe-smart/index.html; retrieved May 30, 2007.

Nelson, C. & Wilson, K. (1998). *Seeding the Process of Multicultural Education.* Plymouth, MN: Minnesota Inclusiveness Program.

New Commission on the Skills of the American Workforce. (2006). *Tough Choices or Tough Times.* Washington, DC: National Center on Education and the Economy.

Northeast Foundation for Children. (2007). What is the Responsive Classroom approach? http://www.responsiveclassroom.org/about/aboutrc.html; retrieved May 29, 2007.

Oakes, J. (1985). *Keeping Track.* New Haven: Yale University Press.

Office for Civil Rights. (1997). *Sexual Harassment: It's Not Academic.* Washington, DC: US Department of Education.

———. (2001). *Revised Sexual Harassment Guidance: Harassment of Students by School Employees, Other Students, or Third Parties.* Washington, DC: US Department of Education.

Olweus, D. (2003, March). A profile of bullying at school. *Educational Leadership* 60(6): 12–17.

O'Neal, C. (2007). How online simulations work in the classroom. Available online at: http://www.edutopia.org/online-simulations-classroom; retrieved February 3, 2010.

Orenstein, P. (2009). Stop your search engines. *New York Times Magazine,* October 25.

Osterman, K. (2000). Students' need for belongingness in the school community. *Review of Educational Research* 70: 323–367.

Oxendine, L. (1989). *Dick and Jane Are Dead: Basal Reader Takes a Back Seat to Student Writing.* Charleston, WV: Appalachia Educational Laboratory, Inc.

Palmer, P. (1998). *The Courage to Teach: Exploring the Inner Landscape of a Teacher's Life.* San Francisco: Jossey-Bass.

Pape, L., Adams, R., & Ribiero, C. (2005). The virtual high school: Collaboration and online professional development. In Z. L. Berge & T. Clark (Eds.), *Virtual Schools: Planning for Success.* New York: Teachers College Press.

Parsad, B. & Jones, J. (2005). *Internet Access in US Public Schools and Classrooms: 1994–2003* (NCES 2005–015). Washington, DC: US Department of Education, National Center for Education Statistics.

Perkins, D. (1993). Teaching for understanding. *American Educator* 17(3): 28–35.

The Pew Forum on Religion and Public Life. (2002). *Americans Struggle with Religion's Role at Home and Abroad.* Washington, DC: Author.

———. (2010). US Religious Landscape Survey. http://religions.pewforum.org/reports/; retrieved March 3, 2010.

Prensky, M. (2001, October). Digital natives, digital immigrants. *On the Horizon* 9(5).

Princiotta, D. & Bielick, S. (2006). *Homeschooling in the United States: 2003* (NCES 2006–042). Washington, DC: US Department of Education, National Center for Education Statistics.

Project Tomorrow. (2007). Speak up 2006: Snapshot of selected national findings from teachers. http://www.tomorrow.org/docs/Speak%20Up%202006%20National%20Snapshot_Teacher.pdf; retrieved May 26, 2007.

Rasmussen, K. (1997). Using real-life problems to make real-world connections. *Curriculum Update,* Summer. Alexandria, VA: Association for Supervision and Curriculum Development.

Ravitch, D. (2012). http://www.thedailybeast.com/articles/2012/02/10/obama-grants-waivers-to-nclb-and-makes-a-bad-situation-worse.html; retrieved Feb 17, 2012.

Ray, B. (2004). *Home Educated and Now Adults.* Salem, OR: National Home Education Research Institute.

Rimm-Kaufman, S. (2006). *Social and Academic Learning Study on the Contribution of the Responsive Classroom Approach.* Turners Falls, MA: Northeast Foundation for Children.

Rivers, C. & Barnett, R. (2011). *The Truth about Girls and Boys: Challenging Toxic Stereotypes about Our Children.* New York: Colombia University Press.

Robinson, K. (2006). Do schools kill creativity? Invited talk at the Technology, Entertainment, Design (TED) Conference, Monterey, CA. http://www.ted.com/index.php/talks/view/id/66; retrieved May 24, 2009.

Rogers, C. R. (1983). *Freedom to Learn for the 80s.* Columbus, OH: Charles Merrill.

Ryan, K. & Cooper, J. M. (2007). *Those Who Can, Teach.* (11th ed.) Boston: Houghton Mifflin.

Ryan, K. & Cooper, J. M. (2013). *Those Who Can, Teach.* Belmont, CA: Wadsworth, Cengage Learning.

Ryan, M. (2010). iPods touch Salem-Keizer schools. *Statesman Journal,* March 31, p. 1.

Sadker, D. M. & Zittleman, K. R. (2007). *Teachers, Schools, and Society: A Brief Introduction to Education.* New York: McGraw-Hill.

———. (2009). *Still Failing at Fairness: How Gender Bias Cheats Girls and Boys and What We Can Do about It.* New York: Scribner.

Sadker, M. & Sadker, D. (1995). *Failing at Fairness: How Our Schools Cheat Girls.* New York: Touchstone/Simon & Schuster.

Sampson, R. (2002). *Bullying in Schools.* Problem-Oriented Guides for Police Series, Guide No. 12. Washington, DC: Office of Community Oriented Policing Services, US Department of Justice. http://www.popcenter.org/problems/PDFs/Bullying_in_Schools.pdf; retrieved January 10, 2010.

Schaffhauser, D. (2010). Realityworks teaches business ed with online simulation games. THE Journal, April 2. Available: http://thejournal.com/articles/2010/04/02/realityworks-teaches-business-ed-with-online-simulation-games.aspx.

Schön, D. A. (1983). *The Reflective Practitioner: How Professionals Think in Action.* New York: Basic Books.

Schwartz, Allan. (2011). Online high schools attracting elite names. *New York Times,* Nov 19, 2011. http://www.nytimes.com/2011/11/20/education/stanfords-online-high-school-raises-the-bar.html?pagewanted=all.

Scott, A. O. (2000). Sense and nonsense. *New York Times Magazine,* November 26. http://partners.nytimes.com/library/magazine/home/20001126mag-seuss.html; retrieved July 28, 2010.

Searls, D. (2005). Getting flat, part 2. *Linux Journal.* http://www.linuxjournal.com/article/8280; retrieved April 29, 2010.

Sears, J. (1991). Teaching for diversity: Student sexual identities. *Educational Leadership* 49(1): 54–57.

Seligman, M. E. P. (2002). *Authentic Happiness.* New York: Free Press.

Seligman, M. E. P., Steen, T. A., Park, N., & Peterson, C. (2005). Positive psychology progress: Empirical validation of interventions. *American Psychologist* 60: 410–421.

Selingo, J. (2004). In the classroom, web logs are the new bulletin boards. *New York Times,* Circuits, August 19.

Shulman, L. (1987). Knowledge and teaching: Foundations of the new reform. *Harvard Educational Review* 57(1):1–22.

Slavin, R. E. & Madden, N. A. (2006). *Success for All: 2006 Summary of Research on Achievement Outcomes.* Baltimore: Johns Hopkins University, Center for Data-Driven Reform in Education.

Smith, T. W. & Lambie, G. W. (2005). Teachers' responsibilities when adolescent abuse and neglect are suspected. *Middle School Journal* 36(3): 33–40.

Snyder, T. & Dillow, S. (2010). *Digest of Education Statistics 2009* (NCES 2010–013). Washington, DC: US Department of Education, National Center for Education Statistics.

Snyder, T. D., ed. (1993). *120 Years of American Education: A Statistical Portrait.* Washington, DC: US Department of Education, National Center for Education Statistics.

Snyder, T. D., Tan, A. G., & Hoffman, C. M. (2006). *Digest of Education Statistics 2005* (NCES 2006–030). Washington, DC: US Department of Education, National Center for Education Statistics, US Government Printing Office.

Stansbury, M. (2009). Can gaming change education? New research on gaming design and brain plasticity offers more perspectives on educational gaming. *eSchool News,* December 9. Available: http://www.eschoolnews.com/2009/12/09/can-gaming-change-education/.

Style, E. (1996). Curriculum as window and mirror. Available: http://www.wcwonline.org/seed/curriculum.html. Originally published in 1988 in *Listening for All Voices: Gender Balancing the School Curriculum.* Summit, NJ: Oak Knoll School Monograph, pp. 6–12.

Thorpe, R. (2003). Getting the center to hold: A funder's perspective. Chapter 5 in N. Dickard (Ed.), *The Sustainability Challenge: Taking Edtech to the Next Level.* Washington, DC: Benton Foundation and the Education Development Center.

Toh, K-A., Ho, B-T., Chew, C. M. K., & Riley, J. (2003). Teaching, teacher knowledge, and constructivism. *Educational Research for Policy and Practice* 3: 195–204.

Tomlinson, C. (2000). Reconcilable differences? Standards-based teaching and differentiation. *Educational Leadership* 58(1): 6–11.

———. (2012). Differentiation grows up. http://www.caroltomlinson.com/Presentations/2012ASCD_DiffGrowsUp_Tomlinson.pdf; retrieved March 25, 2012.

Tomlinson, C. A. & Imbeau, M. B. (2011). *Managing a Differentiated Classroom: A Practical Guide.* New York: Scholastic Inc.

Torp, L. & Sage, S. (2002). *Problems as Possibilities: Problem-Based Learning for K–16 Education.* (2nd ed.) Alexandria, VA: Association of Supervision and Curriculum Development.

Tough, P. (2006). What makes a student? *New York Times Sunday Magazine,* November 26.

US Census Bureau. (2007). *Statistical Abstract of the United States: 2007.* Washington, DC: Author.

US Department of Education. (1998). Achieving excellence in the teaching profession. In *Promising Practices: New Ways to Improve Teacher Quality.* Washington, DC: US Government Printing Office. http://www.ed.gov/pubs/PromPractice/chapter1.html; retrieved January 4, 2010.

US Department of Education, National Center for Education Statistics. (2009). *The Condition of Education 2006* (NCES 2006–071). Washington, DC: US Government Printing Office. http://nces.ed.gov/pubsearch/pubsinfo.asp?pubid=2009081/; retrieved January 15, 2010.

———. (2011). *The Condition of Education 2011.* http://nces.ed.gov/pubsearch/pubsinfo.asp?pubid=2011033; retrieved Feb 5, 2012.

US Department of Education, Office of Special Education and Rehabilitative Services, Office of Special Education Programs. (2005). *25th Annual Report to Congress on the Implementation of the Individuals with Disabilities Education Act.* Washington, DC: US Government Printing Office.

Vacca, R. S. (2004, May). Student records 2004: Issues and policy considerations. *CEPI Education Law Newsletter.* Richmond, VA: Commonwealth Educational Policy Institute. Available: http://www.cepionline.org/newsletter/2003–2004/2004_May_stud_records.html.

Vygotsky, L. (1962). *Thought and Language.* Cambridge, MA: MIT Press.

Wallis, C. & Steptoe, S. (2006). How to bring our schools out of the 20th century. *Time Magazine,* December 18.

Watson, J., Murin, A., Vashaw, L., Gemis, B., & Rapp, C. (2011). Keeping pace with K-12 online learning: An annual review of policy and practice. Evergreen Education Group; retrieved March 2, 2012. http://kpk12.com/cms/wp-content/uploads/KeepingPace2011.pdf.

Weaver, R. (2004). Diverse educators critical to quality teaching. President's Viewpoint, National Education Association, Nov. 10. http://www.nea.org/columns/rw041110.html; retrieved April 17, 2007.

Wells, J. & Lewis, L. (2006). *Internet Access in US Public Schools and Classrooms: 1994–2005 (NCES 2007–020).* Washington, DC: US Department of Education, National Center for Education Statistics.

Winebrenner, S. (2000). Gifted students need an education, too. *Educational Leadership* 58(1): 52–56.

Wisconsin Education Association Council. (2006). Great schools issue paper: The common school movement. http://www.weac.org/professional_resources/great_schools/issues_papers/index.aspx; retrieved March 8, 2010.

Wood, T. & McCarthy, C. (2002). Understanding and preventing teacher burnout. Washington, DC: ERIC Clearinghouse on Teaching and Teacher Education, ED477726.

Young, M. and Slota, S., Cutter, A., Jalette, G., Mullin, G., Lai, B., Simeoni, Z., Tran, M., & Yukhymenko, M. (2012). Our princess is in another castle: A review of trends in serious gaming for education. *Review of Educational Research,* March 2012; vol. 82, 1: pp. 61–89, first published on February 1, 2012.

Zins, J., Weissberg, R., Wang, M., & Wahlberg, H., Eds. (2004). *Building Academic Success on Social and Emotional Learning: What Does the Research Say?* New York: Teachers College Press.

Zuckerbrod, K. (2007). 9 states united on test, standards for high school math. *Philadelphia Inquirer,* April 11.

Index

A

Abuse. *See also* Harassment; Sexual harassment
  child, 95, 132, 177
  cyberbullying, 177–178
  emotional, 132
  online, 178
  reporting, 175
  sexual, 132
  substance, 95, 96, 115
  teen, 177
Academic choice, 172
Academic curriculum, 171
Academic proficiency, 165
Academy
  defined, 48
  Prep Card 3
  In Review Cards 3
Accelerated programs, 113–114
Achievement gap, 121–122
Adler, Mortimer, 56
Advanced placement (AP) courses, 114
Aesthetic education, 58–60
  defined, 58
  Prep Card 3
  In Review Cards 3
African Americans, 53–54
AFT. *See* American Federation of Teachers
Alcohol use, 96
Alice and Jerry Books, 80
Alternative schools
  charter schools, 122–124
  homeschooling, 124–126
  more choices in era of accountability, 122–126
  small urban high schools, 124
American Federation of Teachers (AFT), 40, 191–192
  defined, 15
  Prep Card 1
  In Review Cards 1
Analysis, 71
Anthony, Susan B., 53
AP courses. *See* Advanced placement courses
Application, 71
Apprenticeship, 46
AR. *See* Augmented reality
Assessments
  authentic, 81
  curriculum and standardized, 80
  defined, 81
  embedded, 81
  Prep Card 4

In Review Cards 4
  rubric and, 82
  standardized testing and, 83–85
  teaching portfolio as example of, 82
  types of, 81–83
Assistive technology
  defined, 147
  Prep Card 7
  In Review Cards 7
Assistive technology (AT), 147–148
AT. *See* Assistive technology
Attributes
  personal, 14, 181
  qualities of good teachers, 11, 182
  of teaching and other professions, 12
Auditory learners, 104
Augmented reality (AR), 141
  defined, 140
  Prep Card 7
  In Review Cards 7
Authentic assessments
  defined, 81–82
  Prep Card 4
  In Review Cards 4
  standardized testing and, 83–85
Authentic instruction, 76
Autobiography, educational, 6–8, 19
Autonomy, 171

B

Bagley, William, 55
Basal readers, 80
Beecher, Catherine, 53
Behaviorism
  defined, 72
  Prep Card 4
  In Review Cards 4
Belonging, classroom community and need for, 171
Bethel School District No. 403 v. Fraser, 130
Bible, 49
Bilingual education, 91–92
  defined, 91
  Prep Card 5
  In Review Cards 5
Bilingual Education Act of 1968, 61
Bilingual Education Act of 1974, 61
Blended learning, 151
Blogs, 142–143, 187
  defined, 142
  Prep Card 7
  In Review Cards 7

Bloom's taxonomy of educational objectives, 71–72
Bodily-kinesthetic intelligence, 103
Bolt, David, 146
Boys
  apprenticeships for, 46
  education in the academy, 49
  gender-fair education, 99–100, 115
  hidden curriculum, 36–37
  Latin grammar schools, 46–47
  mathematics scores, 99
  Title IX, Education Amendments and education for, 62
Brooks, Jackie Grennon, 28, 31
Brown v. Board of Education of Topeka, Kansas
  defined, 60
  Prep Card 3
  In Review Cards 3
Bruner, Jerome, 73
Buckley Amendment, 128–130
  defined, 128
  Prep Card 6
  In Review Cards 6
Bullying
  cyberbullying, 145, 177–178
  defined, 176
  lesbian, gay, bisexual, and transgenders, 93
  Prep Card 9
  preventing harassment, 174–178
  reporting, 132
  In Review Cards 9
  teachers' legal responsibilities, 132
  teasing and, 176–177
Burnout, 31–32
Bush, George W., 64
Business Game (online game), 157

C

Cardinal Principles of Secondary Education, 55
Carr, Nicholas, 137
CASEL. *See* Collaborative for Academic, Social, and Emotional Learning
CCSSO. *See* Council of Chief State School Officers
Center for Education Policy, 183
Certification, 16–18, 188–189
  defined, 188
  Prep Card 10
  In Review Cards 10

Gardner, Howard, 102
GED. *See* General Educational Development certificate
Gender-fair education, 99–100, 115
   defined, 99
   Prep Card 5
   In Review Cards 5
General Educational Development (GED) certificate, 95
Gifted and talented students, 113–114
Gifted inclusion, 114
Girls
   colonial education of, 46, 47
   education in the academy, 49
   gender-fair education, 99–100, 115
   hidden curriculum, 36–37
   mathematics scores, 99
   Title IX, Education Amendments and education for, 62
Globalization
   defined, 153
   digitally inclined students, 157–159
   education and, 151–161
   Learning Projects 8
   online education in knowledge economy, 151–155
   Prep Card 8
   In Review Cards 8
   teacher's role in global classroom, 159–160
   teaching in global classroom, 155–156
   teaching with digital media, 156–157
   The World Is Flat (Friedman), 153
   worldwide collaboration, 154–155
Goals
   cooperative learning, 116
   of education, 59, 165
   individualized education program, 110
   of InTASC Model Core Teaching Standards, 189
   middle school concept, 126
   philosophy of teaching statement, 9
   of public education, 183
   social and emotional, 165
   teacher preparation programs, 35
Goodness of fit
   classroom community and, 178–179
   defined, 10
   Prep Card 1
   In Review Cards 1
   teachers and, 181–187
Google, 187
Google for Educators, 187
Graduate School of Education, Harvard University, 82
Greene, Maxine, 58–60

H

Harassment. *See also* Sexual harassment
   preventing bullying and, 174–178
   sexual harassment in school, 174–175
   sexual orientation, 93
Harvard College, 47

Harvard University, 82
Hazelwood School District v. *Kuhlmeier*, 130
Hidden curriculum, 36–37, 78–79
   defined, 31
   Prep Card 2
   In Review Cards 2
High schools
   curriculum, 54–55
   rubric for high school class debate, 84
   small urban, 124
Hispanics, 90
Homelessness, 95
Homeschooling, 124–126
   defined, 124
   Prep Card 6, 124
   In Review Cards 6
Hunger, 95

I

IB program. *See* International Baccalaureate program
iEARN. *See* International Education and Resource Network
Ill-structured problem
   defined, 118
   Prep Card 6
   In Review Cards 6
Immigration, 49, 90
Inclusion
   classroom, 108–113
   defined, 63
   Prep Card 3
   Prep Card 6
   In Review Cards 3
   In Review Cards 6
Individualized education program (IEP)
   defined, 110
   Prep Card 6
   In Review Cards 6
Individuals with Disabilities Education Act (IDEA)
   defined, 63
   Prep Card 3
   In Review Cards 3
Informal curriculum, 78–79
   defined, 79
   Prep Card 4
   In Review Cards 4
Information
   constructing knowledge vs. having, 153–155
   managing new sources of, 155
Information overload, 137–138
Inquiry
   defined, 60
   Prep Card 3
   In Review Cards 3
Instruction
   authentic, 76
   defined, 70
   differentiated, 114–115
   Prep Card 4
   In Review Cards 4

Instructional methods, 70
InTASC Model Core Teaching Standards, 188–189
Intellectual development, 74
Intelligence profile
   defined, 102
   Prep Card 5
   In Review Cards 5
Intelligences
   bodily-kinesthetic, 103
   interpersonal, 103
   intrapersonal, 103
   linguistic, 103
   logical-mathematical, 103
   multiple, 101–103, 187
   musical, 103
   spatial, 103
Interactive whiteboard
   defined, 147
   Prep Card 7
   In Review Cards 7
International Baccalaureate (IB) program, 114
International Education and Resource Network (iEARN), 154
International Schools Services, 190
Internet
   connected classroom, 136
   cyberbullying, 177–178
   digital darting, 136
   flat classrooms and, 136
   guidelines for research, 138
   media convergence on, 187
   safety, 145–146
   use in homeschooling, 125
   ways that technology supports learning, 139–142
   worldwide collaboration, 154–155
Interpersonal intelligence, 103
Interstate New Teacher Assessment and Support Consortium (InTASC)
   In Review Cards 10
   standards, 188–189
Intrapersonal intelligence, 103
iPads, 135, 160
iPods, 160

J

Jackson, Phillip, 36
Jefferson, Thomas, 48, 54, 182
Johnson, Lyndon, 61
Jones, John E., 101
Journaling, 33
Jung, Carl, 18

K

Kierkegaard, Søren, 57
Kinesthetic learners, 104

Chapter Summary

1-1 Reflect on your own educational history and its implications for your future as a teacher. Your views on teaching and learning are shaped by your own experiences and beliefs. Your educational autobiography refers to your own story of your life as a student. Your personal experiences in the classroom, both positive and negative, may be what fuel your desire to explore teaching as a career. A good way to define your beliefs about teaching is to use a metaphor, or comparison. For example, you may think teaching is like: being a tour guide, being a sailor, being a sculptor, climbing a hill, or a toolbox. Whatever your reasons for considering teaching as a career—whether you have always wanted to be a teacher, or you have "fallen into" teaching out of the need for a job—being a reflective practitioner will help you define your personal philosophy of teaching statement. Your philosophy and goals as a teacher should be based on your reflection but also backed up by evidence from research. Most importantly, though, remember that in teaching, your focus should be on the students and their needs and not your own needs.

1-2 Examine the "goodness of fit" between your own personal qualities and the demands of teaching. Teachers do touch students' lives, and you may have had a teacher who stands out for influencing you in a positive way. Perhaps this teacher took a special interest in you, encouraged you to succeed, or challenged you to grow. This teacher may be an inspiration to you as you begin your own journey in the field.

A good teacher needs to be: committed, caring, courageous, conscious and centered. Teaching is a demanding and rewarding career, partly because so many of a teacher's personal qualities are on display every day in the classroom. To honestly assess whether teaching is right for you, you must examine your strengths and weaknesses and the goodness of fit between your personal qualities and the attributes of a good teacher. If you do not possess all of the ideal characteristics, do not be discouraged, but you should realize that you may need to develop certain qualities to be a good fit for teaching.

1-3 Explain the effect that a committed teacher has on the climate and culture within a school. The terms *school climate* and *school culture* refer to the values, cultures, practices, and organization of a school. The general social atmosphere or environment in a school is its climate, which may be described as nurturing, authoritarian, or somewhere in between. A school's climate or culture is the "feeling" that students and teachers have in the school, and it influences relationships and learning. School climate is determined by the administrators and the teachers and, in fact, all the personnel of a school. Teachers should aspire toward a healthy school climate as individuals, which can have an impact throughout the school.

1-4 Examine the importance of being a reflective practitioner. Being a reflective practitioner means looking forward and backward and realizing that we teach who we are. A unique aspect of teaching is that it combines professional knowledge and

Key Terms

reflective practitioner A teacher who consistently reflects on classroom events (both successes and problems) and modifies teaching practices accordingly.

educational autobiography Your own educational history told by you.

philosophy of teaching statement A description of your ideas about teaching and learning and how those ideas will influence your practice. It should be based on your knowledge of educational research.

goodness of fit A term generally used in descriptive statistics to describe the match between a theory and a particular set of observations; in this book, it means the match between a teacher candidate's personal attributes, values, and dispositions and the demands of teaching.

National Education Association (NEA) The largest organization of teachers and other education professionals, headquartered in Washington, D.C.

American Federation of Teachers (ATF) An international union, affiliated with the American Federation of Labor and Congress of Industrial Organizations, representing teachers and other school personnel as well as many college faculty and staff members, healthcare workers, and public employees.

National Association for the Education of Young Children (NAEYC) This professional organization is dedicated to improving the quality of education for all children birth to age eight.

National Board for Professional Teaching Standards (NBPTS) A nonprofit organization that aims to advance the quality of teaching by developing professional standards for teachers.

school climate and **school culture** The values, cultures, practices, and organization of a school.

InTASC Standards

Standard 3: Learning Environments
Standard 9: Professional Learning
and Ethical Practice

Review Questions

1. What reasons did Laura, Sharyn, Derrick, and Christine give for wanting to become teachers?

2. What are some attributes of good teachers?

3. How do teachers rank in the arena of public trust?

4. What is the purpose of the National Board for Professional Teaching Standards?

5. What are some ways in which the culture of a school is evident?

training with the personal attributes of the teacher in cultivating student learning. Teachers must have a heightened sense of self, which can be developed through the use of reflective practices—an honest evaluation of how your own characteristics and background influence your goals and practices in the classroom.

TeachSource Video Case

Advice from the Field

Find the TeachSource Video Case "Becoming a Teacher: Voices and Advice from the Field" on the Education CourseMate at CengageBrain.com. This video showcases several teachers, some new to the field and some who have been teaching for years. Pay special attention to their ideas about what is needed to be a successful teacher. After the main video, view the bonus video called "Essential Qualities That Teachers Must Possess." Ask yourself these questions:

- Jot down the various qualities the teachers mention as essential. How many of them overlap with the attributes listed in the box "Qualities of Good Teachers"? How many are new?
- Begin thinking about whether you have these qualities. Are there some you do not have currently but could work to develop?

Chapter Summary

2-1 Discuss common factors in individuals' decisions to become teachers.
Being a teacher requires an emotional and intellectual commitment, which is why two of the most common reasons cited in the decision to become a teacher are a love of children and a love of learning. These two reasons were echoed again and again in the stories throughout this chapter. But there are many other reasons for becoming a teacher. Often, those who become teachers have worked with children before, as babysitters, camp counselors, or tutors, and enjoyed the experience. Some, like Jane, found they excelled at a teaching opportunity in another setting (e.g., through leading classes at church) and decided to pursue teaching as a career. Others have a passion for a particular content area and wish to share that passion through teaching. Many teachers say they loved school, and found one or more of their own teachers to be inspiring. Parents are another source of inspiration for many people. Although some people, like Amanda, feel that teaching was always their calling, others, like Adam, fall into the profession after being longtime students themselves. Those who become inspiring teachers cite reasons such as these, rather than pay, benefits, or hours.

Though the reasons for becoming a teacher are diverse, the US public school workforce is currently not diverse; the majority of teachers are white (87 percent) and female (70 percent). However, these statistics have improved over the last decade and are trending toward more diversity, which many educators and researchers believe will have a positive effect on children in the classroom. The majority of teachers are also older than forty, and only 10 percent are under age thirty (National Education Association, 2009). In summary, there is a need in US public schools for young teachers from varied ethnic backgrounds.

The nature of teaching makes it both a challenging and rewarding career. Teaching is both demanding and exciting; often what makes it challenging also makes it rewarding. Every day is different, and every student is different—effective teachers admit that being prepared is a challenge in the classroom, but that they are rewarded when they really reach their students and witness learning happening. Another great benefit of teaching is the opportunity it brings to be a lifelong learner yourself.

As you are making your decision whether or not to become a teacher, recognizing the challenges that you may face is important. Some challenges mentioned in the teaching stories are staying focused on true purpose, burnout, pay, paperwork, dealing with parents, navigating relationships with administrators, meeting standardized testing and curriculum requirements, and working extra hours to prepare effective lessons. These stories represent individual perspectives, but being aware of challenges others have experienced can help a new teacher face them if those same challenges are encountered. As Jessica said, "These things shouldn't dissuade people from becoming teachers. You learn how to deal with them effectively and appropriately soon after you begin teaching. They represent difficulties I didn't know about before I entered teaching, but the benefits of this career far outweigh the challenges in the workplace."

2-2 Explain the idea "We teach who we are!" The act of teaching challenges us to consider how we communicate and listen to others. It challenges us to acknowledge our tolerances for differing opinions and multiple types of personalities, as manifested by the students in your classes. It is a dialogic act; teaching face to face requires that you are "on" from the minute the class begins to its completion. Who you are as a person, your level of generosity of spirit, and your ability to speak respectfully to others, will be revealed in your classroom practices.

Key Terms

teacher burnout The condition of teachers who have lost their motivation, desire, sense of purpose, and energy for being effective practitioners.

hidden curriculum What students learn, beyond the academic content, from the experience of attending school.

learning community A classroom, a cluster of classes, or a school organized so as to promote active engagement in learning, collaboration between teachers and students, and a sense that everyone involved shares the experience of being a learner.

professional development Teachers' lifelong effort to improve their skills and professional knowledge. Although professional development often includes advanced courses and workshops, much of your progress will depend on your own continued reading, reflection, and analysis.

InTASC Standards

Standard 3: Learning Environments
Standard 6: Assessment
Standard 7: Planning for Instruction
Standard 9: Professional Learning and Ethical Practice
Standard 10: Leadership and Collaboration

Review Questions

1. Who is the "typical" US public school teacher, statistically speaking (as in race, gender, age, and level of education)?

2. What are two misconceptions about early childhood education?

3. What are at least three signs of teacher burnout? What are some strategies for overcoming teacher burnout?

4. What is the average annual salary for a US public school teacher?

5. What reasons did Ms. Outerbridge give for incorporating movement and music into her second-grade class?

TeachSource Video Case

Surprises of the First Year

There is another story about the challenges and excitement of teaching in the TeachSource Video Cases section of the Education CourseMate at CengageBrain.com. Watch the video "The First Year of Teaching: One Colleague's Story," in which Will Starner talks about his initial year in a classroom. "I've had a lot of situations that I really didn't know would come up," he says. In the bonus video, "Mr. Starner Reflects on the First Year of Teaching," he mentions that he had "all these different theories running through my head," and it felt overwhelming to select the best approach for the context. Ask yourself these questions:

- What are the main challenges Will Starner identifies?
- What ways did he find to cope with these difficulties?
- What is your impression of Mr. Starner? Discuss your reaction to his candid description of his first year of teaching. What attributes do you think make him potentially a very successful teacher?

2-3   Examine how the hidden curriculum may affect the climate in the classroom. Teachers reveal themselves in their classrooms; being conscious of this can help you use your strengths to create a hidden curriculum with positive messages for students. Teachers have a vision of how they want to teach and how their classroom should function; it is a personal vision, informed by scholarship as well as one's own beliefs and unique personality. Your personal interests and life may well intersect with your classroom life, as in the batteries-in-the-pocket story. With or without realizing it, teachers are communicating a hidden curriculum to their students by they way they conduct themselves in the classroom. The hidden curriculum is what students learn, beyond the academic content, from the experience of going to school. Being conscious of the fact that your conduct contributes to the hidden curriculum can help you contribute a positive rather than a negative message to students. In other words, if you are genuinely enthused about learning, your students will notice; if you are frustrated and bored, your students will notice that, too.

2-4   Explore the support systems that are in place for new teachers. New teachers are fully responsible for their students' learning, the same as a veteran teacher. Being new at a job but expected to perform on the same level as someone who has twenty years of experience can be a daunting task! Fortunately, there are many avenues of support for new teachers. Colleagues can be helpful, giving you both professional and emotional support, as well as the "inside scoop" on the routines and procedures of your particular school and district. Many schools and districts have adopted a mentoring program for new teachers, in which the new teacher is partnered with an experienced teacher who has been trained to be a mentor. Professional organizations offer the support of being connected with other teachers across the country and offer access to free online resources. Professional development is often a requirement to keep your certification or licensure current, and many schools and districts offer financial incentives for continuing your education; beyond these reasons, though, many teachers participate in professional development programs simply because they find them valuable. You must always continue to learn and improve if you hope to become an effective teacher or a "centered presence" in your classroom.

2-5   Compare the lifelong learning needs of teachers with those in other professions. Common wisdom states that good teachers are lifelong learners because they are constantly facing new groups of students, actively learning about those students' lives and exploring ways in which to best design instruction. But they are also lifelong learners because teachers immerse themselves in professional development courses and workshops that represent the most cutting edge practices for how to teach effectively and create meaningful experiences for students. Think about other professions; certainly we hope that our doctors are lifelong learners; what about lawyers? Accountants? Office administrators? Most teachers leave the classroom in June and ask themselves how they can do it better in September. Many teachers spend their summers participating in workshops, going to conferences, and seeking professional development on a wide range of topics.

2-6   Create your own teaching story as you explore teaching as a career. One way to practice being a reflective practitioner is to start writing your own teaching story as you begin exploring what it means to become a teacher. You may start by reflecting on your course, what you are learning about teaching that you were unaware of, and how you feel about the prospect of one day having your own class.

Chapter Summary

3-1   **Analyze the ways in which the early pioneers of the US public education shaped the way schools exist today in the United States.** In the New England colonies of the early 1600s, there were few educational options. Primarily, the responsibility of educating children was placed on the family, similar to today's homeschooling movement, but different in that the Puritans focused almost exclusively on the reading and understanding of the Bible. Dame schools were another form of education, for children six to eight years old. Dame schools could be compared to today's day care. This was for the most part the only form of schooling offered for girls, who were usually taught domestic skills at home. Boys could serve an apprenticeship after dame school to learn a trade from a craftsman that they could carry into adulthood. This could be compared to vocational school today.

In 1635, the first Latin grammar school opened in Boston. The sons of the upper social classes studied Latin and Greek language and literature and the Bible. The Latin grammar school is considered a forerunner to the US high school. In 1647, Massachusetts passed a law, known as the Old Deluder Satan Act, that was the first education act in the United States ensuring there would be public schools where children would learn to read and write.

Social class (wealthy), race (white), gender (male), and geography (northern colonies) determined who had better access to education; clearly, today's public education system is more inclusive, but the roots of many of today's educational issues (e.g., equitable schooling, curriculum, government mandates) extend as far back as the early colonies.

3-2   **Explain the dominant philosophies that influenced education.** In the late 1700s, after the American Revolution, the new nation's leaders began an effort to mandate education by setting aside land for public schools. Thomas Jefferson and Benjamin Franklin believed that the new democracy required an educated citizenry for its survival and that an educational system should allow people to succeed on the basis of skill rather than inherited privilege. The idea of a democratic, public education gave rise to the movement of common schools, tax-supported elementary schools. Horace Mann, who championed the common school movement, saw schooling as a way of promoting important civic virtues. By the end of the 1890s, more than 70 percent of children were receiving public schooling. The vision that had been pioneered by Jefferson, Franklin, and Mann was gradually becoming a reality; today, we continue to work toward fulfilling their vision by striving toward the goal of equal educational opportunity for everyone.

Many important reform movements have shaped education since the late nineteenth century. Essentialism, a term coined by William Bagley in the 1930s, is the philosophy that schools should teach certain key elements for students to gain a basic knowledge in core academic disciplines. Today's "back-to-basics" proponents are rooted in essentialist philosophy. This is a teacher-centered approach to learning. In contrast, John Dewey (1859–1952), perhaps the most influential educator of the twentieth century, proposed the philosophy of progressivism, which stresses active learning through problem solving, projects, and hands-on experiences. This is a student-centered approach to learning. Its influence is felt today in "whole language programs." Related to essentialism, perennialism, which was given prominence by Mortimer Adler in the 1980s, stresses that all knowledge is accumulated over time and is represented by the great works of literature, art, and religious texts. Today, this philosophy is manifested in

Key Terms

dame schools   Some colonial women transformed their homes into schools where they taught reading, writing, and computation. These schools became known as dame schools.

Latin grammar school   A type of school that flourished in the New England colonies in the 1600s and 1700s. It emphasized Latin and Greek to prepare young men for college.

academy   A type of private secondary school that arose in the late colonial period and came to dominate US secondary education until the establishment of public high schools. Academies had a more practical curriculum than Latin grammar schools did, and students typically could choose subjects appropriate to their later careers.

common school   A public, tax-supported elementary school. Begun in Massachusetts in the 1820s, common schools aimed to provide a common curriculum for children. Horace Mann, an advocate for the common school, is often considered the "father of the public school."

parochial schools   A school operated by a religious group. Today, in the United States, the term most often refers to a school governed by the local Catholic parish or diocese.

normal schools   A type of teacher education institution begun in the 1830s; forerunner of the teachers' college.

tracking   The practice of placing students in different classes or courses based on achievement test scores or on perceived differences in abilities. Tracks can be identified by ability (high, average, or low) or by the kind of preparation they provide (academic, general, or vocational).

essentialism   An educational philosophy holding that the purpose of education is to learn specific knowledge provided by core academic disciplines such as mathematics, science, literature, and history. Teachers must impart the key elements of these subjects so that all students have access to this basic or "essential" knowledge.

progressivism   An educational philosophy that stresses active learning through problem solving, projects, and hands-on experiences.

perennialism An educational philosophy that emphasizes enduring ideas conveyed through the study of great works of literature and art. Perennialists believe in a single core curriculum for everyone.

aesthetic education Traditionally, this term referred merely to education in the fine arts, such as painting and music. In the broader view of Maxine Greene and other recent philosophers, however, it means education that enables students to use artistic forms and imagination to approach all fields of learning, including the sciences, and to share their perspectives with others.

inquiry A multifaceted activity that involves making observations, posing questions about the subject matter, and conducting research or investigations to develop answers. Inquiry is common to scientific learning but also relevant to other fields.

Brown v. Board of Education of Topeka, Kansas A 1954 case in which the US Supreme Court outlawed segregation in public education.

Title 1 The section of federal education law that provides funds for compensatory education.

Title IX Part of the federal Educational Amendments of 1972, Title IX states that "No person in the United States shall, on the basis of sex, be excluded from participation in, be denied the benefits of, or be subjected to discrimination under any education program or activity receiving Federal financial assistance."

A Nation at Risk: The Imperative for Educational Reform A 1983 federal report that found US schools in serious trouble and inaugurated a new wave of school reform focused on academic basics and higher standards for student achievement.

Individuals with Disabilities Education Act (IDEA) The federal law that guarantees that all children with disabilities receive free, appropriate public education.

inclusion The practice of educating students with disabilities in regular classrooms alongside nondisabled students.

Common Core State Standards A state-led initiative to develop a set of standards that define the knowledge and skills students should have within their K–12 education careers so that they will graduate high school able to succeed in entry-level, credit-bearing academic college courses and in workforce training programs. These standards are consistent from state to state.

Race to the Top (RTTP) A federal competition for state funding that requires applicants to adhere to a fixed set of criteria that include methods of assessing students and teachers.

"great books" courses, for example. More radical theories are social reconstructionism (emphasizing social justice and promoting social reform), critical theory (encouraging students to challenge oppression), and existentialism (seeking meaning out of one's own existence—the extreme of student-centered learning).

3-3 Discuss the impact of federal government legislation, funding priorities, and court cases on the ways that public education has increased accountability in the twenty-first century. Public schools have traditionally been run by local school boards, and the bulk of their funding has come from local taxes, especially property taxes. But the federal government has increasingly influenced schooling through more funding and mandates. The landmark 1954 US Supreme Court case *Brown v. Board of Education of Topeka, Kansas*, outlawed segregation in public education. Federal acts and legislation, especially Title 1 and Title IX, have reinforced equality in education. The 1983 publication *A Nation at Risk* touched of the standards movement that is prominent in education today.

Fostering the rights of individuals with disabilities to receive free, appropriate public education, just like other children, what is now known as the Individuals with Disabilities Education Act (IDEA) originated in 1975 and was most recently updated in 2004. As a result, schools have made efforts to include disabled students in regular classrooms.

The federal government's passage of the No Child Left Behind Act in 2001 dramatically influenced accountability systems in every state. To receive federal funding, states had to provide a great deal of data about schools, teachers, and students, and this ushered in an era of accountability in public education that has become defined by rigorous standardized testing at many grade levels. This has been modified by the Race to the Top Funding (2009) competition that required states to provide accountability data in highly specific ways.

3-4 Create a theme that would describe the period of educational history in which we currently find ourselves. Many individuals describe the current period as assessment-driven curriculum and instruction. Others refer to it as "prep-and-test" education. Still others insist this is a market-driven time in education where publishers that design tests are driving curriculum and instruction and making a fortune in the process. Some people describe this period of time since 2002 as the "Era of Accountability." What historical period does this reform movement remind you of?

TeachSource Video Case

Foundations: Aligning Instruction with Federal Legislation

This video highlights the effects that Federal Legislation, specifically NCLB and IDEA, have had on classroom practice. After reviewing this video and listening to the discussion, ask students the following questions:

- How did IDEA change the composition of students in the classroom?
- What role can mentoring play in your understanding of the implementation of this legislation?
- Why do you think there are significant revisions to NCLB in 2012?
- Do you think that Race to the Top funding has helped ameliorate some of the effects of NCLB? why or why not?

Review Questions

1. What was the first education act in the United States, and why was it passed?
2. What was the driving idea behind the common schools movement?
3. Who was Catherine Beecher?
4. What was Maxine Greene's philosophy?

Chapter Summary

4-1   Explain why there exists the common myth that "anyone can teach."
Teaching is unlike other professions in that most people have spent at least twelve years experiencing the workings of the classroom firsthand. This experience gives some people the illusion that teaching is "easy" or that "anyone can do it" (and some people feel it gives them license to impart their opinions or advice to those serving in the profession). In reality, teaching and learning are complex activities, requiring conscious thought and action on the part of the teacher to employ best practices.

4-2   Compare the art of teaching to the science of teaching. Pedagogy is an art because it is a personal expression of oneself. It is a science because it relies on careful observation of (1) students' dispositions, (2) students' prior knowledge, and (3) students' responses to the lessons. Pedagogy is your personal teaching philosophy based on both who you are and scientific research that has helped us understand the process of learning. It forms the foundation for instruction and the methods and plans you enact on a daily basis in the classroom. Instruction is the manifestation of your philosophy in practice.

4-3   Compare learning theories and examine how neuroscience has influenced current theories about how people learn. Learning theories are formal ideas about how learning may happen, and insight into these theories helps teachers plan effective instruction. Some learning theories that have had an impact on education are: behaviorism (Skinner), cognitive learning theories (Piaget and Bruner), social cognitive learning theories (Vygotsky), and constructivism (Rogers). Discoveries in neuroscience also shape our knowledge of how learning works. Cognitive science provides evidence for understanding that learning is an active process in which individuals attach new knowledge to prior knowledge and define and refine their mental schemes to make meaning of and internalize the new knowledge. Knowing how people learn from the evidence provided by neuroscience helps us frame teaching practices effectively.

4-4   Examine the ways in which curriculum is developed and the promised influence of the Common Core State Standards on mathematics and English curricula. National and state standards define topics to be addressed in a given subject area at each grade level. The standards movement has dominated public education since the early 1990s; it prompted national subject-area associations to state explicitly what students should know and be able to do at each grade level from kindergarten through twelfth grade, resulting in national standards for each subject. The No Child Left Behind Act passed in 2001 mandates that students be held accountable by means of statewide exams that assess their knowledge at various grade levels, often beginning in third grade. Therefore, control over the curriculum moved from individual classrooms and local schools to the state, which is driven by federal guidelines. The statewide assessment is often thought of as a "one size fits all" approach. Teachers have the challenge of teaching the mandated curriculum, but also employing best practices (i.e., presenting it in a way that allows their individual students to learn it). It is the goal of the Common Core State Standards to drive the instruction in each state by the same guiding principles

Key Terms

pedagogy The art and science of teaching; all that you know and believe about teaching.

instruction The act or process of teaching; the way your pedagogy becomes enacted in practice.

personal teaching philosophy
An individual's own pedagogy informed by his or her own beliefs and understanding of how students learn best. A teacher's personal philosophy outs itself through the instructional strategies employed with the students.

pedagogical content knowledge (PCK) The understanding of how particular topics, problems, or issues can be adapted and presented to match the diverse interests and abilities of learners.

learning theories An explanation of how learning typically occurs and about conditions that favor learning.

Knowledge, Comprehension, Application, Analysis, Synthesis, and Evaluation
Bloom's original classes of learning behaviors. They were slightly reorganized and renamed with verbs in the 1990s.

behaviorism The theory that learning takes place in response to reinforcements (e.g., rewards or punishments) from the outside environment.

cognitive learning theories
Explanations of the mental processes that occur during learning.

social cognitive learning theories Explanations that describe the mental processes that occur during learning and how learning involves interactions between the learner and the social environment.

constructivism A group of theories about knowledge and learning, which basic tenet is that all knowledge is constructed by synthesizing new ideas with prior knowledge. Constructivism holds that knowledge is not passively received; rather, it is actively built by the learner as he or she experiences the world.

mental scheme An organizational structure in the brain; a group of foundational concepts that help the individual make sense of the world.

curriculum A plan of studies that includes the ways instructional content is organized and presented at each grade level.

informal curriculum Learning experiences that go beyond the formal curriculum, such as activities the teacher introduces to connect academic concepts to the students' daily lives.

assessment Collecting information to determine the progress of students' learning.

embedded assessments Classroom-based assessments that make use of the actual assignments that students are given as a unit is being taught. These can be used to evaluate developmental stages of student learning.

authentic (performance) assessment An assessment that asks students to perform a task relating what they have learned to some real-world problem or example.

rubric A scoring guide for an authentic assessment or a performance assessment, with descriptions of performance characteristics corresponding to points on a rating scale.

InTASC Standards

Standard 1: Learner Development
Standard 3: Learning Environments
Standard 4: Content Knowledge
Standard 5: Application of Content
Standard 7: Planning for Instruction
Standard 8: Instructional Strategies

Review Questions

1. What are the learning behaviors described by Bloom's revised taxonomy?

2. What is a mental scheme?

3. What does the hidden curriculum refer to?

4. What does it mean to say that curriculum should be a window and a mirror? How do basal readers act as a window but not a mirror?

5. How does a rubric work for assessing a performance?

6. What are at least three tips to keep in mind as you are thinking about how to best teach your students?

of what students should know and be able to do in the areas of language arts and mathematics that are required for future careers and as preparation for college. This ensures that these intellectual standards will not vary from state to state.

4-5 Analyze the statement that "we can teach our students but we cannot learn for them." Teaching and learning may be thought of as two sides of the same coin. As teachers we prepare ways to engage students in a variety of subject areas, and we use the best instructional methods available at this time. The learners, your students, however, must engage actively with the material and make meaning of it on their own terms and in their own personal ways. When we assess their understanding of topics, we can analyze how or if they have learned the material.

4-6 Discuss what it takes to learn to become a teacher. Learning how to teach is a complex process which takes into consideration who you are as a person, what your values and beliefs about teaching may be, your abilities to actively listen to others, to learn new materials, to try new techniques, to make daily life connections for your students, and to plan, plan, plan!

4-7 Explain how understanding how your students learn and what their lives are like influence your role as their teacher. The standards movement has also brought to the forefront of education discussion of the question, "How do we tell when a student has learned something?" Assessment is the process of collecting information to find out what students are learning. Standardized tests (often multiple choice questions), given on a state-wide basis, are only one form of assessment (and are often criticized by educators as being too narrow a way of assessing learning). Embedded assessments and performance assessments give a broader view of student learning. A great way to understand what students are learning is to talk to them about it.

Though teachers have a responsibility to teach the standards set forth by the curriculum, they must realize that a "one size fits all" approach is not the best practice. Figuring out who your students are and how to make learning interesting and meaningful to them, so they truly internalize the lessons, is of paramount importance.

TeachSource Video Case

A High School Debate

When constructivism informs pedagogy, teachers can develop instructional methods known as constructivist teaching. As you can imagine, this type of teaching places a lot of responsibility for learning on the students. It asks them to be actively engaged in creating meaning through experiences in which they take part. Find the TeachSource Video Case "Constructivist Teaching in Action: A High School Classroom Debate" on the student website. Ask yourself these questions:

- In what ways is the teacher, Ms. Levy-Brightman, promoting the tenets of constructivist learning theory?
- How does she structure the learning experience?
- How does the carefully structured debate provide the students with a way to really learn the material?
- What information does the teacher gather from the student debates?

Chapter Summary

5-1   Examine the ways in which students may differ from one another. The population of public school students in the United States represents a broad mosaic of individuals who differ from each other according to their race, ethnicity, social class, native language, and ability to learn. The number of students in schools has been rising rapidly. Between 1985 and 2005, roughly the same time that the standards movement was gaining ground, enrollment in public elementary and secondary schools increased by more than one-fifth. Currently, there are estimated to be more than fifty million students in grades pre-K-12 in public schools, representing a widely diverse population.

5-2   Examine factors that might hinder a child's success in school. By 2010, 43 percent of public school students were considered to be part of a racial or ethnic minority group, and about 20 percent of students spoke a language other than English at home. The needs of English-language learners (ELLs) must be addressed because these young people are at a distinct disadvantage as they attend school where instruction is not conducted in their native tongues. In all student populations, a range of learning and/or emotional disabilities may also hinder student success. Inclusion classrooms with specially trained educators working with general educators often meet the needs of these students.

More than one-fifth of young people under age eighteen live in poverty and more than one-third live in single-parent families. Life outside of the classroom affects students' ability to learn. Generally, socioeconomic disadvantages and emotional turmoil put students at risk of not reaching their full potential or not completing their education at all. Two of the most important issues facing students are teen pregnancy and substance abuse.

5-3   Explain why teachers must have an understanding of their students' lives through the lens of their ethnic, cultural, and daily life experiences. If you are not of the same culture, race, ethnicity, or social class as your students, you should make a special effort to understand how you can meet their needs in the classroom. Remember that to reach your students, you must respect who they are. Diversity can be an advantage in the classroom—an opportunity to celebrate the variety of cultures and ethnic backgrounds found in US schools.

5-4   Analyze how your students' intelligence profiles could explain their performance in your class. Howard Gardner proposed the theory of multiple intelligences, which means that each of us is intelligent in several different ways. What this means for teachers is that different students may learn best in different ways—some perhaps through reading about concepts, and others perhaps through talking and listening, viewing a diagram or video, or hands-on experience, for example. Each learner's intelligence profile consists of a combination of relative strengths and weaknesses among the different types of intelligences. Teachers need to explore topics in multiple ways to reach more students. Types of intelligences include: linguistic, logical-mathematical, musical, kinesthetic, spatial, and interpersonal intelligences. Hence, people can be intelligent in many differing ways.

5-5   Examine your own learning style or styles and relate that to the learning styles you may find among your students. Learning style refers to the particular way you take in a new idea, event, or concept. Some people learn best by

Key Terms

bilingual education   Educating English-language learners by teaching them at least part of the time in their native language.

sexual orientation   An enduring emotional, romantic, sexual, or affectional attraction that a person feels toward people of one or both sexes.

LGBT   An acronym used to represent lesbian, gay, bisexual, and transgender individuals.

socioeconomic status (SES)   A person's or family's status in society, usually based on a combination of income, occupation, and education. Though similar to social class, SES puts more emphasis on the way income affects status.

students at risk   Students in danger of not completing school or not acquiring the education they need to be successful citizens.

dropout rate   The percentage of students who fail to complete high school or earn an equivalency degree.

multicultural education   Education that aims to create equal opportunities for students from diverse racial, ethnic, social class, and cultural groups.

culturally relevant pedagogy   Teaching practices that place the culture of the learner at the center of instruction. Cultural referents become aspects of the formal curriculum.

gender-fair education   Teaching practices that help both females and males achieve their full potential. Gender-fair teachers address cultural and societal stereotypes and overcome them through classroom interactions.

equity   The act of treating individuals and groups fairly and justly, free from bias or favoritism. Gender equity means the state of being fair and just toward both males and females, to show preference to neither and concern for both.

theory of multiple intelligences   The theory that intelligence is not a single, fixed attribute but rather a collection of several different types of abilities.

intelligence profile An individual's unique combination of relative strengths and weaknesses among all the different intelligences.

learning style The dominant way in which we process the information around us. Different people have different learning styles.

InTASC Standards

Standard 2: Learning Differences
Standard 3: Learning Environments
Standard 4: Content Knowledge
Standard 5: Application of Content

Review Questions

1. What are at least three strategies for teaching students who speak English as a second language?

2. What percentages of LGBT students report verbal and physical harassment in school?

3. What are six factors that help to identify students who are at high risk of dropping out?

4. Is single-sex schooling discriminatory under Title IX? Why or why not?

5. What is the difference between treating students equitably and treating them equally?

6. What was the result of the landmark court case in Dover, Pennsylvania?

7. What are the nine (definite) types of intelligence proposed by Gardner?

reading and writing; other basic learning styles are represented by auditory learners, visual learners, and kinesthetic learners. Examining your own learning style helps you to appreciate the presence of many learning styles of the students in your classroom. This requires that teachers vary their approaches to instruction creating learning environments that appeal to many learning styles.

5-6 Assess the importance of knowing who your students are, what their lives are like, and how they learn best. New teachers often draw on their own experiences as learners and base their teaching style on what would work best for them. This chapter explores the many ways that students may differ from each other and from you. Learning about your students' lives helps you to gain an understanding of what conditions in the classroom will help them to be the most successful. Answering questions for yourself such as: do they live with their parents, guardians, single parents, grandparents, two moms, two dads, or in a more typical nuclear family? Do they have breakfast at home or in school? What is their native language? Do any of your students need special services? Do they tend to learn best by doing? Your challenge is to formulate a teaching style that incorporates their diversity along with your own personality.

5-7 Examine the statement that "student diversity is a gift and not a barrier to overcome." Our differences make us unique and honoring them teaches children respect for the human condition. It also helps students become learners, understanding classmates whose identities, cultures, lives, and experiences are different from their own. This is the foundation of education.

TeachSource Video Cases

Bilingual Education in Fourth Grade

To see how a two-way language immersion program can function, find the TeachSource Video Case "Bilingual Education: An Elementary Two-Way Immersion Program" on the student website. As you begin watching the video, note whether all the students are English-language learners. Ask yourself these questions:

- Would you have liked to have been a student in this program? Why or why not?
- In what ways, if any, does the two-way program level the playing field for English-language learners?
- How, if at all, were you able to tell which students were native English speakers?
- Why is communication between the Spanish and English teachers essential?

Multiple Intelligences: Elementary School Instruction

To explore how one teacher accounts for his students' varying intelligence profiles and styles of learning, find the TeachSource Video Case "Multiple Intelligences: Elementary School Instruction" on the student website. The video examines a class writing assignment about the passengers' experience during the ocean voyage of the *Mayflower*.

- In what ways is this lesson informed by multiple intelligences theory?
- If you did not know about multiple intelligences and different learning styles, what would you think of this lesson?
- Why do you think Mr. Won Park asked the students to touch their faces and their clothes and to smell their clothes? What do you think he was hoping for?
- What aspects of this lesson used intrapersonal intelligence? Interpersonal intelligence? Kinesthetic learning?

Chapter Summary

6-1   Explain why inclusion classrooms look no different from mainstream classrooms. The Individuals with Disabilities Education Act mandates that to the greatest extent possible, students with disabilities must be educated with children who are not disabled, which has led to the concept of inclusion. Inclusion means that students with disabilities spend all or part of their day in mainstream classrooms, usually with the support of a special education teacher or inclusion specialist in addition to the regular classroom teacher. In an inclusion classroom, it is often difficult to spot which students have special needs and which do not. That is one of the points of inclusion!

6-2   Analyze the ways in which students are labeled gifted and talented and how inclusion students may also be considered gifted or talented. Research indicates that gifted and talented students are in as much need of special education services as are students with disabilities. It is important for teachers to recognize the unique needs of their high-achieving students and give them appropriate educational opportunities to grow and develop to their fullest potential like any other child. Inclusion students can also be gifted and talented!

6-3   Examine how differentiated instruction meets the needs of *all* the students. Differentiated instruction recognizes the amazing diversity of students and encourages the development of instructional practices that engage all learners through multiple approaches, tasks, and activities. It is the opposite of the "one size fits all" concept of education.

6-4   Evaluate the role of social and emotional learning for classroom teaching. Social and emotional learning (SEL) refers to individuals' abilities to manage their emotions, develop caring and concern for others, make responsible decisions, establish positive relationships, and handle challenging situations effectively. Students vary in their inner social and emotional wellness and their behavior in the classroom reflects this variation. Classroom teaching requires a sense of personal wellness on behalf of the teacher as well. The teacher can then carefully and kindly help students to develop a sense of inner peace in their learning community.

6-5   Compare problem- and project-based learning to each other and to the traditional class discussion. Having students work on problems and projects allows them to explore content areas in-depth, to apply the knowledge they gain, and to work together in groups. Though these teaching strategies require planning and organization from the teacher, the students are usually self-directed and invested in their work. Although problem-based learning focuses on an often messy problem that has a real-world connection and needs a solution, project-based learning often engages groups of students in creating an optimum design or solution for a challenging problem. Unlike traditional instruction, students are working with peers in small groups and the teacher visits each group, offering support through advice and scaffolding strategies.

Key Terms

exceptional learners   Students who require special educational services because of physical, behavioral, or academic needs.

least restrictive environment   A learning environment that, to the maximum extent possible, matches the environment experienced by nondisabled students.

inclusion   The practice of educating students with disabilities in regular classrooms alongside nondisabled students.

special education   The branch of education that deals with services for students with disabilities or other special needs that cannot be met through traditional means.

learning disability   A disorder in the basic psychological processes involved in learning and using language; it may lead to difficulties in listening, speaking, reading, writing, reasoning, or mathematical abilities.

individualized education program (IEP)   A plan, required for every student covered by the Individuals with Disabilities Education Act, specifying instructional goals, services to be provided, and assessment techniques for evaluating progress.

Response to Intervention (RTI)   A service delivery system in schools aimed at preventing academic and behavioral difficulties as well as identifying the best practices for teaching students with disabilities.

differentiated instruction or **differentiation**   The practice of using a variety of instructional strategies to address the different learning needs of students.

cooperative learning   An instructional approach in which students work together in groups to accomplish shared learning goals.

project-based learning A teaching method that engages students in extended inquiry into complex, realistic questions as they work in teams and create presentations to share what they have learned. These presentations may take various forms: an oral or written report, a computer technology-based presentation, a video, the design of a product, and so on.

problem-based learning Focused, experiential learning (minds-on, hands-on) organized around the investigation and resolution of messy, real-world problems.

ill-structured problem A problem that lacks clear procedures for finding the solution.

charter schools Publicly funded elementary or secondary schools that are granted a special charter by the state or local education agency.

homeschooling Educating children at home rather than in a school; parents typically serve as teachers.

Family Educational Rights and Privacy Act (FERPA) or the **Buckley Amendment** A federal law requiring educational agencies to protect the confidentiality of students' educational records.

due process A formal process, such as a legal or administrative proceeding, that follows established rules designed to protect the rights of the people involved.

tenure A status granted to a teacher, usually after a probationary period, that protects him or her from dismissal except for reasons of incompetence, gross misconduct, or other conditions stipulated by the state.

InTASC Standards

Standard 1: Learner Development
Standard 2: Learning Differences
Standard 3: Learning Environments
Standard 5: Application of Content
Standard 9: Professional Learning
     and Ethical Practice

6-6 Examine the affect of standardized testing on curriculum and instruction. Teachers today have a great challenge: To meet the diverse needs of all their students and also to meet the accountability standards provided in federal mandates and upheld through state assessments. Because of the requirement to meet standards, teachers must thoughtfully plan their own classroom instruction to align with the established curriculum. The first decade of the twenty-first century has been called the "era of accountability." The measures of assessment have taken the form of standardized tests in language arts and mathematics and in some states in science. Because many students' futures and teachers' jobs are dependent upon the outcomes of these standardized tests, classroom curriculum and instruction, in many parts of the country, have become test preparation centers in which many educators believe that students are taught how to pass tests and this counts for teaching and learning.

6-7 Analyze the results of experimental school design, initially encouraged by the passage of No Child Left Behind (NCLB) in 2001. Many alternative school models have been developed that are unlike traditional public and private schools. Charter schools and homeschooling are examples of educational models that are gaining prominence today as people look to alternative methodologies for education. Gaining prominence in large urban areas is the small high school movement. Given permission, cities and districts began to experiment with school design and format. Many large urban school districts began to deconstruct their massive overpopulated high schools and create smaller schools sometimes focused on an area of study or a theme and often coexisting on the same large campus. It is unclear what the results have been to this experimental school design. Some studies have shown that students who attend the new smaller urban high school have a better chance of graduating than those in larger urban high schools. But those students who remain in schools that are in the process of closing by losing a grade each year and not enrolling new students have been languishing in the "dying" schools, and their graduation rates are abysmal. The debate continues. What do you think?

6-8 Debate the need for middle schools in today's school culture. In the 1980s, a new "middle school" concept intended to create an educational experience more appropriate for young adolescents than the old junior high school was adopted by many school districts across the country. The goal was to make the old junior high school more developmentally responsive by changing the grade configuration from grades 7–8 or 7–8–9 to grades 6–7–8 and designing new organizational structures such as interdisciplinary teams. The hope was that new grade groupings and teams would foster more responsiveness on the part of teachers and school administrations as children developed into adolescents. The history of the middle school movement suggests that the middle school became the norm because of societal and demographic pressures and not because of hard evidence to support the need for a separate school for young teens. The organization of the middle grades is still in flux, however, many middle school teachers do not have certification in the subject areas they teach or specific training in the development of young adolescents and that has been a cause for concern.

6-9 Examine the precautions that schools and teachers take to prevent violence in the classroom or the school. Establishing a safe school climate requires a commitment from the administrators, parents, school secretaries, custodians, groundskeepers, as well as the teachers and students. The entire school community needs to be sensitive to students who seem to be in trouble, lonely, disturbed, acting as bullies, or feeling like victims. In many schools, students believe that revealing another student's pain or problems breaks a special peer code. This belief often forces troubled students to go it alone. In a safe school climate, students are willing to break the code of silence to get help for a peer. Working together, the US Department of Education and the Secret Service have produced a guide to help schools create a climate of school safety.

6-10 Analyze the legislation ensuring students' rights as part of the US public school system. Family Educational Rights and Privacy Act (FERPA) of 1974, also known as the Buckley Amendment, is a federal law that requires educational agencies and institutions to protect the confidentiality of students' educational records. This law allows students and their parents to have access to the student's records kept by educational institutions. The law also states that no one outside the institution may have access to a student's educational records, nor can the institution disclose any information from the records without the written consent of the student, or, for students under the age of eighteen, their parents. It is a long-standing law that ensures each student the right to privacy and protection from disclosure of records by a school or school system.

6-11 Examine teachers' rights and their legal responsibilities as they perform their professional duties. School is a public institution, and both teachers and students have rights that are protected by law. Being mindful of these rights, as well as the responsibilities that come with them, is an important part of being a teacher. Like students' rights, teachers' rights are protected by the Constitution. As agents of the government, public school teachers are protected by state constitutional provisions, statutes, and regulations as well. They are also held accountable to these regulations and may be dismissed if they are not meeting their obligations. Although private school teachers do not enjoy as much protection as public school teachers, both are protected by the Civil Rights Act of 1964, which prohibits racial, sexual, or religious discrimination in employment. Teachers' employment rights are further protected by the due process clause of the Fourteenth Amendment to the Constitution, which provides that no state may "deprive any person of life, liberty, or property, without due process of law." This due process requirement means that school boards and state agencies must follow established rules when deciding to dismiss or discipline a teacher.

6-12 Debate the merits of standardized testing and the ways that today's contemporary trends pose challenges to teachers. Standardized testing poses challenges to curriculum design and implementation when the stakes attached to student performance are so high that a teacher's job depends on the students' outcomes. Although a teacher is a key figure in a student's success, he or she is not the only factor. Today's testing environment sometimes stifles teachers' creativity because they "teach to the test" instead of creating exciting problem- and project-based lessons, the outcomes of which may be assessed on the test; however, the time it takes to teach in this way may not meet the assessment timeline. Additionally today's teachers are challenged by the weight given to a single assessment event when they also provide classroom assessments that match instruction and that help teachers learn about student progress. Many teachers feel that these assessments are as valid as the standardized test and should be considered when evaluating the progress of a student.

Review Questions

1. What are some ways that gifted students learn differently from their classmates?

2. Why is the problem about milk waste that Ms. Rhodes gave her class considered an ill-structured problem?

3. How does a charter school differ from a public school?

4. What are some characteristics of an effective middle school?

5. What rights of students and parents are provided for by FERPA?

TeachSource Video Cases

Teaching Strategies for the Inclusion Classroom

Find the TeachSource Video Case "Inclusion: Grouping Strategies for Inclusive Classrooms" on the Education CourseMate at CengageBrain.com. Ask yourself these questions:

- In what ways does the general education teacher, Sheryl Cebula, employ teaching strategies that use multiple intelligences theory?
- Which teacher is in charge? How can you tell?
- How would you describe Ms. Cebula's personal pedagogy in her role as the general education teacher?
- The inclusion specialist, Ms. Jordan, intervenes in many ways. How would you describe her role in the classroom?

Teachers Discuss Their Ethical and Legal Responsibilities

Find the TeachSource Video Case "Legal and Ethical Dimensions of Teaching: Reflections from Today's Educators" on the Education CourseMate at CengageBrain. com. Ask yourself these questions:

- In the video, one administrator says, "If you don't know, ask. If you're not sure, don't." What does this mean?
- What did you think of the teacher who reported "disturbing things" she heard during after-school conversations among students? Would you have done the same thing? Why? Why not?

Chapter Summary

7-1 Explain how the digital age has impacted school-age children making technology in the classroom commonplace. Students are digital natives—they have used digital technology all of their lives. Many teachers and schools still rely on traditional instructional methods (e.g., blackboards, textbooks, handouts, pen-or-pencil assignments), but a shift has gradually begun to incorporate technology into the classroom (e.g., electronic whiteboards, Internet, handheld wireless devices called clickers, electronic tablets, and laptops). Although networked devices are becoming more popular for classroom use, significant disparities do exist in many urban and rural areas. Because students commonly use technology in their everyday lives, they are engaged by using technology in the classroom. Teachers are being challenged to not only incorporate technology in their classes, but also to teach students how to assess the vast amount of information accessible to them.

7-2 Assess the value of using digital technology as a tool to foster interactive, real-world learning. Because technology is part of many students' daily lives, it makes sense to use it for more than gathering information and social networking; it can be used as a tool that fosters interactive, real-world learning. With research into the resources available and some planning, teachers can use technology to enhance their lessons in many ways. Students can search for related data on the Internet on nearly any topic and can then use those data to solve a problem or make a comparison. Computer simulations and models make it possible to do experiments and demonstrations that would be difficult or impossible to bring to the classroom otherwise. The Internet is also, for many students who use it for social networking, a natural venue to foster shared learning experiences through a class web page, discussion boards, or blogs.

7-3 Describe the digital tools available to maximize communication with parents and students. Communication is becoming increasingly open with the preponderance of Web 2.0; many teachers participate in blogs or start their own blog as a way to share ideas about teaching and learning. Social networking sites and blogs can be useful tools for teachers and students because they are relatively easy to create with the use of online templates, and they encourage commenting and feedback. Teachers create class Facebook pages to keep parents informed, distribute homework or permission slips, and share photos or videos from classroom activities or field trips. Anyone can "like" a page on Facebook, and students who do will see updates in their News Feed. Parents have additional tools with which to track student progress at school. Several companies have developed software products that allow parents to view a password-protected web-based grade book that tracks student attendance, homework completion, and grades on tests and projects. Teachers maintain these online grade books daily or weekly.

7-4 Explain the most important rules for safeguarding students as they communicate on the Internet. With so much data available online, teachers have often had to rethink their role because all the information we could ever want to know about a topic is a few mouse clicks away. Not so long ago the primary sources of information for students in school were teachers and textbooks; now the Internet makes it possible to retrieve vast amounts of information on any topic in a short amount of time. Teachers must learn to use technology to their and their students' advantage, and they must guide students in negotiating the overload of information so they use their time wisely. Further,

Key Terms

digital natives People who have grown up using the digital "language" of computers, video, games, and the Internet.

flat classroom A classroom in which students, like the teacher, have ready access to information, so that the teacher is not the lone expert.

simulation A computer program or other procedure that imitates a real-world experience.

model A representation of a system or an object, such as a small physical structure that imitates a larger structure or a computer program that parallels the workings of a larger system.

augmented reality (AR) AR is a live, direct or indirect, view of a physical, real-world environment whose elements are *augmented* by computer-generated sensory input such as sound, video, graphics, or GPS data.

virtual reality This type of interface *replaces* the real world with a simulated one that has all the elements of the real world modeled by computer graphics and images.

wiki An online site that allows visitors to add, remove, and otherwise edit or change the available content.

blog (short for weblog) An online journal using software that makes it easy for the user to create frequent entries; typically, visitors can add their own comments and responses.

Twitter An online social networking service that enables its users to send and read text-based posts of up to 140 characters, known as "tweets."

Facebook A social networking service and website that, by 2012, had more than 845 million users worldwide. Users must register before using the site, after which they may create a personal profile, add other users as friends, and exchange messages, including automatic notifications when they update their profile.

technological fluency Proficiency in the use of technology, including an understanding of the way technology systems operate and the ability to use technology to access information from a wide variety of sources.

digital divide The division between people who are "rich" in technological access and expertise and those who are "poor" in this respect.

assistive technology (AT) A device or service that increases the capabilities of people with disabilities.

interactive whiteboard A whiteboard that works together with a computer to display and save information.

InTASC Standards

Standard 3: Learning Environments
Standard 5: Application of Content
Standard 8: Instructional Strategies

Review Questions

1. How is a blog different from a discussion board?

2. How does technology enhance parent–teacher communication?

3. What are some ways handheld wireless devices could be used in the classroom?

4. What are some areas of concern with regard to safety when children are using the Internet?

teachers can help students learn appropriate ways of communicating online and prepare them to safeguard their private information and most personal thoughts. Any inappropriate communications must be reported immediately!

7-5 Analyze why having computer access only at school is not enough in today's knowledge economy. Students are more likely to make regular use of an Internet connection at home than anywhere else. Access to computers at home has been found to be an important factor in students' ability to use computer resources for word processing, information processing and presenting, and other types of communication, including connecting through social media platforms. Students living in poverty are twice as likely as other students to access the Internet at school only. Further, students in poor rural areas lack the coffee shop or library Internet access provided in some urban neighborhoods.

7-6 Analyze how assistive technology in the classroom can benefit students with disabilities. Assistive technology (AT) refers to devices that promote greater independence for students with disabilities by enabling them to perform tasks that would otherwise be difficult or impossible. For example, students with visual impairments would use a keyboard with large symbols that makes it easier for the students to type or a more complex form of AT like speech recognition software that converts the student's spoken words into text on the screen. Similarly, screen reader software can read aloud the information displayed on a computer screen. Computer technology can also allow relevant materials to be converted into Braille and printed on a Braille printer within seconds. This technology makes it possible for the teacher to include blind students in the same activity as the rest of the class, at the same moment. Other AT devices enhance learners with disabilities by providing interactive images through SMART Boards that allow students to manipulate objects and make sense of concepts manually and visually.

7-7 Create an argument for the significance of meaningful integration of technology in the classroom. Meaningful integration of technology refers to using digital devices and media in ways that enhance students' understanding of a concept. Digital natives are not necessarily digital learners. It is important that teachers keep current on the latest trending technologies and use them to facilitate student learning where applicable. This brings the students' lived experiences into the classroom and the classroom becomes a "mirror."

TeachSource Video Case

Integrating Technology to Improve Student Learning

Find the TeachSource Video Case "Integrating Technology to Improve Student Learning: A High School Science Simulation" on the Education CourseMate at CengageBrain.com. In this biology class, Mr. Bateman is using laptops for each student to create a simulation that relates genetic variation to appearance. After watching the video, consider the following questions:

- How do virtual dragons help the students to learn genetics?
- How would you describe Mr. Bateman's pedagogy?
- How do students change the physical appearance of the dragons?
- How does technology help students to understand molecular biology?
- Could students be assigned homework using this website?

Chapter Summary

8-1   Explain how online high schools can foster critical thinking and collaboration in the global marketplace of ideas. The "global" classroom is a reality, with technology making it possible for classrooms all over the world to connect, collaborating on projects and learning from one another. The digital revolution allows people to connect instantly with others all over the globe. Students can now take courses online from anywhere in the world, and online high schools are emerging as the line between virtual- and classroom-based learning continues to blur. Collaboration on a global level will be part of students' lives when they enter the workforce, and our educational system can prepare them accordingly. Technology and globalization are changing the market so rapidly that students need more than core knowledge of academic disciplines—they need the skills to continually keep learning. These are known as twenty-first-century skills: knowing more about the world, thinking outside the box, managing new sources of information, and developing good people skills.

8-2   Explain why globalization can enhance the learning experiences and the lives of today's students. Today's students must possess twenty-first-century skills: to go beyond understanding core concepts and memorizing facts in academic subjects and to think creatively and critically about a problem, work collaboratively with others to find solutions, and see themselves as problem solvers who communicate their ideas clearly. Groups of students from different parts of the world can work together online engaging in problem- and project-based learning. These collaborations foster skills such as: to listening to others, weighing evidence, investigating data, and reaching conclusions through consensus. In the past, students might study about other countries; now students can use technology to actually connect to children in other countries and learn about their cultures and customs directly or collaborate on a course of study with them! Videoconferencing and online courses of study provide opportunities for students to expand their knowledge with experts or subjects that they might not be able to access otherwise. The traditional model must be adapted to bring more connectivity and collaboration into the educational setting, which is an exciting possibility with today's digital technologies.

8-3   Describe how the language of the digital age helps students to take control of their own learning. The purpose of public education is to prepare children to be able to lead successful lives, as citizens and workers. In the digital age, this means that learning how to learn is as important as what we learn. Teachers must demonstrate a passion for learning, seek opportunities created by technology to enhance classroom

Key Terms

knowledge economy An economic system in which the use and exchange of knowledge plays a dominant role. In this kind of economy, knowledge is both an economic asset and a key product.

online learning The use of the Internet to provide programs of study or individual courses that offer instructional materials and interactions between teachers and students.

globalization The increase of global connectivity, integration, and interdependence in economic, cultural, social, and technological spheres.

metacognition The understanding of your own thinking and learning processes.

gaming Used in this context, gaming refers to playing computer and video games. Video game culture is a form of new media that has enormous potential for teaching and learning.

digital learning games These games target the acquisition of knowledge as its own end and foster habits of mind and understanding that are generally useful or used within an academic context.

videoconferencing Real-time audio and video communication allowing individuals or groups at different locations to talk in a face-to-face setting.

digital media Web-interactive video games, podcasts, and lesson plans downloaded to digital devices such as laptops, mobile devices, DVDs, and CDs.

InTASC Standards

Standard 5: Application of Content

Standard 6: Assessment

Standard 8: Instructional Strategies

Review Questions

1. What is meant by metacognition?

2. How is online education affecting global understanding?

3. How can students be engaged in a fully online course?

4. What is the difference between having information and making meaning?

5. What is the value of digital learning games for education?

6. What are some advantages of a virtual school or an online class?

learning, and help students navigate their ever-expanding world of digital access to information. Twenty-first-century teachers must demonstrate a love and a passion for learning and help their students develop skills that foster communication and collaboration. The role of the teacher today is to help students become lifelong creative learners, capable of examining digital content and assessing its value. For teachers, this means embracing the changes that provide opportunities for new ways of learning in the classroom.

Chapter Summary

9-1   Explain how classrooms with diverse students can share a common set of beliefs, values, and goals. A classroom becomes a community when the students can share an understanding of the beliefs, values, and goals that form the basis for the group, despite the diversity among individuals in the group. One of the goals of education is to produce students who are not only academically competent, but also well-rounded community members whose social and emotional development helps them achieve respect for themselves and others. Good communication and collaboration among students and with the teacher are vital for creating a classroom in which everyone feels responsible for managing the environment and working toward the common good. The classroom that accomplishes this fosters the best learning.

9-2   Examine the role of personal power in the abusive behaviors of bullying and sexual harassment. Sexual harassment and bullying, both in class and in cyberspace, refer to abusive behaviors perpetrated by individuals with power over others who feel powerless. Sexually harassing and bullying behaviors happen in school hallways, stairwells, and classrooms, and they have a negative effect on the emotional and educational lives of students. Establishing a sense of community with your students is a vital means of preventing harassment in school. When students feel responsible for one another and care about their learning community, harassing behaviors are less likely to occur; and when they do, they are less likely to persist. The students who appear to have social power over other student and use that position to cause harm in a bullying or sexually harassing manner become apparent in an authentic classroom community.

9-3   Explain how being fully conscious in the classroom can promote a sense of community. Teachers who are "fully conscious" in the classroom have their pulse on the student climate and have an acute awareness of how the students are interacting with each other. These teachers are less likely to "overlook" inappropriate behaviors like name calling or worse. They have clear rules for what is acceptable and what is not under their watch. This behavior builds trust and respect, essential components for building a sense of classroom community.

9-4   Describe the roles of communication and collaboration for classroom communities. Open and honest communication is essential to fostering a classroom community, in which students care about one another and appreciate differences that makes us unique. This communication helps to prevent serious problems like bullying and harassment. Be sure to learn about your district's specific policies regarding sexual harassment and bullying. Communicating with students about how to identify and report sexual harassment and bullying is an important aspect of classroom management. Too often, abusive behaviors go unreported—teachers must strive for an atmosphere in which open communication, even about difficult issues, is encouraged. Students and

Key Terms

classroom management The ways teachers create an effective classroom environment for learning, including all the rules and conditions they establish.

classroom community A sense of common purpose and values shared by the teacher and students in a classroom so that they see themselves as working together in the process of learning; a classroom atmosphere that emphasizes trust, care, and support.

Responsive Classroom An approach to teaching and learning, developed by the Northeast Foundation for Children, that seeks to bring together social and academic learning.

service learning A teaching and learning strategy that integrates meaningful community service with instruction and reflection to enrich the learning experience, teach civic responsibility, and strengthen communities.

sexual harassment Unwelcome sexual advances, requests for sexual favors, or other physical and expressive behavior of a sexual nature that interferes with a person's life.

bullying Repeated cruelty, physical or psychological, by a powerful person toward a less powerful person.

cyberbullying Bullying or harassment through electronic means such as e-mail, website postings, instant messaging, text messaging, blogs, mobile phones, or chat rooms; also called online bullying.

InTASC Standards

Standard 7: Planning for Instruction
Standard 8: Instructional Strategies
Standard 10: Leadership and
Collaboration

Review Questions

1. Why is creating a classroom community the best way to have excellent classroom management?

2. When is noise appropriate in a classroom?

3. What are the goals of a "Morning Meeting"?

4. What are some teaching strategies suggested by the Responsive Classroom model?

5. What are some examples of cyberbullying?

teachers collaborate on the best actions to take when individuals feel threatened or unhappy in the school setting. "Classroom management" is the term typically used when referring to the prevention of disruptive behaviors and the fostering of a smooth-running class. Classroom management is most successful when students are invested in their learning, their environment, and each other and when they understand that their teacher is invested in them. In essence, successful classroom management does not just mean that the students do what the teacher wants them to; it means that the students and the teacher want the same thing—for the students to be so interested in what they are learning that they are naturally attentive and respectful. Rules, procedures, and routines are a necessary part of a smooth-running classroom, but that does not mean the teacher has to be the sole creator of them. Students are more likely to follow rules they have had an opportunity to help create because they can see the benefits to the group. Teacher and students can collaborate to develop rules that maintain order, not silence. A well-run classroom that encourages group learning will not always be silent.

TeachSource Video Case

Teachers Building Community

Find the TeachSource Video Case "Classroom Management: Best Practices" on the Education CourseMate at CengageBrain.com. In this video, several teachers demonstrate and talk about the ways they conduct their classrooms. Notice that in the first segment the elementary teacher talks about investing time in helping the children understand the routines of the classroom. The middle school teacher explicitly addresses the building of a community with shared expectations. The seventh-grade student reminds us that the teacher must be a "listener" before he or she jumps to judgment, and the guidance counselor reminds teachers that if a student is acting up, it is usually not a personal response to the teacher. Ask yourself these questions:

- What do you think the elementary school teacher means when she says that she waits at least six weeks before giving her young students independent activities?
- How does the middle school drama teacher create community?
- Why do you suppose the seventh-grade student urges his teachers not to react first but to listen first?
- Why do you think Ms. Miller spends two hours on grouping students? How does that effort contribute to classroom community?

Chapter Summary

10-1 **Explain how teachers in the twenty-first century are challenged in ways their predecessors were not.** Public education is vital to a thriving democracy, and teachers in the twenty-first century need to foster critical thinking, creativity, collaboration, and communication. Public education serves several purposes in society, notably, to prepare young people to lead productive lives by increasing their academic achievement and improving the readiness to secure jobs in an increasingly global economy and to equip youth to become responsible and active citizens in a democratic society. How are these purposes met? Not by teaching students what to think, but by teaching them how to think. Teaching is no ordinary job. It requires dedication to the well-being of your students and a willingness to reveal your own self in the process. It also requires a commitment to continuous learning, not only on the part of your students, but for yourself. Being a reflective practitioner will help you achieve these goals.

10-2 **Examine the requirements of your state for earning a teaching certificate.** Your state's Department of Education (DOE) website will describe the range of areas for which you can be licensed. Requirements for teacher certificates or licenses vary from state to state. Some states are relatively compatible with other states in their certification requirements; some states are more individualistic. Take this opportunity to examine *your* state's requirements for a teaching certificate. Many states offer temporary and permanent or professional certificates with each requiring a different amount of education and experience.

10-3 **Analyze the roles of the American Federation of Teachers (AFT) and the National Education Association (NEA) for beginning teachers.** Professional organizations have the potential to create learning communities among their members. They offer rich resources for you to use in planning lessons and expanding your professional knowledge. The two most prominent organizations are the AFT and the NEA. In addition to a code of Code of Ethics, the NEA provides job searches, teaching tips and tools, important resources for your professional development, and activities and workshops of interest in your state. The AFT site reveals a wealth of resources for the classroom teacher. For example, the site provides information about professional development opportunities and grants. Both the AFT and NEA act as labor unions, negotiating labor contracts for teachers with school districts ot city governments.

10-4 **Discuss how a teaching portfolio can demonstrate your talents for teaching.** A teaching portfolio can be an excellent way to organize your thinking about teaching and to display some of your accomplishments. Your portfolio should be easily accessible online and at minimum include an essay about yourself and your reasons for becoming a teacher. You could also share your personal philosophy about teaching and what a good teacher needs to understand how people learn. You may also want to include your own familiarity with the Common Core State Standards. If you have field experiences that demonstrate your success in the classroom, be sure to include

Key Terms

public education Education that is publicly financed, tuition-free, accountable to public authorities, and accessible to all students. The term covers various types of public schools, including traditional schools, charter and magnet schools, vocational schools, and alternative schools.

certification The process of obtaining state authorization to teach in the public schools.

The Praxis Series A series of assessments used by many states as part of the teacher certification process.

Interstate New Teacher Assessment and Support Consortium (InTASC) An organization that develops standards and principles to guide the preparation, licensing, and professional development of teachers. InTASC's members are state education agencies and national educational organizations.

InTASC Standards

Standard 6: Assessment
Standard 7: Planning for Instruction
Standard 9: Professional Learning
and Ethical Practice
Standard 10: Leadership and
Collaboration

Review Questions

1. What are some of the attributes of good teachers?

2. What is the overarching mission of public education?

3. What kinds of teaching opportunities exist abroad?

4. What are some tips for new teachers?

5. How did Jamie Barron win over her urban students?

6. What are some items you might include in your teaching portfolio?

stories about them and artifacts, where possible. Some artifacts may be copies (with permission) of student work. Good luck!

10-5 Analyze the self-reflections that lead you to be believe that teaching is for you. Good teachers have specific personal attributes that make them well suited for the profession. Your responsibility is to understand who you are, where your strengths and weaknesses lie, and what your next steps should be in your journey to become a teacher. Becoming a teacher may be something you have always wanted to do, or it may be something you have recently considered. There are many different reasons for deciding to become a teacher, but even if you are certain of your decision and passionate about it, it is not an easy choice. If you decide to be a teacher, you are choosing a career that will constantly challenge you to examine your own self, to keep learning, to express yourself, and most importantly, to do your best by your students. Teaching is not easy, but it is wonderfully satisfying to be able to contribute to your students' development and growth.

TeachSource Video Case

Common Core Standards: A New Lesson Plan for America

Find the TeachSource Video Case on the Education CourseMate at CengageBrain.com, "Common Core Standards: A New Lesson Plan for America." A seventh-grade math teacher in Atlanta shares her thinking about the new Common Core State Standards in mathematics. These standards place all students K–12 on the same track in mathematics and reading. Consider the following questions:

- What do you think motivated the State Governors Association and the Council of Chief State School Officers to develop common standards to be adopted by all the states?
- Many have that these standards will now level the playing field for students all over the country. What do you think that means?
- How do you think the Common Core Standards would raise the level of education in the country?

Building Your Teaching Portfolio

Using the Writing & Reflection activities and questions found throughout this text, you have been asked to reflect on the topics addressed in each chapter as a way of compiling your teaching portfolio. Developing a portfolio is an excellent way to organize your thinking about teaching and to display some of your accomplishments on this journey. You should continue to update the portfolio each year you teach. It is your professional and personal record, and it demonstrates your knowledge and beliefs as well as your accomplishments. What you choose to include in your portfolio is a statement of what you think is important.

When you begin to look for a job, you will need a version of your portfolio to present to prospective employers. This version should be presented electronically. Many of the previous chapters' portfolio suggestions, as well as the additional prompts that follow, can find a place in this presentation version. The portfolio you show others should be concise, clear, readable, and well organized. There are suggestions for preparing your portfolio on the back of the card.

How Do You Document Your Professional Journey?

You may want to document your work in your professional courses and your school field-based experiences. Some teachers collect artifacts, keep a journal, gather their thoughts electronically, or use a formal format to create a portfolio or a personal notebook. Whatever process works best for you, begin to document your journey as a way to reflect on your professional and personal growth as you continue your course work and field work to become a teacher with your own class or classes. Remember, teaching is something you have to work at: It takes time to prepare, it takes time to practice, and it takes time to process feedback from your students and revise your plan accordingly. It will take time to create your portfolio, too; do not try to compile it all at once, but use it continuously as a place to collect your thoughts and document your journey. You can always go back and edit it later.

Additional Portfolio Prompts

Use these additional prompts as you read through the chapters of the book to add to your portfolio your thoughts on the topics presented.

Reflections on Your Journey

Build on your personal philosophy of teaching by reflecting on the teaching stories in Chapter 2. Address the following questions in a document that you can add to your portfolio.

- Do you think you have a "learning life"?
- How do you anticipate working with and communicating with parents?
- What did you learn from your interview with a classroom teacher that can inform your teaching philosophy?
- How does your religion or culture affect your philosophy of teaching?

Building Your Personal Philosophy

Add to your portfolio by identifying elements of essentialism, perennialism, progressivism, and other philosophies discussed in Chapter 3 that you believe in. Use these to build on the personal philosophy that you have already begun to develop.

It is not enough to interpret what you have read. The well-prepared teacher must explain his or her rationale for designing a learning experience in a particular way. Be sure to express why you believe what you do.

Relating Learning Theories to Your Teaching Philosophy

Reflect on the learning theories presented in Chapter 4 and select a theory that can help you make sense of your personal teaching philosophy. You may use more than one theory to pull together a teaching approach that makes sense to you. Include your reflections in your portfolio. Remember, it is subject to change as you progress on your journey.

Reflecting on Student Diversity

After reading Chapter 5, address the following questions in a document that you can add to your portfolio.

- What is your reaction to the various types of student diversity that were discussed and to the ways students can be the same as and different from each other?
- Reflect on where you see yourself headed as a teacher. Do you have a calling, for instance, to work with at-risk students? Are you motivated to create a gender-fair classroom? What, specifically, speaks to you?
- This chapter has an important message: Different is just different; it is not lesser. Can you teach those who are different from you in ways that do not make their difference "lesser"? Describe how you would do so.

Trends You Find Appealing

Think about all of the trends and issues presented in Chapter 6. Add to your portfolio by writing about the current educational trends you find most appealing as a future teacher. Explore the ways you can see yourself involved in this type of change.

Your Thoughts about Using Technology in Teaching

After reading Chapter 7, describe the ways you anticipate integrating your life as a technology user into the work you will do with your students. What are the possibilities? Collect your thoughts in your portfolio.

Designing an Activity to Promote Twenty-First-Century Skills

Chapter 8 emphasizes the importance of developing your students' twenty-first-century skills. As an exercise for your portfolio, imagine you are teaching at a grade level of your choice. Think of one activity you could undertake with your class to enhance your students' capacity to use twenty-first-century skills. Describe this activity as specifically as possible.

Your Plans for Creating a Classroom Community

There is a great deal of content to digest in Chapter 9. In your portfolio, include your plans for creating classroom community. Think deeply about how you will translate the principles discussed in the chapter into your own practice. Be honest with yourself; if you have concerns, write about them.

Your Choice

Upon completing this book, reflect on your choice to become a teacher. How have your coursework and this book informed or influenced your choice? Do you feel more or less sure now than you did at the beginning of the course? What are your fears or anxieties? Your hopes and dreams? Once you have chosen the path of teacher, a wonderful portfolio addition would be a short essay responding to the simple, yet complex, question:

Why did you choose to become a teacher?

Suggestions for Preparing Your Portfolio

Use a website URL or a software program to store the contents of your portfolio. Print the pages and keep one print copy in a folder. Remember, less is more. Select your favorite artifacts and reviews to show your prospective employer.

- You should prepare a version of your portfolio that is available electronically, either on a personal professional website that you have developed (templates for this are available online or as software applications) or on a disk that you give to your prospective employers. You can create a PowerPoint file, a Word document with appropriate images, or a PDF.
- Include a table of contents so viewers can skip to parts that particularly concern them.
- Begin with a short essay introducing yourself. In a few paragraphs, describe your interest in teaching and learning and what you have accomplished. See Chapter 10 for a sample introductory essay.
- Describe your educational philosophy, that is, what you believe a good teacher needs to understand about teaching and learning.
- Discuss your classroom management theory. If your focus is on building community in the classroom, be specific about how you plan to do that.
- Describe your student teaching experience with specific mention of the grade levels you taught and the lessons and activities you prepared. If you have copies of supervisors' observations that attest to your abilities, include them.
- Include photos or electronic files of a few samples of student work from your field experience.
- If you have approved photos of yourself and a class in action, or even a brief video (no more than three minutes long) that you have burned on a DVD, include them. ("Approved" means that you have received consent forms from the other people shown in the photos or video.)
- Include your college transcript, resume, certifications, awards, and letters of reference.
- Do not overdo it. We live in a fast-paced culture, and people do not have a great deal of time to read your portfolio. Be concise and to the point.

Good luck on your journey!